Tell it to the World

Tell it to the World

The Broadway Musical Abroad

DAVID SAVRAN

OXFORD
UNIVERSITY PRESS

Oxford University Press is a department of the University of Oxford. It furthers
the University's objective of excellence in research, scholarship, and education
by publishing worldwide. Oxford is a registered trade mark of Oxford University
Press in the UK and certain other countries.

Published in the United States of America by Oxford University Press
198 Madison Avenue, New York, NY 10016, United States of America.

© Oxford University Press 2024

All rights reserved. No part of this publication may be reproduced, stored in
a retrieval system, or transmitted, in any form or by any means, without the
prior permission in writing of Oxford University Press, or as expressly permitted
by law, by license, or under terms agreed with the appropriate reproduction
rights organization. Inquiries concerning reproduction outside the scope of the
above should be sent to the Rights Department, Oxford University Press, at the
address above.

You must not circulate this work in any other form
and you must impose this same condition on any acquirer.

Library of Congress Cataloging-in-Publication Data
Names: Savran, David, 1950– author.
Title: Tell it to the world : the Broadway musical abroad / David Savran.
Description: New York, NY : Oxford University Press, 2024. |
Includes index.
Identifiers: LCCN 2023036458 (print) | LCCN 2023036459 (ebook) |
ISBN 9780190249533 (hardback) | ISBN 9780190249540 (epub)
Subjects: LCSH: Musicals—Germany—History and criticism. |
Musicals—Korea (South)—History and criticism. |
Musicals—New York (State)—New York—History and criticism. |
Flaherty, Stephen. Rocky. | Krieger, Henry. Dreamgirls.
Classification: LCC ML2054.S28 2024 (print) | LCC ML2054 (ebook) |
DDC 792.6/45—dc23/eng/20230808
LC record available at https://lccn.loc.gov/2023036458
LC ebook record available at https://lccn.loc.gov/2023036459

DOI: 10.1093/oso/9780190249533.001.0001

Printed by Sheridan Books, Inc., United States of America

To my students,
past and present

Contents

Preface   ix
Acknowledgments   xv

PART I: INTRODUCTION

1. Why Musical Theatre?   3

PART II: SOUTH KOREA

2. The New Broadway-Style Musical   37
3. The Sound of Korea   70

PART III: GERMANY

4. Enter the Musical   107
5. Musical Comedy Recalibrated   151
6. Celebrating the Great Tralala   188

Afterword   239
Notes   243
Index   287

Preface

This book was inspired by a profusion of sources. One was provided by Ji Hyon (Kayla) Yuh, a Korean student in my 2008 musical theatre seminar who wrote a final paper about a Seoul production of Michael Bennett's *Dreamgirls* (1981), which was in fact a far-flung, out-of-town tryout for an upcoming New York revival. I was intrigued, to say the least, to learn how Korean performers had transformed a musical I always assumed to be too embedded in US racial politics to travel. A second was Barrie Kosky's super-gay 2008 production of Cole Porter's *Kiss Me, Kate* (1948) at the Komische Oper Berlin, with which I was completely intoxicated. The production's scale—conceptually, musically, theatrically—was so mind-blowing that I wanted all my musical theatre friends to drop what they were doing and fly to Berlin to see it. A third spark for the book came from Ken Nielsen, one of my first students at the CUNY Graduate Center, who in 2011 completed a dissertation on productions of Tony Kushner's *Angels in America* (1993) in Denmark and Germany. Ken's project helped me to recognize that studying the reception of US-American theatre abroad could provide fascinating insights into the love/hate relationship between US culture and the rest of the world.

Draw these three strands together, add fifteen years, dozens of intercontinental flights, and you get *Tell It to the World: The Broadway Musical Abroad*, a study of how performances of musicals have traveled the world, influencing and transforming local idioms and traditions. The title of course is drawn from *West Side Story* (1957), a musical I take up in the last chapter, and is an interjection inserted into Leonard Bernstein and Stephen Sondheim's song "Dear Officer Krupke." The line represents the impassioned (and sarcastic) plea of Action, one of the Jets, who wants to spread the word about his underprivileged childhood: "Lemme tell it to the world!"[1] Unlike Action's caustic interjection, my plea is entirely earnest insofar as I aim to spread the word that some of the most innovative, beautiful, and exciting musical theatre is being made outside the United States. But, I argue, this work remains in implicit or explicit dialogue with US models. The pieces I am documenting and analyzing both adhere to and break with the conventions and formulas of the Broadway musical, some of them to such an extent that I am reluctant even to call them musicals. But having seen popular musical theatre on four continents, I have come to the conclusion that the Broadway musical, which has long set its sights on foreign markets, has indeed succeeded in becoming a lingua franca, a template for musical theatre around the world.

Unable to cover the world in a single volume, I am focusing instead on the indigenization of the musical in South Korea and Germany, the commercial centers for the performance of Broadway musicals in East Asia and continental Europe, respectively. Each country, in addition, has produced some of the most groundbreaking and thrilling original musical theatre I have ever seen. Although the histories of theatre and popular music in the two nations are utterly different, there are important parallels between them. Both were largely destroyed by warfare in the mid-twentieth century and subsequently occupied by the United States, which calculatingly disseminated US-American popular music, jazz, movies, and musical theatre in the belief that these nations, partitioned by the Cold War, needed to rebuild their cultures in accordance with US guidelines. Thus, as early as the summer of 1945, the USO began presenting camp shows featuring US entertainers and the Armed Forces Radio Service started broadcasting jazz and pop music throughout occupied Germany, Austria, Korea, and Japan, as well as other parts of Europe and Asia that had been liberated from the Axis's grip. Flashforward fifty years, and imported musicals were all the rage in Hamburg and Seoul, while local musicals were being fashioned that adapted and utterly transformed the prototypes that had been disseminated by the United States. In the twenty-first century, both nations have seen a proliferation of homegrown musicals that rework US-American conventions while transcending the Broadway models.

The musical is sometimes imagined as a prime example of the weaponization of US culture, but I think the situation is much more complex in part because the US-Americanness of the musical is increasingly up for grabs. The contours of the genre, moreover, have become so protean that it is by no means clear what the musical designates today. Although this book focuses on twenty-first-century work, it also looks back through the twentieth century to plot the evolution of musical theatre in both Korea and Germany. Part I, the introductory chapter, tries to answer the fundamental questions: What is a musical? Why is it the great success story of US theatre? And how US-American can it be if it has been so easily assimilated to and transformed by musical theatre traditions all over the world? Part II focuses on musical theatre in South Korea. Chapter 2 studies the import/export business in large-scale musicals about Korean history, and Chapter 3 reviews innovative hybrid experiments that mix Korean performance traditions with the Broadway vernacular. Part III moves to Europe and takes as its backdrop the conflicted attitudes toward musicals in the German-speaking world—both the siren song of Broadway and the many attempts by German artists and intellectuals to stop their ears to it. Chapter 4 surveys the history of musicals in Germany from 1945 until the fall of the Berlin Wall. Chapter 5 provides a close-up of the work of director Herbert Fritsch in order to chart the absorption and reconfiguration of musical theatre conventions by experimental directors making category-defying performance work. Chapter 6 studies the groundbreaking German-language productions of Broadway classics by Barrie Kosky and other innovative directors.

This volume is very much a product of my own fieldwork, that is, thousands of evenings of theatregoing, massive amounts of reading and research, and conversations over many years with friends, colleagues, students, former students, and theatre professionals. Above all, it is an attempt to understand the contexts for innovative performances in South Korea and Germany that have fascinated and moved me, despite—or more likely, because of—my foreignness. Because I reside in Germany whereas have only visited South Korea, my foreignness relative to the two countries is very different. This book, as a result, evinces a palpable asymmetry. My familiarity with German art, music, and literature dates back to my childhood, whereas I started studying Korean music and culture only in 2008. Although I remain an outsider in both countries, my long-term immersion in German theatrical culture has made me feel more like an insider than I ever could in South Korea. This distinction, for better or worse, also plays itself out in my research and writing and induces me to provide more historical background on Korea than Germany.

From my perspective, the key issues in Korean musical theatre are different from the ones that dominate the debates in the German-speaking world. The Korean chapters focus on the dialectic between Western and Korean forms, styles, and conventions, while the German chapters focus more on the dialectic between high and low, art and entertainment, avant-garde and commercial. These different points of focus, however, also represent responses to the modes of critical debate that prevail in each society. Thus, for example, cultural nationalism is a much more pressing issue in South Korea than in Germany, in which nationalism (at least since World War II) is shunned but questions of cultural legitimacy continue to dog work that does not fit neatly into established categories.

These asymmetries are linked to profound dissimilarities between theatre's institutional structures in South Korea and Germany. Except for replica productions of blockbusters such as *The Lion King*, one-to-one analogies are elusive. Original musical theatre pieces in Korea are in the main work of commercial producers (sometimes with government support), while comparable German examples are usually performed in state-subsidized houses. The one example that most clearly links the two nations is the German rock musical *Linie 1* (Subway Line #1), which opened in West Berlin in 1986 and continues in the repertoire. Several years later, *Linie 1* was rewritten for the Korean stage, opening in 1994 and playing until 2008, when it was crowned the most popular "Korean" musical of all time.[2] Because *Linie 1*, like most of the work about which I am writing, is unlikely to be familiar to Anglophone readers, this book includes links to audio and video clips, trailers, and in a few instances, full videos of the productions I am studying. Despite most readers' unfamiliarity with many of my examples, I hope that my thick descriptions, and my use of Anglophone points of reference and analytical frameworks borrowed from the study of the Broadway canon, will make them accessible. In the last chapter, I do finally return to Barrie Kosky's *Kiss Me, Kate* and perform detailed analyses of his and others' groundbreaking productions of Broadway classics.

The task of a preface is to explain what a book is doing, rather than what it does not do, but I feel obliged to set forth a caveat. I have deliberately sidestepped musicals such as the Disney shows, which happen to have the highest profile in the global marketplace, and of which analyses can be found elsewhere. Rather, most of the musical theatre for which this volume serves as a guidebook has not made it onto the typical tourist itinerary. Nor has it toured to the Anglophone world, since theatres and producing organizations erect considerable barriers to the circulation of foreign-language work. Another obstacle to circulation is the obsessive classification by producing organizations, marketing professionals, and critics of the entire range of musical theatre practices and the shoehorning of musicals, opera, operetta, and experimental music theatre into discrete categories. The hierarchy of categories inevitably reinforces the constant and regrettable revitalization of the opposition, especially in the German-speaking world, between elite and popular cultures. These classifications, moreover, represent the very foundation of the global theatre economy, which comprises a vast array of commercial, nonprofit, and state-subsidized houses and production companies. The durability of this economy poses a challenge for new work that is performed in languages, styles, and genres that are not immediately comprehensible. This iconoclastic work, however, is precisely what interests me most and what I would describe as the artwork of the future, if that term were not so tainted by Richard Wagner's megalomania and antisemitism. For I firmly believe that the theatre that has the greatest potential to reach people and change attitudes is precisely that which undermines aesthetic categories, seduces and challenges, overflows national boundaries, and explodes the distinction between art and life.

Acknowledgments

I have never felt so indebted to so many people for their assistance on a project. I must start by singling out my South Korean students and former students, Ji Hyon (Kayla) Yuh, Hansol Oh, Dohyun (Gracia) Shin, and Kyungjin Jo, who played invaluable roles in bringing material to my attention, as well as translating, interpreting, and elucidating Korean texts, contexts, and performances. I think of them almost as coauthors of portions of this book.

Next, I want to thank my German friends, Kevin Clarke, for introducing me to operetta and challenging so many of my preconceptions about musical theatre, and Prosper Schücking, for teaching me everything I always wanted to know about German culture. Marvin Carlson first alerted me to the wonders of German theatre, while Matt Cornish and Elmar Juchem have offered invaluable support, feedback, and assistance. I also want to thank Dagmar Sonnak and my academic friends and acquaintances, David Roesner, Ilka Saal, Kerstin Schmidt, Birgit Bauridl, Udo Hebel, Florian Weinzierl, Jennifer Reimer, Olivia Frech, and the Music Theatre Working Group at IFTR.

I owe a great debt to the International Research Center "Interweaving Performance Cultures" at the Freie Universität Berlin, especially Erika Fischer-Lichte and Christel Weiler, and fellows Proshot Kalami, Susan Manning, Jung-Soon Shim, Carol Fisher Sorgenfrei, and Susan Leigh Foster. I also want to thank the German directors, dramaturgs, and actors who have given so generously of their time: Herbert Fritsch, Barrie Kosky, Ersan Mondtag, Till Briegleb, Helmut Baumann, Rainer Luhn, Maximilian Hagemeyer, Ruth Rosenfeld, Matthias Davids, Fred Berndt, and Christian Weise.

I thank my many academic friends on this side of the Atlantic, especially Laura MacDonald, my interlocutor and theatregoing pal in Germany, Austria, and China, as well as Ryan Donovan and Andrew Friedman for many years of thoughtful dialogue. My thanks to Norm Hirschy at Oxford University Press for his patience and encouragement and to the Press's editorial team. To Dave Stein and Brady Sansone at the Kurt Weill Foundation and to the theatres that have provided me with access to videos of productions,

Deutsches Schauspielhaus (Hamburg), Schauspielhaus Zürich, Volksbühne am Rosa-Luxemburg-Platz, Schaubühne am Lehniner Platz, Burgtheater (Vienna), Maxim Gorki Theater, and Theater Bremen, as well as producer Lisa Wagner.

I owe a debt to my colleagues at the CUNY Graduate Center, Jean Graham-Jones, Peter Eckersall, Jim Wilson, and Erika Lin, for their long-term friendship and support and their indulgence for my many mid-semester excursions to Berlin.

I want to express my gratitude to and love for my wonderful teammates in the Musical Theatre Forum who for many years have offered me enormous intellectual and emotional support and inspiration, Stacy Wolf, Raymond Knapp, Dominic Symonds, Jeff Magee, Liza Gennaro, Joanna Dee Das, Doug Reside, Jessica Sternfeld, Tamsen Wolff, and especially Elizabeth Wollman, who has given me precious feedback every step of the way. Thanks to my old friends in New York and Berlin who have patiently nurtured me over the years, KC Witherell, Annette Saddik, Paula Vogel, Libby Koponen, Paula Greenman, Dan Fox, Charles Curkin, Penina Scher, and Janet Williams. And to Daniel Gundlach in Berlin, who has been my editor, goad, sounding board, and faithful and loving helpmate and friend.

Most of all, I want to express my deep gratitude to my many students and former students who have inspired and propelled me over the years to broaden my horizons, experiment with new methods, question doxa, explicate the inexplicable, and seek out innovative theatre and performance wherever I roam.

PART I
INTRODUCTION

1
Why Musical Theatre?

In the twenty-first century, live theatre enjoys unprecedented mobility. Performances circulate in myriad forms around six continents and are disseminated across countless platforms. Among theatrical genres, one, which I am calling the Broadway-style musical, has become exceptionally nomadic and pervasive. It migrates not only as a discrete body of globetrotting works such as *The Lion King* (1997)—which, with cumulative worldwide ticket sales of almost $10 billion, overtook *The Phantom of the Opera* (1986) in 2014 to become the largest-grossing theatre piece of all time—but also as a set of musical theatrical forms and conventions uniquely adaptable to local traditions.[1] I borrow the phrase "Broadway-style musical" from the South Korean director-producer Ho Jin Yun, whose musical theatre works, like those of so many theatre artists around the world, use as a model what he terms the "'Western' framework called the 'Broadway-style musical.'"[2] Despite this genre's obviously syncretic character, its "Western" conventions, forms, and idioms are ineluctably associated with the United States, which for over one hundred years has been a locus for the invention and propagation of popular music styles. As a result of its flexibility, and despite its US-Americanness, the Broadway-style musical has succeeded in saturating theatrical genres around the world. From Seoul to Hamburg, it has proven invaluable as a lingua franca, a kind of theatrical envelope into which indigenous vernaculars, musical and otherwise, are inserted and celebrated.

Although the musical's saturation of theatrical genres around the world might seem to be yet another example of cultural homogenization, the situation is far more complex. As anthropologist Richard Wilk notes, the global cultural market always balances transnational and local, different and familiar, universal and particular. This is especially true of cultural forms that defy mass production, such as live theatre. In order to travel, a globalized system of music theatre has developed in the twenty-first century that always distinguishes, implicitly or explicitly, between form and content. Wilk emphasizes that, despite the handwringing over alleged standardization, the global circulation of cultural goods does not and cannot iron out differences: *"we are not all becoming the same, but we are portraying, dramatizing and communicating our differences to each other in ways that are more widely intelligible."* In other words, the "globalized system exercises hegemony not through content, but through form."[3] On the one hand, a limited repertoire of popular musical theatrical forms and idioms has become increasingly pervasive. On the other hand, in order to be articulated and understood, these forms and idioms must be filled with local content.

Trying to track the dynamic relationship between form and content, global and local, I will analyze the very different ways the musical has been embraced and indigenized in the regional hubs for musicals in continental Europe and East Asia, respectively, Germany and South Korea. Despite their obvious differences, these nations since World War II evince many similarities: both were devastated by war in the mid-twentieth century, occupied by the United States, and subsequently partitioned by the Cold War. Because the United States played the role of guarantor power over both nations, they have repeatedly been characterized as the most US-Americanized countries in their geopolitical spheres—or, more precisely, ones in which US-Americanization has been especially pronounced and contested. While there are many reasons for this Americanization, the postwar proliferation of broadcasting facilities for the Armed Forces Radio Service (later the Armed Forces Network) was crucial in disseminating US-American popular music, and later television, as well as English, the language of the occupying forces.[4] The many Armed Forces installations and associated bars and clubs in both West Germany and South Korea were also instrumental in schooling musicians and singers in US vernaculars while propagandizing for US-American style democracy. Although West Germany's reindustrialization occurred twenty-five years before South Korea's, both nations have since the 1990s seen a boom in Broadway-style entertainments as local producers have bought, renovated, and built theatres to accommodate Broadway shows. Despite well-founded anxieties over globalization, one of the most creative and productive signs of syncretism, I believe, can be found in the many innovative popular musical theatre hybrids that have developed in both nations that mix global and local, commercial and esoteric, orthodox and avant-garde. The musical theatre that results is prodigiously wide in its compass, ranging from large-scale populist rock musicals aimed at young audiences to more specialized, almost operatic forays into smaller-scale, experimental music theatre. Yet in all the cases I cite, twentieth-century popular musical theatre provides these new hybrids with a vocabulary and syntax that allow them to be understood, valued, and loved.

What Is a Musical?

To begin, I want to provide at least provisional answers to two foundational questions. First, what is a Broadway musical? And second, how stable is the national identity of a theatrical genre named after a New York thoroughfare? In the Anglophone world, the meaning of the term is often taken to be self-evident: a musical is a collaboratively made, narrative play composed of an amalgamation of spoken dialogue and popular song. It is typically centered on a romantic couple, has a happy ending, includes discrete songs and usually dance, and provides an occasion, both onstage and off, for the consolidation of communities. Its combination of song, dance, and readily understandable narrative succeeded in making it a uniquely popular genre in the United States, which started during the nineteenth century in the commercial theatre but since World War II has migrated to the nonprofit realm, as well as to elementary schools, summer camps, community centers, and amusement parks. Despite the musical's ubiquity, its native soil is still regarded as the forty-one large-scale theatres on or near Broadway in Midtown Manhattan. At the same time, for many specialists and nonspecialists alike, the Broadway musical is a still-evolving genre whose history, topography, and possibilities are delineated by canonical works such as *Show Boat* (1927), *Oklahoma!* (1943), *Kiss Me, Kate* (1948), *West Side Story* (1957), *Fiddler on the Roof* (1964), *Hair* (1968), *A Chorus Line* (1975), *The Phantom of the Opera* (1986), *The Lion King* (1997), and *Hamilton* (2015).

However, the more pressure one applies to the designation *musical*, the more indistinct it becomes. For by any definition, it represents a remarkably heterogeneous compendium of works whose subgenres include musical comedy, rock musical, megamusical, musical play, jukebox musical, boutique musical, and many others. Revue and operetta are usually described as forerunners of the musical yet often incorporated into the category as subgenres. Most musicals feature discrete songs, but some are sung-through; most employ popular musical idioms, dance, and target mass audiences, but some choose more esoteric or even avant-gardist styles and aim for coterie audiences; most are enacted by performers trained in popular musical theatre, but some by actors, dancers, and singers trained in classical or heritage performance traditions. The definition of a musical is thus as contested, historically contingent, and unstable as that of a novel or an opera.

The question of the national identity of the musical similarly defies a straightforward answer. Just as Hollywood is identified with a particular brand of narrative cinema, so is Broadway identified first and foremost as the home of the musical. Although large-scale, popular musical theatre developed in many countries during the second half of the nineteenth century, the musical consolidated its identity as the emblematic US-American theatrical genre early in the twentieth century, despite the fact that popular music theatre always mixes national styles and vernaculars. Before World War I, musicals and operettas (genres that were sometimes indistinguishable) proved their cosmopolitanism by playing the circuit: Paris, Vienna, Berlin, London, and New York. In most cases, they were translated, adapted, and indigenized for local markets, often retaining little more than a few songs and characters from the originals. But even at the turn of the twentieth century, the United States held a privileged place in the popular imagination. As early as 1903, the Berlin journalist Erich Urban extolled musicals for their "Americanism": "These swinging rhythms, these syncopations . . . met the continent's ears like stinging blows," bringing "to Europe's slackened nerves a long-desired new sensation."[5] Even in these years, the United States was already supplanting Europe as the prime source of inspiration for popular music.[6]

In the early twentieth-century United States, meanwhile, musicals proved their modernity and their "Americanism" by provocatively mixing ragtime, vaudeville, jazz, Tin Pan Alley, and tap dance with the plots and conventions of geographically designated genres such as French and Viennese operetta, and British music hall. Through two world wars and countless changes in musical fashion, the United States has retained its privileged position, despite the fact that several musicals that were especially important in opening up new markets are more aptly described as British. Megamusicals, notably Andrew Lloyd Webber's *Cats* (1981) and *The Phantom of the Opera*, along with Schönberg and Boublil's French/British hybrid *Les Misérables* (1985), were the first to be mass-marketed and franchised on a large scale and became worldwide sensations during the 1980s, whetting the appetites of theatregoers in China, South Korea, South Africa, and elsewhere. These megamusicals, or "poperettas," injected musical and dramatic characteristics associated with both opera and operetta into the Broadway idiom and eschewed the topicality of musical comedy for the presumed universality of

European classics. Although they dominated the world market in the late twentieth century, they have since been superseded by a more heterogeneous body of work that draws freely on an array of musical and theatrical idioms. I will continue to call them Broadway musicals, though this designation elides questions of national origins and traditions, even in the case of a piece such as *The Lion King*, which premiered in New York and was written, produced, and directed by US-born artists but whose songs are penned by a British songwriting team and whose appeal depends in part on its exploitation of Africanist exoticism.

My quibbles about the national identity of the Broadway musical make it clear that the thoroughfare embedded in its name is less a real street than a fantasmatic origin and terminus in the global culture industry. The fantasy of Broadway, with its dazzle, lights, and syncopated dance music, remains as potent as the fantasy of Vienna was in the late nineteenth century, when it was evoked by the waltzes of Johann Strauss II and operettas such as the Strauss pastiche *Wiener Blut* (Viennese Blood, 1899). Thanks to these operettas, many of which premiered not in Vienna but Berlin, the Austrian capital became inextricably associated with *Eleganz*, sophistication, and three-quarter time. In the twenty-first century, what theatregoers call a Broadway musical no longer need originate or even play in the United States to glow with an unmistakably US-American aura. And wherever it travels, it seems to be singing that old chestnut, "Give My Regards to Broadway."

The Crackle of Difference

Before analyzing the musical's migration, I want to focus more closely on the decisive question: why the musical? Why has a musical theatre genre, whose English-language, Roman-character appellation is employed worldwide, become a template for so many different kinds of music theatre? First, let me single out its dependence on popular musical idioms, all of which evince the impact of US-American jazz, pop, or rock 'n' roll. As became clear already in the 1920s with the rapid worldwide dissemination of jazz, US-American popular music styles, which are intertwined and often synonymous with African American musical forms, have proven uniquely irresistible and adaptable. Indeed, their historical evolution can effectively be traced through the chronological sequencing of African American musical traditions, from ragtime, jazz, and the blues to rock 'n' roll, gospel, soul, and hip-hop. Most important, the worldwide dissemination of these styles has meant that Western popular music, with its distinctively African American roots, has become a kind of musical Esperanto.

Second, if I were forced to describe the essence of the Broadway-style musical, I would say: the disjuncture between spoken dialogue and song, or what Scott McMillin memorably calls "the crackle of difference" between book and music. The musical hinges on the contrast between these two components, which, he argues, are emblematic of two different temporal modes: the progressive time of the plot and the repetitive time of song.[7] Raymond Knapp stresses less these temporal differences than the cognitive and emotional ramifications of this "crackle." He does so by theorizing that the latter produces an "artificiality" that requires that we, the audience,

> pay attention to both the emotional realities that music seems to body forth and the performance of that music by the actor-singers on stage. Indeed, we are almost forced into this mode of dual attention, since music notoriously does not unfold in "real time," but rather imposes a kind of suspended animation so as to intensify selected emotional moments, and through this dramatic hiatus directs us all the more urgently to see behind the mask/makeup/costume of the performer—even as he or she embodies the role being played even more fully through the enactment of song.[8]

For Knapp, the Broadway musical is in essence a self-reflexive enterprise whose metatheatricality makes it especially rich, complex, and productive both as performance practice and as a cognitive and affective experience for audiences.

The compulsory theatricality and double-consciousness of the actor-singer—and of the very soul of the musical—has been a recurring theme in the study of musical theatre, which helps distinguish the genre from both spoken drama and opera. The effects generated by what Millie Taylor calls the "self-referential quality" of musicals moreover, are far-reaching.[9] Stephen Banfield, for example, points out that in musicals, song

> has traditionally behaved much more self-consciously and *presentationally* [than in opera], that is, as one mode of representation rather than its governing medium, and indeed we could say the same of dance, comic dialogue, and all the other stage topoi that make up a show. Correspondingly, music is often . . . the *subject* of representation on the stage; it can often not

just move in and out of the drama but in and out of itself, and is more dramatically agile, perhaps therefore even more epistemologically aware (thus serving as a model of human self-knowledge), than in most opera

and, I would add, most spoken theatre.[10]

The theatrical self-consciousness of the musical is doubtlessly linked to the fact that so many musicals are about the stage or about performing. Especially in the Anglophone world, many of the most celebrated works are backstage musicals, that is, plays (like *Show Boat* or *The Phantom of the Opera*) about the making of theatre. But every live musical, regardless of its subject matter, spotlights the song-ness of song and the embodied presence of the performer. In doing so, it becomes self-reflexive, questioning and slyly undermining the distinction between diegetic and non-diegetic music, between music that originates in and emanates from the fictional world of the play and music whose source is invisible (coming from offstage, the orchestra pit, or an imagined locale). Although many musicals feature songs presented *as* songs, the meaning and emotional force of even diegetic music always exceed its function within the fiction. As a result, every musical functions in some way as a reflection upon performance itself. The locus classicus for the deconstruction of the difference between diegetic and non-diegetic is certainly "Rose's Turn" from *Gypsy* (1959), which represents both an explicitly real, live performance and an imaginary performance, a fantasy, for both the character Rose and the actor playing her. The song thus renders the audience simultaneously real and imaginary, visible and invisible, while providing them—us—with the kind of deliberately over-the-top, bravura performance and show business razzle-dazzle that have always been principal attractions of popular musical theatre. This number thereby exemplifies the "moment of physical and emotional excess" described by Millie Taylor, whose "thrill" binds the listener to the performer.[11]

Musicals are unexceptional in the history of world theatre insofar as almost all theatrical performances use some kind of music or song. In fact, the development of a sharp distinction between diegetic and non-diegetic is very much tied to the rise of theatrical realism in the West in the nineteenth century, which paralleled the consolidation of the musical as a discrete genre. In the context of world theatre, however, realism, despite its pervasiveness during the long twentieth century, represents a historical exception and aberration. The theatrical and musical self-consciousness of the Broadway musical, in contrast, is related stylistically to countless theatrical traditions ranging from Japanese kabuki and Chinese *jingju* to various strands of opera, melodrama, and operetta. But the musical is often smaller-scale, and while its performers must train in multiple modes in the hope of becoming "triple threats," their schooling is usually not as highly specialized as the training processes these other forms (e.g., kabuki and opera) require. As a self-aware composite of speech and song that foregrounds its own theatricality, the musical becomes almost infinitely pliable, a kind of portable collage that proves remarkably proficient at incorporating different musical and theatrical styles and traditions. This pliability and integrative ability, as well as those of the Western tonal system, make it unique among theatrical forms in the possibilities it offers theatre-makers worldwide for hybridization and indigenization.

Given its requisite comprehensibility, and despite its collage-like nature, a musical must be more than a nonsensical grab bag or catch-all of songs. Like any intelligible play, it requires a certain dramatic coherence—it tells a story—which means it has what is usually identified as a plot with a certain logic and a beginning, middle, and end. Most important, however, the musical requires that songs, in Brian Valencia's words, "expand the range of expressive possibilities conventionally available to realistic spoken drama," often by "jolt[ing] the hierarchical balance" between different structural and affective properties and registers. In other words, songs always perform a dramatic function; they advance, "stop," or "accelerate narrative," alter character, and/or stage-manage ideas.[12] Although song functions and styles have changed and continue to change, the most common way of categorizing them is by type. In 1977, for example, Lehman Engel, in his guidebook *The Making of a Musical*, categorizes songs by their character or function: ballads, comedy songs, charm songs, rhythm songs, character songs, and a few others.[13] One could add to this list the "I want" song, list song, hypothetical love song, narrative song, waltz, and 11 o'clock number, among others. This list is complicated by the fact that these labels describe different qualities and functions. Some single out a song's musical characteristics, some its dramatic utility, some its verbal constitution, and some its placement in the arc of the show. Most songs, moreover, perform several functions simultaneously. But whatever a song's form, style, or function, it is always set in opposition to the spoken word and to other songs. It thereby accomplishes tasks dramaturgically and theatrically.

Despite the changes in song types and styles, I think the most useful way of understanding a song's function, especially when it does not explicitly forward the plot, would be by appealing to Kenneth Burke's theorization of form, which he understands less as an indwelling quality of art than a matter of reception. For Burke, form is in the eyes and ears of the beholder. It is a rhetorical construction, "the creation of an appetite in the mind of the auditor, and the adequate satisfying of that appetite."[14] In his "Lexicon Rhetoricae," Burke outlines five aspects of form, three of which I find especially helpful in theorizing both the shapes of musicals and the functions of songs within them. The first of Burke's categories he calls syllogistic form (labeled progressive form by Scott McMillin), "a perfectly conducted argument, advancing step by step." Not all musicals may have "perfectly conducted" plots but all, even revues, have intelligible narrative spines. In terms of song form, the clearest example of syllogistic form would be the narrative song. Although they are relative rarities in musical theatre, a notable and complex example is "The Saga of Jenny," a specialty number from the second act of Kurt Weill, Ira Gershwin, and Moss Hart's *Lady in the Dark* (1941). Written as the 11 o'clock number for Gertrude Lawrence, the star of the show, the song tells the life story and erotic misadventures of the notorious, eponymous Jenny, who, unlike the musical's indecisive heroine Liza Elliott, "would make up her mind."[15] Rather than furthering the plot, the song represents a performative eruption that resists a narrowly syllogistic reading, a swinging boogie-woogie which, on the show's opening night in Boston, Lawrence suddenly and spectacularly turned into a show-stopping, bump and grind number.[16]

Burke's first alternative to syllogistic form is qualitative (or associative) progression, by which "the presence of one quality" or mood or state of mind "prepares us for the introduction of another." Liza's virtuosic turn and defense of her indecision represents an explosive, exhibitionist recoil from the focus on inwardness in this first musical about psychoanalysis. It also represents a boisterously comedic rejoinder to Liza's melancholy, meditative theme song, "My Ship," that haunts her obsessively over the course of the show. Burke's second alternative is repetitive form, which Burke defines as "the consistent maintaining of a principle under new guises," which is to say, "the restatement of the same thing in different ways." This use of repetition describes in fact one of the most pervasive conventions of musical theatre songs, which almost always utilize stanzaic formulas. In the case of "Jenny," the refrain in fact consists of six repeated, sixteen-measure, A-B stanzas, each of which illustrates the song's moral, a warning against decisiveness.[17] Despite the song's many blue notes and harmonic eccentricities, "The Saga of Jenny" is still a manifestly repetitive, minor-key pseudo-blues whose structure alternates refrain and release, solo and chorus, which step by step builds an argument that supports Liza's case. It exemplifies the fact that a musical theatre song is always a mode of dramatic action: something happens in and through its performance.

The Interwar Musical

I choose *Lady in the Dark* as a representative work not because of its structural innovations but rather its ingenious repurposing, despite these innovations, of a musical theatre vernacular that had evolved during the 1920s and 1930s. Although Broadway (like Hollywood) had become a world leader in popular culture by the time the show opened, the musicals that filled its theatres represented the results of decades of generic and formal development on both sides of the Atlantic. They were also linked to a lively transatlantic trade in musicians, composers, singers, and writers, as well as various media, especially sheet music and gramophone records. This trade facilitated the mobility of musical styles and theatrical conventions that, in the years before World War I, led to the consolidation of an international style epitomized by the cosmopolitan modernity of Berlin and New York, the trendsetting hubs in both music and theatre. In Berlin, a vibrant center for operetta, revue, and cabaret, "*Amerikanismus*" became all the rage, "serv[ing] as a metaphor for Germany's own modernity."[18] In the United States, meanwhile, both imported and homegrown operetta was wildly popular as a more elite, Europeanized alternative to musical comedy and revue, with which, however, it became more and more intertwined. Even a landmark show such as Jerome Kern's *Show Boat* suffers from what Katherine Axtell describes as a "generic 'identity crisis,'" defying easy categorization by combining the structure and musical dramaturgy of operetta with the conventions of revue and musical comedy.[19]

Even though US jazz had a decisive influence on German popular and concert music as well as opera, the early twentieth-century traffic in musical plays between continental Europe and the US remained primarily east to west. Operettas by Franz Lehár, Emmerich Kálmán, and many others were successfully adapted for the Broadway stage, but the German-language originals were far more satirical, topical, politically provocative, and bawdy than their US-American adaptations or, for that matter, the original Broadway operettas of Victor Herbert, Sigmund Romberg, and others. The ascension of the Nazis in 1933, however, put a damper on the trade and like Kurt Weill himself, the musical's center of gravity migrated from Europe to the United States. The last pre-Hitler German work to open on Broadway during the 1930s was Ralph Benatzky's *White Horse Inn*, in 1936, by which time the piece had become a worldwide hit and had changed the rules governing the transnational trade in musicals. Blurring distinctions among operetta, revue, and musical, as well as different popular musical styles, the lavish production of *Im weißen Rössl* that premiered in 1930 in Berlin's 3,000-seat Großes Schauspielhaus was so spectacular and popular that for the first time, a musical was marketed as "a complete package" that included direction (by Erik Charell), scene and costume design, "Tyrolese singers and dancers, Bavarian zither players, and its own continental version of a jazz band."[20] (*Im weißen Rössl* was thus the first real precursor of franchised musicals like *Cats* and *Phantom of the Opera*, which would travel the world in the 1980s.) After its Berlin premiere, it quickly crossed the English Channel, where it was turned into a "rapturously received" *White Horse Inn* in 1931. The next year, it opened in Paris as *L'auberge du cheval blanc* but did not debut on Broadway until stopping along the way in Italy, Hungary, Spain, Denmark, Palestine, Australia, and the Belgian Congo.[21] Its peregrinations well suited this "mythical rural idyll" about tourists vacationing at a picturesque inn in the Salzkammergut of Upper Austria. Len Platt and Tobias Becker aptly describe the piece as an "appealing chocolate box fantasy of Germany as 'Austria'" and note that in the first years after the show opened, the Baedeker travel guide praised the region "in terms derived from the show itself" and even awarded the real inn a Baedeker star.[22] Despite, or more likely because of, its exploitation of local color, *Im weißen Rössl* was almost completely Anglicized or Americanized for its runs in London and New York (Figure 1.1).

Although the Austrian protagonists and setting remained, in London the tourists became British, while in the US version they hailed from Brooklyn. Both adaptations included most of the songs, while localizing characters, dialogue, and song lyrics. The Broadway version, with swinging, colloquialized lyrics by Irving Caesar, turns it so completely into a musical comedy that it makes one almost forget its German roots.[23] Even in Germany and Austria, *Rössl* is repeatedly referenced not as an operetta but as the "first" homegrown "musical."[24]

Despite the differences among the adaptations of *Rössl*, the basic plot and songs traveled with it because they exemplify the conventions associated with the transnationalized Broadway-style musical during its so-called

14 INTRODUCTION

Figure 1.1 Cover, souvenir program, *The White Horse Inn*, Center Theatre, New York, 1939. Photo courtesy Operetta Research Center, Amsterdam.

Golden Age, between World War I and the late 1960s.[25] Like most musicals, its plot has several pairs of would-be lovers of different social classes who are brought together by the finale. Like most, *Rössl* is strewn with songs whose different styles are predicated on their function. These songs, moreover, usually employ a three-part modular structure that renders them both dramatic and theatrical: an introductory verse, a refrain (the most memorable part of the song), and a contrasting bridge or release that links to a repeated statement of the refrain. This modular structure, which both advances and suspends the narrative, guarantees that it has a dramatic arc. *Im weißen Rössl* remains, along with *Die Fledermaus*, one of the two most popular and widely performed operettas in the German-speaking world, and its score, which interpolates music by several other composers, indulges both the skillful parody and romance central to musical comedy (and operetta) while also spotlighting atypical reversals of gender and class relations.[26] The main couple, whose songs are closest in style to operetta, are neither royalty nor rich sophisticates, but an independent, prosperous woman innkeeper and her lovesick head waiter. (There are notable similarities between the main plots of *Rössl* and *Lady in the Dark*, both centered on a successful businesswoman and a dissatisfied male underling.) Furthermore, the moneyed guests, most with ridiculously comic flaws, are two-dimensional buffoons and the subjects of satire. The placement of the gainfully employed bourgeoisie front and center and the piece's persistent focus on the labor involved in running a hotel full of international tourists are crucial in giving *Rössl* consequence and portability.

The appeal of works like *Im weißen Rössl* (in all its incarnations) to an internationalized middle class is indissolubly linked to questions about the relative class position of musicals in different cultural traditions. For there is no question but that the cultural dispensation in Germany and Austria was—and is—more clearly hierarchized and inflexible than that which obtains in the United States. In the United States, a theatrical hierarchy was consolidated after World War I predicated on the opposition between highbrow literary theatre and low- to middlebrow popular entertainments. But the regime that set Eugene O'Neill against musical comedy gradually broke down, especially in the wake of the social, political, and cultural revolutions of the 1960s, as rock 'n' roll became the dominant musical idiom and avant-gardism began to signal commercial viability as well as prestige. In musical theatre, this revolution was epitomized by *Hair*, which debuted Off Broadway in 1967, opening the next year on Broadway, and quickly jetting to London, Stockholm, and Munich. By the end of the twentieth century, the kind of work that used to be called highbrow, whether theatre or classical music, had become more accessible and sometimes shameless in its cannibalization of popular styles. So too, formerly lowbrow forms like pop music, Hollywood films, and Broadway musicals had become more experimental formally and stylistically. The disintegration of the cultural hierarchy in the United States was attended by a disruption of class-based and race-based identities and identifications. Even a style like hip-hop, which began in the 1970s as an African American street vernacular, has been incorporated into opera and musical theatre. The most celebrated example of the latter is *Hamilton*, which has been such a runaway hit in New York, Chicago, London, and on the Disney+ channel, that its producers are planning productions all over the world. Its first foreign-language production, in Hamburg in October 2022, translated into idiomatic German by a veteran musical theatre translator and a songwriter/rapper, was greeted with glowing reviews.[27] Ironically, its hyper-US-Americanness seems to have made it ripe for a global invasion.

Glocalizing Musical Theatre

In 2012 and 2013, the *New York Times* published high-profile lead stories by Patrick Healy about the boom of Broadway musicals in Germany and South Korea, both hit shows from New York and flops that are granted a second life abroad. The *Times* was correct to single out Hamburg and Seoul as centers for the production of US-American work and to consider the transnational commercial and institutional structures that facilitate the musical's mobility. But Healy missed the fact that theatre-makers in both countries have since the 1990s become highly skilled at making their own versions of a hybrid musical theatre that mixes local stories, musical forms, and theatrical conventions with the idiom of the transnationalized Broadway-style musical. Because this hybrid musical theatre tends to be more locally oriented, it rarely travels outside or far from its homeland. But in many places, this homegrown work is more calculatingly innovative than transnational musicals and more keyed into the concerns and preoccupations of local audiences. This is the work on which this book is focused, which, I argue could not exist without the global circulation of *The Lion King* and *Phantom of the Opera*. This homegrown work exemplifies the fruits of what is sometimes described with the neologism "glocalization."

The world conquest engineered by Broadway-style musical theatre over the past century, despite two world wars and countless social, cultural, and technological revolutions, has been one of the great success stories of US culture. Yet as Healy's articles demonstrate, this success has never given

Broadway producers monopolistic powers outside the United States. Rather, the hegemony of the Broadway musical has always been more formal and ideological than economic, and has been achieved increasingly at the expense of the deterritorialization of Broadway, its dematerialization and transformation into a brand or marketing ploy. This dematerialization happened to take place concurrently with the 1997 decision of the Broadway League, the trade association of the Broadway theatre industry, to brand itself and so protect its identity with a red and white logo and the registered trademark, "Live Broadway."[28] The League understood that since the nineteenth century, Broadway has been shorthand for the commercial theatre in New York City, and it trademarked itself at a moment when neoliberal globalization was at once reinforcing and compromising the identity of Broadway as a uniquely US-American resource.

Since the 1990s, the deterritorialization of Broadway has coincided with the coming of age, in large metropolitan centers such as Hamburg, Vienna, and Seoul, of several generations of producers, songwriters, playwrights, directors, and performers who have collaborated on internationally and/or locally produced Broadway musicals and absorbed the genre's conventions and idioms. This absorption has been facilitated and fueled by local arts institutions and conservatories as well as the worldwide reach of entertainment conglomerates such as Disney and Cameron Mackintosh and other transnational corporations that have succeeded in mounting musicals with a decidedly international appeal.

The large corporations that dominate the commercial theatre industries in Germany and South Korea, the two countries singled out by the *Times*, have excelled both at importing large-scale popular work from abroad and at mounting new work in their own posh venues. The commercial musical theatre industry in Germany is far more monopolistic than in the United States and is dominated by one conglomerate, Stage Entertainment. Austrian commercial theatre is similarly dominated by one company, Vereinigte Bühnen Wien [United Stages Vienna], a private corporation owned by the city of Vienna. These models contrast with South Korea, whose less centralized musical theatre industry is closer to the New York template, providing opportunities for both major and minor production companies. Although my choice of Germany and South Korea follows the *Times*'s lead, I think it is crucially important to understand how and why they became such creative regional hubs. Before becoming major centers for musical theatre, both countries had long-standing traditions in the performing arts, especially music, and both specialized in the manufacture of consumer goods and benefited considerably from the relaxation of trade restrictions engineered in the 1990s by the World Trade Organization and the World Bank. Although West Germany was committed from its founding in 1949 to a social market economy (*Soziale Marktwirtschaft*)—which in fact evolved from a subspecies of neoliberalism called ordoliberalism—reunified Germany (like Austria) has become increasingly, if complexly, neoliberalized.[29] South Korea, on the other hand, which has a more centrally planned economy, initiated a government-mandated program in 1993 of economic and cultural globalization (*segyehwa*), which, in alliance with a renewed cultural nationalism tied to the fall of the dictatorship, has produced extraordinary results.[30] With the rise of neoliberal globalization, Broadway-style musicals have thrived in both countries as German and South Korean producers began investing in Broadway shows (Stage Entertainment co-produced twenty-three between 1993 and 2022).[31] At the same time, South Korea, Germany, Austria, and other non-Anglophone nations started to ship a small number of large-scale productions to New York, such as the Korean musical *The Last Empress* (1995) in 1997, and German-language musicals rewritten for New York, like Vereinigte Bühnen Wien's *Dance of the Vampires* in 2002 (based on *Tanz der Vampire*, 1997, based in turn on Roman Polanski's *The Fearless Vampire Killers*, 1967) and Stage Entertainment's *Rocky the Musical* in 2014 (originally *Rocky: Das Musical*, 2012).

Recognizing the impossibility of writing a comprehensive survey of recent intercontinental migration, I want here instead to provide snapshots of two pivotal productions whose transfers to New York demonstrate the complex socioeconomics and aesthetics of Broadway musicals as global properties in the twenty-first century. The first is a 2009 revival of *Dreamgirls* (1981) that transferred from Seoul to New York six months after its South Korean premiere. The second is the 2014 remounting on Broadway of the original production of *Rocky: Das Musical*, which had opened two years earlier in Hamburg.

Because production costs for musicals in the United States run so high (usually between $5 million and $20 million), producers in the twenty-first century began to look overseas for co-producers in countries that hunger for musicals but in which labor costs are significantly lower than in the United States.[32] In 2009, one New York producer even launched an out-of-town tryout 7,000 miles from Broadway. The success of the 2006 film adaptation of Michael Bennett's hit musical *Dreamgirls* induced John F. Breglio, entertainment lawyer and executor of Bennett's estate, to bet he could further exploit his intellectual property by teaming up with a South Korean producer. "After the [2006] movie," Breglio declared, "I started getting interest all over the world.... The show became an international brand."[33] So his company, Vienna Waits Productions, went into partnership in 2009 with Chun-soo Shin, whose OD Musical Company exemplifies, in the words of the *New York Times*, "South Korea's new, voracious appetite for musical theater."[34] For producers like Shin, *Dreamgirls* represents a dream of a brand: an opportunity for "the expansion of Korean musicals into the world stage."[35] The Seoul production was staged by a prestigious US-American design team, helmed by director Robert Longbottom, allowing Breglio to save $6 to $7 million, about 60 percent of the estimated budget.[36] The Korean backers meanwhile covered "the lion's share of the entire tryout costs," including scene and costume designs and wages and expenses for the twenty-member, US-based creative team. For the scheduled New York opening, all 580 costumes had to be rebuilt (in Korea) for US actors, and the production was given "an American makeover."[37] But because "the cost of labor was vastly less expensive" in South Korea, the price tag for the new costumes proved to be $850,000 instead of $2.5 million.[38] The Seoul tryout thus represented a cost-saving enterprise, as well as an attempt both to tap "a new market of investors"[39] and dodge "the prying eyes of theater columnists."[40] For Shin, the production was most of all a valuable outlay because it allowed him to create "networks with producers across the globe.... I now have credit in Broadway and it has made my dream come much closer to reality."[41]

Although the original *Dreamgirls* is regarded as a landmark Black musical, despite its white production team,[42] the Korean production, with an all-Korean cast, did not employ blackface or Afro wigs, "essentially eliminate[ing]," in Ji Hyon (Kayla) Yuh's words, "the show's racial elements." Thus, the souvenir program noted, "issues of race will be excluded [in this production] while the story behind an unknown singer's journey of becoming a glamorous star will be emphasized for a tighter drama that will move the Korean audience."[43] Yet at the same time, the program remained intent on "educating the audience about the backdrop of the story by providing cultural and historical references for the original story." Because Chun-soo Shin "believed that the crux of the drama dealt with such universal values as family, friendship, and success, ... he felt *Dreamgirls* could resonate with Korean audiences just as well as audiences in the US or any other part of the world."[44] This point was underlined by Choe Sang-Hun in the

New York Times, who argued that the film adaptation's "universal themes" and celebration of "the power of sisterhood" especially resonated in South Korea, where "a new generation of assertive women [were] moving from the margins of society to the center."[45] The Seoul *Dreamgirls* premiered in February 2009, earned strong reviews, ran for six months, and won six Korea Musical Awards, including best foreign musical.[46] However, as Ji Hyon (Kayla) Yuh writes, "Korean audiences seemed to be divided, writing performance reviews noting the limitations of the Korean cast, who could not reproduce the 'feel that is unique to African American performances' of soul and R&B."[47] Recast with African American actors, it opened at Harlem's Apollo Theater on November 22, 2009, as the kick-off to a national tour in partnership with Broadway Across America.[48] The production earned positive reviews in *Variety*, which foregrounded news of the trans-Pacific partnership, while Ben Brantley's mostly negative review in the *New York Times* never mentioned the Seoul tryout, preferring to criticize the production's "intense and unshaded" hard sell that "doesn't do justice to the show's genuine complexity."[49]

The de-racialization of *Dreamgirls* in South Korea, that is, the production's success at stripping away its social and cultural specificity, points to the remarkable ability of so many Broadway musicals to tell a culturally—and often ethnically or racially—particularized story while making it seem "universal." If the choice of *Dreamgirls* seems especially ironic, it is because the piece itself centrally concerns—and critiques—the stripping away of cultural specificity, the commercialization of soul and gospel in the 1960s, and the rise of the much less heavily blues-inflected Motown sound. From a different perspective, however, *Dreamgirls* may well be a perfect choice for Korean performers on whom, Kyung Hyun Kim notes, "the impact of 'blackness'" that results from the long-term US military presence is "profound and unerasable." He argues in fact that Koreans in the twenty-first century have been positioned as "somewhere between" Black and white, resistant and compliant, because the "blackish or off-white Korean subjectivity that emerged in the era of social media" could evade "the continuing racial-cultural war between whiteness and blackness" and "self-correct the potential errors and insults that could risk damaging one's reputation around the issue of race."[50] The Korean *Dreamgirls*, when exported back to the United States several months after its Seoul premiere, re-acquired its Blackness and its aura via its re-casting and its run at the legendary Apollo Theater, the setting of the musical's opening scene, a venue chosen by Breglio despite the fact that it had "never presented a legit [Broadway] production on the scale of 'Dreamgirls.'" He justified his choice of the Apollo over a Broadway house by claiming that it allowed the musical to "tap African-American and music-enthusiast auds [*sic*] who may not have turned out so readily for a Broadway run."[51] With Breglio's assistance, Chun-soo Shin had accomplished his mission.

Broadway on the Elbe

Although exponentially larger than OD Musical Company, Stage Entertainment is similarly ambitious and has succeeded in becoming a major player in the global musical theatre sweepstakes. It was incorporated in 1998 by Joop van der Ende, a then already well-established Dutch theatre entrepreneur, who combined several of his companies to form a new multinational conglomerate. In 2022, it owns sixteen "world class theatres" while committed to strengthening its "position as industry leader and 'go-to' partner for content" that is tailored to "broad audiences in local languages." Its theatres, in seven European countries, offer 10,000 performances per year, drawing 7 million visitors.[52] It boasts 3,000 employees, 1,500 in Germany alone, its largest subdivision, and ticket sales of 310 million euros,[53] thanks in part to its acquisition in 2000 of then-bankrupt Stella Entertainment, a builder of large-scale theatres and producer of numerous megamusicals in Germany during the 1980s and 1990s. Stage Entertainment oversees the production, distribution, and consumption of its product: by producing new work (six world premieres) as well as continental premieres of Broadway and West End hits, while handling its advertising and marketing in house.[54] It maintains a portfolio of about seventy productions and has almost singlehandedly turned Hamburg into "the Broadway of Europe"[55] by fostering what the *New York Times* in 2012 described as an "enormous audience appetite for musicals—an appetite encouraged by 25 years of producers splashing television ads and billboards across Germany . . . to market Hamburg as the home of Broadway-style shows."[56] Stage Entertainment's website, meanwhile, promises customers what audiences have always expected of Broadway: "the highest level of production of musicals and shows, with unique staging, fantastic scene design, high-class artists, and thrilling music. People will be snatched out of their everyday lives, touched, and brought into impressive and atmospheric theatres for unforgettable moments."[57]

Most of Stage Entertainment's musicals have been launched in partnership with producers like Disney Theatricals, the Really Useful Group, Blue Man Productions, Cameron Mackintosh, and Vereinigte Bühnen Wien. And most of its original productions have been tailor-made for the German market, including *Ich war noch niemals in New York* (I Have Never Been to New York, 2007), a jukebox musical featuring the hits of the Austrian singer Udo Jürgens; *Hinterm Horizont* (Beyond the Horizon, 2011), a jukebox musical based on the music of pop star Udo Lindenberg; and *Das Wunder von Bern* (The Miracle of Bern, 2014), based on the 2003 film about Germany's 1954 victory at the World Cup. Stage Entertainment's most high-profile bid for global success, however, was its extravagant production of *Rocky: Das Musical*, which won the 2013 Best Musical of Germany Award. This 15 million euro[58] adaptation of the 1976 Sylvester Stallone all-American blockbuster was coproduced by Stallone, engaged an A-list, all-US-American, non-German-speaking production team (including Stephen Flaherty, Lynn Ahrens, Thomas Meehan, and Alex Timbers), and received "a rapturous critical reception" upon opening in November 2012 at the swank Operettenhaus in Hamburg's red-light district.[59] *Rocky* delivered a knockout punch in Hamburg, but in a perhaps unexpectedly old-fashioned way, by employing a tuneful, carefully constructed score and overlaying an intimate version of the Rodgers and Hammerstein formula (think: *Carousel*) with spectacular scenic and visual effects. Despite its large scale, the first act, set in Philadelphia, concentrates on the story of awakening love between Rocky and Adrian while the second opens up the story to focus on the heavyweight championship, both Rocky's intensive physical training and the prize fight itself. The climactic fight is turned into an astonishing display as the spectators seated in the first seven rows of the orchestra, the "Golden Circle," are brought up onstage to sit in bleachers facing the house, after which a boxing ring rolls out over the vacated seats and video screens are lowered from the ceiling. This radical remaking of the performance space ratchets up the excitement and changes everyone's point of view, turning *Rocky* into an immersive event.

Opening just before the rise of neo-fascist populist leaders like Viktor Orbán, Marine Le Pen, and Donald Trump, *Rocky* looks back nostalgically to a time when heroism was deemed a less problematic concept than it became in the 2010s. Both film and musical use Rocky Balboa to symbolize nationalist and entrepreneurial aspirations, focusing on his transformation into a hero who, through the loss of one critical battle (the prizefight), wins more precious and longer-lasting prizes, Adrian's love—and a Best Picture

Academy Award. The score of *Rocky*, like that of most post-Sondheim musicals, is deliberately polystylistic, mixing contemporary pop-rock with 1970s pastiche, especially Philly soul. In *Rocky*, soul alternates with a contemporary Broadway pop-rock vernacular while it also borrows two well-known songs indelibly associated with the Rocky story, Bill Conti's "Gonna Fly Now," the hit song from the original *Rocky*, and Survivor's "Eye of the Tiger," written for *Rocky III* (1982). These songs give the musical period flavor and ensure audiences familiar with the Rocky films that they will not be disappointed by their absence.[60]

Although *Rocky: Das Musical* was calculated to appeal to Germans' love of US popular culture and was developed in part to bolster Stage Entertainment's symbolic capital in the eyes of German musical theatre fans, it, like the Korean *Dreamgirls*, represents an extremely far-flung, out-of-town tryout.[61] Even before the announced transfer, *Stern* magazine noted that Hamburg may cast "a constant, worried eye [*Argusaugen*] on Broadway," but "for the first time, a major international musical" would be traveling "from Germany into the world."[62] *Stern* articulated what musical theatre aficionados long suspected, for *Rocky the Musical* did indeed begin a run at New York's Winter Garden Theatre in February 2014. Before its opening, Stage Entertainment touted its prestige as the first company to export a "German" musical to Broadway, indeed, to the theatre that once housed *West Side Story* and *Funny Girl*.[63] In the words of Johannes Mock-O'Hara, Stage Entertainment Germany's managing director, "This is a milestone for Stage [Entertainment], the cultural city of Hamburg, and the musical genre altogether. Before, all the major musical productions shown in Germany came from the U.S. or the U.K. But never before has a German musical made it into the *Mutterland* of the musical."[64] This pride is also reflected in the three trailers made for the German premiere, which emphasize the production's bicontinental loyalties. Two of the trailers are set unmistakably not in Rocky's Philadelphia, but along the River Elbe in Stage Entertainment's Hamburg, which, like the fighter himself, is imagined as a scrappy "underdog," an ambitious pursuer of the "typical American Dream" in the shape of a heavyweight title.[65] Stallone himself, moreover, emphasized the musical's relevance to its adopted hometown: "The story fits Hamburg. Hamburg is a 'Rocky' city."[66]

Although *Rocky* was staged by a US-based creative team, its bicontinental identity is emphasized by the fact that its co-producers in Germany included the Klitschko brothers, two Ukrainian-born, former heavyweight champions who made their professional debuts in Hamburg, were strongly associated with the city, and were featured in two of the trailers made after the show's opening. The subjects of a celebrated German film documentary (*Klitschko*, 2011), they are especially lionized in Germany where they are seen as Rocky-like prizefighters, sexy media stars who also happen to be more potent sites of identification for young audiences than the now-septuagenarian Stallone. Although the presence of their names above the title complicates Stage Entertainment's cultural nationalism, it does not change the fact that *Rocky* is less a specifically German cultural production than an exemplar of the multiple allegiances of large-scale, transnational musicals.

When *Rocky* opened at the Winter Garden in March 2014, it was shorn of the Klitschko brothers and other noticeable links to Germany. Stage Entertainment remained the primary producer, but it was joined by fourteen co-producers (including Chun-soo Shin and his OD Musical Company). In Hamburg, *Rocky* had been staged and promoted as an old-fashioned musical to attract the middle-class, middlebrow audiences that routinely patronize German musical theatre. It scored a three-year run in Hamburg followed by a year and a half in Stuttgart. On Broadway, in contrast, it was marketed to a more male, sports-minded public less as musical love story than staged prizefight. New York audiences, but not the critics, cheered the reproduction of iconic scenes from the movie as well as the high-testosterone performances, especially of Andy Karl in the title role. Although the simulated prizefight became *Rocky*'s Broadway calling card, its immersive mise en scène was ill-suited to what *Chicago Tribune* critic Chris Jones calls an "old-fashioned theater" like the Winter Garden. The musical will, he "suspect[s], be yet more visually dazzling once it gets restaged in a neutral space in Las Vegas or Korea or somewhere."[67] Most of the reviewers forgot the particular "somewhere" the musical had premiered, with the notable exception of Ben Brantley in the *Times*, who panned the "leaden show" except for its last sixteen minutes, the prizefight. While noting the musical's all-American subject matter, Brantley quipped snidely that it was "[p]reviously staged to big box office in German in Hamburg (I said, no snickers)."[68]

Against McTheatre

The presumed snickers that would greet the idea that Germans could manufacture and appreciate a Broadway-style musical with a populist, US-identified hero point more to the snobbish xenophobia of New York critics than to the provincialism of Hamburgers. It also represents the flip side (on the other side of the Atlantic) of the elitism of the "unruly-haired intellectuals who run" Hamburg's two major state-subsidized theatres, the Thalia and Deutsches Schauspielhaus. According to the *Times*, the mere mention to them of new musicals draws "winces and barnyard epithets."[69] Although these snide reactions betray two very different kinds of snobbism, they both point to the anxiety that attends the global circulation of Broadway-style musical theatre, which, it is presumed, is either misunderstood and mismanaged by non-US-Americans or else is simply mass-produced garbage force-fed to innocent consumers. While the former reaction represents a narrow-minded provincialism, the latter, which has long prevailed among many anxious intellectuals outside (and sometimes inside) the United States, represents what Jonathan Matusitz describes as "a monolithic or one-dimensional view of globalization or Americanization, a thesis that portrays icons of American culture spreading by design worldwide and riding roughshod over local conditions and practices."[70]

For critics and intellectuals who consider musicals, in the words of one Hamburg Senate member, merely "loud entertainment" utterly devoid of "cultural significance,"[71] it is tempting to run to Theodor W. Adorno for cover and label Disney, Cameron Mackintosh, and Stage Entertainment as the conquistadors of the culture industry who invade and overrun the defenseless indigenous peoples. Yet that characterization is inaccurate. For despite the concentrations of capital that neoliberal globalization has enabled and expedited, the traffic in cultural goods has changed radically since the 1980 UNESCO-sponsored MacBride Report set forth its now-classic description of cultural imperialism as the "cultural invasion" by the "worst" commodities of "[t]ransnational companies" that stifle "creative artists in developing countries." According to this hypothesis, these wares impose "external values" and enforce "uniformity of taste, style and content" in order to serve the political and economic interests of the imperializing power while subjugating those of the target culture.[72] Because plays from the United States, including Broadway musicals, are almost always performed in translation outside the Anglophone world, they are inevitably mediated by local producers, directors, actors, and performance traditions, unlike popular music, which, at least since the 1960s has as a rule been broadcast, marketed, and sold "as is," that is, as audio or video recordings, as well as Hollywood movies and television, which are routinely dubbed for foreign markets but usually presented with minimal or discreet editing. While the Disney musicals, with the notable exception of *The Lion King*, may aim to approximate the animated film originals, they are carefully tailored when exported to engage and cater to local audiences.

Laura MacDonald reports that for Disney executives, the goal of the Chinese premiere of *The Lion King* that welcomed visitors to Shanghai Disneyland when it opened in 2016 was to be "authentically Disney and distinctly Chinese." Thus, it was indigenized and partially restaged to incorporate elements of "Chinese culture such as the Monkey King and acrobats." MacDonald summarizes the impact of this dual tactic: "Hedging its bets, Disney sought to please different kinds of Chinese consumers—those who might feel more secure in purchasing a ticket to a Broadway replica, as well as those wanting a unique Shanghai *The Lion King*."[73] She emphasizes that this mode of giving audiences what they think they want is always Disney's strategy when exporting its musicals.

Despite the many well-documented changes incorporated into franchised Broadway musicals outside the Anglophone world, the "cultural invasion" thesis retains a certain political and analytical leverage for those preoccupied with the politics of performance. For a sizable group of Anglophone critics, scholars, and theatre aficionados intent on separating the esoteric theatre they love from mere entertainment, transnational musical theatre has become the poster child for an allegedly standardized, mass-produced commodity they call McTheatre. Jonathan Burston, Dan Rebellato, and others are correct to note the efficient production and distribution machinery that multinational corporations deploy. Burston decries producers' "rationalising, industrial logic," while Rebellato notes the megamusical's status less as "an event in itself" than "as part of a transnational entertainment corporation's marketing strategy."[74] Although their attack on McTheatre dates back to the 1990s, the label continues to be trotted out, especially by scholars who have never seen a non-English language *The Lion King* or scrutinized the performance of franchised musicals outside the Anglophone world.[75] The McTheatre label, in fact, is an evocation of George Ritzer's *The McDonaldization of Society* (1993), which launches a thoroughgoing critique of what he describes as the standardization and "routinization of interactive service work."[76] But unlike Ritzer, the critics of McTheatre misjudge the level of standardization and focus exclusively on relations of production, overlooking the geographically and historically specific responses of spectators. A musical, however, is not a hamburger and consumers develop a much more active and complex relationship with a two-and-a-half-hour musical spectacle than with a Big Mac.

For the laboring bodies on stage produce not a thing to be chewed up and swallowed but an experience, no matter how predictable, as elusive as it is ephemeral.

Contemporaneously with the theorization of McTheatre, media scholars such as Ien Ang emphasized the pressing need for an analysis of how cultural productions are "actively and differentially responded to and negotiated in concrete local contexts and conditions."[77] Or as Elihu Katz and Tamar Liebes put it in their now classic ethnographic study of different interpretative communities' readings of the television show *Dallas*: "in addition to the reader constructed by the text there is a real reader, who may or may not act as instructed."[78] The work of Katz and Liebes demonstrates that for decades communities have developed active relationships with texts and that entrenched attitudes and beliefs "shape what, if anything, of the program will penetrate the culture." Presumably, a live performance of *The Lion King* would be at least as "open" to interpretation as an episode of *Dallas*, open enough "to permit" audience involvement on different—and often competing—semantic, moral, and ideological levels.[79]

Although the study of theatre spectatorship is, at best, an inexact and subjective science and has been the subject of far less ethnographic research than televisual reception, a critical observer like Laura MacDonald who has attended productions of the same musical inside and outside the United States can see plainly that they are transformed by cultural middlemen and received by consumers in often utterly different ways. To provide another example, let me take Stage Entertainment's 2008 production of Disney's *Tarzan* in Hamburg, which was a revision of the Broadway original that had opened two years prior. Reviews and online postings suggest that the audience experience of the long-running Hamburg hit was very different from that of the notorious Broadway flop, which, although it played fourteen months, lost Disney Theatrical Productions $12 million. With music and lyrics by Phil Collins and a book by David Henry Hwang, it was damned by Ben Brantley in the *New York Times* as a "giant, writhing green blob with music"[80] but celebrated two years later in the Hamburg press as "an intoxicating orgy of colored fabric that grows into fantastic plant and animal forms."[81] The German reviews suggest that the piece's spectacularly acrobatic effects were far better served in the giant, steeply raked auditorium of Stage Entertainment's Theater Neue Flora than in New York's more intimate Richard Rodgers Theatre. As one Disney executive noted, "the visual language and expressionistic environment and special effects of 'Tarzan' have much more appeal in Hamburg," where the Tarzan story is better known than in the United States.[82] Even five years into its run, the Hamburg fans found it exciting, moving, and "simply fantastic." "Grief, joy, anger, emotion, longing, and love. ONLY MUSIC AND THEATRE TOGETHER CAN DO THAT!"[83] The attack on McTheatre ignores both the changes prompted by translation and the uniquely communicative nature of musical theatre, which always practices a kind of intermedial counterpoint of story, text, music, lyrics, singing, dancing, acting, and mise en scène. Social media postings suggest that in Hamburg, *Tarzan* was able to produce "a *super* atmosphere in the whole theatre" and make people "really feel the actors' passion," feel that they are giving "such an outstanding performance that they sweep the audience away."[84] And Hamburg is not unique. The world over, audiences seem to expect that a ticket for a musical, which costs roughly ten times that for a movie, will buy them "goose bumps," liveness, dazzle, and transcendence.[85] The dismissal of dozens of shows whole-cloth for "bland, boring music" reveals little more than the critic's unfamiliarity with the genre he attacks, combined with a snobbish anti-populism.[86] For it is neither fair nor respectful to say that the class fractions that love these musicals are simply deer in the headlights, immobilized targets blinded by the commodity fetishism perpetrated by the global culture industry. As Jessica Sternfeld notes tartly, "audiences are not that inept."[87]

The attack on McTheatre also betrays a nostalgia for a mode of cultural production that, because it has been declared archaic, is viewed as being better and more authentic than contemporary modes. This nostalgia, moreover, is not unique to those who decry the globalization of musical theatre. Some conservative musical theatre scholars, most notably Mark Grant, argue that the "fall" of the musical began back in 1966. He mercilessly condemns what he refers to as the McMusical, "corporately franchised staged happenings" that leave the "brain . . . numbed and narcotized," which "are actually music videos packaged for theatre."[88] And he is particularly critical of those purportedly over-miked shows in which, he writes, sound designers feel obligated "to replicate the recorded sound."[89] Jacques Attali points out, however, that the displacement of live musical performance by recording represents a structural change that dates back not to the 1960s but to the early years of phonography, and that it signals "a very deep transformation" of the listener's relationship to music. Recording may have been invented as a means of preserving sound, but it quickly turned into "the driving force of the economy of music," a force that impels "public performance" to become "a simulacrum of the record."[90]

Rather than rehearse the McTheatre thesis, I want to argue that multinational corporations such as Stage Entertainment are well aware of the dangers of standardization and have responded to audiences' anxieties about mass-produced live entertainment by practicing what Luc Boltanski and Eve Chiapello refer to as codification, which is distinct from commodification and "makes it possible to operate on a combinatory and introduce variations" "element by element . . . in such a way as to obtain products that are relatively different, but of the same style." Codification thus manages to "preserve something of the uniqueness" that has always been expected of a theatrical performance.[91] Even franchised musicals must be translated and adapted to local markets through changes to script, mise en scène, topical references, casting, and advertising. Corporations like Disney, Stage Entertainment, and Vereinigte Bühnen Wien have become so successful at producing and exporting live musicals because they are cognizant of the tastes and desires of consumers and have learned how to practice what marketing guru Mark Gobé calls the "emotional customization" of both product and advertising as a way of responding to local tastes and predispositions while also catering more widely to the desire for pleasure, adventure, and liveness.[92] One might deplore the motives behind "emotional customization," but it is incorrect to assume that it always results in cultural homogenization and economic exploitation.

Although franchised musicals represent the most conspicuous part of the transnational trade in musical theatre, many small-scale musicals also ride the international circuit in localized adaptations that rehearse more politically progressive intercessions. One of the most widely traveled is *Linie 1* (Subway Line #1), which premiered in West Berlin three years before the fall of the Berlin Wall. With a text by Volker Ludwig and music by Birger Heymann, it has become the most widely toured and the most frequently performed German musical after *Die Dreigroschenoper* (*The Threepenny Opera*, 1928), with which it shares a trenchant critique of the economic and social chasm between rich and poor. *Linie 1* appeals cross-culturally because of the transferability of its story, which details the fallout that has resulted from rapid, unchecked urbanization. Its plotline tracks the peregrinations of a young woman from the provinces newly arrived in the big city looking for the rock 'n' roller who fathered her soon to-be-born child. Riding a subway line that cuts through the heart of the city, the unnamed girl happens upon a panoply of colorful locals, most of whom are on the losing side of the class war. After confronting opportunists and misfits, she finally ends up meeting the father of her child but realizes he is not the man of her dreams and she exits with a different young man whom she met on the subway earlier in the day. The German-language production has toured to dozens of theatres on six continents, while the musical has been translated and adapted to local conditions in many cities, like Berlin, that harbor many casualties left in the wake of the neoliberal turn of the 1990s. Its most successful adaptation was in Seoul, where, after a fifteen-year run, it was even dubbed "the national musical."[93] *Linie 1* was also translated and adapted to local conditions in Hong Kong, Barcelona, Kolkata, Vilnius (Latvia), Windhoek (Namibia), Aden (Yemen), and Maputo (Mozambique).[94] It seems especially apt that this most portable of musicals, which is centrally concerned with the literal and symbolic mobility of persons, is set in a subway line. The mobility of *Linie 1*'s constantly moving subway car, its premise and promise, also points to the portability of the musical itself, a supremely adaptable set of conventions that is as likely to critique and satirize the ruling classes as to reaffirm the status quo.

It's a Small World

In 2009, the webpage promoting "Disney Musicals Around the World" used as backdrop an image of a megapolis after dark, stretching across the curvature of the globe, whose only recognizable landmark was the Statue of Liberty. Disney's graphic seemed to announce: "It's a small world," evoking the Sherman brothers' song penned for the Disney "centerpiece" of the UNICEF pavilion at the 1964 New York World's Fair, a boat ride that "took visitors to more than 100 countries with child-like *Audio-Animatronics* figures."[95] This evocation is uncannily appropriate for the webpage, considering that "It's a Small World," deemed "one of the most well-known [songs] of all time," was written to Walt Disney's specification as one "that could be sung by all of the children" of the world. It has been translated into countless languages, spawned a musical boat ride in Disney theme parks, and was even interpolated into the film *The Lion King* (1994).[96] The "Musicals Around the World" webpage, meanwhile, included links to all the satellite companies' websites, which sell tickets and feature videos, photo galleries, postings by fans, and of course excerpts of the songs performed in local languages.[97] The Statue of Liberty would seem to announce that New York remains the primary point of dissemination for Disney product. But as I am arguing in this book, Broadway since 2009 has increasingly become merely one node or distribution center in a global network of live and electronic performances with little regard for national borders. Broadway has become a fantasy kingdom, "a world of laughter, a world of tears," where shows try out or to which they aspire to alight in this "small world."[98]

Despite its deterritorialization, the Broadway brand continues to mobilize desires and fears, aspirations and anxieties in relation to the United States. After all, the landmark on Disney's website is not a municipal symbol like the Empire State Building but a national one. And although the United States is demonstrably an empire in decline, it remains, in Hyunjung Lee's words, "the great symbol of affluence and . . . the epitome of the global."[99] It is not by chance that the original German graphics for *Rocky: Das Musical* are red, white, and blue; that Apollo Creed, Rocky's African American opponent, shouts out his national spirit in a song entitled "Patriotic"; and that Creed puts in a brief appearance as Uncle Sam before the climactic fight (as he does in the film). Yet the United States envisioned in *Rocky* and other transnational musicals is as fantasmatic as Broadway itself. Stripped of its militarist and imperialist trappings, and condensed in the image of the Statue of Liberty or Uncle Sam, it is imagined not as the wholesaler of neoliberalism but as the homeland of that hoary delusion, the American Dream.

Rocky's jingoism notwithstanding, productions of Broadway hit musicals outside the United States by no means merely rubber-stamp US cultural nationalism. On the contrary, they are often mobilized to critique the American Dream. By way of example, let me cite a summer 2017 production by Staatstheater Braunschweig (Germany) of Marc Shaiman and Scott Wittman's *Hairspray* (2002), based on John Waters's 1988 film of the same title. The musical, set in 1962 Baltimore, is an attack on racial segregation and, like so many musicals, uses differently racially or ethnically identified songs to dramatize social conflict. Like *Rocky*, it builds to a final spectacular performance that is also a kind of prizefight, a contest of strength and skill between protagonist and antagonist. *Hairspray*'s battle pitches liberal women against reactionaries, anti-racism against racism, gospel-style soul against white-identified rock 'n' roll, and engineers a fairy-tale happy ending in which girl gets boy and racial integration is miraculously achieved. Although *Hairspray* aims to be politically progressive, its plot is still focused squarely on a white heroine, Tracy Turnblad, and her mother (famously played by Divine, a male actor in drag) and, like so many other well-intentioned, white-centered narratives, relegates the African American characters to supporters and helpmates. Nonetheless, soul music does triumph in the end in Motormouth Maybelle's powerful 11 o'clock gospel number, "I Know Where I've Been," and the show's finale, "You Can't Stop the Beat." The latter is a rousing song-and-dance showstopper, a utopian soul anthem to the supposedly unstoppable progress that reconciles races, musical styles, and even political enemies.

Hairspray, whose theme of racial integration is congenial to liberal, Western European theatregoing audiences,[100] received its German-language premiere in St. Gallen, Switzerland, in 2008 and was staged the next year in Cologne in a Broadway replica production. The musical has been performed on six continents and is now staged periodically in German-speaking state-subsidized theatres. The open-air Braunschweig production, directed by Sebastian Welker and opening six months after Donald Trump's inauguration, was designed in part to protest his administration and so interpolated a Trump imitator's narration (in English) over the high school PA system, shouting out orders to the students. More intriguingly, it also incorporated a mute, glitter-clad, presumably invisible Statue of Liberty (played by a male actor) who shadowed the characters and even ended up in jail with them, comforting the ill-used Tracy. Bathed in a blue-green spot, this ghost-like figure stood in Tracy's prison cell weeping, mourning Trump's resuscitation of the racism and white supremacy that the musical roundly condemns as well as his desecration of the freedom and welcome promised by the Statue of Liberty.

Although the Broadway musical abroad can serve all too easily as a focal point for contradictory attitudes toward the United States, it also demonstrates the veracity of the Sherman brothers' claim that this is indeed "a small world after all." And while one might deprecate the consumerism of the Disney theme parks that play "It's a Small World" on endless loops, the song does stake a claim to being "the most performed, and most translated, song of all time."[101] The original version alone, recorded by the Disneyland Children's Chorus, features the lyric in five languages (English, Japanese, Swedish, Italian, and Spanish) and its jingle-like simplicity guarantees its maddening infectiousness. According to Richard Corliss, the Sherman brothers composed it in the wake of the Cuban missile crisis as a "Cold War peace anthem: a prayer to find 'so much that we share' in 'a world of fears.'"[102] Sixty years later, fears of nuclear annihilation have been multiplied by war, neo-fascism, climate change, and an awareness of the precarity of life on an increasingly uninhabitable planet.

Fully cognizant of these dangers, I am not in this book going to debate further the ethics and ecology of the glocalization of franchised musicals, whether by Disney or other multinationals. I am instead focusing on a different kind of circulation, that is, on the many different ways cultures adopt, adapt, and transform the conventions of the Broadway-style musical to perform global citizenship. At the risk of putting too propitious a spin on global citizenship, I want as a coda to endorse the utopianism of both "It's a Small World" and "You Can't Stop the Beat" and suggest that social, political, and economic reform is not possible without a propulsive vision of the global community. For all its pie-in-the-sky romanticism, "You Can't Stop the Beat" provides exactly that propulsion in its evocation of song and dance as a performance that produces the irrepressible pulse and harmony it describes:

> 'Cause the world keeps spinning
> Round and round
> And my heart's keeping time
> To the speed of sound
> I was lost 'till I heard the drums
> Then I found my way
> 'Cause you can't stop the beat.[103]

PART II
SOUTH KOREA

2
The New Broadway-Style Musical

The Korean peninsula presents a fascinating clash of cultures. Neighbor to China and Japan, it has long been subject to incursions from both, having paid tribute to China for centuries only to be annexed by Japan from 1910 until 1945. Its connections with Japan are especially fraught because the latter, during the colonial period, tried to suppress Korean language and culture; brutally exploited Korea's natural, industrial, and human resources; and conscripted Korean men as workers and soldiers and women as sex slaves, so-called comfort women. After World War II, the peninsula was divided between the United States and the Soviet Union, and in 1948 the US occupation zone became the Republic of Korea (South Korea) while the Soviet zone became the Democratic People's Republic of Korea (North Korea). The former retains close ties to the United States but long refused diplomatic and trade relations with Japan, not lifting all restrictions on Japanese cultural imports until 2002.[1] Although the United States is a relative newcomer to the Korean peninsula, its postwar dominion over the south (like its postwar occupation of West Germany and West Berlin) has had profound and far-reaching consequences on art, culture, and society.

In June 1950, North Korea invaded the South and the United States came to its aid in what became the Korean War, which ended three years later when a truce (not a treaty) was coordinated with the North, and the United States and South Korea signed a still-binding Mutual Defense Treaty. Both nations have since maintained close military, economic, and cultural links and war-generation Koreans still "have strong emotional ties to the US, an 'ally tied by blood' rather than interests, based on shared Cold War experiences and zeitgeist."[2] This shared zeitgeist has been greatly strengthened by the persistent influx since the Korean War of US capital, consumer goods, pop music, movies, television, and fast food, which rapidly and radically transformed South Korean society and culture. As Kyung Hyun Kim notes, "There was probably no other place in the era of Pax Americana outside the United States where the learning of the American—the aesthetics, styles, and language— was as intense and durable as it was in Korea."[3] During the 1980s and 1990s,

Broadway musicals were added to the mix, and in 2013, an account of their "head-spinning popularity" was even splashed across the front page of the Sunday *New York Times*.[4] After decades of a barrage of US culture, Korean writers and directors have become so adept at mounting musicals that they have turned Seoul into the preeminent center in East Asia for the production of "Broadway-style" musicals.

But the *New York Times* missed the most provocative part of the story. Even more remarkable than Koreans' skill at staging US-American musicals has been their proficiency at fashioning groundbreaking, ingenious musical theatre pieces that fuse Western and Korean styles. These original works (*changjak*) present, in the words of director Ho Jin Yun, a creative and innovative injection of "a uniquely Korean spirit" into "Broadway-style" musical theatre.[5] *Changjak* also represent a dimension of *hallyu*, the Korean Wave, which includes K-pop, film, television, opera, and various crossbred forms. In this chapter, I examine the impact of Western music in South Korea, the construction of K-pop as a global commodity, and the meaning of "Broadway-style" in the Korean context. In the subsequent chapter, I focus on the construction of tradition and the ways in which "a uniquely Korean spirit" is fashioned and performed in South Korean musical theatre. This chapter studies "Westernization"; the next, "Koreanization."

The Arrival of Western Music in Korea

Western culture was introduced to Korea long before the US occupation. In 1876, Korea opened its doors first to Japan, and in 1882, to the United States. During this period, Western music, using the heptatonic rather than the traditional pentatonic scale, was brought by Christian missionaries from the United States and later, a German musician, Franz Eckert, who was invited to the Korean court, taught composition and trained early Korean composers. At the turn of the twentieth century, the singing of hymns and children's songs led to the elaboration and spread of "Western-style songs" (*changga*) that used the tonal structure of Western music.[6] Ironically, it was only after 1910, which is to say, under Japanese rule, that modernization was effected, along with the dissemination of Western-style performing arts. Choi Yujun explains that as a result of colonialism, Korean modernization is a "very complicated and multilayered" phenomenon. It initially "intermingled with the colonial domination by Japan" and then was "complicated even more by the engagement of American culture," which became "absolutely dominant" after the Korean War. Choi emphasizes how problematic this history has been and how the "very concept of 'Korean music,'" in particular, "epitomizes this colonial structure . . . and creates a conundrum that Korean musicians and musicologists have faced over the last century."[7] The category *gugak*, traditional (or national) Korean music, could not exist without its opposite, the conjoined concepts of Western and modern. This conjunction, moreover, inevitably reinforces a Eurocentric logic that continues to dominate the analysis of both music and theatre in South Korea. That logic constructs the modern and the Western as universals with which, Dipesh Chakrabarty argues, "there is no easy way of dispensing," while the Korean is constructed as the particular, the other. Even with the unprecedented mobility of cultural productions in the twenty-first century, especially music, this bipolar opposition remains necessary for analytical purposes, despite its inadequacy, "a necessary placeholder in our attempt to think through questions of modernity."[8] Recognizing this inadequacy, I will continue to use the terms Western and Korean, traditional and modern, because I see no way around them.

In studies of Korean performance cultures, Andrew Killick notes, "art forms that are considered traditional, and hence protected from change (most conspicuously by the Intangible Cultural Properties system), are generally those that are believed to have developed on the Korean peninsula to a form that would be recognizable today before the end of the Choson dynasty in 1910."[9] Heritage performance, including puppet and masked performances and shamanic rites, all of which use music and song, are probably the oldest theatre forms, while *pansori*, deemed the Korean traditional theatrical genre par excellence, is a sung narrative performed by a vocalist and drummer that dates back to the eighteenth century.[10] None of these, however, constitutes a dramatic, dialogic, internationally renowned lyric theatre, comparable to Peking Opera (*jingju*) or Japanese kabuki. Only in 1908 was Korean opera, *changgeuk*, invented, a "'hybrid-popular theater' form" based on *pansori*, which Killick calls "traditionesque," and which was constructed to be comparable to those which were already well-established in East Asia.[11]

Because spoken theatre was even more conspicuously absent than music theatre, Korea was regarded by Koreans and non-Koreans alike, Killick notes, "as a 'land without theatre'" until the twentieth century. This absence is a result of the fact that "only with the dawn of the twentieth century" did a "commercial indoor theatre with separate stage and auditorium" come "to the peninsula."[12] Moreover, as Robert Nichols writes, "[i]n the years surrounding the 1910 annexation, there were no indigenous dramas on which to build a 'modern' Korean version." Melodramatic, partially improvised plays (*shinpaguk*), which in fact were a Korean imitation of Japanese *shinpa* (an amalgamation of kabuki "and what the Japanese perceived to be Western realism") were first performed in 1911 but disappeared by the 1930s.[13] Not until the 1920s, under the influence of Japanese *shingeki* (realist drama), was the work of Chekhov, Strindberg, Shaw, and Tolstoy first performed in Korea.[14] And not until 1935 was a theatre constructed in Seoul dedicated exclusively to presenting drama.[15]

The Japanese occupation, therefore, paradoxically effected the Westernization, or "colonial modernization," of Korean society, as the Japanese engineered and administered Korean industrialization,[16] along with what Andreas Reckwitz identifies as the "three grand narratives of modernity": capitalization, rationalization, and functional differentiation.[17] Although street lighting had been introduced to Seoul in 1900 and trains began running on a new rail line, Korean mass media and transportation systems were greatly expanded under colonial rule while Western musical and theatrical styles, heavily filtered through Japan, increasingly impacted Korean practices. Under the Japanese occupation, a new Western-influenced song form developed in the 1920s "similar to the German lied" or parlor song.[18] Sound recording and radio broadcasting hastened Westernization as records began to arouse attention due in part to the popularity of soprano Yun Sim-deok's 1926 recording of "Hymn of Death"—followed by her love suicide later that year with her paramour Kim U-jin, "a pioneer of modern Korean drama."[19] Yun was the first Korean woman to study Western classical singing and her recording is a skillfully rendered, Western-style performance of the slow, minor-mode waltz "Waves of the Danube" (1880) by the Romanian composer Iosif Ivanovici, with a text by Yun herself. Yun has been mythologized in Korean culture and is even the protagonist of a small-scale original musical about the tragic love affair entitled *Hymn of Death* (사의찬미, 2012), which boasts a Western-style score and continues to run in the repertoire ten years after its premiere. As Dohyun (Gracia) Shin notes, Yun is constructed and celebrated in the musical as a proto-feminist hero, a "strong and desiring woman."[20]

Yun Sim-deok's fame during the late 1920s "served as an impetus for the birth of popular music as a full-fledged industry,"[21] as phonographs "made their way into the daily lives of the upper class" and Western record labels opened offices in Seoul.[22] The decade also bore witness to a jazz boom and the formation of the Korean Jazz Band by musicians who had first heard jazz in Tokyo and Shanghai and fostered a generation of urbanized "modern girls" and "modern boys" who started questioning traditional values.[23] Simultaneously, a group of Korean composers arose who were trained in Japan or the West and well versed in the Western classical tradition. Among them, the best known is Ahn Eak-tai, who was educated first by missionaries and then studied in Japan, the United States, and Europe. He is best known for his lavish showpiece *Symphonic Fantasia Korea*, for large orchestra and chorus, first performed in Dublin, Ireland, in 1937. Using a late romantic/ early modernist style and incorporating traditional Korean melodies, it remains intermittently performed in South Korea in part because its choral finale has been adopted as the South Korean national anthem, "Aegukga."[24]

Under the aegis of a colonial modernization, filtered through Japan, the genre *gugak* was constructed in a binary opposition to *yangak*, modernized Western music,[25] along with the categories popular music and concert (or classical) music. During the 1930s, jazz, new folk songs, comic songs, and slow triple-meter songs, like "Hymn of Death," persisted while a new kind of popular song called "trot" became dominant. The name is short for "foxtrot" and is derived from Japanese popular song, to which it is closely related. Trots were usually written in a moderate duple meter, employed the minor mode and pentatonic scale, and featured Western-style "pure and clear ringing vocalization."[26] As John Lie notes, the trot, which "was a genre borne of Western musical form and Japanese soundscape," remained enormously popular and influential in Korea even into the 1980s.[27]

Because Japanese colonialism in Korea was especially ruthless, it represented yet another upheaval that jeopardized "a sense of Koreanness," a national identity that had long been subject to "fundamental and total civilizational transitions."[28] Indeed, beginning at the end of the nineteenth century, with the so-called Korean Enlightenment, controversy over modernization, Korean identity, and folk culture raged and these issues continue to be contested into the twenty-first century and even underlie debates about the Koreanness of K-pop.[29] Some musicologists, for example, hold a primordialist view that claims that Korean musical traditions are rooted in the ancient past, despite the fact that the term *minyo* (folk songs), as Keith Howard points out, only began to be used in the early twentieth century with the importation of commercial phonograph records from Japan.[30] It is little wonder that the repressive dictatorship of Park Chung-hee (1961–1979), fearing the threat that industrialization posed to recently invented traditions like *minyo* and *changgeuk*, launched a massive program in the 1960s to consolidate folk culture. Even "Arirang," Korea's "'national' folk song," which, the *Korea Times* claims, "has been sung for more than 600 years," can in fact be dated back conclusively only to the 1890s.[31] Its "elusive" provenance, however, did not stop the Korean government from lobbying UNESCO to get the song registered on its Intangible Cultural Heritage of Humanity list (it finally succeeded in 2012).[32]

After the defeat of Japan in 1945, the controversies over the definition of Koreanness were rekindled when almost overnight the southern part of the peninsula became a US-American outpost in East Asia, while the United States "served as the engine for South Korea's economic development."[33] As US-style capitalism was consolidated, the Americanization of Korean mass-cultural, musical, and theatrical cultures proceeded apace. In cultural discourse, the term "modern" started to be used for the first time as both popular and concert music sought to leave colonialism behind.[34] The ongoing presence of large numbers of US troops "prompted American culture, including its popular music, to spread rapidly across the nation." The war allowed the public to become acquainted with American soldiers and their culture, and "this inclination toward the United States translated into an unconditional preference."[35] The American Forces Korea Radio Network, meanwhile, "construct[ed] a nationwide network targeting the American troops," which, together with dance halls and "private music listening salons," were "dedicated to ... American popular music," including "boogie-woogie, mambo, blues, and cha-cha-cha."[36] By the mid-1950s, big-name entertainers, including Marilyn Monroe, Louis Armstrong, and Nat King Cole, made live appearances for the Eighth US Army. Camptown clubs, meanwhile, trained and employed Korean musicians, signaling US goodwill and spreading what were considered the most appealing aspects of US culture. In Seoul and the Demilitarized Zone alone there were reportedly 264 clubs that were supplied with singers by quickly sprouting Korean entertainment agencies.[37] These camptown clubs, which remained racially segregated until the mid-1970s, were in fact instrumental in disseminating Black musical idioms since it "was the black variety of Americanness that needed to be copied ... in order to survive as an entertainer during postwar poverty-ridden Korea."[38] As Lee Kee-woong reports, in the war-ravaged country, employment in "the U.S. camp club shows were a jackpot that guaranteed huge profits." However, "Korean-style music and originality were rejected; conversely, the more closely American-style music was emulated, the bigger the reward." Most valued were "'Good English pronunciation,' 'ability to convey emotions naturally and attractively' and 'good showmanship'" as "Korean performers had to internalize" the "techniques and practices" of "American entertainment."[39] Unless they learned "each and every song with a sincere and positive attitude," they would be mocked for their diction, fail "the constant tests, get kicked off the tour, and lose [their] livelihood."[40]

It should come as no surprise that club shows "should be credited for shortening the development process of Korea's popular music"[41] and that by the late 1950s, Korean popular songs started systematically employing US song types; singing styles; English words, phrases, or images; and the syncopations of US pop. This system "created a cascade of Korean popular hits"[42] and led to South Korea's first cultural export to the US, the Kim Sisters, who began entertaining US troops in 1953 singing English songs learned phonetically.[43] Traveling to the United States in 1959, they performed in Las Vegas as the "China Doll Revue" and appeared twenty-two times on the *Ed Sullivan Show*, becoming the "face of Korea."[44] Back in Korea, pop singers of the 1960s like Patti Kim and groups like the Pearl Sisters and Add4 developed large followings singing original songs that employed a wide variety of different styles, including Motown, classic rock 'n' roll, folk-rock, rhythm and blues, and even psychedelic rock.

But popular music was not the only target of a sweeping Americanization. In the classical field, composers of Korean concert music studied "the latest composing techniques of the West," including atonal, twelve-tone composition, and electronic music, while nationalist "[e]fforts to include Korean themes and spirits . . . became buried in the breathless sprint toward modernization."[45] To advance the musical modernist cause, many Korean composers studied in the United States or Germany, where they became familiar with avant-gardist trends. Although contemporary music societies and festivals were inaugurated in the 1960s, not all Korean composers were convinced of the need to forsake traditional styles, and the 1970s bore witness to debates between modernists and traditionalists, the latter striving to appeal to "human emotions and sensibilities."[46]

The repressive Park Chung-hee dictatorship (handsomely supported by the United States) engineered a period of explosive, export-centered economic growth that has persisted to the present. The oft-cited Miracle on the Han River enabled South Korea to have "risen from war and destitution (with a per capita GDP of $67 in 1953)" to become the world's tenth largest economy,[47] with a per capita income of $31,327 in 2021.[48] But the price, in terms of civil liberties, was staggering. Thousands were arrested as suspected communists while "[b]ureaucrats and university professors were purged... and there was an absolute ban on political activity or discussion."[49] This crackdown was especially damaging to a new, restive youth culture, which as a result lagged behind the cultural revolution in the United States and Western Europe, and whose music was subject to wholesale censorship as "authorities banned hundreds of songs under the pretext of purifying music," as well as long hair on men and miniskirts.[50] Youth culture, in other words, was constrained from the start because of the dictatorship's iron fist and heavy censorship of the mass media and performing arts. Nonetheless, one the most important cultural developments of the 1970s was acoustic folk music by young singer-songwriters based on US models, which continues to find echoes in contemporary musical theatre. The government required this new style of folk music to steer clear of political protest and, indeed, every variety of Korean popular music was "severely censored for its melodies— which were considered 'too Japanese' or 'too Western'—and its lyrics—which were deemed 'politically subversive,' 'pro-North Korean,' or 'containing improper cultural messages.'"[51] Nonetheless, many folk songs of the period exercised a kind of "passive resistance" by rehearsing "a distinctive pursuit of abstract freedom in a pristine world unstained by outside reality."[52] Even into the twenty-first century, many Korean films, musicals, and song lyrics continue to use luxuriant natural imagery that remains an evocation of "abstract freedom."

Following the 1979 assassination of Park Chung-hee, the military regime of Chun Doo-hwan became even more oppressive than Park's. Nonetheless, popular music thrived during the 1980s as teenagers emerged as "a major consumer group." Two streams of popular music dominated the field, both of which fed into the development of K-pop, *changjak*, and post-rock: pop ballads and dance music, on the one hand, and so-called underground music, on the other, which "carried on the legacy of folk music" and remained "outside the mainstream."[53] Although it was not explicitly politically subversive, underground music was strongly associated with the student-led Minjung movement of the 1980s, "*minjung* meaning 'the people' or 'the masses.'"[54] Although "an eclectic blend of Marxism and nationalism heavily influenced by Third World anticolonial, antiwar, [and] antinuclear thinking," Minjung helped pave the way for the democratization that began at the end of the 1980s.[55] Young writers of concert music, meanwhile, formed a new movement in the 1980s calling themselves the Third Generation, which began to turn away from the European avant-garde toward *gugak* and Korean popular music and produced new music dramas that incorporated popular and vernacular styles.[56]

The constantly changing attitudes to traditional music during the postwar era meant that, as Howard notes, most Koreans did not wake "up to the passing of the old" until the 1980s, "as economic success created room for nostalgia."[57] In other words, it was only with the runaway success of Korean consumer goods in the neoliberal marketplace that heritage performance began to be highly prized as an antidote to mass cultural forms. Moreover, the weakening of the dictatorship in the late 1980s and its control over culture allowed an unprecedented flourishing of the performing arts. With the dictatorship's fall in 1988, the election of the first civilian president (Kim Young-sam) in 1992, and Korea's membership in the World Trade Organization in 1995, preemptive censorship of culture finally ended (for theatre in 1988 and music in 1996). Korean performing arts organizations were intent on participating internationally and founded arts festivals, while under the aegis of Korean "turbo capitalism," the domestic market was opened to "the transnational entertainment industry."[58] All these events, plus the revitalization of the Korean film industry in the 1990s, were instrumental in turning Seoul into one of the leading cultural centers in East Asia, "globalizing Korean performing arts," and setting the stage for *hallyu*, the Korean Wave.[59]

The Korean Wave

Hallyu broke in the wake of the 1997 Asian financial crisis with the large-scale overseas distribution and promotion of Korean television programs, films, online games, animation, and K-pop. *Hallyu*'s initial impact was felt in China and Japan, which for the first time started importing significant quantities of Korean cultural goods. The television romance drama series *Winter Sonata* became a blockbuster success in Japan in 2004, while other forms of Korean popular culture, especially K-pop, quickly penetrated the rest of East and Southeast Asia, soon thereafter becoming a worldwide craze. By the late 2000s, John Lie notes, "the driving force of the Korean Wave—at times dubbed the Korean Wave 2.0—seemed to have shifted to the rapid ascent of K-pop."[60] Thanks to innovations such as YouTube and social media networks, the generous financial support of the Korean government, the

Korean diaspora, and the undeniable savvy of producers, Korea's shipments of culture came to rival its exports of Hyundai, Samsung, and LG. Between 2008 and 2020, cultural exports jumped from $1.8 billion to $9.8 billion, and they continue to rise.[61] By 2018, Youjeong Oh notes, *hallyu* had so transformed Korea "that everybody now seems to be riding the Korean Wave," using a "K-" prefix for drama, games, food, and beauty.[62]

Despite K-pop's global success, musicals have not yet quite caught the wave. They became big business in Korea in the 1980s and 1990s but Korean theatre producers and promoters only began "to turn their attention overseas" around 2000, and in the 2010s started shipping musicals to China and (especially) Japan.[63] The domestic Korean market for musicals has thrived in the twenty-first century with a "steady annual growth of 15–17 percent" while Korea has become a leader in touring shows to its neighbors, licensing Chinese and Japanese versions of Korean originals, and adapting foreign musicals that are then re-exported. Although Korean homegrown musicals are closely related to K-pop and, producers claim, "are poised to become the next frontier of Hallyu,"[64] they have yet to follow K-pop's lead and make major inroads into Western markets.

Since 2010, K-pop has become the economic engine not only for *hallyu* but also for the entire Korean cultural economy. As Joseph Kim and Seung-Ho Kwon report, the "export revenue of K-pop and its music videos rose fivefold between 2017 and 2021." Although K-pop was initially popularized in East Asia, the United States is now as K-smitten as the rest of the world. During 2020 and 2021, the boy group BTS became "the top selling digital music artist" in the United States while "the group's estimated contribution to the Korean economy in 2019 was USD 4.6 billion, or 0.3 percent to the nation's GDP."[65] K-pop's unprecedented success has turned the heads not only of legions of fans around the world, but also of critics and scholars who are seeking to explain K-pop's success, analyze its system of production, and assess its Koreanness.

Because K-pop is difficult to pin down stylistically, both Korean and Anglophone critics are more attentive to its systems of production, distribution, and consumption than to its formal characteristics. Hee-sun Kim defines it as "globally consumed idol dance music" that incorporates "Hip hop, R&B, electronic, [and] rock-based dance music" and is "produced by the Korean entertainment industry."[66] Hyunjoon Shin describes it as "cosmopolitan pop music," a "polished audiovisual package" performed by "bright-skinned, sharp-faced, and slim-bodied Asian boys and girls."[67] Hit songs by bands called idol groups are released as spectacularly (over)produced music videos, fabricated by *gihoeksa*, large entertainment companies and management agencies. A K-pop idol is a young singer who begins training in childhood and is essentially constructed by the *gihoeksa*, using a vertically integrated production system "of artist selection, training, image making, song writing, management, contracting, and album production." Since an idol is "someone who is to be admired for their attractiveness, musical talent is not necessarily the best quality to have." Under the in-house factory system, which owes a significant debt to Berry Gordy's Motown, "trainees get many years of instruction in singing, dancing, acting, foreign languages, and communication techniques," while the *gihoeksa* "controls every aspect of the idols' public image and career."[68] The idol groups are single-sex and, despite producing songs that are tightly synchronized choreographically and vocally, members are coached to develop "distinct personalities."[69] Like musical training programs the world over, this huge, sprawling system produces "endless competition among trainees," among whom only a small proportion become stars.[70]

Although K-pop dramatically raised the profile of Korean performers and cultural producers, the Koreanness of this total entertainment package remains hotly debated. Some critics see K-pop as nothing more than a capitulation to global capital engineered by the Korean government, an assembly line that manufactures and exploits "extremely photogenic" young performers who, in John Lie's damning assessment, "exemplify [a] sort of pop perfectionism: catchy tunes, good singing, attractive bodies, cool clothes, mesmerizing movements, and other attractive attributes in a nonthreatening, pleasant package." For Lie, "there is almost nothing 'Korean' about K-pop." It may be "identified as part of Brand (South) Korea," but is in reality "a globally competitive product without encumbrance of traditional Korea."[71] For others, such as Youna Kim, K-pop represents a new musical cosmopolitanism, a multimedia paradise, "a futuristic pastiche that sounds like a utopian blending of all contemporary musical genres."[72] For Kim, it is culturally and politically productive, an "alternative horizon" that "self-reflexively interrogate[s] and unsettle[s] the global hegemony of Euro-America."[73] Focusing on its historical development, Hee-sun Kim argues that what began as "nationless," "globally standardized pop music" has grown more and more obviously Korean. Beginning around 2012, she notes, K-pop has selectively incorporated Korean elements, including *gugak*, traditional Korean dress, traditional houses, and old palaces, thereby "redefining" and disseminating "'K-heritage' for music consumers worldwide." Because innovative K-pop has increasingly borrowed from both *gugak* and *pansori*, it "remains unclear and arguable whether these hybrid kinds of music should be called *gugak* or K-pop."[74]

K-pop superstar Psy's "Gangnam Style," the first video to score one billion YouTube hits (in December 2012), illuminates the stakes in constructing K-pop, and Korean popular culture more widely, as a source of nationalist pride.[75] In May 2014, the song surpassed two billion YouTube hits, more than double what was then the second most-watched video (Justin Bieber's "Baby").[76] But the national identity of the video's musical and visual style was hotly debated. That "Gangnam Style" provoked considerable anxiety over its Koreanness is evident among bloggers, some of whom attempted to make Psy an upholder of Korean tradition, by claiming, for example, that his horse dance "looks uncannily like"—and is modeled after—a "bas-relief sculpture" at "Seokbulsa Temple in Busan, South Korea."[77] Kyung Hyun Kim elucidates the complexity of the song's cultural positionality and offers a multifaceted reading of it as a theatricalized, "carnivalesque" performance, "the most ironic cultural sensation in the first two decades of the twenty-first century." The video, Kim notes, which has its roots in Korean television comedy, "creates an awkward humor" in its depiction of "a slightly chubby Asian performer singing a dance tune with Korean lyrics accompanied by horse-dance choreography" while appropriating "American pop references such as Westerns, fast cars, and race-car girls." Kim explains that many US-Americans misunderstood "Gangnam Style" in a condescending, racist way as a "poor imitation," and he argues instead that the song represents a crystallization of "the political predicament" of contemporary South Korea, "a minor culture trapped between the globally perceived advanced culture of American pop and Hollywood and the presumed backward copycat that is K-pop."[78] Because Psy's mimicry is calculatedly "wrong," the song exposes, in Choi Yu-jun's words, the double bind of a "colonial modernity that can describe the subject only through the 'eyes of the others.'"[79]

Youna Kim argues that *hallyu*'s double bind is inescapable. For her, it is less a question of choosing between Koreanness and neoliberal cosmopolitanism than recognizing their interdependence. *Hallyu*, in other words, both enables and diminishes "cultural diversity in a digital cosmopolitan world"; it represents a real challenge to Euro-American cultural hegemony and a new consumerism; it is "a highly interactive ongoing process that is created, and . . . sustained, by digitally empowered fan consumers" yet epitomizes commodity fetishism; it both modernizes and repudiates traditional Korean performance practices; it is a sign of "a newly found [Korean] self-confidence" and the "anxiety" generated by "an increasingly mediated and precarious world of everyday life."[80] It is, as Anandam Kavoori points out, at once "national, regional, transnational, and diasporic."[81] Because it functions differently on each of these levels, these contradictions are less a regrettable byproduct of *hallyu* than its lifeblood. They arise not from the idiosyncrasies of producers and fans, but from the social, economic, and cultural networks in which *hallyu* flourishes.

These networks in turn are the result of the Korean government's policy of fostering a distinctively South Korean brand of capitalist globalization called *segyehwa*, of which *hallyu* is a consequence. As early as 1995, the newly democratized Korean government set forth the goals of *segyehwa*: "first, to become a leading nation in the world; second, to reform irrational social customs and consciousness; third, to unite all Koreans north and south; fourth, to advance Korea's unique value system and traditional culture onto the world stage; finally, to participate in solving global problems."[82] *Segyehwa* requires not a rejection but incorporation of heritage: "Koreans should march out into the world on the strength of their unique culture and traditional values."[83] It thus crystallizes the contradictions that have structured modernization in Korea since the end of the nineteenth century: the double mission of Westernizing and Koreanizing, of learning from and surpassing Euro-America while celebrating Korean traditions. As a result, the Korean government continues to subsidize not only traditional cultural practices but also K-pop with "gargantuan amounts of cash."[84] Unlike the United States and Western Europe, where the popular culture industries are privately capitalized, Korea has engineered a synergistic interlinking of public and private funds. The Ministry of Foreign Affairs and Trade, however, supports more than mass-cultural forms. Every year it also "sends Korean performance troupes abroad and organizes Korean art exhibitions and film festivals."[85]

Recognizing the symbolic capital of opera as export, the Korean government has diversified its investments. In 2006, for example, it sent to Frankfurt, Germany, Lim Jun-hee's opera *Soul Mate*, a hybrid of Korean heritage performance and European high culture. The opera's two performances at Oper Frankfurt by two hundred singers, dancers, and instrumentalists cost the Korean state 1.2 million euros.[86] Titled *Der Hochzeitstag* (The Wedding Day) in Frankfurt, it is a European-style comic opera that features passionate, Puccinian arias and duets, and was critically acclaimed, according to the press office of the Korea National Opera, "for the ideal blend of Korean culture and European formality."[87] Even more widely traveled is the National Changgeuk Company's updated realization of Euripides' *The Trojan Women* (2016), directed by the Singaporean Ong Keng Sen. This through-composed music theatre piece, a collaboration between a K-pop composer and a *pansori* master, clearly aims for elite cultural status. Toward this end, the piece employs Korean instruments (plus piano for Helen of Troy), *pansori* singing for the soloists, and percussion-driven choral music, which according to the company's promotional material "draws on K-pop," although if there was any resemblance, I did not hear it.[88] With a futuristic set and elaborate projections, it has been marketed as a mix of traditional and avant-garde and has toured to prestigious festivals in Singapore, Vienna, London, Amsterdam, and New York. These two hybridized works thus testify to the Korean government's determination to rebrand Korean high culture as "the epitome of cool."[89] Simultaneously, with its huge investments in *hallyu*, Korea is refashioning itself as the epicenter of a "pop Asianism" that both reconceives and enlarges the traditional modes that have defined Korean performance cultures.[90] It is within this expansive network that the Broadway-style musical has flourished in South Korea, as an exemplar of pop cosmopolitanism, serious music theatre, and nationalist spectacle.

Although historically, musicals have often championed national identity, it is important to recognize that nationalist culture in South Korea has an urgency and innocence it lacks in many other parts of the world. This urgency results from Koreans' belief that their identity was "robbed multiple times in the twentieth century, through the collapse of the independent nationhood, Japanese colonialism, national division, fratricidal war, and the Cold War."[91] This long, troubled history means that nationalism is less fraught in South Korea than in Japan, Germany, or the United States. As Ronald Meinardus points out, Korea "has not led aggressive wars and has not attacked its neighbors."[92] Korean nationalism, moreover, is usually considered benign because South Korea is seen in most parts of the world "as 'non-offensive'—a political tabula rasa" with a "'non-confrontational image . . . whereas with brands like the U.S., . . . Russia, . . . China, you have immediate polarization."[93] Given Korea's positive image on the world stage and "the mountain of investment that the government" has poured into cultural promotion and export since 1990, it is difficult to dispute Euny Hong's claim that South

Korea is aiming for nothing less than "becoming the world's top exporter of popular culture."[94]

Broadway on the Han

Although some Korean producers and promoters are hoping to make original Korean musicals "the next frontier of Hallyu,"[95] Korean theatre has not yet been able to ride the Korean wave as film, television, and pop music have. Because spoken theatre is a handmade product, it defies the kind of mass production and distribution (via YouTube, cable, and elsewhere) that have made K-pop a global phenomenon. Rather, the big success story in twenty-first-century Korean theatre is Broadway-style musical theatre. As Patrick Healy reported in 2013 in the *New York Times*, "Seoul has become a boomtown for American musicals," with ticket sales for "American and European musicals," and "a sprinkling of Korean originals,"[96] rising "from $9 million in 2000 to an estimated $316 million" in 2019.[97] In fact, there is far more than a "sprinkling" of original Korean musicals, and Healy largely ignores the most exciting and innovative developments in Korean theatre.

The success of musicals in South Korea has depended on the cultivation of a huge fan base comprised primarily of young women raised on what Healy condescendingly describes as "the bombast of Korean pop and the histrionics of television soap operas."[98] In Seoul, 70 percent of the musicals audience is "made up of young people in their 20s to 40s," while 16 percent of Koreans said they had seen at least one musical per year.[99]

These figures are significant in part because audiences for musicals on average are considerably more affluent than those for K-pop and television, and stage musicals occupy a relatively elevated position in the cultural hierarchies in both South Korea and the United States. In both nations, ticket prices for musicals are significantly higher than for plays, which are in turn many times higher than movie tickets. And ticket prices in Seoul and New York are comparable. In 2014, large-scale Korean musicals (the equivalent of Broadway) cost per ticket between $125 and $60, while small-scale (the equivalent of Off Broadway) run between $70 and $35.[100] In the United States, the $261,000 average household income for Broadway theatregoers in 2018–2019—who are also far better educated than the average US-American—was more than three times the national median.[101] And in both Seoul and New York, most musical theatre ticket buyers choose to see more than one show in the course of a year.[102] In both countries, musical theatre remains an artisanal luxury good in relation to mass-cultural forms.

Although the boom in musicals began in earnest only in the 1990s with the explosion of neoliberal globalization, Western music theatre has a history in Korea that long predates the arrival of *Cats* in 1994. In 1948, Giuseppe Verdi's *La traviata*, with an all-Korean cast, was the first opera staged in Korea. Its five performances "won great éclat," created "a big stir," and occasioned a "great turnout." These performances initiated "opera fever" in Seoul and were followed by productions of Gounod's *Faust* and Bizet's *Carmen*.[103] After a lengthy hiatus during the Korean War and the first postwar years, they were followed in 1962 by *Porgy and Bess* by George and Ira Gershwin and DuBose Heyward and a series of smaller-scale US and Korean musicals that, Ji Hyon (Kayla) Yuh argues, followed the "tradition of American musicals." *Porgy*, Yuh notes, was pointedly redesigned by its director "as a musical, which he saw as a genre with the potential to revitalize Korean theatre, which was then competing with the rising popularity of films and other forms of popular entertainment." At the same time, musicals became ammunition in a Cold War offensive that "allowed South Korea to demonstrate its competency in adapting/appropriating an American genre." The first Korean musical production company Yegrin Akdan was founded in 1961 and both privately funded and richly subsidized by the government because it was designed "from its inception to serve a political purpose by providing South Korea a means of culturally upstaging North Korea's big-budgeted, visual-centric propagandistic productions." Yegrin Akdan produced several well-received original musicals during the 1960s, while in 1965, a touring production of *Hello, Dolly!* with Mary Martin in the title role played two nights in Seoul.[104]

Although original musicals flourished during the 1970s, the Hyundai corporation in 1980 sponsored the first Seoul production of *Jesus Christ Superstar*, which played for one and a half years and sold more than 300,000 tickets (and whose popularity was linked to the growth of evangelical Christianity in South Korea). This was followed by canonical Broadway and West End musicals, including *The Sound of Music, Guys and Dolls, Fiddler on the Roof, Cabaret, Evita, Cats,* and *Les Misérables* (Figure 2.1).[105] Because South Korea did not sign on to the Berne Convention for copyright until 1996, most of these productions were unlicensed and took considerable liberties with the originals.[106] All told, however, the productions of musicals, both imported and Korean, increased tenfold between 1962 and 1991. Although Seoul had long provided stages for small-scale Korean musicals,

Figure 2.1 Two fans awaiting a performance of *Les Misérables*, Blue Square Theater, Seoul, 2013. Photo by the author.

by the 1980s, "Broadway-style imports" had become far more popular than Korean musicals. During that decade, "several musical companies and theaters were established while public appreciation of musicals increased dramatically enough to threaten the conventional drama genre." According to Yoo, the "most notable event" during the following decade "was the 1992 production of *The Sound of Music*" staged by a Broadway touring company that gave the Korean public "a taste of real Broadway."[107] By 1997, US musicals had become "the most active form of music theater in Korea" and were "strongly influenc[ing] the development" of Korean musical theatre.[108]

The most popular Korean musical dates from this period, *Subway Line 1*, which premiered in 1994 and is adapted from the first globally successful German musical, *Linie 1*. The latter, protesting the conservativism and class divisions of West German society, premiered at the GRIPS Theater in West Berlin in 1986.[109] The Korean version was adapted and directed by Kim

Min-gi, the composer of the 1971 hit "Morning Dew," the "most well-known and iconic [Korean] protest song."[110] The plot of the adaptation details the impact of the social and economic changes in South Korea in the early 1990s. It sticks closely to the German book, music, lyrics, and scene design, but so thoroughly Koreanizes the colorful cast of characters that in 1999 the GRIPS Theater waived copyright fees.[111] By the time it closed in Seoul in 2008 after more than 4,000 performances, *Subway Line 1* had become the longest-running musical in Korean theatre history and had launched the career of several Korean musical theatre stars.[112] Many other small-scale Korean musicals followed in its wake, while large-scale shows such as *Wicked*, *Mamma Mia!*, and *Guys and Dolls* drew enthusiastic crowds to the most high-priced of Seoul's 300 theatres.[113]

The explosion of musical theatre in Seoul is unquestionably a product of the unprecedented growth of the performing arts in South Korea since the 1990s. It is, moreover, a tribute to the fact that Korea has long been the most US-Americanized of East Asian cultures. This is not to say that South Koreans have unambiguously positive feelings about the United States and its art. On the contrary. Although Koreans, Meredith Woo-Cumings argues, "do not possess the kind of historical and cultural vocabulary others have employed for ridiculing and despising the United States," its long-term superordinate position has ensured that Koreans have developed nuanced attitudes toward its sometime protector.[114] Since the fall of the dictatorship, opinions have fluctuated dramatically, in part because most Koreans harbor an undisguised ambivalence about the US–South Korea relationship.[115] As the wartime generation has been superseded by Koreans who know the US government best through its thirty-nine military installations and its often bellicose rhetoric, attitudes have become increasingly polarized.[116] Many younger men and women condemned the United States' role in supporting repressive anticommunist governments all over the world, including South Korea. During the military dictatorship, although "the 'good' image of the U.S. as the best friend" and primary bulwark against North Korea was "widely shared and ideologically hegemonic," many Koreans correctly assumed that the United States was helping prop up Korea's despotic, antidemocratic regimes.[117] Since democratization, younger, more progressive Koreans, "especially students, sympathize with . . . radical groups' . . . aspirations for peaceful unification, opposition to war on the peninsula, wariness of U.S. unilateralism, and . . . the U.S. military presence in Korea."[118] For many South Koreans, the United States represents more an obstacle to reunification than a democratic safeguard. Nonetheless, North Korea's acquisition of nuclear weapons has led most South Koreans to believe in the necessity of the alliance.

As in many other parts of the world, disapproval of the United States as a political actor does not necessarily translate into displeasure with US culture. For decades, Koreans have sent their children to schools and universities in the United States in far greater numbers per capita than has any other country. Between 2001 and 2012 alone, the figure rose more than 40 percent, and in 2019 South Koreans in US universities were outnumbered only by students from two immensely more populous countries, China and India.[119] US-American popular music and music videos have long been ubiquitous in Korea, and Black music, in particular, has been the single greatest influence on the development of K-pop. Hollywood cinema has also been tremendously successful in Korea, as in most of the world, so much so that Korea in 1966 introduced a quota system to limit the importation of US films and protect the Korean film industry. Given the global success of Korean movies beginning in the 1990s, however, the government agreed in 2006 to reduce the required number of days per cinema for the screening of domestic films from 146 to 73.[120]

Because non-Korean theatre has not been subject to quotas since the Japanese occupation, US-American musicals have boomed. While most of the hits in Seoul have also been Broadway hits, Korea is increasingly welcoming Austrian musicals (produced by Vereinigte Bühnen Wien) and small-cast US shows that would strike most New York theatregoers as unlikely hits, including Off-Broadway flops such as Julia Jordan and Juliana Nash's *Murder Ballad* (2013), and modest successes, such as Stephen Dolginoff's *Thrill Me* (2003). The musicals of Frank Wildhorn, meanwhile, a Broadway composer whom New York critics love to hate, have been far more popular in Seoul than in the United States. "His musical 'Jekyll & Hyde,' which lost money in New York," drew large crowds in Korea starting in 2004 "and is considered one of the most financially successful American musicals" in Seoul.[121] As the *Times* reports, these unlikely hits have "changed the game for New York producers looking" to invest abroad and "to extend the lives of their shows."[122]

But US producers are by no means the only ones cashing in on Broadway musicals in Korea. Because the name Broadway carries so much cultural and symbolic capital and because the financial success rate for musicals in Seoul is even lower than in New York (10 to 20 percent versus 25 percent on Broadway), Korean producers are eager to invest in the United States. According to Broadway producer James Nederlander Jr., they are cultivating "a 'wild, wild West'" investment mentality.[123] One producer, Byeong-seok Kim, poured $1 million into *Kinky Boots*, thus bringing back to Seoul the 2013 Tony Award for Best Musical.[124] Kim's pride in this award is proof that Korean producers acquire significant economic, cultural, and symbolic capital through their investment in Broadway. The most prominent producer during the 2010s, however, was Chun-soo Shin, whose OD Musical Company (whose name stands for "Open the Door") teamed up with John Breglio for *Dreamgirls* and then invested in numerous Broadway shows, including *Jesus Christ Superstar* (2012), *Jekyll & Hyde* (2013), *Rocky* (2014), and *Doctor Zhivago* (2015). OD Musical Company, founded in 2001, touts their Seoul productions of dozens of Broadway musicals, original Korean musicals, as well as overseas investments in the United States and Japan, all of which have made them, they claim, "a high-profile producing company leading the Korean musical theatre industry." OD believes, moreover, that although they are diversifying into film and television, their investment in Broadway musicals will earn them more glory in Korea (and abroad) than the development of new Korean musicals.[125] "'Do I care about losing money on Broadway? Not really,'" Shin told the *New York Times*. "What matters is that American producers notice us, see our market, understand what Asia can become. Broadway is the place of origin for musicals; once it's on Broadway, it's likely to spread around the world."[126]

Chun-soo Shin's assertion was seconded by Simone Genatt, executive producer of Broadway Asia, who argued in 2011 that

> Broadway is an incredibly powerful brand. Much more powerful [abroad] . . . than in the American system. It really denotes money, the best of the West, and non-political entertainment, which crosses cultural barriers everywhere and which draws a lot of financial support and sponsorship. And when . . . an economy emerges, they tend to brand themselves with Broadway. That's what's happened over the last twenty years, so that as the emerging markets have come into the system, whether Latin America or China or Dubai, . . . they tend to brand themselves with Broadway to show that they are a market to be reckoned with and a market that has clout and money.[127]

The explosion of Broadway musicals in Seoul beginning in the 1990s neatly corresponds to Genatt's chronology. It is also related to the Korean diaspora, especially to the United States and the UK, and to the fact that, according to US producer Judy Craymer, "Koreans travel so much to New York and London, and they care deeply about brands—like Broadway."[128]

Although Genatt, a seasoned producer, describes the musical as being "non-political entertainment," her observation is misleading. Granted, very few musicals could be described as agitprop, but many canonical musicals, from *Show Boat* to *Cabaret*, *South Pacific* to *Hairspray*, have been used to score political points, albeit points that are not especially contentious for the vast majority of the educated, middle- to upper-middle-class US theatregoing public. She is correct insofar as the most popular transnational musicals from the United States, the UK, and Austria place a premium on spectacle, romance, and entertainment value, that is, pleasure, and take relatively uncontroversial positions on social issues. Despite a history of politically motivated art in Korea that goes back to the Japanese occupation, the most successful imported musicals tend not to challenge the preconceptions of cosmopolitan, upper-middle-class Korean audiences. Transnational musicals made in Korea, however, tell a different story.

Staging Korean History

In the twenty-first century, Korean producers and digital ticketing platforms distinguish among three different kinds of musicals. According to Dohyun (Gracia) Shin, the first category, somewhat misleadingly called "original," refers to internationally produced touring productions of large-scale musicals such as *Chicago* and *Les Misérables*. The second category is called "licensed" and designates Korean-produced and -acted productions, replica or non-replica, of large- or medium-scale musicals such as *Man of La Mancha* or *Thrill Me*. The third category—and the one on which I am focusing—is *changjak*, or homegrown musicals. This category (almost completely ignored by the *New York Times*) is the most diverse and ranges from large- to small-scale works that employ a Western-style musical theatre syntax and take Korean history as subject matter or adapt European novels.[129] Especially when they take up Korean historical subjects, *changjak* do not merely dramatize history but also reference or rehearse Korean musical or theatrical traditions. Their skill at mixing these dissimilar idioms is what has made original Korean musicals so innovative, culturally significant, and (at times) difficult to categorize.

Given the huge public and private financial investment in branding and disseminating Korean art and culture, Korean producers and the Korean government have been eager to export original work that celebrates Korean heritage, buttresses Korean nationalism, and shows off the undeniable skill of Korean musical theatre writers and performers. Among the production companies developing Korean musicals for the global market, none has had a higher profile than ACOM International (Arts Communication International). It was founded in 1991 as Korea's first professional corporate producer of musicals and has toured two of its original productions to the United States, Canada, and the UK. *The Last Empress* (명성황후) premiered in Seoul in 1995, directed by Ho Jin Yun, and played New York's Lincoln Center in both 1997 and 1998 before moving on to other Anglophone theatre capitals. It was followed by *Hero: The Musical* (영웅), also directed by Yun, which premiered in 2009 and played Lincoln Center two years later. Korea's two most widely traveled bids for global recognition, *The Last Empress* and *Hero*, are large-scale, spectacularly designed, uncompromisingly nationalistic historical dramas about Korea's struggle against Japanese imperialism; each has a title character who champions Korean independence and is martyred by the Japanese. Although both toured outside Korea, the New York performances earned ACOM the most symbolic capital. In fact, the venue at which they played, the David H. Koch Theater (until 2008, the New York State Theater), is not contractually a Broadway house, but its location several hundred feet from the Great White Way seems to have authorized ACOM to promote both musicals as having been performed "on Broadway."[130] Hyunjung Lee suggests that this disingenuous claim is symptomatic of the fact that because in South Korea, "the idea of Broadway evokes visions of magnificent glamor, global success," Korean musicals "adopt and internalize Broadway as a yardstick of South Korea's cultural capacity." In Korea, the designation "Broadway" was and remains both highly particularized and vague, local and universal. " 'Broadway' " represents "a fantastic . . . image that stands for the United States," which, in turn, is a metonymy for "the West."[131] So it was crucially important for ACOM to be able to claim that *The Last Empress* and *Hero* were performed "on Broadway" and received enthusiastically by critics, several of whom did indeed note the newly found ability of Korean musicals "to compete with worldly [*sic*] renowned musicals."[132] "The Korean musical is going to boom," Ho Jin Yun predicted in 1998. "We are the frontiersmen. . . . The musical is here to stay."[133]

The Last Empress and *Hero* are quite unlike two other Korean theatre exports, *Cookin'* (*Nanta*) and *Jump*, first performed Off Broadway in 2003 and 2007 respectively, "high-energy spectacles" that use almost no spoken language and are aimed at children and others looking for non-literary, live entertainment.[134] *The Last Empress* and *Hero*, in contrast, are elite cultural enterprises, expansive and lush historical costume dramas. Although both musicals boast nationalist messages, they are "unapologetic" adaptations of the musical and dramatic conventions of Broadway and West End musicals.[135] Yet both are also committed to reclaiming Korean history and heritage, not only in the story they tell, but also stylistically, overlaying Euro-American musical styles with traditional Korean melody, harmony, and instrumentation. Yun, the director of both shows, explains that "The form is Western-style, the sets are Western, but the songs carry a lot of Korean rhythm and emotion," despite the fact that the prevailing musical style is unambiguously "Western."[136]

Because musicals require a far greater investment per potential consumer than mass-cultural forms, ACOM had to recruit Korean corporations and government agencies to back its work. The tours of *The Last Empress* were underwritten by large corporations such as Samsung and the Seoul Broadcasting System, as well as the South Korean Ministry of Culture and Tourism.[137] For *Hero*, which reportedly cost $4.6 million to produce, ACOM chose to forfeit economic capital for symbolic capital: "We will see some $1 million deficit even if all performances [at Lincoln Center] are sold out."[138] ACOM, in other words, was able to line up supporters like the Seoul Foundation for Arts and Culture, Asiana Airlines, and the New York offices of the Korean Consulate General and Korean Cultural Service because they believed that the promotional value of the musical would outweigh its cost. As an elite cultural event, *Hero* succeeded in bringing to its New York premiere dignitaries on the order of United Nations Secretary-General Ban Ki-moon and South Korea's Permanent Representative to the United Nations, Kim Sook, "who noted the significance of the show's vast Lincoln Center staging for the homeland of its creators."[139]

The Last Empress (with music by Hee Gab Kim, lyrics by In Ja Yang, and book by Mun Yol Yi) is a colorful historical drama notable for its use of musical and theatrical styles reminiscent of Italian grand opera. It tells the story of the strong-willed, Eva Perón–like Queen Min (or Empress Myeongseong) who wed King Kojong in 1866 and, seeking to protect and modernize Korea, was assassinated by the Japanese in 1895. To reinforce its Korean nationalist story, this "[v]isually stunning" costume drama was further Koreanized in 1997 for its New York premiere by incorporating heritage performance, a "Shamanic Rite" in which a female shaman and her assistants dance a "feverish . . . mystic ritual." The play favorably impressed the critic for *Variety* who noted that "Korean craftsmen have probed the machinery of Broadway musicals in a heady attempt for commercial success."[140] Another observed that "[s]plendor obviously means the same thing in Korean as it does in English" and likened it to *Ragtime* because of its foregrounding of a large chorus.[141] Although the musical uses many Broadway conventions, as well as Broadway-style choreography (plus a martial-arts movement vocabulary), it also adapts many features from opera, including the clear distinction between aria, arioso, recitative, and speech. It requires operatically trained singers, and the vocal casting is reminiscent of Italian opera: lyric soprano heroine, tenor hero, bass-baritone villain, comic comprimario sidekick, and so forth. And although the prevailing musical style is unmistakably "Western," *The Last Empress* makes spare, but carefully spotlighted use of the pentatonic scale and traditional Korean percussion.[142] The musical's adroit use of Western conventions is nowhere more visible than in its grand, tableau-like finale, "Rise, People of Chosun [Korea]," which "stages Queen Min's resurrection as she blesses Korea's eternal prosperity."[143] It begins, like some traditional Korean music, as a solemn chorus, over which sounds a passionate, minor-key aria for the Queen, who is bathed in blue light. Then, as the scene brightens and the music modulates to the major, the finale turns into a cross between Rodgers and Hammerstein's "Climb Ev'ry Mountain" and the final nationalistic chorus of Verdi's *Macbeth*: a stirring, slow march in praise of Korea that gradually gathers speed and volume, capped by a sustained high B for the soprano heroine.

The Last Empress aims to display Korean writers and directors' knowing use of Western conventions by mobilizing the musical and dramatic machinery of highbrow Western music theatre in order to celebrate and monumentalize Korean history and heritage performance. Director Yun explains:

> We conceived *The Last Empress* as a way of refashioning a part of "our culture" and promoting it in the world market. From now on, it is crucial for one to repackage their own national culture, provoking financial interest in the global market. This is our way to build a "cultural nation" [*munhwa kuka*] in order to fully arrive at a "world-class society." Otherwise, we will remain as a country that is "culturally subordinated."[144]

The defensive tone of Yun's statement is a reminder of the deeply contradictory nature of *segyehwa*, which represents both a nationalist project and a cultural uprooting for the sake of "the global market." It is also symptomatic of the fact that the urgency to consecrate heritage performance is felt especially acutely among those who believe themselves to be "culturally subordinated," that is, the victims of an imperialism that brands their culture as inferior. In the case of Korea, the sense of inferiority is rooted, as the *Hero* souvenir program reminds readers, in the long history of "Western aggression in Asia," in the economic and cultural dominance of Korea by its larger neighbors, and specifically, by the Japanese during its annexation, a period that inflicted "incalculable and unspeakable damage on the Korean people."[145]

Both *The Last Empress* and *Hero* were constructed as commemorative pieces that "repackage" and disseminate a "cultural nation."[146] *Hero*, however, with music by Oh Sang-joon and book and lyrics by Han A-reum, jettisons the operatic trappings of the earlier piece and hews much more closely to the conventions of the mid-twentieth-century Broadway musical. Although *Hero*'s musical style owes a good deal to the megamusical, its dramaturgy would be clearly recognizable to Rodgers and Hammerstein. Like *South Pacific* and *The King and I*, *Hero* constructs a leading male character who is martyred to a nationalist cause and makes limited and highly particularized use of musical orientalisms. And while it does not depict the clash of East and West, as do the aforementioned Rodgers and Hammerstein musicals, it does dramatize a violent conflict between different East Asian political and cultural traditions. *Hero* tells the story of An Chunggun (portrayed in Seoul and New York by Sung Hwa Chung), a Korean nationalist activist, pan-Asianist, and Roman Catholic who in 1909 assassinated Ito Hirobumi, the first Japanese Resident-General of Korea, at the Harbin Railway Station in Manchuria. The musical focuses on An's plotting with his confederates, his murder of Ito, and subsequent imprisonment, trial, and execution. While the emphasis is squarely on An's exploits, it also introduces An's mother, Cho Maria, plus two fictitious women characters, Sorhui, who witnessed the execution of Queen Min (and so provides a link to *The Last Empress*), and Lingling, who has a "secret crush" on An.[147] The latter provides a love interest to spice up the political plot, while each of the female characters is given a soulful ballad that offers respite from the purely male solo and choral singing. Like An, Sorhui and Lingling are martyred for Korean independence. Although *Hero* foregrounds the deaths of most of its major characters and resembles tragedy structurally, it, like *The Last Empress*, figures the resurrection of its title character in the spirit of modern-day Korea. Immediately after the ringing high A-flat that ends An's plea from the gallows, "Heaven, guard me that I may accomplish my resolve!" a title flashes on the screen that signals the answer to his prayer: "*Korea achieved independence in 1945.*"[148]

The New Transnational Musical

With its nationalist content and straightforward use of the conventions of the musical, *Hero* exemplifies the ways in which Broadway musical and dramatic conventions are adapted to make the twenty-first-century transnational musical, variations of which one can find all over the world. It was hailed by Korean critics for its "'intensity,' 'universality,' and 'timeliness,'" and its demonstration "of the astonishing evolution of Korean original musical shows."[149] It swept the 2010 Korea Musical Awards and was developed, the program notes, like *The Last Empress*, "with the goal of globalizing the Korean musical."[150] On opening night at Lincoln Center, it drew "a bevy of international diplomats" and elicited unanimously positive, if slightly patronizing, reviews, before moving on to Los Angeles, Toronto, and London.[151] It has been remounted repeatedly since its premiere, including a "tenth anniversary production in Seoul in 2019."[152] Employing song conventions long familiar from Golden Age musicals, rock musicals, and megamusicals, as well as "Broadway-type razzle-dazzle," *Hero* provides a casebook study in how local stories and theatrical idioms are incorporated into the "'Western' framework called the 'Broadway-style' musical."[153]

Yun uses the phrase "'Broadway-style' musical" because it is capacious enough to include the assimilation of national traditions. Often in Korea that moniker is shortened, for *Hero* is not the only home-grown musical whose local advertisements include one—and sometimes only one—English word: "Musical." Its eclectic "'Western' framework," meanwhile, includes musical comedy, the Rodgers and Hammerstein formula, the rock musical, Italian and French grand opera, and the British megamusical. To this list of theatrical subgenres must be added contemporary pop, Europop, and film music, especially the scores of John Williams and Hans Zimmer, which have had a palpable impact on musical theatre dramaturgy, orchestration, and underscoring. The "Broadway-style" designation is further complicated by the fact that each of these subgenres, especially the rock musical and the megamusical, embraces a multiplicity of forms and styles. *Hair, Rent,* and *Kinky Boots* may all have rock-based scores, but their musical and dramatic languages are completely different. Jessica Sternfeld's description of the megamusicals' stylistic pastiche gives a clear sense of the broad range of styles incorporated into the new transnational " 'Broadway-style' musical," in its mixture of broadly based "pop music . . . with theatrical music," including "ballads . . . tinged with pop, country, blues, or cabaret influences." These musicals, she notes, also feature "hard-driving up-tempo numbers and love duets that could work just as well in the movies or on television as they do onstage, . . . alongside quasi-operatic ensembles and purely [musical] theatrical styles."[154] In a piece such as *Hero,* this eclecticism is carefully calculated, a reminder that the musical has long been the most hybridized of theatrical genres, dating back at least to *Shuffle Along* (1921), mixing different musical styles (often with distinctive national, ethnic, or racial genealogies) while exploiting them for their associations and dramatic impact. As Elizabeth Wollman emphasizes, the megamusical—like the new transnational musical—"offers not only more sophisticated sound than its predecessors, but also a more thorough blend of popular music and traditional theater fare."[155]

Ho Jin Yun's use of scare quotes around the phrase "Broadway-style" seems to signal a deliberately non-specific usage, one general enough to accommodate all these different forms and styles and yet remain recognizable as a musical. If I take *Hero* to be a paradigm for the new transnational musical that circulates in the global marketplace, it is because the polystylism of its score makes it similar to the widely traveled historical musicals of Vereinigte Bühnen Wien. The criticism of *Hero* voiced by one New York critic, Gregory Bernard, could be leveled against many of these transnational musicals. He described it as "a living sampling of the best and worst attributes of modern musical theater" and enumerated its alleged echoes of *Les Misérables, Miss Saigon, Martin Guerre, Chess, Evita, Jesus Christ Superstar, Billy Elliott,* and *West Side Story.*[156] In his review, Bernard seems to have forgotten that the musical has always been one of the most highly conventionalized of theatrical genres, using and reusing song forms in a way that sometimes suggests deliberate or accidental pastiche. Like K-pop or many other Korean exports, *Hero* illustrates a complex mode of assimilation that, by producing a "Broadway-style" score, represents what Kyung Hyun Kim describes as "hegemonic mimicry" that "simulate[s] and reinvent[s] American cultural artifacts, styles, and pop products," a "simultaneous appropriation and misappropriation" that "open[s] the door for innovation."[157] Like other musicals that circulate transnationally, *Hero* makes use of the many song types that Broadway has long favored: love duets, novelty and charm songs (generally in triple meter), plot songs, power ballads, rousing choruses, and passionate soliloquies. Yet unlike *The Last Empress*, *Hero* requires muscular, Broadway-style singers who can negotiate the Broadway belt with aplomb. Most of the songs, accordingly, opt for the modular structure of rock songs rather than the thirty-two-bar A-A-B-A refrain long favored by Broadway and Tin Pan Alley. Their typical form (verse-transition-refrain-release-refrain-coda) usually blurs clear-cut distinctions between sections in favor of a gradual build to a surging or poignant emotional and musical climax.

Despite *Hero*'s use of rock song structures and a Rodgers and Hammerstein–style musical dramaturgy, it is not simply "Western-style," as most US critics labeled it.[158] Like an increasing number of Korean musicals, it incorporates components of K-pop: elaborate projections, synchronized choreography, and synthesized musical timbres. It also includes numbers that evoke heritage performance, in this case, both Japanese and Korean. It contains no scene as distinctively Korean as the "Shamanic Rite" in *The Last Empress*, but the score, like Korean concert music of the 1990s and 2000s, undermines the "dichotomies between tradition and modernism, traditional Korean music and Western-style music."[159] Most of the songs for the Japanese characters use an orientalist pastiche of pentatonic melodies and harmonies that imitate or incorporate the Japanese three-string samisen. Musical orientalisms and archaicisms, kimonos, and a black and "[b]loody-red" costume color palette are reserved for Ito and the geishas while the Korean women are costumed in traditional dress and are figured as the embodiment of Korean history. While the penultimate number, Cho Maria's pentatonically inflected "My Beloved Son, Thomas," suggests a Korean folk-like lullaby, Sorhui's songs would not be out of place on US radio. The Korean "freedom fighters" also sing contemporary-sounding, Western-style music and wear more up-to-date, less historically marked costumes.[160] These choices make it clear that *Hero*, like the orientalist musicals of Rodgers and Hammerstein, contrives to render foreign cultures exotic musically and socially while portraying the protagonists (in this case, Korean nationalists) as sympathetic, modernized figures who employ a transnational pop vernacular.

Hero's Broadway style is closely correlated with its Westernized, Christian protagonist. At age nineteen, An Chunggun was baptized in the Roman Catholic Church with the name Thomas. Moreover, as the program explains, "He learned to embrace Western culture while learning French."[161] In the musical, An is portrayed as a devout Christian, who, just before he assassinates Ito, enters a Catholic church in Harbin "and prays on bended knees for courage and forgiveness."[162] His prayer becomes a song, "Before the Crucifix," a slow, minor-mode prayer, accompanied by harp arpeggios, tubular bells, and strings, which aims to convey a hushed, uplifting piety reminiscent of Rodgers and Hammerstein's "You'll Never Walk Alone" and "La vergine degli angeli" from Verdi's *La forza del destino*. Because this song is one of the few moments in the piece that seems to reference elite Euro-American culture, it serves to elevate An socially and strengthen his tacit link to "economic, political, and social modernization," of which the Korean Roman Catholic church has long been a champion.[163] More important, it makes him especially sympathetic to the many affluent Christians who attend musical theatre in Korea. Because the "explosive growth" of Christianity after the Korean War "accompanied that of the economy," Christianity for many Koreans is associated with Westernization and worldly success.[164] Although conservative Protestant sects spread especially quickly through the 1980s, Catholicism has flourished more recently and, since 1995, Catholic conversions have outpaced Protestant ones. Polls show, moreover, that Korean Roman Catholics "are mostly drawn from the upper and middle classes" and that although only 10 percent of the population is Catholic, 55 percent of the upper classes are.[165] Thus, An's dedication to the "'American' religion" serves as the sign not only of his Westernization, but of the piece's identification with that most US-American of theatre forms, the Broadway musical.[166]

In comparison with *The Last Empress*, *Hero* seems to have positioned itself to ride the Korean Wave. While both musicals take anti-colonialist positions and are highly critical of Japan, *Hero* adopts a much more nuanced and sympathetic view of the Japanese. Set during the consolidation of modern Korean nationalism, both musicals revisit a period when nationalism and pan-Asianism were at odds. Nationalism, trying to construct a uniquely Korean identity and culture, saw the greatest threat from its Asian neighbor, Japan, and not the West. Pan-Asianism, in contrast, "viewed race as the basic category of distinction in the world" and conceived the "global situation as one of racial struggle" between the "white" and "yellow" races. For Korean Pan-Asianists like An, "cooperation and solidarity among the yellow race . . . would be necessary for defending not only the region but Korea itself."[167] In its demonization of the Japanese, *The Last Empress* unequivocally sides with Korean nationalists and the finale, "Rise, People of Chosun," leaves no question where the play's sympathies lie:

> People: Graceful land and fertile field were raped,
> And our dear Queen has left in our grief.
> The humiliation brought by wicked Japan,
> Will they [sic] ever vanish from our minds?[168]

Hero, in contrast, presents the Japanese colonizers as colorful, if exploitative adventurers. In its second scene, the Japanese sing a comic, pentatonic waltz that exults that Japan—much like postwar South Korea—"will reveal her power like America and the great European Powers." Even more instructive is the musical's penultimate scene, in which the condemned prisoner An Chunggun is visited by the spirit of Ito Hirobumi and they sing a tragic, minor-key duet distinguished by its ghostly, chromatic string figurations that provide a portrait of the tangled and sinuous relationship between both characters and nations. An explains to his enemy that "There was no personal rancor" and that he "pulled the trigger" only to "avoid further bloodshed." This number is followed by a second Korean-Japanese duet, "Peace in Asia," a simple, lyrical waltz sung by An and his jailer, Chiba:

> Aware of each other, we live in peace;
> Guarding each other, we live in harmony.
> This is the wisdom that makes for peace in Asia.[169]

In their eagerness to reconcile two historically opposed formulations, Korean nationalism and pan-Asianism, the *Hero* production team implicitly acknowledges that the Japanese in 2009 were the leading consumers of *hallyu* outside Korea.[170] If K-pop and Korean television can become hugely successful in Japan, which has almost three times the population of South Korea, then why not a musical that preaches peace? *Hero* in 2015 was performed in Harbin, China, where Ito was assassinated, and director Yun hopes to tour it to Japan and China. "The two countries," he says, "are perfect locations for the musical as it conveys a message of pan-Asia peace."[171] In its reconciliation of opposing ideologies and nations, *Hero* yet again proves its Broadway pedigree, for what dramatic form has been quite as successful as the musical at seducing audiences to support and cheer irreconcilable positions?

A Rite of Return

Hero: The Musical, with, on the one hand, its nationalist message, and on the other, its Broadway-style songs, musical dramaturgy, choreography, and singing, exemplifies the incongruities that define the transnationalized musical. For this new musical tries at once to assert and disavow a unique national identity. If such a work is to travel, it must speak a cosmopolitan, that is, Western musical theatrical language and employ the generic conventions to which local theatregoing audiences are accustomed. But in order to entice international audiences, such large-scale Korean examples also need to embody a national brand that stokes colorful, seductive fantasies. It must, in short, be at once familiar and exotic. This contradiction is one that K-pop has negotiated with great success, even though when *hallyu* broke, most Western consumers had no idea what made Korean culture unique. Thus, in branding itself as cosmopolitan, K-pop has had to construct the Koreanness it purportedly expresses.

This mix of familiarity and exoticism finds expression in the first Broadway show with Korean subject matter, a musical about the K-pop industry, *KPOP*, which opened in November 2022. Though both librettist (Jason Kim) and co–songwriter (Helen Park) were born in Korea, and most of the rest of the production team is European American, *KPOP* capitalizes on the trendiness of K-pop and casts K-pop idols in leading roles. It is fashioned not as a K-pop concert, but as a traditional book musical and was first presented Off Broadway in 2017 in a sold-out, immersive production, only to be radically reconceived for Broadway. *KPOP* apes the structure of a biographical jukebox musical but with an original score. Its premise is the purported filming of a "mockumentary" by a US-American director "about an upcoming American tour for a K-pop entertainment company's roster": the boy band, F8; girl group, RTMIS; and the solo idol, MwE.[172] *KPOP* is a hybrid, with Korean and Korean American actors and two title pages in the *Playbill* (one in English, one in Korean). While many of the song lyrics are in Korean, almost all the spoken dialogue is English, the non-stop projections avoid traditional Korean imagery, and the techno/hip-hop/dance music does not sample Korean musical instruments. Its skillfully written songs are diegetic, as in a jukebox musical, but they function, in typical Broadway fashion, to advance the plot, entertain, and allow the characters to express their thoughts and feelings. Many are traditional "I want" and "I am" songs, beginning with the opening number, "This Is My Korea," in which the band imagines its sensational reception in the United States: "The future's standing right in front of [us]!"[173]

KPOP's plot places it squarely in the tradition of backstage musicals such as *Gypsy*, foregrounding the trials and tribulations of performers, chiefly the vulnerable, orphaned MwE, whose association with the company's imperious owner, Ruby, clearly seems to reference the vexed mother/daughter relationship between Mama Rose and Louise at the heart of *Gypsy*. Like *Gypsy*, *KPOP* focuses on aspiration, providing a close-up of the arduous, multiyear process that manufactures, packages, and markets idols. The particulars of that process, however, have long been familiar to Koreans, since Korean television broadcast more than forty idol reality shows between 2009 and 2015.[174] *KPOP* thus seems to be directed at a US audience that is less aware of its pastiche of stereotypes. Although it was not a financial success on Broadway, its very production illustrates not only the global popularity of K-pop but also the centrality of K-pop to both Korean and global media cultures, especially since (former) idols are popping up more and more frequently in films, television programs, and musicals.

Most important, *KPOP* represents a rite of return. Sixty-five years before the show's debut, South Korean postwar pop was cobbled together from trot, jazz, rock 'n' roll, rhythm and blues, and showtunes "through a lengthy postwar tutelage under the American military occupation." In the span of three generations, it has developed its own uniquely sexy and communicative vernacular that went viral in the 2010s and proves, in Kyung Hyun Kim's words, that "Koreans [have] finally come of age."[175] In 2022, Korean culture stormed the citadel of the Great White Way it had so long and so skillfully mimicked with a musical with a catchy score, extravagant costumes, and high-powered singing and dancing. Although countless musicals have been produced about the music business, *KPOP* is only the third, after *Bombay Dreams* (2002 West End, 2004 Broadway) and *Fela!* (2009), about non-Western pop cultures. These shows may have had mixed rates of success, but their appearance on Broadway, now inundated by jukebox musicals, seems to signal a wave of hybrid, transnational musicals that originate in the metropole but take as subject matter and style non-Western musical vogues. The global success of K-pop and its reinvention as a Broadway musical proves that South Koreans have acquired the power "to become the very origin of the cultural hegemony," which once upon a time "they had grown up mimicking in the poverty-stricken, war-ridden camptowns."[176] *KPOP* thus fashions itself the first Korean Broadway musical by mixing musical, dramatic, scenic, and choreographic idioms with very different pedigrees in order to celebrate the invented tradition that goes by the name of Koreanness.

3
The Sound of Korea

South Koreans' flair for creating innovative musicals is correlated to their skill at composing unique musical hybrids that mix Western and Korean national styles. Indeed, the twenty-first century has seen a blossoming of innovative music—utterly unlike K-pop—that not only combines Korean traditions (*gugak*) with Western international styles (*yangak*), but also deconstructs the binary opposition between popular and classical. Many of these innovations offer a creative mixture of idioms and musical instruments in order to resist being pigeonholed. Choi Yu-jun argues that this mixture makes South Korean music inherently diasporic, "an experimental mechanism for cultural assimilation and multicultural exchanges" that "started at least a century before" the recent flowering of category-defying music. "Music's unique characteristic of crossing national borders" has been exploited by Korean artists and cultural institutions to promote "musical imaginings" that freely transgress institutional and aesthetic "borders drawn between Western and traditional." In South Korea, both music and theatre have become especially important sites for provocative experiments in "globalization and multiculturalism."[1]

In Korea, these experiments include even popular musical theatre, which is not typically considered an experimental genre. Not all Korean musicals transgress these borders, but several of the most celebrated have devised uniquely stirring combinations of Western and Korean traditions. In Korea, traditional music (*gugak*) is an enormously complex and powerful invention, an assemblage of indigenous musical instruments, institutions, and practices, of which recordings, sheet music, and performances are only a part. As a set of practices and social relations, tradition is always evolving not only technologically, but also through affective registers that are both individual and community-based. In the case of musical theatre, Koreanness may be vested less in song form and tonal structure than in an emotional palette and musical dramaturgy. Certain affects, notably *han*, or sadness, have long been defined as uniquely Korean. *Han*, which has been closely identified with Korean art and culture, is usually explained to mean resentment, spite,

Tell it to the World. David Savran, Oxford University Press. © Oxford University Press 2024.
DOI: 10.1093/oso/9780190249533.003.0003

sorrow, and regret. The apparent clarity of this definition obscures the fact that although *han* is frequently applied, D. Bannon notes, to "nearly every aspect of Korean life and culture," its meaning is notoriously elusive and its very being contested.[2] Usually, Daniel Tudor observes, *han* is described as "an unresolved resentment or emotional pain, . . . a kind of grudge, but an internalized one," usually "accompanied by an inward sense of despair and injustice."[3] Because of *han*'s strongly nationalist character, many scholars believe it to be rooted in the "long history of foreign invasions; colonization; prolonged poverty and starvation under oppression; the tyranny of ruling classes, first in the feudal caste system as well as later, during the period of rapid industrialization; the abuses of power by one authoritarian military regime after another in the postwar period; oppressions of religious ideologies."[4] As victims of this terrible history, Koreans, Chang-Hee Son claims, "are more *haan*ful than any other race on earth."[5]

As a marker of Koreanness, *han* would seem to clash with the formulas of popular musical theatre, which, as a rule, shun tragedy. But it is precisely this clash between *han* and Broadway, *gugak* and *yangak*, tragedy and comedy, East and West, that has been so productive for Korean musical theatre. I analyze three examples in this chapter, proceeding from the least obviously Korean musical to the one most deeply embedded in heritage performance.

The International Style

Although both *The Last Empress* and *Hero* mine Korean history, their scores make parsimonious use of traditional Korean musical styles. Their Koreanness lies more in their subject matter, plotting, and scenic and costume design—and of course their use of the Korean language. Since *Hero*'s tour to the United States, this careful and spare apportionment of Koreanness has become standard practice in many of the homegrown musicals (*changjak*) that attempt to ride the Korean Wave and circulate in the global marketplace. Many, in fact, are based on Western source material and, at first glance, seem to mimic Korean consumer goods such as Samsung phones and Hyundai cars, which lack obvious visual signifiers that mark them as Korean. K-pop, on the other hand, despite its cosmopolitanism, is becoming more conspicuously Korean not only in its occasional pastiche of *gugak* but also in its futuristic techno-pop sonic and televisual landscapes.

As Choi emphasizes, K-pop songs such as "Gangnam Style" instantiate "a phase of Korean materialistic modernization on a global scale" through its distribution on "heterogeneous media centers... such as YouTube."[6] Korean musicals, in contrast, are live events not accessible at the click of a mouse. Most are aimed primarily at East Asian consumers, both local audiences and tourists from Japan and China. Because Seoul is a two-hour flight from Tokyo, Beijing, and Shanghai, many are even starting to employ Japanese and Chinese titles.[7]

Some producers shy away from Korean content, bemoaning the reliance of musicals like *Hero* on Korean stories and claiming that "[l]ocally produced musicals had a difficult time in overseas markets because of the extremely localized, Korean nature of the subject matter."[8] As a result, instead of looking to Korean sources, they have produced large-scale musical adaptations of Western classics, among them Mary Shelley's *Frankenstein* (2014) and Lew Wallace's *Ben-Hur* (2017), both written and directed by Wang Yongbum, with music by Lee Sang-jun. Produced in Seoul with all-star casts, they are clearly transnational in their ambitions and musical theatrical styles. The former, which was pointedly "produced for overseas markets,"[9] resembles other spectacular, European-style costume dramas set in the nineteenth century that have been hits in Seoul, including imports such as *The Phantom of the Opera*, Maury Yeston's *Phantom*, *Les Misérables*, and a locally made *Sherlock Holmes*. Set during the Napoleonic Wars, *Frankenstein* features sumptuously designed sets and costumes, high-energy choreography, a fast-moving plot, and an eclectic Western-style score that aims for an operatic emotional grandeur, or in the words of one blogger, "a classy feel."[10]

But *Frankenstein* is by no means a paint-by-numbers musical. On the contrary, it is "grim," "gruesome," and spine-chilling, with full Gothic accessories: an ominous, looming castle, guillotine, high body count, and decapitated head—not exactly a proven formula for success.[11] The production, however, was so successful that it was revived in 2016 and 2018 and has been hailed as a "guiding light to Korea's original musical industry."[12] Because of *Frankenstein*'s initial success, Asian producers were "calling in to purchase the rights," and the piece was even singled out by critics as setting "the necessary tracks for the next generation of Korea's Hallyu."[13] Its sold-out performances in Seoul earned a large enough profit that the producers decided to open the show in Japan in 2017, where it also sold out its twenty-three performances.[14]

Although *Frankenstein* has capitalized on inventive design and special effects, a large part of its success is owed, I believe, to its unusually memorable and effective score. It uses a preponderance of songs in the minor mode that range from large-scale quasi-operatic scenes and Spanish-style dances to *han*-drenched, chromatic, introspective solos that bestow real substance on both Dr. Frankenstein and his Creature. *Frankenstein*'s relatively spare orchestrations, moreover, give the piece an emotional directness that distinguishes it from the megamusical's sometime pomposity. Although the plot differs substantially from the novel's, the musical's themes and its gravitas are very much derived from Shelley. The musical retains the over-reaching scientist Victor Frankenstein, but introduces his new, intimate friend Henry Dupre, who initially opposes Victor but is won over to the scientist's cause, takes the blame for a homicide committed by Victor, is guillotined, and is brought back to life as the Creature (Figure 3.1). The musical adds many plot twists, including scenes in a pub, dance hall, and fight club, all of which allow for diegetic numbers and pastiches of European musical styles. It ends with Victor shooting the Creature (i.e., Henry) dead on a polar ice floe and "left to live in guilt and agony, a fate more terrible than death."[15] The picaresque, apocalyptic quality of the narrative produces Victor and Henry as tragic doppelgängers entwined and ensnared by ambition, crime, and guilt. It underlines the Faustian edge to the original story, which is complemented by

Figure 3.1 The Creature awakes, *Frankenstein*, 2017, screenshot from YouTube clip.

magical, science fiction–style stage effects. Victor, moreover, as in Shelley's original, is clearly undone by his arrogance, his attempts to become a second God, to heal (in his words) a world in crisis (with "epidemics, natural disaster, danger of extinction," "wars and genocide"), a world that human beings have made "such a hell."

> The science I pursue isn't to unlock some distant future
> I'm saying let's change right now.[16]

But Victor's soteriological plan fails of course and he is unable to effect the changes for which he aims.

The *han*-filled climax of *Frankenstein* is the Creature's final number, "Wounded," which he sings to a lost, crying boy he encounters wandering through a wood at night. The song, which substitutes an intimate, contemplative solo for the usual rousing eleven o'clock number, is the most despairing in the piece, which makes it unusual as a climactic number. Given the Creature's distracted state, it would seem that the child is simultaneously hallucination, ghost, and palimpsest of both young Henry and young Victor. In the production, the Creature enters to comfort the boy and they sit down by the side of a lake. The Creature's hushed song unfolds over repeated, syncopated, chromatic piano vamps:

> There lived a man, just a weak man,
> Who admired the sky so much that he decided to become a god himself.
> He made a creature that resembled himself,
> But he realized he was not ready.
> . . .
> His ambition to become a god was nothing but reckless greed.
> What makes humans think they own this world?

The boy, noticing the wound on his protector's neck, asks softly if he is the Creature. The latter responds,

> Yes, I was wounded. When you grow up, you will pretend to be a man, too.
> Do not do that.

The Creature lifts his hand to stroke the back of the boy's head but instead of comforting him, throws him into the water, in a moment that echoes one of the most famous scenes from both the novel and James Whale's 1931 Hollywood classic *Frankenstein*. The Creature then sings the final stanza:

> There lived a monster
> Trapped in wounds
> At the end of the world.[17]

I find it difficult to imagine a more unlikely—or more wrenching—climax to a musical. The song's quiet despair is underlined by the fact that the Creature and the boy are facing upstage, so the focus is not on the actors' faces, but on the entire starlit scene, the music, and the lyric. The shocking murder, at once real and symbolic, certainly undercuts one's sympathy for the Creature, but it also functions to rent temporality itself, as if the Creature/Henry were trying to foreclose the very story in which he appears.

KBS Radio hailed *Frankenstein* as the first Korean musical that has "satisfied both artistry and commercial profitability." One reviewer's praise, moreover, was all-too-revealing of the aspirations of Korean producers and audiences: "Often, people leave the theater thinking that 'Frankenstein' was imported from Broadway, and cannot hide their shock when they learn that the show was produced by an all-Korean staff."[18] A producer declared that his "long-term goal is to show this production on Broadway or West End," while the director voiced his hope of seeing "Korea transform from a contents consumer, which mainly imports musicals from other countries, into a contents creator."[19] Playing at a subsidized theatre, the $3.85 million production benefited from considerable state support.[20] The Chungmu Art Hall, at which *Frankenstein* opened, had decided "to support original musical productions" from "the planning stage" in order to give them a "Korean spin" and provide "a new paradigm for local productions" in the global market.[21] I suspect, however, that the producers of *Frankenstein* have underestimated how profoundly this "Korean spin" changes the vernacular of the Euro-American musical. Attempts at making musical theatre for export usually result in endless compromise. But the opposite proves true for *Frankenstein*, which rigorously follows through with its tragic logic. Indeed, only a small handful of Broadway musicals, among them *Sweeney Todd*, *Assassins*, and *American Psycho*, refuse a happy, consolatory ending as aggressively as *Frankenstein*. Thus, the challenge, I believe, in exporting *Frankenstein* to the United States is not its sensationalism, but its *han*, its uncompromisingly dark vision of humankind.

Musical Theatre Performers

The blossoming of Broadway-style musical theatre in South Korea and its popularity with East Asian audiences is the result not only of gifted composers, writers, and directors. Just as important are two tangentially related performance features: the casting of K-pop stars and the remarkable talents and skills of Korean singers and musicians. Regarding K-pop stars, Patrick Healy, in the second of his three *New York Times* stories about musicals in Korea, quotes a Korean producer who claims that the casting of K-pop stars is especially important in those shows aimed at Japanese and Chinese tourists. One Korean producer noted that since 2010, "K-pop casting has become the No. 1 criteria for a lot of shows" in order to attract young adoring fans. In 2022 alone, twenty Korean musicals, both original and imported, starred at least one K-pop idol (most featured multiple idols), in addition to the Broadway *KPOP*, which starred four. Unlike musicals in New York, London, or Hamburg, those in Seoul rotate leading roles and often cast K-pop stars and film and television actors in differing configurations to turn "women in their teens, 20s and 30s into devoted and repeat customers."[22] This policy means that medium- and large-scale musicals employ multiple sets of stars, and although casts are usually announced in advance, one sometimes does not know the casting of the leads until one arrives at the theatre. As Healy's remarks imply, Korea has a highly developed musical theatre fan culture, especially among young women, many of whom write about the musicals they have seen on social media. Indeed, one of the privileges of attending a musical is the opportunity to pose and be photographed next to life-size cutouts of one's favorite stars, and sometimes, after the show, next to the stars themselves. Moreover, while videotaping performances is illegal and strictly policed, curtain calls are fair game and YouTube commonly features dozens of curtain call postings by fans for every Korean musical, especially those that feature K-pop stars. But the casting of K-pop stars is not ubiquitous. *Frankenstein*'s director emphasizes that they avoided K-pop stars because they wanted to "make an artistic musical," choosing "actors who fit the roles perfectly and who were remarkably talented, not those who could sell tickets."[23] It is also worth noting that given the overwhelmingly female fan-cultures, it is not by accident that shows like *Frankenstein* and *Ben-Hur* are very much centered on male characters and male stars and that both musicals repeatedly place on display large choruses of well-built, sometimes scantily clad young men.[24]

The second and more important performance feature that makes Korean musical theatre (and opera) notable is the superb technique and musicianship of so many Korean music theatre performers. Although Korean popular singers hit the airwaves in the 1930s, internationally recognized Korean classical musicians first appeared on the scene in the 1950s. With the steady growth of Western-style musical training programs in schools and universities, there has been an unprecedented boom in Korean classical musicians, many of whom have attended conservatories in the United States or Europe, won prestigious international prizes, and performed in high-profile venues. Although the best-known are conductor Myung-whun Chung, violinist Sarah Chang, and sopranos Sumi Jo and Hei-Kyung Hong, the phenomenal success of so many Korean musicians inspired the Belgian journalist Thierry Loreau to collaborate with film director Pierre Barré to make *Le mystère musical coréen* in 2012 to try to explain the Korean talent "avalanche."[25] Loreau was motivated to make the film because of his "amazement at how South Korea with its population of 50 million can continue to produce more prizewinners and competition laureates than the United States or Russia." According to media reports, Korean musicians between 2010 and 2012 "comprised at least a quarter of all participants in prestigious international competitions." In 2001, the Queen Elisabeth Music Competition in Belgium "had no Korean participants but in 2011, five of the twelve finalists were Korean," with sopranos Hong Hae-ran (in 2011) and Sumi Hwang (in 2014) winning the Grand Prize in the voice competition in two consecutive rounds.[26] The reasons for this blossoming are many and also help to account for the explosion of musical theatre talent in Korea: the long history of Western music in the country, the high quality of music education, the financial and emotional support of parents, and the tenacity of young performers. Indeed, the flowering of the full spectrum of singers and musicians in South Korea proves, according to Fred Brouwers, "that music is closely linked to the standard of living and the economic development of a nation."[27] And, I would add, to the international educational and performance opportunities available to young musicians.

Although there is no necessary correlation between the training of opera singers and musical theatre performers, singing techniques tend to be highly culturally specific, and the differences between and among US-American, German, and Korean musical theatre singers are striking. In fact, however, musical theatre singing styles are determined by more than taste and tradition. They are also symptomatic of the musical's relative position in the cultural hierarchy in all three countries. In the United States, musicals are extraordinarily diverse and so occupy a wide swath of the cultural field. In many popular shows, especially rock musicals, singers resort to the Broadway belt, of which Ethel Merman and Patti LuPone have been the acknowledged masters. But the New York theatre also features many performers unafraid of a quasi-operatic style (singing from their diaphragms and properly negotiating their head voices), including Audra McDonald, Victoria Clark, Laura Benanti, Kelli O'Hara, Rebecca Luker, Brian Stokes Mitchell, Brian d'Arcy James, and Matthew Morrison. Germany, in contrast, has a strictly hierarchized theatrical culture, and the method of voice production employed by musical theatre actors in the commercial theatre is very different from that used by opera singers. Many celebrated German musical theatre stars, like Pia Douwes, Wietske van Tongeren, Katharine Mehrling, Thomas Borchert, and Uwe Kröger, may be skilled actors, but they deliberately aim for a vibrato-less, penetrating sound, as if they were intent on proving that musicals in Germany belong to a different—and inferior—cultural realm than opera and classical vocal music.

In Korea, where musicals accrue considerable symbolic capital, singers use a mode of voice production much closer to the US model. As a result, most Korean musical theatre stars are fine technicians and expressive actors—and major draws for the many East Asian tourists who visit Seoul expressly to see musicals. By way of example, let me cite the 2013 Korean revival of *Les Misérables*, a variant of the same twenty-fifth anniversary production that was being staged in North America, Europe, Australia, and Japan.[28] With an all-Korean cast and a large-scale, fine-tuned production, it was designed, staged, and miked to produce the greatest emotional effects. Sung Hwa Chung, who was so widely acclaimed for playing the title role in *Hero*, delivered a stirring performance as Jean Valjean that belies Jonathan Burston's contention that the megamusical actor is transformed into a machine or moving prop.[29] As Chung proved in *Hero*, he is a magnetic singer and deeply communicative actor with an almost operatic-style vocal technique, and has the power and affect associated with US musical theatre baritones like Alfred Drake and Brian Stokes Mitchell. Although he began his acting career as a television comedian, he is a master of the Broadway idiom with virtuosity, power, and sense of theatre.[30] He does not, like most singers, croon his way mawkishly through Valjean's big number, "Bring Him Home." Instead, he moves confidently from a grounded pianissimo to ringing, heroic full voice.[31] Despite the opprobrium sometimes cast on virtuosos, Chung's virtuosity, charismatic power, and presence do not represent an act of what Richard Wagner referred to scornfully as the "intractable self-love which is characteristic of all virtuosos,"[32] but of customization, of claiming ownership. His live performance, like that of virtuosos elsewhere, "evokes a distinctive affecting presence," an expansive quality that transforms "ways of viewing the potentialities of human agency." Moreover, as anyone who has seen a virtuosic, show-stopping performance knows, the shared recognition and appreciation of Chung's artistry can generate "an acute sense" of excitement and "community" among audience members.[33]

Given the eagerness of Korean producers and the government's support for Broadway-style musicals with both Korean and European settings, it is impossible to predict the future for the Korean musical on the world stage, especially given the "drying up" of some private funding at exactly the moment when the *New York Times* was touting the musical's hotness 7,000 miles from Broadway.[34] Even if *Frankenstein* were to make it to Broadway, it would only reinforce the unfortunate truth that an original Korean story would be a much tougher sell in New York than a European classic.

The Sound of Tradition

The South Korean musicals on which I have focused thus far use Western-style musical idioms and song forms and seem to eschew obviously Korean music. But this statement begs the question, what exactly is Korean music? One might offer the imprecise answer that the use of pentatonic scales and Korean musical instruments identifies Korean traditional music. But that definition is overgeneralized and inadequate. Although *gugak* is characterized as "'traditional music that remains in the past,'"[35] it endures in Korea as a living art practiced by many amateurs and professionals and supported by the South Korean government since the founding of the Republic. The National Gugak Center, established in Seoul in 1951 with the aim of teaching and promoting traditional Korean music, has thrived, despite the ups and downs of government and popular support, as well as the lack of a clear definition of what *gugak* designates. The Center opened a museum in 1995[36] and underwrites four performance groups, including the Contemporary Gugak Orchestra, devoted to transmitting "traditional music as well as . . . produc[ing] new performances which reflect the musical need of our era."[37] The Center's work targets not only professionals but also "people's daily lives" and includes multiple educational and performance programs aiming for the "Expansion of Gugak through Global Communication."[38] Its publications, in both Korean and English, provide detailed analyses of and guides to many different kinds of heritage performance as well as practical handbooks for composers in the use of traditional musical instruments.[39] Choi Yu-jun hails the novelty of what he calls this "deterritorialization of traditional music" through which "encounters of different musical materials with each other are highlighted." Most important, he points out that the new *gugak* "dismantles the boundaries of musical institutions and embraces virtually all genres of music." On the one hand, some composers who mix Western and Korean instruments and styles, such as Na Hyo-shin and Lim Jun-hee, are usually labeled classical. On the other hand, there has been an explosion of "progressive" ensembles and soloists that mix *gugak*, rock, jazz, classical, and postrock, including Ensemble Sinawi, Jambinai, Geomungo Factory, SB Circle, Dongyang Gozupa, and Park Jiha, that both compose and perform their own music and make it available on widely distributed platforms. Their work is sometimes dubbed fusion *gugak* or post-*gugak* and is usually categorized as popular.[40] But what of musical theatre, which practices even more diverse modes of hybridization?

Given the "deterritorialization of traditional music," I want to try to map the field of musical theatre by analyzing the construction of national identity and culture in two Korean-themed musicals, *The Days* (그날들, 2013) and *Seopyeonje* (서편제, 2010). These are relevant examples because they employ contrasting musical vernaculars and offer two utterly different, ingenious possibilities for reclaiming Korean performance traditions. Both are tragic chronicles of postwar Korea, the former peopled by characters from the high reaches of South Korean government service, the latter by lowly itinerant musicians who perform *pansori*, the oldest and most highly prized indigenous music theatre (which forms the basis for *changgeuk* and other kinds of heritage performance). *The Days* is a jukebox musical based on the songs of Kim Kwang-seok, a popular singer-songwriter of the 1980s who committed suicide in 1996 at the age of thirty-one. *Seopyeonje* in contrast has an original fusion *gugak* score and is based on a landmark 1993 film of the same title by Im Kwon-taek. Like *Frankenstein*, these pieces represent serious essays in popular music theatre, a genre not usually known for its gravity. Unlike *Frankenstein*, however, with its use of European source material, both *The Days* and *Seopyeonje* explore the tragic dimensions of South Korean history. Both have plots that span several decades, and both, because they swing between different temporalities, are haunted by literal or figurative ghosts. Both have memorable scores and build noteworthy songs on baroque-style sequences of descending fifths that underline the serious aspirations of both musicals. Despite these many similarities, however, they rehearse contradictory modes of Koreanness, the first glamorously, if soberly modern, the second primordial and conjured by the world of heritage performance. In order to explain their similarities, however, I need to make a brief detour from content to context, and dig into the affective registers these musicals mine.

When Korean writers and critics are asked what makes their nation and culture unique, they are most likely to answer *han*, which an authoritative Korean-English dictionary translates as "a grudge; resentment; a bitter feeling; spite; hatred; rancor; (*hant'an*) a mixed feeling of sorrow and regret (unique to Korean); an unsatisfied desire."[41] As an affect, it is identified both as "an individual emotion" and "a larger, national sentiment or ethos."[42] Given *han*'s link to the oft-cited "intensity of Korean emotive culture" as well as its social and psychological character, its origins remain much debated.[43] Because of *han*'s strongly nationalist character, many scholars believe it to be rooted in the long history of oppression and colonialism that Koreans have endured. According to Suh Nam-dong,

> Koreans have suffered numerous invasions by powerful surrounding nations so that the very existence of the Korean nation has come to be understood as *Han*.... At a certain point in Korean history, about half of the population were registered as hereditary slaves and were treated as property rather than as people of the nation.[44]

Although *han*'s facticity, character, and uniqueness remain contested, it has become, Tudor notes, "a part of the psychological landscape of Korea in that it affects people's behavior as well as the music, art, and drama they produce," including *hallyu*.[45] Youna Kim understands this "deeply felt sense of oppression and deep-seated grief" to be a vital component of television and film romance dramas like *Winter Sonata*. K-pop is less obviously inflected by *han*, but most other kinds of Korean vocal and concert music are thought to be imbued with *han*, from *pansori* to the Westernized musical language of the symphonic poem. *Han*, moreover, like tragedy, is understood to be an ennobling affect, one that raises up both a suffering protagonist (in a musical like *Hero*) as well as the artifact itself in the cultural hierarchy, and is opposed to *hung*, "a communal concept of joy."[46] Generally, *han* is associated with more elite cultural forms—opera, classical and heritage music, poetry, and serious plays and prose works—as opposed to K-pop or comedy, which are associated with *hung*. Although the qualities in *The Days* and *Seopyeonje* I am identifying as tragic could more precisely be labeled as *han*-ful, the *han*-fulness they describe looks uncannily like what in the West passes for tragedy.

Han in art is usually judged an asset and a cause of Korean performances' uniqueness, but the term carries the risk, as do all cultural stereotypes, of essentializing, exoticizing, and objectifying the subjects with which it is associated. Indeed, Sandra So Hee Chi Kim argues forcefully that the ubiquity of *han* dates back only to the Japanese colonial period, when it was "anachronistically imposed on Koreans" in order to orientalize them "while making the Japanese seem more Western." She sees it accordingly as a Japanese-derived "Korean aesthetics of sorrow [that] helped to legitimize the Japanese colonial project of helping a sorrowful, naïve people," but which, since the colonial period, "Koreans themselves embraced as a special and unique racial essence." Even Kim acknowledges, however, that despite *han*'s colonial heritage, this "ethnonational, biologistic badge of Korean uniqueness... is not just a social construct; it names an embodied experience of shared grief."[47] In short, *han* is real insofar as most Koreans *believe* in its power and act on those beliefs. In music, its sound has often been analogized with the African American "song of sorrow" or the so-called tear in the voice that allegedly underlies the "Jewish vocal aesthetic."[48] Though *han* can thus be framed as an orientalist trope or melodramatic trick, the fact that so many Koreans believe in its passionate intensity helps explain why Korean classical musicians fill concert and opera stages around the world, and why Korean musical theatre actors are so soulful and powerful.

Although *han* is firstly understood as a negative affect, it also functions as the impetus for an expressive culture that triumphs over catastrophe. According to Tudor, *han* aims not to undo tragedy but to survive and transcend it, to use it, like a funeral, "to sublimate the grief and darkness of death into the happiness and brightness of life."[49] He also cites *han* as a way of explaining the function of the shamanic ritual *gut* for the dead, in which singing and dancing "release" energy, offering a psychological reward through "the catharsis it brings."[50] So too with musicals. By embracing their tragic subject matter, both *The Days* and *Seopyeonje* offer this catharsis and, most important, the transmutation of pain and loss into beauty. In that sense, the *han* raised by both pieces designates not death but continuing life.[51]

The Days

The characteristics that make Korean musicals remarkable—K-pop stars, high-quality musical talent, and *han*—come together in *The Days* (2013), one of the most successful, widely performed, and honored recent Korean musicals. Unusually for a jukebox musical, it has serious cultural ambitions, and features the songbook of the celebrated singer-songwriter, Kim Kwang-seok. *The Days* is an elaborately plotted, designed, and choreographed piece with a Korean nationalist theme, a kind of musical thriller about the multiple intersections between public and private, politics and love, and has impressive credentials, having been written by the playwright and director of the 2006 hit musical (and later film) *Finding Mr. Destiny* (Yu-jeong Jang) and designed by the scene designer of *The Last Empress* and *Hero* (Dong Woo Park). It won several 2013 Musical Awards, including Best Original Musical and Best Director. Although its original "star-studded cast" featured "A-list performers," most of the show's leads made their names in film and television.[52] One of the original rotating leads, Oh Jeong-hyuk, is a K-pop star, while a second, Ji Chang-wook (who won the Best New Actor Award), is a movie and TV actor with a huge fan base.[53] Given the overwhelming femaleness of Korean musical theatre audiences and fan cultures, it is little wonder that this popular piece would feature male actors on display far more prominently than female actors, both in military uniforms and bare-chested in a locker room scene.

Although not immediately apparent to a non-Korean audience, the musical's biggest selling point is unquestionably its score, which includes almost all of Kim Kwang-seok's most famous songs. A charismatic musician who committed suicide by hanging in 1996 at the age of thirty-one, Kim may not be the subject of the musical, but the writers are clearly capitalizing upon the audience's knowledge not only of his songs but also of his unfortunate and, some say, mysterious death.[54] A short promotional video for the musical that uses only typewritten Korean texts begins with the date of Kim's suicide, as if it were a news flash coming through the wire. His end, it seems to be saying, is where we begin. Although Kim did not write all his own songs, he is sometimes compared with Bob Dylan and is regularly considered one of Korea's finest singer-songwriters, who, during the 1980s was part of the folk-rock band Dongmulwon that "played a large part in Korea's democratization movement by providing many songs with the underlying message of resistance."[55] He went solo in 1989, but remained an underground artist whose albums sold poorly during his lifetime but whose renown has risen steadily. His best-known later songs, many of which are used in *The Days*, are more melancholy, introspective, and confessional than political, but he remains associated in the minds of many Koreans with the *minjung* movement, the civic activism and street demonstrations of the 1980s.[56]

Although Kim toured to the United States in 1995, he is best-known in Europe because of the commemorative song "Kim Kwang Seok" (2009) by the German hip-hop band, Die Orsons. The song lyric describes Kim as South Korea's Bob Dylan and Kurt Cobain, a misunderstood, reclusive genius who sang "the saddest songs in the world" but "did not like to sing on the radio or on TV but in front of the audience." The Orsons' video meanwhile shows the assorted band members foiling a number of suicide attempts in quick succession.[57] In Korea, Kim remains one of the most popular and esteemed singers of his generation, the "barer of Korean soul of [the] late 1980s," whose albums have sold more than five million copies since 2000.[58] Given Kim's charismatic artistry, his preference for live performance, his *han*-drenched legend and repertoire, and the love and devotion his music has inspired, the writers faced serious challenges in incorporating his best-known songs into an elaborately plotted, fictional musical.

The Days uses a double time frame and multiple flashbacks, its action moving back and forth between 2012 and 1992, the year South Korea and China established diplomatic relations. Quick scene changes are facilitated by movable set pieces and the creative use of projections and lighting. It tells of two political intrigues and two mysterious disappearances, one in 1992 of a woman identified only as "She," a translator working for the Korean negotiating team whose life is in jeopardy, and the other in 2012 of Hana, the daughter of the president of Korea. The main characters, however, are two military bodyguards, friends, and rivals, the stern and dedicated Han Jeong-hak and the "free-spirited" Kang Mu-yeong, who are both smitten with "She" and exist side by side only in the 1992 plot.[59] In 1992, Mu-yeong disappears with "She" while Jeong-hak, some years after the incident, is promoted to Chief Bodyguard at the Blue House, the Korean presidential residence. Although Han Jeong-hak is the linchpin to both stories, there are many twists in the interwoven plots, and, as he investigates Hana's disappearance on the eve of the anniversary of the normalization of relations between South Korea and China, he gradually discovers the truth about how Mu-yeong helped the translator to escape and how, to protect the woman he loves, he ignited an explosion of cedar pollen as a decoy and so sacrificed his own life. Although the parallel between Kang Mu-yeong and Kim Kwang-seok is never explicitly drawn, the former's suicide is clearly meant to echo Kim's. Jeong-hak, meanwhile, is constructed as a conscience-stricken man who feels remorse (*han*) for not having been able to save his friend Mu-yeong, just as some of Kim Kwang-seok's fans feel remorse for not having been able to prevent his suicide.

Rather than using only flashbacks to tell the backstory, *The Days* (like *Seopyeonje*) superimposes the present onto the past so that in several scenes, characters from 1992 and 2012 exist side by side, moving through the same space simultaneously. This temporal superimposition is one at which musical theatre historically has excelled because of the evocative possibilities offered by underscoring as well as the convention of the reprise, both of which have the power to evoke that which has been heard before, to repeat with a difference, to call up an absent character, situation, or idea.[60] The locus classicus for these powers of evocation is arguably Stephen Sondheim's *Follies*, in which all the leading characters are ghosted by the persons they used to be and the songs they used to embrace. Although *The Days* does not use younger doubles, it similarly stages memory itself in order to pose two mysteries, both of which are solved at the same time and in the same place, Mount Bukhansan, which rises in Seoul behind the Blue House and is regarded by shaman practitioners "as the most sacred of mountains." Because Bukhansan remains "a wellspring of shaman belief," on which shamanistic rituals are still regularly performed,[61] the musical also becomes a kind of *ssitgimgut* or shamanistic grievance cleansing ritual for the survivors of the deceased, in this case, both the character Kang Mu-yeong and the singer Kim Kwang-seok.[62]

The score of *The Days*, like all of Kim Kwang-seok's songs, is not obviously Korean to one unfamiliar with Kim's legend. Like *Frankenstein* and *Hero*, it is written in a Euro-American musical style and includes the conventional song types used in new (and old) musicals. For Korean audiences of the musical, however, the songs' Koreanness lies in their context, their evocation of Kim's role in *minjung* culture of the 1980s, the resistance to the military dictatorship on the part of "the working class, farmers and college students," of which a "significant component" were sometimes illegally released protest songs.[63] Kim's folk-rock style, moreover, places more emphasis on the lyrics than is usually the case with rock or K-pop. In concert, he accompanied himself on an acoustic guitar (and sometimes harmonica) and showcased songs in a folk-rock style evocative of the early work of Dylan, Joan Baez, Simon and Garfunkel, and Joni Mitchell. His live performances display an immediacy and austerity at odds with some of his studio recordings, many of which sport overblown, over-synthesized arrangements in the style of 1990s pop.[64] But even when undermined by an overheated accompaniment, Kim's plaintive, reedy tenor and impassioned mode of delivery give his work an unusually intimate forthrightness and seem to be confessional, even if they are not. The musical's spotlighting of a solo harmonica at the very beginning and end, as well as its use in several songs, seems clearly an attempt to evoke if not the man himself, then at least the ongoing presence of Kim's musical signature. *The Days*, moreover, seems intent on commemorating less his sentimental side, than his impassioned gravitas, his *han*. The musical's orchestrations, for a twelve-piece orchestra, are accordingly richer yet more refined than Kim's studio arrangements, and often foreground obbligato solo strings, which are, in fact, an element in the musical's plot. Hana is an aspiring violinist (like so many South Korean teenagers!) and in a student competition in Act 1 plays the "Air" from J. S. Bach's Orchestral Suite No. 3, commonly known as "Air on the G String." This well-known piece's musical pulse is repeated several times during the musical, most notably after Mu-yeong's death, when it is transformed into a gentle dirge. But elsewhere in the second act especially, the musical uses songs, notably "Becoming Dust" and "Flowers," which are marked by their dependence on sequences of descending fifths in the minor mode as well as a restrained orchestral palette that at times sounds more like a consort of strings than a standard Broadway pit band.[65] These choices suggest that *The Days* is aiming for somewhat more elite cultural status than that usually accorded musical theatre in South Korea.

The Days exploits Kim's songs skillfully, but as with the Bob Dylan musical *Girl from the North Country* (2017) and so many other jukebox musicals that use songs for non-diegetic purposes, there is an inherent tension between the self-contained, reflective songs and the narrative conventions of musical theatre. Although the reviewers were correct to note that "the songs and the plot" do not completely "meld together," they perhaps overestimate the integration possible in a book musical that uses well-known, preexisting songs that are more confessional than most musical theatre songs.[66] The modes of address, conventions, and structures of the introspective songs that are the hallmark of singer-songwriters like Kim make them difficult to insert into a complex narrative, especially a thriller. In *The Days*, the songs do not advance the plot so much as reflect on the characters' thoughts and feelings. A second criticism voiced by some critics and disgruntled fans was the trivialization of the confessional work of a revered songwriter, "the lame repacking of the authentic."[67] But this, too, is a risk that jukebox and rock musicals always take, since both have been accused relentlessly of being commercialized and fake.[68] On the other hand, Kim's songs, so many of which are about loss, also function in the musical as a spur to retrospection, since they stimulate "people [to] think back on their" own "sorrow and frustration from a time when Korean society was struggling in the early stages of democracy."[69] Moreover, the short overture's prominent use of harmonica and wailing electric guitar seems clearly to signal the emotional authenticity for which the piece strives.

The Days' passion and refinement, when combined with its references to Bach, generous underscoring, insertion of countermelodies, restrained orchestrations, politically driven plot, use of temporal superimpositions, austerely black-suited male characters, and *han*-soaked atmosphere, turn it into a relatively highbrow affair. Although almost all the songs are unmistakably pop in style, with memorable tunes and (at times) prominent electric guitar, *The Days*, like *The Last Empress*, seems to be aiming for an almost operatic-scale narrative and emotional and scenic grandeur. The second act opens with a funeral service during a rainstorm (presumably for Kang Mu-yeong) at which a solemn "Kyrie eleison" is intoned and Jeong-hak sings Kim's final recorded song, the valedictory "A Letter That Did Not Get Sent." Mu-yeong's leave-taking in the musical's third from last scene is an emotion-charged final encounter with "She." After their escape up Mount Bukhansan, the wounded Mu-yeong begs her to leave him behind and she very reluctantly agrees. At her departure, he writes her a farewell letter and sings "Though I Loved You," the musical's climactic, heart-wrenching ballad. Written in 1991 by Han Dong-jun, "Though I Loved You" has a modular structure, with a verse-like introduction, refrain, and repeated contrasting sections that gradually raise the pitch and intensity. The sad, regretful lyric grieves over lost love:

> Yesterday rain fell from morning til night
> Descending in thick cloud[s]
> through the dust
> Your delicate voice that filled my ears
> Vanished into the rain.

The contrasting, high-flying climax of the song soars:

> Though I loved you
> I was just only able to look at you from afar.[70]

And the song closes with a quiet, sorrowful repetition of the title.

Although written as a standalone ballad for Kim Kwang-seok, "Though I Loved You" epitomizes the *han*, the sense of personal loss at the heart of *The Days*. As sung at the Korean Musical Awards by Ji Chang-wook with a passionate simplicity and directness, and a sob in his voice, the song's power was enhanced by the scene design.[71] The LED backdrop depicts what, like an M. C. Escher graphic, appears to be either a blue-and-black, canopied mountainside crevice, or peaks that disappear into the ether, telegraphing a sense both of entrapment and the sublime. The explosion that kills Mu-yeong is followed by a throbbing dirge and, as time flashes forward twenty years, Hana's recovery of his letter, which, in the next scene, she gives to Jeong-hak, who finally and belatedly understands what happened that fateful day.

Although *The Days* is a thriller, the identity of the person or persons out to assassinate the translator is never revealed. Those unfamiliar with the details of Northeast Asian history might not understand the sensitive politics linked to the musical's commemoration of diplomatic relations between a democratic South Korea and China, its much larger, more threatening, non-democratic neighbor. The 1992 agreement in fact marked a turning point in dismantling some of "the last remnants of the age-old war structure in Northeast Asia and herald[ing] the expansion of détente on the Korean Peninsula."[72] Because in 2013 (and 2023), a divided Korea remains the most acute example of the persistence of bipolar Cold War logic, the agreement between South Korea and China, coming in the wake of the collapse of the Soviet empire, marked a political and economic watershed that greatly expanded trade, tourism, and goodwill. Most of the negotiations were conducted by a "secret task force" charged with the delicate mission, which both Taiwan and North Korea "attempt[ed] to block or delay." Taiwan realized that the establishment of diplomatic ties with China would require South Korea "to sever her diplomatic relations with Taiwan," while North Korea feared that the agreement would weaken its relations with its primary protector.[73] These facts provide motivations for representatives from both countries to try to sabotage the negotiations, as well as those South Koreans and Chinese whose interests, economic and otherwise, lay in forestalling bilateral ties.

Although the unresolved mystery of "She" echoes the unresolved mystery of the suicide of Kim Kwang-seok, the plot's casualty is Mu-yeong, whose sacrifice saves the life of a negotiator engaged in reconstructing pan-Asian security. This loss, however, is felt most acutely by Jeong-hak, the only character who goes back and forth between the two temporalities, and whose remorse (call it *han*) over the death of his friend/rival places him at the center of the musical. As a political parable, *The Days* honors the *han*-steeped Korean singer's association not only with the oppositional *minjung* movement but also with the capitalist modernization of South Korea and its turn to democracy during the last eight years of Kim's short life. Indeed, some of the most visually arresting scenes in the musical involve the ceremonial pomp and circumstance and the comings and goings of Korean soldiers, among whom must be numbered the two heroes, especially the soldiers' martial arts–inspired dances and acrobatics in the second act. The Koreanness that *The Days* champions resides both in its commemoration of the iconic figure of Kim Kwang-seok and in its celebration of Korean democratization, modernization, and diplomacy. In its commitment to pan-Asian modernity, *The Days*, unlike my next example, *Seopyeonje*, never cites Korean traditional performances, unless one includes the work of Kim Kwang-seok as part of that tradition. As with composers like Chopin or Tchaikovsky, it is less the cosmopolitan style of Kim's music that bestows a national identity upon him than his legend. *Seopyeonje*, in contrast, not only rescues heritage performance but, more daringly, combines it with the conventions of the Broadway-style musical to produce a pathbreaking hybrid.

The Sound of *Han*

The musical *Seopyeonje* is based on two 1976 short stories by the celebrated novelist Yi Chung-jun and the landmark 1993 film of the same name by Im Kwon-taek, which broke all previous box office records for Korean films and was "the first Korean film to garner a million tickets in Seoul."[74] The film (whose title translates as western songs, one of the two stylistic schools of *pansori*) helped launch *hallyu* and "became an international festival favorite that drew unprecedented attention to the Korean cinema."[75] Yet what makes the musical *Seopyeonje* remarkable, besides its string of awards and continuing performances, is the fact that its protagonists are singers of *pansori*, the indigenous music theatre form that is commonly considered the most *han*-steeped of all Korean performance genres and the one whose mode of vocalization is deemed most antithetical to that used in both bel canto singing and musical theatre performance. By taking up *pansori*, and incorporating a *pansori* performance into its second act, *Seopyeonje* manages to produce a unique—and uniquely *han*-filled—amalgamation of two utterly dissimilar performance traditions, Korean heritage performance and the transnationalized Broadway-style musical.

The source for both the film and musical is a set of five interlinked and interwoven short stories by Yi Chung-jun. The first two stories, "Seopyeonje" and "The Light of Songs," which supply most of the material for movie and musical, were published in 1976, but Yi continued to elaborate on the fiction by writing three more stories that intersect with, parallel, and extend the narrative (the collection was first published as *Seopyeonje* in 1993). Because Yi's narrative technique is fragmentary and elliptical, Im Kwon-taek's film, which in Korea "elicited a collective outpouring of *han*," filled in some of the narrative gaps and gave Yi's unnamed characters names.[76] It weaves a more straightforward narrative about a man from the city (Dong-ho) who arrives at a tavern in a mountain village looking for a renowned female *pansori* singer. In flashbacks, Im tells the story of Dong-ho's stepfather, Yu-bong, an itinerant *pansori* singer, his adopted daughter, Song-hwa, and Dong-ho himself.[77] Set during the years after the Korean War, the film and musical picture a quickly modernizing Korea in which *pansori* is being eclipsed by US-American-style popular culture. The makeshift family barely scrapes by because Yu-bong insists on teaching his children what in the postwar years was considered an obsolescent and dying art. Both film and musical focus on "the process of 'giving' and 'receiving' the *sori*," Yu-bong's monomaniacal effort at imparting to his children the "voice [that] not only reflects but also shapes one's character."[78] Frustrated and angered by his disdainful, abusive father, Dong-ho flees to the city and the movie focuses on his search years later for his sister, who, he discovers, has been deliberately blinded by Yu-bong with poison in order to force her to experience the depths of *han*—and thereby become a great *pansori* singer. In the last part of the film they meet—but never acknowledge their kinship—and together perform one of the most celebrated *pansori* plays, *Simcheong*, whose tragic narrative about blindness and filial love resonates powerfully with that of *Seopyeonje*. (*Simcheong* tells the story of a daughter who sacrifices herself out of devotion to her blind father and whose piety so moves the Dragon King of the Sea that he sends her back to earth, makes her an empress, and finally reunites her with her father, whose eyesight she restores.)

Because of its renown both in Korea and abroad, and its extraordinarily evocative and *han*-filled potency, Im Kwon-taek's *Seopyeonje*, made shortly after the democratization of South Korea, has inspired considerable debate. Critics read it contradictorily as a valiant reclamation of Korean heritage performance in the face of capitalist modernity, a populist protest against authoritarianism and forced modernization, an allegory in which "the victimized woman is given the role of redeemer of the nation," and a "self-orientalizing affirmation of imperialist nostalgia and misogynist nationalism."[79] Despite these disagreements, critics are unanimous in noting that the film was instrumental is fostering a renaissance of *pansori*, which in 2008 was inscribed on UNESCO's Representative List of the Intangible Cultural Heritage of Humanity. When the musical premiered in 2010, it swept the Korean Musical Awards, winning five, including Best Original Musical, and has remained in the repertoire of the commercial theatres. The plot of the musical follows the same outline as the film, but the musical also introduces several scenes of Dong-ho's life in Seoul as a member of a US-American-style rock band with the English name Spring Boys.[80] This detour is contained in neither short stories nor film, but it works to retain the focus on music-making and elaborates on the antithesis constructed in all versions between the ethos of *pansori* and a quickly Westernizing, urbanizing South Korea, while preserving Dong-ho's identity as a musician. In the musical, it is an ingenious addition because it allows the show to thematize the collision of utterly different musical vernaculars. The second act, in particular, repeatedly performs the violent clash between the two kinds of music and the contradictory values and ways of life associated with each.

The success of film and musical is doubtless a result of the fact that both are tailored to their respective media and exploit genre-specific conventions. The film presents memories as flashbacks and includes a celebrated five-minute long shot in which the static camera films the three protagonists snaking down a road, singing the traditional "Chindo Arirang," dancing first toward the camera and then away from it. The musical, meanwhile, uses post-Golden-Age-style modular songs, a Broadway-esque palette of song types, a climactic first-act finale that hones the conflict, and a series of leitmotifs (both melodic and harmonic) whose recurrence and development provide the musical with a narrative arc.

Given *Seopyeonje*'s focus (in all its versions) on heritage performance, its inclusion of *pansori* performance, and its complex contrapuntal relation to *Simcheong*, I cannot analyze it without providing some information about the history of the genre and the embodied experiences of *pansori* singers. Since the premiere of *Seopyeonje* the musical, moreover, many singers of post-*gugak*, post-rock, and even K-pop have started using *pansori*'s mode of vocalization. Although the origins of *pansori*, Andrew Killick notes, are lost "in the mists of oral tradition,"[81] it probably grew out of the performances of (male) epic storytellers and (female) hereditary shamans. It was consolidated in the eighteenth century as a comic performance genre catering to rural audiences, but it also functioned to "express the anguish and grievances of the lower classes."[82] These early performances (given by itinerant actor/musicians) were often "bawdy, scatological, or satirical," but over the course of the nineteenth century they attracted elite patronage and became more elevated in tone, while still portraying the ruling classes "in a less than flattering light."[83] Originally, there were twelve *pansori* plays but only five survive, transcribed (and doubtlessly expurgated) by a minor civil servant, Sin Chae-hyo, in the mid-nineteenth century. All are basically melodramas with happy endings that illustrate at least one of the Confucian virtues and dramatize conflicts produced by the inflexible class system and the trials and tribulations of heroes who, after considerable suffering, are redeemed in the end. The two most celebrated and widely performed are the aforementioned *Simcheong*, an illustration of filial devotion, and *Chunhyang*, the tale of the forced separation of two lovers and the courage of the man who heroically saves his affianced bride.

Pansori is also the performance form that is most closely related to and derived from *musok*, Korean shamanism, which similarly has been constructed as an indigenous or folk practice. Like *pansori*, *musok* is performed as a series of *gut*, or rituals, conducted by a female shaman (*mudong*) to placate the spirits of the deceased. Francisca Cho claims that *pansori* in fact is a "cultural legacy of *muga*," shamanistic songs, among which numbers the tale of *Simcheong*. The shaman, like a skilled *pansori* performer, requires "a good performing voice" and the "ability to improvise upon a standard oral text and to customize it in interaction with the audience."[84] Beginning in the Japanese colonial period, shamanism was reconceived through the lens of a romantic primitivism as the exemplary indigenous Korean religious practice, despite the fact its belief system borrows heavily from Buddhism, Confucianism, and Taoism.[85] In the musical, the funeral for Yu-bong derives from shamanic ritual, reinforcing a sense of *pansori*'s essential Koreanness, in stark opposition to the standardized, commercial "Yankee pop song[s]" the Spring Boys play.[86] Moreover, the association of shamanism during the 1970s and 1980s with the oppositional *minjung* political movement underlines the musical's construction of *pansori* as a cultural practice that may be grueling and perilous but is also resistant, transcendent, and emancipatory.[87]

Originally, *pansori* was performed exclusively by men, but in the late nineteenth century, women also took it up and since the Korean War have become its primary exponents. The name *pansori* is a compound of the words *pan*, meaning "a place where many people gather," and *sori*, meaning sound, song, singing, or voice (especially its employment in traditional music). The latter word is particularly important in the musical, which centers on the characters' searches for their *sori*. The *pansori* singer usually performs holding a fan, which she manipulates as a prop, accompanied by a drummer who not only beats time but also interjects *chuimsae*, verbal exclamations that encourage the singer. The drummer, moreover, has a repertoire of a discrete number of modes of rhythm and tempi that are selected "to represent different sentiments, such as sadness, happiness, idleness, and urgency, as well as to indicate the appearance of a specific character."[88] The *pansori* singer must be skilled at using a range of rural and elite dialects, both declamation and the impersonation of characters, and the interpolation of songs in distinctive melodic modes.

Yet Koreans recognize that what make *pansori* uniquely *han*-ful and challenging to perform are its extreme dramatic qualities that are emphasized by the harsh, husky, powerful timbre it requires. *Pansori* singers practice outdoors (this is depicted in both the movie and musical) in order to develop their diaphragm muscles and are famous—or notorious—for singing in the middle of a forest, from a mountaintop, or by a waterfall (which they try to drown out!). Unlike bel canto singing, *pansori* is vocalized "as the air is forcefully thrust through taut vocal cords and larynx, thereby creating a harsh or rough tone quality."[89] As Nicholas Harkness emphasizes, the "higher larynx, restricted pharynx, and higher subglottal pressure delivers a sound (e.g., raspy, harsh, rough) and a bodily experience (tense, squeezed, painful) that is understood to [be] opposite to the values of Western classical singing." Legend has it (and there are many legends linked to the training of *pansori* singers) that one cannot be a fully developed *pansori* performer until one drinks feces water, one's throat bleeds, and one undergoes a "regimen that combines often corporeally painful vocal practice with suffering and hardship in one's broader life experience."[90] One *pansori* master explains that singers developed the aesthetic

> [b]ecause people have experienced *han*. *Han* is also a personal, internal experience—an experience of difficulty from birth. There is a proverb: [birth-endeavor-sickness-death.] This is the experience of life, one accumulates sorrow throughout life—everyone does, all throughout the world. But in Korea's case there is another aspect to *han*. The life and way of practicing for a *p'ansori* singer is extremely lonely and utterly exhausting. You study and study, trying to become great. You are always striving for a higher artistic state (*kyongji*). But you cannot climb to that high state without loneliness. And so you must live alone. That is the sound of *han*.[91]

Collisions East and West

The unique communicative power of *han* performance is essential to understanding the emotional impact of *Seopyeonje* in all its versions, and why it affects so many Koreans so deeply. And while Song-hwa is a fictional character, she is analogous to several early twentieth-century Korean artists and writers who lived under Japanese colonialism and around whom tragic mythologies have been constructed. These include two singers who committed suicide, Yun Sim-deok (with her famous "Hymn of Death") and Kim Kwang-seok, as well as artists who died under unhappy circumstances, the painter Na Hye-seok and writers Kim U-jin, Jeon Hye-rin, and Yi Sang.

The tragic Song-hwa who sacrifices herself to art also finds analogues in Western culture. Indeed, the myth of the suffering artist who surrenders his or her happiness and even life to be rewarded (sometimes only posthumously) with immortality has become stock-in-trade in the West since the eighteenth century. Consider, for example, Goethe's *The Sorrows of Young Werther*, Thomas Chatterton, and Vincent van Gogh, as well as many classical antecedents. The myth of Orpheus, the grieving musician, forms the basis for some of the earliest surviving works of the European lyric theatre.[92] During the eighteenth and nineteenth centuries, the suffering artist was almost always imagined to be male, but during the twentieth century, more and more women, especially singers, have been immortalized as sacrificing themselves for their art (Billie Holiday, Judy Garland, Edith Piaf, Maria Callas, Janis Joplin, and many others). Like Song-hwa in *Seopyeonje*, Holiday,

Garland, and Callas have been constructed as tragic figures whose voices are understood to be simultaneously the source of their genius and the vehicle for their downfall.

I draw these correspondences not to try to universalize the particularities of Korean history but to point out analogies in Western musical traditions closely related to the Broadway musical. Moreover, these cross-cultural analogies provide a key to understanding *Seopyeonje*'s position as a hybrid of the performance practice that Koreans have embraced as uniquely their own (and in which their tragic history is telescoped) and the most transnationalized of musical theatre genres, the Broadway musical. The piece's unlikely mixture of tradition and modernity, its juxtaposition of two radically different theatrical vernaculars and modes of vocalization, provides a key to understanding why Korean musical theatre has been so successfully transnationalized.[93]

Written by award-winning composer and K-pop singer Yun Il-sang, with a book by Cho Kwang-hwa, *Seopyeonje* the musical evinces a mastery of the conventions of Broadway-style musicals.[94] Like many post–Golden Age musicals, it is extremely eclectic in its use of musical styles, drawing not only on *pansori*, but also on pop, rock, folk, jazz, and classical vernaculars. These range from hard rock (for Dong-ho's band) to the Broadway ballad (solos for both Song-hwa and Dong-ho), from pseudo-folk song (for Dong-ho) to baroque-style passacaglia. *Pansori* moreover, is not the only Korean musical convention that the piece cites. The overall musical language is thoroughly Westernized, but the orchestrations (by the composer) make extensive use of Korean instrumental timbres. The score is arranged for keyboards, strings, guitars, flute, *gayageum* (twelve-string zither), and percussion, but the transverse flute sometimes mimics the Korean bamboo flute, and the solo violin the Korean bowed fiddle. The percussion, moreover, is often dominated not by snare drum and hi-hat cymbals, but by the motoric beat of Korean-style barrel drums, which are also used extensively in shamanic rites (the snare drum and hi-hat are used in *Seopyeonje* only in the most rock-inflected songs). These choices, combined with a selective use of pentatonic scales and the minor mode, gives *Seopyeonje*'s score a distinctively Korean inflection that pays tribute to heritage performance.

Seopyeonje the film is focused on the middle-aged Dong-ho, his search for his sister, and his memories, which are told in flashbacks, a well-established cinematic convention. The musical, in contrast, is a kind of backstage musical (with tragic dimensions) that performs the dynamics of remembrance and grief by creating multiple temporalities and persons. Relative to the film, it adopts a much more supple movement between past and present and double-casts Dong-ho and Song-hwa with both child and adult actors. This temporal dynamism is enabled by the scene design, which jibes with *pansori*'s "minimalist visual aesthetics"[95] and consists of a painted backdrop of mountains disappearing into mist as well as sliding screens covered with *jijeon*, white paper money used in shamanic rites, especially in Jeolla province in southern Korea, which is also home to the *pansori* performance style *seopyeonje*.[96] Indeed, the color scheme for both costumes and screens is white, which facilitates the frequent use of projected images from traditional Korean painting and calligraphy, and is also the color of mourning. White robes are especially prominent in the long funeral scene for Yu-bong, which is based on the shamanistic *ssitgimgut*, or grievance cleansing ceremony. Indeed, the entire musical can be seen as an elaboration on the *ssitgimgut*, or three-stage series of rituals that serves as an entry rite to the underworld.[97] This ritualistic element also links *Seopyeonje* to what in the West is the most revered dramatic genre, Greek tragedy. And while the plot bears little obvious resemblance to Sophocles' *Oedipus the King*, the musical clearly portrays several Oedipal triangles (in both the Sophoclean and Freudian senses) and features the emblem of the tragic victim: blindness, both literal and figurative.[98]

Seopyeonje's superimposition of multiple temporalities (like that of *The Days*) theatricalizes the narrative by exploiting the ontology of the stage as a place traversed by ghosts, a place whose live-ness is always haunted by those who came before. Although Dong-ho's mother appears briefly in the film, she is turned into a ghost in the musical and given much greater dramatic weight (she sings several solos and is one of the quartet in the climactic first act finale). The superimposition also transforms the set's turntable into a kind of temporal and spatial merry-go-round on which the past keeps moving onward while constantly repeating itself.

Another choice the musical makes that sharpens Yi's focus in the short stories on the opposition between rural and urban, traditional and Westernized, is its fleshing out of Dong-ho's life in Seoul, where he forges a successful career as a rock musician with the Spring Boys. (The US-American bona fides of the band is proven by their performance in English in Act 1 of Creedence Clearwater Revival's 1969 hit, "Proud Mary.") Moreover, by retaining Dong-ho's calling as a musician (unlike the stories and film, in which he is a salesman of traditional herbal remedies), the musical demonstrates that Dong-ho's flight from his father (and sister) represents not a repudiation of his *sori* but a search for it in a different place. He escapes from what he sees as a stultifying tradition as well as his role as foster son to an abusive father he blames for his mother's death.[99] Although in the musical, the child actors' roles are much less prominent than those of the adults, they usually appear in tandem with their older doubles, with whom they sometimes interact, often on opposite sides of the turntable. The sliding screens, meanwhile, like the play of memory, facilitate the sudden appearance and disappearance of characters.

Seopyeonje's musical eclecticism reflects not only the idioms of the US-American musical, but also of *pansori*, whose stylistic borders, Killick notes, "were never impermeable." Throughout *pansori*'s development, "existing folk songs" as well as shamanistic songs and "new melodic modes" were "woven into the texture as 'interpolated songs.'"[100] Like most popular theatre forms boasting long histories, *pansori* is deeply syncretic and was only elevated to elite cultural status (and in effect, frozen) in the post–Korean War era, in an attempt, David E. James writes, "to sustain a specifically Korean culture against its debasement and neglect, as well as against the encroachments of foreign media."[101] Although both film and musical represent an embrace of foreign media, the musical retains the melodramatic conventions of the *pansori* narrative, which are leavened by traditional musical theatres songs. Many of *Seopyeonje*'s songs represent the classic "I want" formula, as each character sings of his or her quest for *sori*, the ability to sing with perfect expressivity and so heal their wounds. Like desire itself, however, the quests remain unfulfilled (and unfulfillable). At the same time, the death of Dong-ho's mother in childbirth and Yu-bong's horrific blinding of his daughter inspire a furious drive for revenge on the part of both children. The climax of the musical, a classic if atypical eleven o'clock number, is an extraordinary second act scene in which brother and sister briefly reunite—without ever acknowledging they recognize each other—to perform the final scene of the *pansori* play *Simcheong* and the make the past, as if in a shamanic funerary ritual, dissolve into a perpetual present to purify those who are departed and—impossibly—to acknowledge, make palpable, and restitute that which has been irrevocably lost.

The drive both to recover and release a vanished past is also inscribed in the musical's use of leitmotifs that undergo a series of transformations over the course of the piece (the recurrence of the leitmotif is itself an act of reminiscence). These leitmotifs musicalize both the changing locations and the play of memory itself. Like many of Wagner's leitmotifs, they are linked variously to characters, situations, objects, places, or ideas. But they are in the main abstract, associated more with affects, desires, and drives than specific personalities, process rather than product. Because these leitmotifs are more situational than characterological, they also become transferable and shared. Two leitmotifs (defined harmonically, melodically, and rhythmically) are especially prominent, both passacaglias whose most recognizable feature is their harmonic sequencing, along with the slowly sinking bass that usually grounds this most serious of musical figurations. The first, subject to constant variation, is stated initially in the opening number and the harmonic sequence, or portions of it, repeatedly return in different guises, differently orchestrated. In the Prologue, the adult Dong-ho sings it as he remembers the burning sun, "The Massive Body of Light" that beats down on him when, as a young boy, his mother tethered him to a post while she worked in the fields. (This torturous situation is taken directly from Yi's stories.) Dong-ho remembers it as nightmarish, but his *han* is always entwined with the sound of his mother's glorious singing (her *sori*):

> The *sori* I remember
> A summer day when I was bound, playing by myself
> Mother works in the field, I'm bound
> The sound of Mother's singing, her singing sounds
> Mother works in the field, I'm bound. The *sori*.[102]

This motif is introduced by the children, but it quickly loses its characterological specificity and becomes the emblem of all the characters' quest for their *sori*. Although this passacaglia is in the major mode, it remains a solemn, implacable, slowly repeating harmonic figuration that instantiates both the eternally present and the eternally fugitive nature of their *sori* and their *han*.

The second passacaglia is introduced in the second number, "The Sister's Theme," in which the young girl sings of her quest:

> Come with me on this journey
> Let's go together
> The heart follows our footsteps. Let's go.

This is a minor-key song that resembles many Korean folk songs (including "Arirang") as well as Western folk songs (such as "Greensleeves"). The writers use it, however, to dramatize both continuity with the past and the process by which heritage performance is commodified. In the second act, the now urbanized Dong-ho takes it up (in a version strongly evocative of the folk song and 1960s pop song "The House of the Rising Sun"), playing it first on his acoustic guitar and then with his full rock band. But this change from solo to ensemble leads to a third iteration, as the now hit song is heard again by Song-hwa on a static-y transistor radio. Despite the three-stage commercialization, this passacaglia remains a slow, melancholy lament that invokes the burning sun and never-ending quest:

> Midsummer, midday
> On the asphalt road with no shade
> Do you know why I'm singing?
> It's because my youth
> Doesn't know where it's headed.[103]

Like the first passacaglia, this one instantiates *han*, the eternal recurrence of traumatic memory, both curse and cure.

Although the passacaglia represents a deep-seated Western musical tradition, *Seopyeonje*'s second act dramatizes an increasingly violent collision between Korean and Western idioms. The most acute example is the song "Time, Please Pass," which contrasts the different musical worlds of brother and sister. Onstage, Dong-ho launches into a dissonant, bluesy, hard rock lament, as from offstage, Song-hwa's keening voice slowly rises singing an excerpt from *Simcheong*. Because the two musical styles so patently collide, the dissonance musicalizes each character's isolation and literalizes the deep disharmony between internationalized rock 'n' roll and Korean heritage performance. Prior to this, there is an extended scene that depicts Yu-bong's death followed immediately by his shamanic-style funeral, in which Dong-ho's wailing guitar both synchronizes and clashes with the music of a choral funeral dance accompanied by thundering Korean barrel drums. At the end of the funeral, Song-hwa's keening voice cries out a powerful, agonized lament: she finds her *sori*.

The final ten-minute, second-act reunion of brother and sister is a performance of the ending of *Simcheong* (Figure 3.2). Accompanying his sister on the drum, Dong-ho seems mesmerized by Song-hwa, whose performance builds in speed and intensity, as the slow, solemn major-mode passacaglia quietly creeps in as non-diegetic underscoring and gradually rises to a

Figure 3.2 Final scene of *Seopyeonje*, Lee Ja-ram and Song Yooguen, 2013. Photo courtesy of Page 1 Company.

powerful crescendo. This moment of transcendence is visualized by the dematerialization of place as slowly dancing stars are projected onto the entire playing area as the turntable revolves.

This elaborate set piece, the musical's climactic monumentalization of Korean heritage performance (and of *han*) has such a powerful theatrical impact because it brings Korean and Western musical traditions, and diegetic and non-diegetic music, into a new and startling alignment, as the slow, solemn passacaglia ("the *sori* I remember") creeps in as underscoring and gradually engulfs both sister and brother. In the end, the weight of literal and figurative blindness engineers a synesthetic miracle, in which "sound is seen and visual is heard."[104] The curtain slowly falls as the pair disappears into the stars.

In *Seopyeonje* the musical, as in the short stories and film, Dong-ho is the structural center. It is he whose quest and memories construct the piece's narrative spine. But his transformation in the musical from older to younger sibling allows Song-hwa to gain more theatrical heft and illuminates telling differences between cinematic and musical theatrical conventions. Like most musicals, *Seopyeonje* gives its starring role to a woman. As D. A. Miller famously notes, in musical theatre "the female performer will always enjoy the advantage of also being thought to *represent* this stage, as its sign, its celebrant, its essence, and its glory."[105] In contrast to the film, the musical vividly dramatizes Song-hwa's transformation and gives her a musical and theatrical tour de force in Act 2. Despite the musical's embrace of Broadway conventions, her performance of this ten-minute scene, which requires extraordinary concentration and virtuosity, is reminiscent less of a traditional eleven o'clock number than an operatic mad scene. Like most mad scenes (the locus classicus is the title character's in Donizetti's *Lucia di Lammermoor*), Song-hwa's performance of the climax of *Simcheong* in *pansori* style is set off stylistically and performatively from the rest of the piece. Because, as Choi Yu-jun points out, the performative dimension of *sori* "cannot be applied properly to written music," "it has its own meaning only in the context of improvisational performance."[106] Song-hwa's overwhelming performance, like the operatic mad scene, "bears the glory of the composition" and is "its raison d'être."[107] Crucially, however, Song-wha, unlike Lucia, is not mad. On the contrary, her *pansori* performance with her brother is utterly lucid and an act of revelation and fulfillment, the long-awaited arrival and performance of *sori* and of love. Its climactic power is underscored by the piercing clarity of her musical voice, which brings the play to its end.

Seopyeonje the musical's transposition of dramatic focus is underlined by its casting and the fact that it, like all Korean musicals, features a rotating cast. In this case, however, its two original female stars, Lee Ja-ram and Cha Ji-yeon, were already distinguished performers (both won Best Actress at the Musical Awards for their work in the piece). Lee especially is an actor with a broad repertoire who has become one of the leading and most creative *pansori* performers and has been instrumental in extending its canon by writing and performing *pansori* adaptations of Western plays (most famously, solo versions of Bertolt Brecht's *Mother Courage* and *The Good Person of Szechuan*). What otherwise might be a minor change in emphasis between film and musical in fact carries great theatrical weight insofar as the history and power that Song-hwa claims work as a counterweight to the film. The latter, several critics agree, presents a seriously misogynist narrative in which "a daughter is blinded for the perfection of a cultural nationalist artifact that fulfills the masculinist desire" of her father.[108] Song-hwa in the musical, however, voices her hatred of her father and desire for revenge much more powerfully than in the film.[109] Moreover, it becomes clear in Song-hwa's final scene with her brother that *she* is the one who chooses not to acknowledge him, or to acknowledge him only in and through her *sori*, which thereby becomes a visionary practice. Most important, however, the live performance of both Lee and Cha as the blinded singer-seer is so awe-inspiring that it nearly upends the misogynist paradigm. As such, her embodiment becomes an illustration of the contradictory position of the female star in many musicals who, Stacy Wolf notes, may be misogynistically characterized but is given "tremendous performance opportunities in portraying complicated psychologies through rich music and engaging lyrics."[110] Both Lee and Cha make the most of those opportunities.[111]

The emotional and theatrical power of *Seopyeonje* the musical testifies to an irreducible contradiction between ends and means, between its avowed cultural nationalist project and the thoroughly transnationalized idiom it employs. For it is even more adept than the film in championing Korean heritage performance, all the while testifying to the ultimate triumph of the Broadway-style musical as a composite, synoptic genre capable of absorbing even antithetical performance traditions. By the finale, one is ready to echo Julian Stringer on the film: "What was ... an endangered cultural form ... has now been culturally reconstructed as a living, breathing national treasure" that "symbolize[s] the very endurance and vitality of Korea."[112] *Seopyeonje* the musical thereby succeeds at a seemingly impossible project, using modern technology (in this case, the dramaturgy of the Broadway musical) to celebrate the somatic and affective power not only of Korean heritage performance but also of the "spiritual culture" with which it is associated.[113]

Both the film and musical of *Seopyeonje* helped rescue *pansori* from cultural oblivion and thereby made an invaluable contribution to the preservation of that most vulnerable of cultural practices, intangible heritage. UNESCO's mission statement regarding that heritage, moreover, emphasizes its pivotal function as a fragile link between and among national history, personal identity, community, and sustainable development.[114] Unlike museums, which tend to decontextualize artworks, this live performance restores and revitalizes *pansori*'s affective history. I would suggest, moreover, that metatheatricality makes musical theatre deeply productive epistemologically, to paraphrase Stephen Banfield's point I cited in Chapter 1. I think he is correct to note that because music is often "the *subject* of representation" in musical theatre, as it is in *Seopyeonje*, it bestows on the genre a great dramatic agility and an epistemological awareness that allow it to serve "as a model" for "human self-knowledge"[115] and self-fashioning. *Seopyeonje*, after all, is preeminently about pedagogy, and it takes its place in a long genealogy of musicals (including *The Music Man*, *The Sound of Music*, and *Jelly's Last Jam*) that draw on popular musical forms to revive the didactic and oracular functions of expressive culture and restore a sense of rootedness. It also serves as proof that live musical theatre is uniquely capable of carrying listeners away by the very force of its self-conscious theatricality and musical sweep. This capability, moreover, is inextricably tied to its liveness, especially today, when we are so saturated with mediated cultural experiences. In the case of *Seopyeonje*, the thrill of seeing, hearing, and feeling the intertwining of a uniquely Korean and *han*-filled music with an internationalized musical theatre idiom produces—for me, at least—an epistemological shiver and models a constructive cosmopolitanism that, I believe, is becoming increasingly urgent for engineering productive and innovative cultural encounters.

In these two chapters, I have tried to demonstrate that the Koreanization of the Broadway musical represents a multifaceted, dynamic undertaking. There are as many modes of Koreanization as there are ideas of what constitutes tradition, which is a practice that must be constantly renewed, a social relation, a dynamic network that includes human and non-human actors. That network stretches from the primordial past into the present, and on into the promise of a future. In linking past to future, the musical allows Koreans, in Choi Yu-jun's words, as well "human beings in general" to "hear the otherized *sori* within their historicized bodies."[116] Those, like Michael Billington, who see in *The Last Empress* merely evidence of selling out, "the artistic equivalent of the process by which local Korean companies have surrendered to foreign control," miss the point.[117] There is no unspoiled Korean tradition to surrender. Each of the musicals on which I have focused performs a modernization of tradition in which the latter is at once preserved, canceled, and transcended. Choi strongly advocates for this mode of hybridization, arguing that bringing "the past to present" allows one to confront tradition "in a new way." As he emphasizes, "*sori* can resonate with the auditory sense of 'now-here' only through the unfamiliar and vivid experience of encounters."[118] In the twenty-first century, these encounters have led to the worldwide popularity of K-pop, Korean cinema, and Korean opera stars; tours of *changgeuk* to Western theatre capitals; a Broadway musical about the K-pop industry; and the development of an homegrown popular music theatre that mixes Korean with Western traditions in innovative and potentially transformative ways. These are singular and monumental achievements unimaginable thirty years ago.

PART III
GERMANY

4
Enter the Musical

In contrast to Korea, the German-speaking world has a tradition of concert music, opera, and drama dating back hundreds of years, which has been decisive for the very definition of Western culture. With Beethoven as its figurehead and epitome, German and Austrian music became virtually synonymous in the nineteenth century with what is called classical music, while German opera and operetta became fixtures of the standard repertoire. German drama, meanwhile, standing in the very long shadow of Shakespeare, may not be as renowned as German music, but the works of Schiller, Büchner, and Brecht remain central to the theatrical canon. Despite revolutions, two world wars, Germany's perpetration of the most terrible genocide in history, and its Cold War partition, its masterpieces are esteemed and performed the world over.

The towering renown of German music and drama is inseparable from Germany's establishment of the largest and most generously state-subsidized theatre system in the world. Aristocratic and civic support for the arts dates back to the Holy Roman Empire of the German Nation (1512–1806), which, like the later German Confederation, was compounded of many small sovereign states and cities, each with its own performing arts traditions and set of institutions. Middle-class citizens also supported the arts, erecting, for example, the Oper am Gänsemarkt in Hamburg, which opened to the public in 1678 and remained under the administration of artists until its demolition a century later. Even after German unification in 1871, the German Empire's twenty-six kingdoms, principalities, duchies, and free cities maintained supervision of the arts, and the decentralized system that developed has survived, with some modifications, to the present. Because theatre in Germany has long been charged with a vital moral and educational mission, the many states have competed with each other to proffer ever better and more lavish venues, productions, and performances.

At the end of World War I, with the fall of the Kaiser and establishment of the Weimar Republic, the court theatres, concert halls, and opera houses were turned into state-run institutions that flourished during the golden

1920s alongside civic and private opera and operetta houses, theatres, and cabarets. When the Nazis came to power in 1933, they instituted a policy of coordination aimed at destroying the freedom of the arts (*Gleichschaltung*), confiscating private theatres, and integrating the performing arts into a centralized system, over which they exercised totalitarian control. After World War II, the administration of the public theatres in the Federal Republic of Germany (FRG or West Germany) reverted back to the newly reorganized federal states and to the cities while private venues were returned to their owners. The German Democratic Republic (GDR or East Germany), on the other hand, continued the integrated system inherited from the Nazis. With reunification in 1990, the East German system was absorbed into the Federal Republic's and almost all the major performing arts institutions were again administered and subsidized by states and municipalities, not the federal government (except for some of Berlin's theatres, which also receive federal subsidy). In former East Germany, which was the country most densely packed with theatres in the world, some venues were closed or consolidated to bring the scale of the system more into line with that of the former West.

Although Germany continues to have a decentralized theatre system (unlike the United States, UK, and France), there is an umbrella organization for theatres, opera houses, and orchestras, the Deutscher Bühnenverein (German stages association), which every year publishes detailed statistics about live performances. These statistics break the theatre landscape down by genre according to a complex classification scheme, which works efficiently for Schiller, Wagner, or Pina Bausch, but not for musicals (to use the word the German language borrows from the English lexicon). Music theatre in the German system is an anthology of genres, which stand at the intersection of so many histories, economies, and performance traditions that it is difficult to discern what makes musicals a discrete category. The Bühnenverein does indeed recognize the genre in its division of the theatre arts into seven major fields (*Sparten*): opera, dance, operetta, spoken drama (*Schauspiel*), concerts, youth theatre, and musicals; and three minor ones: puppet theatre, revue, and multi-genre performances and projects.[1] Their statistics, meanwhile, which embrace the 142 state-subsidized theatres, 199 private theatres, 128 orchestras (including 69 theatre orchestras), and 84 festivals in Germany alone, provide the clearest anatomization of what is by far the largest state-subsidized performing arts system in the world.[2] In this system, most theatres have permanent homes and employ full-time ensembles as well as administrators, costumers, designers, musicians, and stage technicians.

Because German spoken theatres (*Sprechtheater*) and music theatres in 2019 covered only 15.2 percent of their expenses at the box office, they were bankrolled by city, state, and sometimes federal governments to the tune of 2.90 billion euros per year (or about 34 euros per capita).[3] The Austrian and Swiss systems are smaller than the German, but they too are well subsidized. Austria divides 945 million euros among 17 major theatres, most of them with multiple performance spaces, while Switzerland divides 801 million Swiss francs among 28 major theatres.[4]

Despite the immense size of these subsidized systems, permanent theatres represent only a part of the performing arts landscape, which also includes a large independent scene (*freie Szene*) made up of freelance artists who are awarded government and foundation funding on a project-by-project basis but sometimes collaborate with permanent institutions. The landscape also contains a network of commercial theatres that produce musicals exclusively, but which are excluded from the Bühnenverein's statistics.

In the German-speaking theatre world, musicals are unusual insofar as their domain is divided between for-profit producers who mount commercial properties in private theatres and government-funded theatres that perform classic works. These spheres represent different institutional systems with different repertoires, audiences, and admission prices. The large commercial houses, most of which are owned and operated by Stage Entertainment, Mehr-BB Entertainment, and Vereinigte Bühnen Wien, play post-*Cats* musicals, while the state-subsidized houses perform older shows that enjoy canonical status in the Anglophone and German-speaking worlds, as well as original German works. But the differences between these two spheres run far deeper than repertoire. While the musicals performed in the two dozen or so commercial theatres would be immediately recognizable to habitues of Broadway or the West End, the state-subsidized work is astonishingly diverse, ranging from large-scale, often wildly heterodox reimaginings of classics like *The Threepenny Opera* or *Kiss Me, Kate* to new, smaller-scale, music theatre works aimed at local and/or coterie audiences. Yet for statistical purposes, they are collapsed into a single category, musicals, of which there were 5,261 performances (excluding the big commercial houses) in 2018–2019, the last full pre-Covid season. They drew about 2.65 million spectators, which is modest in comparison with opera's 5.17 million spectators and spoken theatre's 9.24 million.[5] It is also modest in comparison with the 11 to 12 million spectators per annum who patronize Broadway musicals in New York.[6]

At the end of each season, the Bühnenverein publishes a meticulously researched, 400-page book, *Wer spielte was?* (Who played what?), that lists and categorizes every theatrical production in Germany, Austria, and the German-speaking part of Switzerland (except for those in the large commercial theatres).[7] Like most catalogues, it aims for transparency and completeness, and despite its scrupulous classification system, it explains neither the boundaries of the ten genres nor the criteria used to discriminate among them. The classification of most work is conventional and plausible, but there are also generic particularities unique to the German theatre system: for example, the large category of adaptations, about 40 percent of the total *Schauspiele* and youth theatre, is indexed as being "*nach*" (after) the author of the source material, usually a play or novel. Although opera, operetta, and musical are all parts of the supra-category *Musiktheater*,[8] the composition of these three genres is by far the most indistinct and, at times, downright deceptive. Consider, for example, the labeling of the category-defying works of Kurt Weill, a bicontinental musical dramatist who was hyperconscious—and suspicious—of generic boundaries. According to the Bühnenverein, two works designated operas by Weill, *The Rise and Fall of the City of Mahagonny* and *Der Jasager* (The Yes-Sayer), are listed under opera. But so is *Der Silbersee* (Silverlake), which Weill pointedly called not an opera but a "play with music."[9] Among musicals, one finds listed the musical comedy *One Touch of Venus* as well as Weill's so-designated "Broadway opera," *Street Scene*. *The Threepenny Opera*, meanwhile, by far the most popular of his works and the most performed musical in German history, is listed not as musical theatre at all, but as a *Schauspiel* by Bertolt Brecht (with music by Weill). I am less interested, however, in quibbling over these categories than in demonstrating how challenging generic classification is. Music theatre is the most obviously impacted, but *Schauspiel* is arguably even more problematic because in Germany it constantly shades over into music theatre. Most German theatrical productions use live music not only as incidental accompaniment but also as a part of the theatrical action and often a generative element in the creative and rehearsal processes. Since around 1990, so many *Schauspiele* have been produced, both original pieces and refashionings of non-musical plays, that integrate music and singing into their fabric that they often become, in my view, formally indistinguishable from musicals.

U- und E-

German theatre professionals, academics, and critics refuse an expansive use of the term musical principally because of the opprobrium it carries. Indeed, the German academic and critical prejudice against musicals is far more intense and programmatic than that which obtains—or used to obtain—in the United States. Although musical theatre studies has been legitimized in the Anglophone world, that is by no means the case in Germany and Austria, where Adorno's ghost continues to terrorize the arbiters of taste. For all but a handful of theatre scholars, musicologists, and critics, musicals (and even operettas) represent commercial, middlebrow, sentimental entertainment at its most mind-numbingly trivial. This judgment is doubtless tied to the very popularity of musicals, which in Germany is second only to that of rock and pop concerts (soccer is ranked third).[10] The widespread prejudice against this widely loved genre means that every attempt at definition also represents a judgment, in most cases negative.

The problematic position of musicals in Germany is also related to the niceties of the music classification system that has long distinguished between *Unterhaltungsmusik* (entertainment music) and *ernste Musik* (serious or art music). *U-* and *E-* continues to be bandied about by critics and is also written into the German Copyright Administration Act, which singles out "culturally significant works and achievements"[11] for preferment by the distribution practices of copyright collectives such as GEMA (the German counterpart to ASCAP). Mandy Risch and Andreas Kerst emphasize that although *E-Musik* and classical music are by no means synonymous, the distinction between *U-* and *E-* is "fundamental" to GEMA's mission of promoting "this demanding, but not particularly lucrative art." Its determination *U-* or *E-* is made by a panel of "experts" who take into consideration "the type of music, admission price, venue size, and the necessity—or not—for public funding."[12] Although the distinction was abolished in Switzerland in 1983 and Austria in 2020, it remains widespread in Germany. In 2020, the president of the German Composers' Union, Moritz Eggert, who claims not to take the dichotomy into account when composing, tried to minimize the differences but finally opted to discriminate between music such as Bach's, which has "sustainability," and the "average mainstream pop music of today" whose chance of remaining "interesting in 100 years is close to zero."[13]

Director Barrie Kosky points out that despite such halfhearted protests to the contrary, the opposition between *U-* and *E-* in the German-speaking world remains a crippling distinction.[14]

As an example of the uncomfortably liminal position occupied by musicals (as *U-Musik*) in Germany, let me cite a magazine article by Marianne Wellershoff, whose carefully weighed ambivalence seems calculated to give it an aura of objectivity. Although it dates from 2014, it remains regrettably up to date. In September of that year, the newsweekly *Der Spiegel* published a showcase of coming cultural attractions. The magazine, founded in Hamburg in 1947, is a widely respected, left-liberal opinion-maker known for its investigative journalism. Its preview included a grudging defense of musicals and other allegedly beleaguered cultural goods (caraway schnaps, soap operas, Ariana Grande, and children's books). Headquartered in Hamburg, the magazine focused on the commercial theatre giant Stage Entertainment, many of whose theatres and whose German headquarters are also located in the city, and whose musicalization of the soccer championship film *Das Wunder von Bern* (*The Miracle of Bern*) was to open there two months later. Attempting to "rescue the honor" of musicals, Wellershoff begins her essay by questioning what for most Germans is obvious: "if you want to be a person with a serious taste for culture," there is "a tacit agreement that you have to find musicals not good, and not worth taking seriously." Her interrogation of this position becomes increasingly disingenuous insofar as it quickly becomes clear that she does indeed regard musicals as extravagant, simple-minded baubles designed to divert mass audiences. Wellershoff's examples of musicals' "intellectual rigor or profundity"—*Hair* is about the Vietnam War and *The Lion King* is a variation on *Hamlet*—are unlikely to convince skeptical readers of musicals' consequence.[15] *Spiegel*'s teaser, meanwhile, that "musicals are not necessarily worse than avant-garde theatre,"[16] is laughable in the eyes of almost all German theatre scholars, for whom musical theatre does not even count as theatre.[17] Hans-Thies Lehmann, one of the few even to mention musicals—in passing—dismisses them contemptuously as "profitable and ridiculous mass entertainment."[18] Thus *Spiegel*'s feature, despite its apologetic pose, ends up reinforcing the highly prejudicial judgments that make it a challenge even to define this embattled category with precision.

The identity of the musical in Germany and Austria is very different from what prevails in the United States, despite certain obvious similarities and a modest overlap in repertoire. It is moreover irreducibly complicated by the fact that the history and historiography of the musical are so entwined with those of operetta that it is impossible to disentangle them. Because there are no indisputably canonical German-language operettas following Paul Burkhard's *Das Feuerwerk* (Fireworks, 1950),[19] I would argue that musicals, which gained traction in Germany and Austria just as operetta as a living art form was stagnating, are the post–World War II transformation of operetta. They represent the continuation of operetta by other means. The formal similarities between them are undeniable, although Volker Klotz, in his synoptic and authoritative book on operetta, considers musicals vastly inferior. In an attack that would do Adorno proud, Klotz rails against musicals' "sentimentality," "melodramatic passages," "obvious scenic situations," clichéd scores, and "random and unspecific" songs. Unafraid of parading his ignorance of the genre, he hails them as nothing but the products of "industrial production."[20]

Klotz's attempt to rescue operetta from the deadly embrace of the musical cannot disguise the fact that operetta, from its birth in the mid-nineteenth century until today, has been the subject of debates and controversies in Germany and Austria no less heated than those fought over the musical. And while the character and particulars of these debates have changed, they remain centered on the status of operetta as an uncomfortable mixture of high culture and popular entertainment. Although several scholars have carefully surveyed these debates, let me cite Micaela Baranello, whose work lucidly explicates the "uneasy zone" operetta inhabits, "between art and entertainment, . . . encompassing both vaudeville and Wagner, alternating quasi-operatic arias with the latest international dance styles."[21] Like the Broadway musical, operetta was the product of an expansive "family tree" that allowed it "to build its rich vocabulary of conventions and codes with remarkable speed." And Vienna, like New York in the 1920s, had a diverse mix of theatres and audiences "that made these codes intelligible."[22] Like Vienna and Paris before it, New York City in the jazz age was rife with a panoply of determinedly modern art and entertainment venues that birthed that misbegotten bastard, the musical. I have elsewhere described the long history of US-American musical theatre as a middlebrow genre, a "promiscuous mixture of commerce and art, entertainment and politics, the banal and the auratic, profane and sacred, spectacular and personal, erotic and intellectual."[23] The middlebrow status of musical theatre, trapped between elite and plebian, is not unique to the Anglophone world, but is anticipated, paralleled, and echoed by operetta's stubbornly liminal status in the German-speaking world.

On the Genealogy of Musicals

Despite the anxiety generated by the musical's mixed pedigree, it is further complicated by the history of its introduction to Germany and Austria, a troubled history that is reflected in a highly selective canon that is even more clearly delineated in the German-speaking world than in the United States. That delineation, moreover, underscores the inevitably retrospective and tautological dimension of canonicity: in both the Anglophone and German-speaking worlds, local theatres, critics, and audiences define the musical only through the canons they are always already in the process of (re)constructing. German scholars agree that although the real history of the musical in Germany and Austria does not begin until after World War II, there is a prehistory that starts with the importation of US-American music—and the modernity it instantiated—at the beginning of the twentieth century. Berlin's Metropol-Theater, a leading venue during the Weimar Republic for popular music theatre, especially operetta, staged *No, No, Nanette* with an all-star cast in 1925, shortly after it opened in New York and London. Hailed as unmistakably US-American, with its blend of "jazz, Charleston, and the newest light music," it was performed shortly thereafter in Vienna, Paris, and Budapest.[24] Although dismissed by the Berlin feuilletons as "musical flailing" (*musikalischen Dreschflegel*), this popular, dance-filled "alternative to romantic and tragic operettas"[25] was enormously successful and set the pattern for the jazz operettas and revues of the later 1920s by Paul Abraham, Ralph Benatzky, Mischa Spoliansky, and others that formally are almost indistinguishable from Broadway musicals of the period.

Despite its success, *Nanette* was exceptional and, given the aforesaid development of homegrown jazz operetta/revue and the rise of the Nazis, US-American musicals did not again travel to Germany or Austria until after World War II. During the Cold War, which began even as the rubble was being cleared from German cities, art was turned into a formidable weapon. In the FRG, the brashness and fantasy of US-American popular culture was pitted against Beethoven and Goethe, while in the GDR, the decadent culture of the West posed a threat to sober, didactic, socialist realist work. Uta Poiger points out that in postwar German society, far more was at stake in this struggle than the marketing of Coca-Cola and Hollywood films. The occupation by the Western Allies forced Germans to come to terms with their Nazi past and with the United States' role as cultural colossus. As she emphasizes, both Germanys had to manipulate the image of the United

States, "long recognized as [having] the most developed consumer culture," to lay "claim to a German heritage and . . . define what it meant to be German."[26] Although the United States was depicted uniformly negatively in the East, it remained in the West a source of constant ambivalence, both savior and subjugator, a model both to imitate and reject. The divided city of Berlin, especially after the erection of the Berlin Wall on August 13, 1961, became the site of a serious and sustained culture war. As the eminent theatre critic Friedrich Luft wrote one month after the Wall went up: "Berlin was and is a political sore spot. Berlin's theatre (whether one wants it so or not) was and is political theatre, even when it seems to be completely unpolitical."[27] Musical theatre, an unmistakably US-American cultural product, became especially weaponized in both West and East Germany, along with jazz, gangster movies, Westerns, and rock 'n' roll.[28] But unlike movies and popular music, musicals were aimed at not the youth market, but the temperate, older middle class for whom they came without the Nazi baggage that invariably accompanied operetta. As a result, their spectacular arrival in Germany and Austria in the first postwar decades was far more complexly politically charged than that of *No, No, Nanette* in the 1920s.

Three leading German musical theatre historians, Nils Grosch, Wolfgang Jansen, and Thomas Siedhoff, agree about the shape of the history of postwar musical theatre and in particular the landmark productions that changed attitudes and expanded the repertoire. As in South Korea, the first show to make a splash was the Gershwins' and DuBose Heyward's *Porgy and Bess*, which was performed in Zurich by local actors in blackface in June 1945, one month after the surrender of Nazi Germany. It was hailed in the local press as a "sensation" that paved the way for the legendary State Department tour in 1952 with Leontyne Price and William Warfield that played both Berlin and Vienna.[29] The next example is the much less well-received national touring production of Rodgers and Hammerstein's *Oklahoma!* which, courtesy of the Theatre Guild and the State Department, was performed in English in 1951 at West Berlin's Titania-Palast with Celeste Holm repeating her New York triumph as Ado Annie. In Berlin, however, the piece was anything but triumphant. Critics were unsure what to make of it: "Who or what is a musical?"[30] Undecided of its ontology, they described this suspicious protean piece variously as a "folk play with music," "musical comedy," "musical play," "operetta,"[31] or "mish-mash of operetta, revue, comedy, and pantomime."[32] For some, it seemed romantic and sentimental, a "thin rehash of good, old operetta" with "lasso-swinging cowboys instead of singing gypsies."[33] Knowing, however, that *Oklahoma!* was a proudly cultural nationalist product of an occupying power, most West German critics seemed inclined to flatter their Cold War protectors and reluctant to attack the musical's "optimism" and its "galvanic, full, swinging feeling for life," which were seen as an antidote to the "modern neuroses," "emotional trauma," and "life pessimism of [Arthur] Miller and [Tennessee] Williams."[34] In the East Berlin press, meanwhile, the Cold War had heated sufficiently for critic Hans Preuß to use the production to attack "American 'culture'" relentlessly, contemptuously dismissing *Oklahoma!*'s score, plot, design, choreography, and "amateurish" performances as examples of "American imperialism." It was "frighteningly clear" to Preuß that *Oklahoma!*'s attempt at "'modern American operetta revue'" was "disgustingly banal, bumbling, and downright rude." "Art?" Preuß asks, "No, fairground." Describing it as "the end and death of art," he cautioned that there could be "no better sign of the deadly effect of America's presumption to 'save' European culture."[35]

Hans Preuß's response to *Oklahoma!* may be extreme, but it, like Marianne Wellershoff's, is symptomatic of the discomfort many Germans have felt and continue to feel with the musical as a genre. In 1978, when *Oklahoma!* received its first East German production, in Erfurt, it was again dismissed, while its German-language West Berlin premiere at Theater des Westens in 1982 was deemed "unsuccessful."[36] Although *Oklahoma!* remains arguably the most culturally nationalist and optimistic piece in the Rodgers and Hammerstein canon, none of their work, Elmar Juchem reports, has found a home in Germany or Austria. This is in part a result of serious qualms on the part of the Rodgers and Hammerstein Organization about licensing German productions.[37] *The Sound of Music* has enjoyed some recent modest success, but as Juchem emphasizes, Rodgers and Hammerstein musicals—which remain absolutely central to the Anglophone canon—face a number of challenges that are emblematic of the obstacles any US-American musical must face in the German-speaking world. These include the inadequacy of translations, the resistance of the "classic (that is, the committed classic modernist) feuilletons to newer popular culture," "a latent anti-Americanism" from both the left and the right, and a sometime disparagement of their works relative to those of their jazzier predecessors.[38]

If the Rodgers and Hammerstein musicals never made the splash in Germany and Austria that they did elsewhere, a 1955 Frankfurt production of Cole Porter's *Kiss Me, Kate* proved the "Big Bang" for the development of Broadway-style musical theatre in the German-speaking world.[39] It was cast not with opera singers but with renowned actors and dancers who were able to do justice to the mischievous Shakespearean borrowings and the operetta-type songs, which doubtless helped the piece ingratiate itself to German audiences. Even the exacting Friedrich Luft gushed, "It was invigorating, cosmopolitan, one of the most important events in the theatre in recent years. I want to spend every night there! Hurrah—the musical is here! It came, we saw, it conquered!"[40] Luft's words were indeed prophetic, as *Kiss Me, Kate* initiated the first wave of Broadway musicals to be integrated into the German repertoire. It was quickly produced elsewhere in Germany, Austria, and Switzerland, and it remains one of the best-known and most widely performed musicals in state-subsidized theatres.

If *Kiss Me, Kate* opened the door, it was *My Fair Lady* that made the triumphal entrance. When staged at Berlin's Theater des Westens in October 1961, it was rapturously received, a "theatrical miracle" that rendered the musical "an integral and permanent part of the German stage repertoire."[41] Opening just two months after the erection of the Wall, the much-ballyhooed production was received by critics and audiences alike as a theatre historical event of unique importance: "Nothing like this had been seen before."[42] With music by the Berlin-born Frederick Loewe and book and lyrics by Alan Jay Lerner translated into German by renowned lyricist and librettist (and childhood friend of Loewe) Robert Gilbert, *My Fair Lady* was marketed as groundbreaking yet familiar, new but traditional. Indeed, the first page of the program includes "A Word on the Theme 'Musical'" by Hellmut Kotschenreuther that defines it as "a new form of music theatre" that is in fact "a new word for an old thing, namely the waltz-happy operetta." (In fact, there are very few waltzes in *My Fair Lady*.) Even in 1961, however, Kotschenreuther felt a need to defend the musical and he argued that, unlike operetta, it does not shy away from literary sources and sometimes even manages to revive the "socially critical aggressivity" of Offenbach.[43] The next year, the Cold War at its height, the souvenir program touted "Eliza's triumphal procession around the world" and boasted that her very name represents "the personification of the word success." (For skeptical observers in both the West and East, that would have meant the US-American culture industry.) Even though Germany had "no tradition of musicals," *My Fair Lady* staked its claim as the "definitive breakthrough for musicals in Germany."[44]

The jubilation that greeted *My Fair Lady*'s arrival on the West German stage was inextricably tied to its political mission as an ambassador for US culture at its most captivating. Because almost all Berlin's operetta and revue houses were located in the East, they had, after the erection of the Wall, become virtually inaccessible to West Berliners. As a result, this lavish production became a "test case for the will to live and the vitality of the Berlin theatre."[45] Its Berlin-centricity was bolstered by the fact that Robert Gilbert translated Lerner's cockney into a pungent Berlin accent. Because West Berlin, an island of two million people, remained occupied by the Allies until reunification, it was not officially a part of the FRG and had fragile links to the West. Its precarity became frighteningly apparent during the 1948–1949 Berlin Blockade, when the US- and UK-administered Berlin Airlift dispatched planes twenty-four hours a day to keep the city alive. Who would have imagined that eleven years later, a Broadway musical written and directed by Jews and based on an Anglo-Irish play would be hailed as a "Musical Airlift" that would save West Berlin from cultural isolation and despair?[46] Because the Wall had turned West Berlin into a virtual prison, tourism had been devastated. (Who would want to holiday in a city that had been cordoned off by a "death strip" guarded by heavily armed soldiers with shoot to kill orders?) As an attempted remedy, *My Fair Lady*'s producers, tourist agencies, and hotels partnered beginning in January 1962 to sponsor package tours to Berlin that included airfare from West Germany, hotel, and tickets to the show. These packages, Wolfgang Jansen reports, were hugely successful, a "new method of marketing," and became "the talk of all Germany," keeping the show—and the city—alive until its last performance in July 1964.[47] "The play," one critic crowed, "which in New York and London was harmless fun, became in Berlin a coup" and "a symbol" for the city's "will to live."[48] An unprecedented success, *My Fair Lady* then opened in Munich in 1962, Hamburg and Vienna in 1963, and Zurich in 1964, utterly changing Germans' perceptions of the musical. Not until 1966, however, was it performed in East Berlin, at the Metropol-Theater, and the following year in Leipzig. Even before its performances in the East, however, it had a profound influence on the development of East German *heiteres Musiktheater* (light music theatre), a catch-all term that conveniently obscured the distinction between operetta and musical, East and West.[49] *My Fair Lady*'s admittance to the German canon was guaranteed when it became the first Broadway musical to be produced in opera houses, in Frankfurt in 1973 and Hamburg in 1984.[50] While today it is staged more frequently in *Schauspielhaüser* than opera houses, it remains one of the most widely performed pieces of music theatre in the German-speaking world.

My Fair Lady's central position in the German popular music theatre canon makes it paradigmatic of the genre as a whole, in the way that *Hamlet* is often taken to be paradigmatic of tragedy. Both these pieces are centrally about performance, deception, and the enactment of roles. Contemplating *My Fair Lady*'s singularity, I am tempted to read it allegorically as a fable about the genre it typifies. Setting social classes and musical styles in battle against each other, is it not, like its heroine, trying above all to pass, to establish its own legitimacy? Are not its plot and score a three-hour-long negotiation of the conventions of operetta and musical, or to paraphrase one German critic, "high culture" and the "underclass"?[51] I would argue that *My Fair Lady* has become the paradigmatic musical in Germany because it so deftly performs precisely the generic sleight of hand that Arthur Maria Rabenalt contends lies at the heart of operetta:

> It is notable that the storytelling invention of operetta goes almost entirely in one direction: namely toward rectifying its own illegitimacy, to rehabilitate itself in society. The only theme of operetta is misalliance, the only conflict is social difference. So thus operetta, in the false tragedy of its plot, reflects back the problem of its heritage.[52]

Pace Rabenalt, not every musical (or operetta, for that matter) is about misalliance or class conflict, but *My Fair Lady* quite exactly fits that description, carefully performing the balancing act that the genre, like operetta before it, mastered in order to thrive in Germany and Austria. Although the meaning (and gender politics) of the musical's final scene have been much debated, it does arguably represent an entente between Eliza and Professor Higgins, or if you prefer, between popular and learned vernaculars.[53]

Among Broadway musicals performed in state-subsidized theatres, *My Fair Lady*'s most serious competition are five shows that in very different ways also evince the influence of operetta, *Kiss Me, Kate*; *West Side Story* (German-language premiere 1968); *Fiddler on the Roof* (renamed *Anatevka* in Germany, 1968); *Cabaret* (1970); and *La Cage aux Folles* (1985), as well as a rock musical, *Hair* (1969), that vigorously breaks with and problematizes that very tradition. These remain the most widely performed Broadway musicals in the German-speaking world. To this short list must be added several pieces that made big splashes when premiered but today are less regularly performed, including two prototypical old-fashioned musicals, *Hello, Dolly!* (1966) and *Man of La Mancha* (1968), as well as the rock musical *The*

Rocky Horror Show (1980), which first played in London in 1973, flopped miserably in New York in 1975, but then went on to become a worldwide hit (primarily because of the 1975 cult film based upon it).

This relatively short list of canonical Broadway musicals in the German-speaking world might suggest that the musical is defined there much as it in the United States. Most of this first generation was premiered in Germany and Austria in the 1960s, during which decade the musical established itself as a more or less legitimate, if suspect and contested genre. Were one to construct a family tree of German-language musical theatre with these canonical musicals as its trunk, it would have a number of branches, of which I want to single out four limbs, three of which I will survey in the remainder of this chapter. First are the East German musicals produced between 1960 and 1990, which represent idiosyncratic syntheses of the idioms of Broadway and operetta, bent (in principle, at least) to the requirements of socialist dogma. Second are small- and medium-scale West German musicals, none of which stayed long in the repertoire until *Linie 1* (1986), a path-breaking rock musical whose action takes place in the stations of West Berlin's subway line number 1 and features a kaleidoscope of urban eccentrics. No musical theatre work is as typical of West Berlin as *Linie 1*, which premiered in the divided city, was made into a film, continues in the repertoire, and is arguably the progenitor of countless German musicals performed in smaller theatres and conservatories.[54] Third is the large body of German theatre pieces performed since reunification, both original pieces and adaptations of preexistent texts, that borrow the conventions of the musical even if they are not so designated. The year of reunification, 1990, marked the world premiere of the iconoclastic Robert Wilson/Tom Waits/William S. Burroughs piece *The Black Rider* at the Thalia Theater in Hamburg, which is now hailed by the press as a "legendary musical." Despite its avant-gardist patrimony, the original production toured the world and the piece continues to be widely produced in Germany.[55] *The Black Rider* may not be the earliest, but it is certainly one of the first examples of a feuilleton-approved German theatre piece that nonetheless manages to smuggle the conventions of the Broadway musical into high art. Finally, I must acknowledge the explosive 1983 premiere of Andrew Lloyd Webber's *Cats* at Vienna's Theater an der Wien, which, in popularizing the megamusical, greatly expanded the reach of the musical and helped establish a thriving commercial musical theatre industry in Germany and Austria. *Cats* broke box office records, helped to redefine the genre formally, and became the first musical to be successfully marketed worldwide. Like the birth of Jesus Christ (the subject of a previous Lloyd Webber hit), *Cats* divides time into a before and after.

Musical Theatre in a Bell Jar

In histories of Broadway, the years between the early 1940s and the late 1960s are routinely designated the Golden Age of musical theatre.[56] This label is extremely problematic for many reasons, not least of all because it establishes a hierarchy of cultural values in which certain forms, conventions, and styles are celebrated and immortalized while others are systematically disparaged or simply forgotten. Such hierarchies almost always discriminate against the popular arts in relation to the fine arts and function all too conveniently as lodestones for prejudice: racism, sexism, anti-Semitism, classism, among others. Besides dubiously periodizing, the term "Golden Age" assumes a critical consensus, which is by no means the case, despite the fact that many musicologists and theatre scholars seem to accept the mythology on faith. On the other hand, the concept is tantalizingly useful, as Jessica Sternfeld and Elizabeth Wollman point out, and its "continued application is understandable,"[57] if only because it allows one to posit, as I have, a shared musical theatrical language. In Germany and Austria, as I have noted, all but one (*Hair*) of the first wave of imported US musicals to enter the canon of the state-subsidized theatres belong to this purported Golden Age. (And *Hair* ironically is often cited as the musical that killed it.) They are all book musicals with discrete songs that take up the musical and lyric conventions established in Tin Pan Alley and on Broadway during the first half of the twentieth century, while retaining certain features commonly identified with operetta.

This first wave of musical imports entered the repertoire in West Germany much more uncomplicatedly than in East Germany, which viewed them initially as "ideologically suspect."[58] With the densest concentration of theatres and orchestras in the world (64 subsidized theatres for 17 million people, of which 44 had music theatre ensembles), the GDR theatre system demanded the constant production of new work.[59] Because the economic, social, and political circumstances in East and West were so dissimilar, the indigenization of the musical took very different, if related, paths. In the GDR, debates about both the form and content of musical theatre, and all performance genres, for that matter, were much more politically charged than in the West. During the forty years of national division, 130 US and British musicals were premiered in West Germany, Austria, and Switzerland, while only 33 made it to East Germany.[60] To say that this inequity was balanced by the 80 musicals, operettas, and rock operas imported from the Soviet Union and its European satellites misunderstands the aesthetic and political differences between Broadway and the *heiteres Musiktheater* of the East, whose very appellation is an invention, Katrin Stöck argues, to deflect attention away from the generic disparities between two suspiciously "late-bourgeois" forms, operetta and musical.[61] And while the scarcity in East Germany of the hard Western currency needed to pay Broadway-sized royalties was part of the challenge, a state-mandated commitment to "social relevance" and the "dialectics of tradition and innovation" were always more unpredictable parts of the equation.[62] Despite these obstacles, distinctive musicals by several accomplished East German composers managed—improbably—to combine the conventions of the Broadway musical with the demands of a socialist realism aiming both to maintain the "popular character of the arts" and "build the new socialist human being."[63] Yet East German authorities also recognized that the political task for musical theatre was not propagandistic: "spoken theatre can activate people, but operetta can only unmask,"[64] that is, offer a critique of bourgeois society. This critique, however, is not a passive enterprise, but an active crusade, in the words of one GDR official, to make "'[p]etit-bourgeois' and reactionary-feudal characteristics . . . ridiculous."[65] While the vast majority of original West German musicals are now relegated to footnotes, the two most widely performed musicals from the East, Gerd Natschinski's *Mein Freund Bunbury* (My Friend Bunbury, 1964) and Guido Masanetz's *In Frisco ist der Teufel los* (The Devil Runs Loose in Frisco, 1962),[66] are skillfully composed pieces that, in utterly different ways, "unmask" capitalist norms while providing examples of workable musical theatre formulas. In retrospect, and less premeditatedly, they also "unmask" the aesthetic and political contradictions that structured East German art and society.

Roland Dippel argues that the 1960s represented the high water mark for *heiteres Musiktheater* in the GDR. "In no decade," he writes, "was its development as diverse and creative."[67] It was, in other words, the closest thing to a Golden Age of homegrown, Broadway-style musical theatre one can find in the divided Germanys. In this almost Golden Age, *Mein Freund Bunbury* (Figure 4.1) and *In Frisco ist der Teufel los* provide very different answers to two key questions: how does one conjoin operetta and musical, and how does one incorporate a social message into entertainment? If *Bunbury* updates *The Importance of Being Earnest* to the 1920s in an attempt to duplicate the

Figure 4.1 Cover, cast recording, *Mein Freund Bunbury*, Nova Records 8 85 031, 1974.

success (and even evoke the title) of *My Fair Lady*, *Frisco* redrafts Western-themed US musicals like *Oklahoma!* and *Annie Get Your Gun* in order to celebrate the solidarity of the working classes in the face of cutthroat capitalism. Both moreover are inherently contradictory, exploiting the very un-socialist local color of their settings and the very un-socialist glamour of musical and dance styles of the Americas (the Charleston, black bottom, boogie-woogie, tango, beguine, and the blues) to provide scenic, musical, and choreographic allure. *Bunbury* proves a very free adaptation of Wilde's play that retains his characters while giving them all gainful employment and double lives. Cecily has the leading role and together with Jack, her guardian, collects money for the Salvation Army while "flee[ing] her hypocritical environment" to moonlight as the Sunshine Girl, a music-hall singer and dancer.[68]

The musical juxtaposition of Christian goodwill with nightclub decadence allows Natschinski to build collages of hymns and jazz dances, with a few paraphrases of *The Magic Flute* thrown in to make *Bunbury* even more eclectic and bolster its legitimacy. The dandy Algernon becomes a writer of mysteries who falls for the Sunshine Girl and is assisted in his writing by the widowed, impoverished, yet wickedly sympathetic Lady Bracknell, who supplements her income by secretly spicing up his detective novels with "A Little Horror and a Little Sex." As in Wilde, the men repeatedly use an imaginary, chronically ill friend Bunbury as their alibi to escape the monied, restrictive society of "The Upper Ten," which the diplomatic Natschinski, ever mindful of political correctness, described in an interview as "degenerate" (*morbiden*).[69] In the musical, however, unlike the play, Bunbury turns out to be real, the surname of the man who has made a double income by playing Bunbury and masquerading as Algernon's butler, Jeremias, and ends the musical happily betrothed to Lady Bracknell.[70]

Mein Freund Bunbury was East Germany's great musical theatre success, chalking up over 5,000 performances by 1994 in 152 different productions, 25 of them in West Germany.[71] It was even filmed for West German television and broadcast in 1970. The piece helped establish Gerd Natschinski (1928–2015), a prolific, multitalented composer, arranger, and bandleader, as the preeminent East German writer of a genre whose very deliciousness made it suspicious to communist cultural authorities. As in *The Importance of Being Earnest*, *Bunbury*'s characters compose their double lives as havens from everyday drudgery. In *Bunbury*, however, the emancipatory power of escape is both heightened and literally jazzed-up. Although the LP liner notes acknowledge that listeners might find reference in their own lives to the "double-standard morals and two-faced behavior" shown in the musical, the East German critics predictably interpreted the characters' conduct as emblematic of capitalist alienation and decadence.[72] Rather than acknowledge the secrecy and double-dealing practiced by East Germans constrained and persecuted by the communist regime, the critics hailed it an "attack on the hollowness of bourgeois morals" and a satirical denunciation of "the inner untruthfulness and crass profiteering of the ruling classes."[73] East German hypocrisy, harassment, the secret police (Stasi), and the apparatchiki went unremarked. Yet critics also recognized its musical and lyric achievements: "It is a musical with wit, flair, and character—and half a dozen instantly memorable tunes" whose "effervescent dialogue" and "electric rhythms" made it much too effective to dismiss as mere propaganda.[74]

With its depiction of 1920s smart London society and its substitution of Berlin dialect for cockney, *Mein Freund Bunbury* opened at the Metropol-Theater as an obvious attempt to capitalize on *My Fair Lady*'s unprecedented success at Theater des Westens five kilometers to the west. Like its model, it mixes different popular song styles, including a very un-*Lady*like potpourri of US-American dances that even throws in the Twist, an interpolation that was not well appreciated by the East German cultural bureaucracy.[75] The score features several songs that are clearly analogous to *My Fair Lady*'s, including Chasuble's Alfred P. Doolittle-like eleven o'clock number, "Gluck, gluck, ein guter Schluck" (Glug, glug, a good gulp) and the chorus's "Ascot Gavotte"–like "The Upper Ten." Most of the songs use a standard thirty-two-bar, verse-refrain-release structure and in fact remind me (and critic Horst Koegler)[76] less of *My Fair Lady* than *Hello, Dolly!*, which opened only nine months before *Bunbury*. Like *Dolly*, *Bunbury* boasts a charmingly old-fashioned setting and a collection of winningly infectious songs. *Bunbury*'s includes an old-fashioned operetta-style waltz duet, jazzy dance numbers, a tango, and a lilting, dreamy soprano aria. It also features a brassy title song evocative of *Dolly*'s number-one, round-the-world hit. Especially rousing is the song's elaborate ending, which begins as a speedy pileup of the word "Bunbury" (a name that does not fall trippingly off the German tongue), climaxing in a half-tempo, kick line–inspired coda. Although these similarities to Broadway classics might suggest that *Bunbury* is merely derivative, that judgment does not credit Natschinski's skill as a musical dramatist with "an elegant personal style" and a knack for catchy tunes.[77] Especially impressive is his skill at crafting a sophisticated, tuneful verse that leads inexorably to a memorable refrain and contrasting release. In other words, Natschinski understood the formal requirements of musical theatre numbers and how they differ from *Schlager* (middle-of-the-road Europop songs).

If Natschinski's work manages gracefully to avoid Cold War politics, Masanetz's *In Frisco ist der Teufel los* jumps into the fray. A revised version of a 1956 original (*Wer braucht Geld?* [Who needs money?]), *Frisco* premiered at the Metropol-Theater as an operetta not about the Old West, but the new melting pot known as California. Its plot centers on a seaman, Anatol Brown, who inherits the Hotel Nevada from a relation who once ill-advisedly borrowed $10,000 from the greedy, scheming Xonga Miller, proprietress of the Tampico Bar, a nightclub and watering hole for racially and ethnically diverse clientele. The bighearted Anatol, who wants to turn the hotel into a home for old seamen and sailors, has only twenty-four hours to repay the debt to keep it from Xonga's filthy, capitalist clutches. The plot details the many complications, from escaped madmen to a barroom brawl, that Xonga and Anatol engineer to try to realize their plans. Anatol, with the help of his girlfriend Virginia, finally triumphs by launching a crowdfunding venture (*avant la lettre*), and his friends and acquaintances band together to raise the money to defeat Xonga. *Frisco*'s record jacket tidily explains its moral: "It is only with the coming together of working people that a meaningful life can be made, a life that must be wrested from the exploiters through the solidarity of the working class."[78]

This plot summary of *Frisco* does not even begin to describe the elements that made the work a big success. This hybrid of operetta and musical paints a devilishly tuneful portrait of the gorgeously evil temptations of capitalism—scantily clad barmaids, liquor smugglers, cowboy-booted chorus girls, corrupt police, and singing and dancing sailors—all the while condemning US-American materialism. Given its portrait of a fantasy United States as the homeland of capitalism, and its focus on the seamy side of the big city, *Frisco* seems almost to be socialist realist rewriting of Kurt Weill and Bertolt Brecht's *The Rise and Fall of the City of Mahagonny*, but with a happy ending in which the benevolent hero and joyful community celebrate their collective victory over greed. Instead of apocalypse, Masanetz gives us festivity. Although the LP liner notes highlight Masanetz's deliberate use of operetta-style conventions for Anatol and Virginia, the score's distinction comes from its exploitation of California's Latin American legacy. The piece, in other words, is a hodgepodge operetta, with the musical and choreographic vernaculars of the Americas substituting for Central European folk dances. The piece's highpoints include several extensive ballet sequences that patently imitate the dance and theatre works of George Gershwin, Aaron Copland, and Leonard Bernstein. Masanetz, who had wanted to become a concert pianist, clearly seems to have learned about Latin music through the works of those US-American composers. The polyglot Bernstein, in particular, looms large, and *Frisco*'s setting and musical style render it closer to Bernstein's *On the Town* or *Fancy Free* than to other East German operettas. Its symphonic scale and elaborate orchestrations also afford it a musical and choreographic grandeur to which *Bunbury* does not aspire.

Guido Masanetz (1914–2015), who was born in what today is the Czech Republic, was a serious-minded composer of *heiteres Musiktheater* in the GDR who composed operas and film scores as well as operettas. Although *In Frisco*'s liner notes are unequivocal about the work's anti-capitalist message, the piece is very generous to the denizens of San Francisco, who are exploited for their racial, ethnic, and musical diversity. The Latin American–influenced numbers predominate while the piece's villain, Xonga Miller, is made as mysterious as her name is remarkable. According to the work's creators, "Xonga can be young or old, thin or fat—but one thing she must be: fascinating! The more extraordinary she is, the greater Brown's victory over her."[79] It is not clear from what her name is derived, but its initial "X" guarantees her a non-European exoticism and if one judges from her one song, "Schaut mich einer an" (Look me over), she seems almost to be channeling one of the Kurt Weill's Jennys, especially the *Mahagonny* Jenny (from Havana!), in her teasing, bluesy, femme fatalité. But the more important character in terms of Frisco's message is Bessie, the "Negerin" (negress), who sings the score's sole "Blues," its most plaintive song. Although the character's name echoes that of the best-known African American heroine in musical theatre and the best-known blues singer, she was played initially by a white actor in blackface and the text and dramatic function of her "Blues" make the song into a pastiche less of Gershwin than "Ol' Man River." Like the latter, "Blues" is a pseudo-spiritual in AABA form, but it is determinedly in the minor mode and launches a much more mournful protest than the Kern-Hammerstein anthem. Yet its pivotal placement just before the finale is a sign of the importance of this African American character as a key to parsing the piece's anti-Americanism. Priscilla Layne points out that during the Cold War, "U.S. minority groups, like Native Americans and African Americans, ... were treated" by the East Germans "as potential allies in the fight against American imperialism."[80] Indeed, this attitude is part of a long, complicated history in the Soviet bloc of sympathy for and solidarity with leftist African American activists like Paul Robeson, who put his "art in the service of class struggle,"[81] and whom GDR official policy championed as providing "proof of socialist countries' superior treatment of minorities."[82] Ironically, however, white East Germans, who as a rule had no contact with US-Americans, would use these figures, and Black popular culture more generally, especially Black music, as surrogates for their own rebellious feelings against "their highly structured and monitored communities."[83] Thus *Frisco*'s romanticization of Bessie and her "Blues" is utterly disingenuous, flying in the face of the highly prejudicial "everyday reality" and "racial hatred" that Blacks faced in East Germany.[84]

Whatever their flaws and virtues, *Bunbury* and *Frisco* were uniquely successful and their popularity was never replicated in the divided Germany.

Roland Dippel argues that they represent a high point and that the 1970s marked the beginning of a period of stagnation as younger composers' works, the "analogs to the genre-expanding, contemporary theatre forms in the West like the rock musical," were unable to find permanent homes in the repertoire.[85] Although the tightly censored East German theatre system had serious, chronic problems, it did offer three houses dedicated to *heiteres Musiktheater* (in Berlin, Dresden, and Leipzig) and a fixed ensemble structure that guaranteed continuing employment and financial security for actors, playwrights, designers, musicians, and other theatre-makers. Despite the high quality of a handful of East German musicals, they were never as popular or novel as imports from New York, which provided Germans on both sides of the Wall with the "international flair" that audiences craved.[86] In the East, people unable to vacation in London or New York could (as of 1966, at least) attend *My Fair Lady* at the Metropol-Theater and get a taste of a world tantalizingly out of reach. In the West, meanwhile, with the German Economic Miracle in full swing, Broadway musicals held a different promise of both reviving a moribund musical theatre tradition and certifying West Germany's status as rehabilitated, cosmopolitan, and rich. Not until 1986 did a West German musical open that unashamedly celebrated West Berlin, doing for the rock musical in Germany what *Hair* had done eighteen years earlier in the United States. *Linie 1* succeeded by embracing its status as a progress report from a city that then seemed to lie both at the center of the world and to teeter on its edge. Employing a rock vernacular, it tells a story that is so totally West Berlin, about urban discontents on a well-traveled subway line, that it ended up being adapted and indigenized all over the world to tell the story of urban discontents on well-traveled subway (or bus) lines in cities suffering fallout from neoliberalism.

Krautrock

The rock 'n' roll that *Linie 1* celebrates arrived in Germany from the English-speaking world and even today sports its Anglophone colors, despite the fact that Germany has produced its own distinctive rock bands since the 1960s. Like South Korea's economic and social infrastructure, Germany's was destroyed by warfare and the subsequent postwar occupation by the Western Allies permanently transformed the nation's culture. As Uwe Schütte notes, "broadcasts by the American Forces Network (AFN) and British

Forces Broadcasting Services (BFBS)," which included top 40 chart shows, "acquainted young German listeners with pop-musical developments" in the United States and the UK that had been suppressed by the Nazis. The first sign of "rock 'n' roll's coming victory march was shown by the rapturous reception of Bill Haley's 'Rock Around The Clock'" among young Germans after the 1955 release of the film *Blackboard Jungle*. Haley's own 1958 concert tour of West Germany "caused outbreaks of violence," which "left behind a shocked generation of parents who rightly sensed that this inflammatory new music from America would create a shared sense of rebellion amongst the post-war youth."[87] The second sign was the media-fueled "'Elvis mania' amongst German teenagers" occasioned by Elvis Presley's stint as a GI in Hesse between 1958 and 1960. His 1959 #1 single, "A Big Hunk o' Love," even featured a cover photo of the star backed by the Burgpforte in the town of Bad Nauheim where he was stationed. As Schütte writes, "While Haley's music demonstrated the unruly aspect of pop music, Elvis stood for the physical, sexualized side of rock 'n' roll. He was the very incarnation of rock 'n' roll on German soil and represented the disruptive spirit of this new music that was there to stay."[88] During the following decade, rock 'n' roll became "by far the most explosive" import from the Anglophone world, the focal point of an ongoing culture war that culminated in a Rolling Stones concert at West Berlin's Waldbühne in 1965. After the Stones sang "Satisfaction," the concert suddenly turned into "a pitched battle between young fans and police" that tore the stadium apart and continued on the S-Bahn, destroying "seventeen city train cars, . . . four so badly that they had to be taken permanently out of service."[89] As one activist later noted, "for the first time I saw otherwise totally unpolitical people [develop] a maniacal hatred and frustration against the cops."[90]

In West Germany in the 1960s, the Rolling Stones (not the Beatles, despite their Hamburg performances) became figureheads for a popular insurgency that contested social, political, and cultural paradigms and destroyed the postwar consensus. This insurgency was part of a widespread rebellion in Western Europe, the United States, and many other parts of the world whose objectives and methods mixed different combinations of Marxism, Leninism, Maoism, anarchism, and pacifism. These revolts climaxed in 1968 with the most violent, and most theatrical, assaults on conservative institutions and traditions. As Timothy Scott Brown notes, the year was especially dramatic in West Germany, "a watershed event," during which young Germans rebelled "against a stifling atmosphere of cultural conformity, challenging anti-Communist Cold War hysteria, and demanding an accounting with the crimes of the Nazi era" and "a democratic renewal of society from the ground up." Although Brown correctly emphasizes the global dimension of this insurrection, these "demands, explosive wherever they were made, acquired a special potency in a West Germany poised precipitously on the front line of the Cold War and struggling with the legacy of a recent past marked by fascism, war, and genocide."[91] Even more dramatically in West Germany than the United States or France, 1968 permanently changed the political and cultural settlement. Given the centrality of the performing arts to German national identity, especially music and theatre, the "new democratic politics of self-invention from below" signaled "an explosion of creativity across a range of artistic and political media."[92] Even though "English-language rock music," Schütte notes, "became the soundtrack of . . . cultural revolution and political rebellion,"[93] it also spurred the development of an iconoclastic, politically activist German-language rock 'n' roll called Agitrock. If Anglophone rock's revolutionism was predominantly countercultural rather than militantly leftist, West German rock reversed that paradigm to become at least as much a political avant-garde as an aesthetic one. Theatre, moreover, was always an essential ingredient.

Agitrock had two major branches, according to David Robb, both deeply theatrical and key sources for the German concoction of a rock-based music theatre of the 1980s and 1990s. Both performed *Protestlieder* (protest songs) and both "made music an outspoken mouthpiece of social critique and political agitation."[94] The first branch comprised the *Liedermacher* (song makers), singer-songwriters whose protest songs mixed the traditions of cabaret, chanson, Brecht/Weill, Brecht/Eisler, and US-American folk singers such as Woody Guthrie, Pete Seeger, Joan Baez, and Bob Dylan. The two most celebrated exemplars were Franz Josef Degenhardt in the West and Wolf Biermann in the East, both of whom specialized in narrative and satirical songs as well as *Rollengedichte* (dramatic monologues). Robb explains that Degenhardt would often don "a character mask and—via an ironic self-exposure—reveal . . . that character's hypocrisy or self-interest."[95] This Brechtian formula was similarly taken up by Biermann, and both singers, accompanying themselves on acoustic guitars, embraced class struggle and a Marxist critique of capitalism. The second key component of Agitrock was labeled Krautrock, a slur initially concocted by the British press that homogenizes what was in fact an extremely diverse set of "underground" musical practices. The best-known Krautrock bands outside Germany (Kraftwerk, Tangerine Dream, Amon Düül II, and others) epitomized "the psychedelic revolution"[96] with work sometimes called *kosmische Musik* (cosmic music). But other leading Krautrock bands, aiming for national rather than international audiences, were far more deeply committed to left-wing militancy than US or British rockers, and their concerts and social performances were designed as political actions.[97] Determinedly electric (unlike the *Liedermacher*), Krautrock was central to the German countercultural scene, especially in West Berlin. Most intriguingly, several of the best-known Krautrock bands were also fully committed to theatrical practices that were inseparable from their music-making and politicking. Rather than merely fashioning both music and theatre, they began from the premise that live performance and political protest constitute an explosive music theatre that shatters the distinctions between art and life. Indeed, the always already theatricalized nature of Krautrock makes it an essential part of the genealogy that leads to *Linie 1*, *The Black Rider*, and countless avant-gardist music theatre hybrids that followed.

Among Krautrock bands, three are especially important as both musical visionaries and political activists whose *Liedertheater* (song theatre) was aimed at the working classes and without which *Linie 1* is unimaginable. The best-known group is the now legendary Ton Steine Scherben (clay [or sound] stone shards), which developed as an extension of the radical street theatre collective Hoffmanns Comic Teater [*sic*], founded in 1964,[98] which aimed to "liberate the consciousness of young workers and apprentices in order to facilitate their political action." Under the leadership of Ralph Möbius, who became known professionally (and highly celebrated) as Rio Reiser, they performed pieces that "depicted the conflicts of daily life" for students, apprentices, and working-class West Berliners, wearing colorful costumes and masks, "accompanied by a live band for which Ralph wrote the songs." From the beginning, Hoffmanns was a participatory theatre in which "young workers" were given masks and "invited onto the stage to play out scenes from their own lives."[99] The records that the Scherben started releasing in 1971 were a direct outgrowth of these street performances and other political interventions in which they participated, and in some cases, commandeered. The second group is Floh (Flea) de Cologne, founded by Cologne university theatre students in 1966, which developed a leftist cabaret-meets-rock-opera style and "supplied the soundtrack for a more staunchly Marxist, heavily didactic leftism" than the Scherben, whose work fell more on the anarchist end of the spectrum (and who were more accomplished and creative musicians).[100] Finally, Lokomotive Kreuzberg, "Germany's musically most perfect political rock band" (according to *Rock in Deutschland*), is more appropriately described as "rock 'n' roll theatre," which mixes music with street theatre "for concrete political engagement."[101] Lokomotive thrived during the early 1970s, playing in West Berlin clubs and recording four albums, all of which employ narrative threads to tie songs together. Their first, *Kollege Klatt—Rock Story*, tells of the political awakening of a factory worker, Klatt, his story split between spoken inner monologues and part-sung, part-spoken scenes set in his local bar. Over the course of the forty-minute piece, Klatt gradually becomes politically enlightened, and the album's finale features the band singing an adaptation of the Brecht/Eisler proletariat anthem, "Solidaritätslied" (Solidarity Song).

This Agitrock shares many features with the blues-inflected rock of the Rolling Stones as well as the musically—but not politically—more adventurous psychedelic rock of the Grateful Dead, Jefferson Airplane, Pink Floyd, and others. An electric guitar, bass, and drum kit–driven sound, it manages to negotiate both the "new sonic possibilities offered"[102] by the international rock style and the intensively local social and political concerns of working-class districts in Berlin and other cities. Most of the bands sang in gritty, colloquial German, often heavily inflected by local dialect, unlike earlier German rock bands for whom English was the language of choice. The anti-capitalist dedication of the three bands meant they eschewed commercial record labels and incorporated chanting and political sloganeering into their songs. Whether their albums have narrative spines or not, most fall into the category of concept albums in the tradition of the Beatles' *Sgt. Pepper's Lonely Hearts Club Band*, but with an aggressive political edge for which the Beatles never strove. Scherben's performance work (as Hoffmann's Comic Teater) represents activist musical theatre, of which *Rita und Paul* (1969) is the "flagship" work. The piece illustrates what for Hoffmanns Comic Teater is the "first goal of the theater group, . . . to turn the theater into a practical and transferable weapon."[103] The musical, a retelling of the Romeo and Juliet story but with class antagonism substituting for familial enmity, ends with Paul (Rio Reiser) smashing a television and launching into what would become the Scherben's first single, "Macht kaputt, was euch kaputt macht" (Destroy what destroys you). Like most of their songs, "Macht kaputt" uses a repeated AB stanzaic structure in the minor mode propelled by a driving, syncopated beat. Over a recurring guitar riff, it catalogues a litany of the things that should be destroyed: radios, TVs, cannons, tanks, dollars, police, soldiers, the state. It ends with a rendition of the Brecht/Eisler 1934 communist anthem "Einheitsfrontlied" (United Front Song). On the Scherben's second and most famous album, *Keine Macht für Niemand* (No power for nobody) (1972), Rio Reiser plays a squatter anarchist who is both his real self and a theatricalized version of that self. In David Robb's words,

> Each song tells a different story of life in their community: street battles with police; occupying houses; dodging fares on the Berlin public transport system; the communal squat as a haven from the boredom of apprenticeships; the quest for freedom from the constraints of the postwar Economic Miracle; the longing for utopian alternatives to capitalist reality.[104]

All these subjects would be taken up in *Linie 1*.

Given West Berlin's precarious political position, the city authorities felt particularly threatened by Krautrock's cultural offensive. And the Scherben, the musical mouthpiece—and sometimes leader—of the squat movement of the early 1970s, became especially fearsome political actors whose music was banned by the public radio stations. (In the 1980s, Rio Reiser was one of the first German rockers to come out as gay. He is also the hero of a 2019 jukebox musical about his life, *Rio Reiser—Mein Name ist Mensch* [Rio Reiser—My name is mankind].) It is little wonder that director Frank Castorf was and is an admirer of the Scherben and incorporated their music into his groundbreaking *Räuber von Schiller* (1990, Volksbühne Berlin). For Castorf, the band represents "a voice that bursts out and sings against the judges and prosecutors, against all who betray us."[105]

A rich example of Hoffmanns Comic Teater/Ton Steine Scherben's activist musical theatre is preserved in recorded form as *Herr Fressack und die Bremer Stadtmusikanten* (Mister Glutton and the Bremen Town Musicians), a 1973 audiobook for children that is really a Marxist, fairy-tale musical. Turning the Brothers Grimm story into a fifty-three-minute teaching play, *Herr Fressack* is a rough-and-tumble, artfully constructed piece that inserts the Grimms' rebellious animals into an *Animal Farm*–type frame, but with a happy end, which in turn is inserted into a Scheherazade-like frame (in which a frog successfully diverts a hungry stork).[106] In the innermost story, Fressack is a wizard (and only human character) who, to deceive the animals into working for him, promises them the same conveniences the German Miracle provided: washing machines, refrigerators, vacuum cleaners, cars, and televisions. After he enslaves the music makers and sends them into battle against the other animals to capture a pot of gold, they finally realize

Fressack's villainy, turn on him, and drive him out. The Scherbens recorded the piece in their large Kreuzberg house with their "extended family,"[107] friends and neighborhood children who enact the many partly improvised roles with wit, style, and gusto. The songs are simpler than most of their canon, with a folk-rock character that suits the source material. It has a memorable, minor-key finale (accompanied by guitar, Jew's harp, and winds), "Ich will nicht mehr das arme Schwein sein" (I don't want to be that poor pig anymore), an anthem of resistance whose narrative recapitulates the victory against Fressack: "That will cost you your life, Fressack / We are getting rid of you now, you bag of trash!"

> I don't want to be that blind chicken anymore
> I don't want to be that poor pig anymore
> I don't want to be that stupid dog anymore
> I don't want to be that old donkey anymore![108]

Like many folk songs, it gives each animal a stanza and the piece ends with a slow fade on the echoing refrain. *Fressack* ends confidently on this note of defiance, but its musical perpetuum mobile also suggests—ominously—that the battle against tyranny never ends.

Take the U-Bahn

Although in the United States, politically radical rock 'n' roll is usually considered antithetical to musical theatre,[109] that was not the case in a divided Germany. Thus, there is a definite synergy between Ton Steine Scherben's activist musical theatre and *Linie 1*, a musical developed by GRIPS Theater, a youth theatre company that is another "product of the West German student movement of 1968."[110] GRIPS was founded in 1969, the same year as Hoffmanns Comic Teater, as a children's theatre cum political cabaret designed as "a means of affecting social circumstances" and correcting "the political excesses of the capitalist class." For Volker Ludwig, GRIPS' founding artistic director and librettist/lyricist of *Linie 1*, children constitute an "oppressed class" insulted by the "ironical, schmaltzy, cheap ballet and operetta trimmings" of conventional children's theatre.[111] GRIPS' "emancipatory children's theatre," in contrast, repeatedly took up hot-button issues—the Vietnam War, the environment, squatters' rights, divorce, disability, the children of guest workers, and neo-fascism—and served them up in plays that were regularly attacked by the press for practicing "'communist indoctrination' or 'left wing agit-prop for children.'"[112] In 1980, GRIPS performed their first adult play, A Left History, an autobiographical piece that follows the lives of three students who had met years before at a Vietnam War protest. In 1986, GRIPS put together their first musical, Linie 1, a low-budget piece that uses a Berlin subway line as a unifying thread. Although Ludwig is credited as author, the piece developed out of his work with the ensemble, since the cast and crew, he writes, "came regularly to tell me of their experiences" on the subway. He collaborated with composer Birger Heymann and the band No Ticket, and the piece became a surprise hit that has been performed more than any other German musical except The Threepenny Opera, has toured to fifteen countries (including the United States), and continues in the GRIPS repertoire.

Like the Agitrock that preceded it, Linie 1 practices a fierce political critique, in Erika Hughes's words, of "the capitalist greed of the West, which pits old against young, rich against poor, immigrant against German street thug, ticket takers against those who ride the train without paying."[113] But unlike Krautrock, with its knack for narrative and musical experimentation, it is unabashedly a traditional musical and embraces not only a conventional Broadway structure but also its message of hope: "Have the courage to dream."[114] Hellmut Kotschenreuther, the same critic who, twenty-five years before Linie 1, felt that he needed to explain to My Fair Lady ticket buyers what a musical was, greeted it euphorically: "the enthusiastic audience . . . applauded not just one revue; it applauded the birth of the Berlin musical, a genre whose existence has hitherto only been whispered about."[115] Although Linie 1 features a large dramatis personae, many discrete scenes, and the constant mobility of people, trains, and events, it has a clear and simple narrative structure. This clarity is underlined by the piece's bare-bones mise en scène that gives it the do-it-yourself character for which GRIPS' theatre, like Krautrock, is famous. Its spine is a quest: a young woman arrives at Berlin's Zoologischer Garten (the main West Berlin train station) looking for Johnnie, a rock musician whom she met when he played her West German hometown and with whose child she is pregnant. A set of contemporary variations on The Odyssey or an expressionist station drama, the musical depicts her travels on the central #1 U-Bahn line that runs through the heart of West Berlin. (Most of its stations are in Kreuzberg, which was then the center of the student, rock 'n' roll, and squatter movements.) Its scenes dramatize the Girl's encounters with the many opportunists, waifs, pimps, activists, truant students, pensioners, Turks, Nazi widows, squatters, addicts, and assorted misfits, several of whom befriend her and help her locate Johnnie (Figure 4.2).

In the final scene, Johnnie makes his glitzy rock-star entrance on the steps of the Zoologischer Garten station, like a deus ex machina, and serenades her with a trite, flashy rock song. But when he finishes, the Girl (who is never named and whom the kindly drug-dealer, Bambi, affectionately, if reproachfully, calls the fairy-tale princess) recognizes that Johnnie is not the Prince Charming of her dreams and she (literally) walks off into the sunset with another Young Man in a trench coat whom she had just met on the U-Bahn.

With its kaleidoscopic view of the city, *Linie 1* is awash in local color and its many list songs catalogue the people, places, and events that made West Berlin unique. It was clearly fashioned to be, and remains, the paradigmatic Berlin musical despite (or perhaps because of) the fact that the stereotyped characters turn out to be more contradictory and sympathetic than their labels would suggest. The opportunistic Bambi is the one who finds Johnnie; the ugly duckling Maria becomes the Girl's guardian angel; and the down-and-out Schlucki and chic, unhappy Lady turn out to have hearts of

Figure 4.2 The Girl (Lisa Klabunde) rides the Berlin U-Bahn, *Linie 1*, 2006. Photo © david baltzer/bildbuehne.de.

gold. Yet *Linie 1* flirts with these sentimental tropes in very self-conscious, unsentimental ways and ends up, like the works of Stephen Sondheim, problematizing the very musical theatre conventions it mobilizes. Perhaps the most hard-hitting example of that strategy is a list song titled "Berlin Song," sung *Liedermacher*-style by a solo acoustic guitarist, that rehearses a jaundiced, angry, obscene salute to the city that ends,

> With my feet in dogshit,
> My head in carbon dioxide,
> I sing your song, Berlin.[116]

The sarcasm of the *Liedermacher*'s complaint is answered later in the piece by its most satirical, show-stopping number, "Wilmersdorf Widows," an oompah, oom-pah, beer hall–style march, performed by four male actors in full drag, playing moneyed, unrepentant widows of high-ranking Nazi officers. Like a pack of wolves on the subway car, they sing merrily about the luxuries West Berlin has to offer while berating Turks, asylum-seekers, communists, and everyone to the left of Goebbels. The most formidable part of the song is a menacing *molto ritardando* that grinds the verse to a halt as they bear down threateningly on everyone in the car—and the audience—only to snap back into their original march tempo as if nothing had happened. (This musical trick in effect allegorizes the fantasy that the devastation of 1945 marked "Germany Year Zero," after which everything started afresh.) In good Broadway-style, the song closes with a lurid, half-tempo, kick line coda.

Although Kotschenreuther was absolutely correct about *Linie 1*'s deliberately parochial stance, he jumped the gun when he wrote that the piece shows that "the German musical has emancipated itself from its American role models."[117] In fact, *Linie 1* closely follows the rock musical canons established by *Hair* and its successors, with its episodic structure, musical eclecticism, and plethora of list songs. Although the piece's principal musical idiom is pop-rock (with saxophone obbligatos that give it a jazzy feel), it also uses a pastiche of folk and hard rock songs, a comic operetta number, torch song, and march to help characterize persons and events. Most of its songs use an AB or ABC rock sequential form with a memorable refrain as its centerpiece. Its musical dramaturgy, moreover, is extremely, if creatively traditional, with the time-honored "I am" song, "I want" song, eleven o'clock number, and final romantic duet. But *Linie 1* puts a dark, angry spin on these conventions to place them in dialogue with the leftist political activism of the 1960s, 1970s, and 1980s. Most important, the musical has a group protagonist: the people, the many, the crowd, who sing several of its most important and memorable songs. To the end, the Girl, whose quest drives the narrative, remains nameless, like the Young Man with whom she pairs off in the finale. Indeed, the Girl and Young Man are given none of the musical's personal, confessional songs and end up being more anonymous than the many eccentrics they meet. *Linie 1*'s most exemplary number perhaps is its "I want" song sung by the ensemble early in the show, "Waiting," a list song and pseudo-blues over a throbbing bass, as they wait anxiously for the U-Bahn and dream about what the future might hold:

> The apartment with a terrace
> The wife for life
> The truly good job.

But these prizes, they decide, have already passed them by. Instead, the lonely crowd is left adrift in an urban wasteland,

> Waiting—for the next full train
> Waiting—for the next little swig
> Waiting—to be fired from the job
> For a life, empty as a cracked sieve
> Waiting—for the day to be done
> Waiting—for my heart to go snap
> Waiting—for the last big bang
> From rheumatism, cancer, dementia.[118]

The despair that drives this "I want" song is calculatedly set against the characters' hopes, which are not quite as broken as the refrain might suggest. Instead, the musical repeatedly runs opposites against each other, "always changing perspectives," in Wolfgang Jansen's words, setting misery against "bursts of wit,"[119] anomie against belonging, endurance against the ephemeral, mobility against stasis, security against dread, collectivism against individualism.

The ensemble number in *Linie 1* that answers back to "Waiting" is the eleven o'clock number "Mut zum Träumen" (Dare imagine), another bluesy, minor-mode song with a locomotive beat (it is sung on the train rather than the platform). In performance, though, the singers nearly freeze as they speed along:

> Have courage—DARE IMAGINE
> That your spirit's aflame
> DARE IMAGINE
> You can break free from all shame
> DARE IMAGINE
> Or they'll kick till we fall
> DARE IMAGINE
> Or there's no love at all.[120]

No other song in *Linie 1* epitomizes the sense of hope and aspiration for which the Broadway musical is so often celebrated—and so often derided. But it is not the show's real/parodistic finale, which, in Alisa Solomon's words, "is so kitsch," like "the self-conscious endings of Shakespeare's romances," that "you can enjoy it only by recognizing its artifice."[121]

The mobility that is the subject of *Linie 1* has not coincidentally become its distinguishing feature in the international musical theatre marketplace. In Kotschenreuther's review, he announced proudly that "the German musical has . . . come of age in a witty, very Berliner way." Little did he know how clairvoyant he was when he then declared that it "finally [has] become cosmopolitan and exportable."[122] He seems to have understood that *Linie 1*'s very particularity, its DIY close-up of the eccentricities of a thriving yet punishing city, made it ripe for adaptation in many parts of the world. Thanks to neo-liberalization, economic and social inequities have persistently widened and the distresses the musical spotlights have become even more severe and endemic. At the same time, the individual and collective hopes and dreams the piece echoes have become even more pervasive. This contradiction is precisely the reason for the musical's appeal in so many parts of the world that, like Germany, must continue to wrestle with the social and political nightmares of their recent past. In 1990s Korea, for example, the Nazi widows were handily translated into the widows of despotic generals who thrived under the dictatorship while the opportunists and drifters were transformed into the denizens of Seoul's then thriving demimonde. The success of the Korean version, adapted by Kim Min-gi, testifies to the similarities between the fallout from urbanization and industrialization in both West Germany and South Korea, as well as to the plights of the many casualties of neo-liberalization in both nations. Critic Yu-Sun Lee's explication of the Korean version's mode of engagement helps explain why *Linie 1* became the iconic transnational musical—one built to travel—at the turn of the twenty-first century:

> Although Kim's *Linie 1* depicts the unhappy everyday life of suffering people, it does so sensitively, lyrically, powerfully, and amusingly—with a live rock band. The characters may be dejected, but they are no longer humbled, instead singing and dancing happily, wittily, and mockingly. . . . The long-running success of Kim's *Linie 1* is based on this gripping dramaturgy. The comic aesthetic distance provided by powerful live rock music appeals to a Korean audience that, looking back, can also identify its later economic success and outstanding political achievements: Once upon a time it was like this. . . . We keep going forward and forward![123]

Because German musical theatre comes in all shapes and sizes, *Linie 1* marks a paradigm-shift for small- and medium-scale German musicals, which similarly aim at local markets and often run in repertory for years. A long-term success in Hamburg has been the musical *Heiße Ecke—Das St. Pauli Musical* (2003), with music by Martin Lingnau and lyrics by Heiko Wohlgemuth, about a snack bar where locals gather, play, bicker, and fall in love. Until the 2020 Covid lockdown, it drew a total of 2.5 million spectators.[124] A more recent example, catering to former East Germans, is *Go Trabi Go* (2018), based on the 1991 film about newly liberated East Germans vacationing for the first time in the West. With music by Dominik Walenciak and lyrics by Carsten Golbeck, it enjoyed a successful run in Dresden before being closed down by Covid. Finally, I want to single out the work of Peter Lund, librettist, lyricist, translator, and adaptor, who has collaborated on over a dozen, inventive small-scale musicals since the mid-1990s, mainly with composer Thomas Zaufke, many of them premiering at the Neuköllner Oper Berlin.[125] All these works continue to develop, relocate, and recalibrate *Linie 1*'s abiding appeal using German subject matter but taking the US-American musical as a kind of Platonic ideal it imitates from afar.

Sympathy for the Devil

Four years—and the fall of the Berlin Wall—separate the premieres of *Linie 1* and *The Black Rider* (1990). But the world of difference between them is about more than that once-in-a-lifetime geopolitical shift. If *Linie 1* is an intensively local, small-scale musical that happens to have ridden the rails around the world, *The Black Rider*, premiering at Hamburg's Thalia Theater, was designed from the beginning as a large-scale, cosmopolitan venture. While the former put its creators on the cultural map, the latter was the invention of three superstar artists. If the former embraces a do-it-yourself aesthetic, the latter is spectacularly and immaculately artful. If the former was mounted on a very tight budget, the latter was designed as a multi-million Deutsche Mark extravaganza. If the former's ability to go viral was an accidental dividend, the latter was carefully and deliberately planned to be a global sensation. If the former spotlights its actors as quirky, urban misfits, the latter turns actors into a hybrid of kabuki-style characters and manic puppets. If the former identifies as a dyed-in-the-wool Berliner, the latter proclaims itself a citizen of the world. If the former forges a politically activist musical theatre, the latter prefers an apparently apolitical aestheticism. Despite these vast differences, however, each piece helped legitimize a musical theatrical paradigm with far-reaching, long-term effects.

The Black Rider: The Casting of the Magic Bullets, a "cosmic vaudeville show,"[126] was directed and designed by Robert Wilson, with music by Tom Waits, book by William S. Burroughs, and lyrics by Waits and Burroughs. Although Wilson was the central creative force, the piece was constructed collaboratively and is based on "Der Freischütz" [The freeshooter]—not the opera by Carl Maria von Weber (1821), but Weber's source, a tale included in *Gespensterbuch* [Ghost book] (1811), a collection of German ghost stories edited by August Apel and Friedrich Laun. Although the tale dates back several centuries before Apel and Laun, their volume popularized it during the height of the craze for Gothic fiction and melodrama, and it was translated into English by Thomas De Quincey as "The Fatal Marksman" (1823). (It also served as an inspiration for Mary Shelley's *Frankenstein* [1818].) *The Black Rider*'s *Faust*-like narrative is about a would-be marksman, named Wilhelm (William in De Quincey), who, to become a successful hunter and win the hand of the woman he loves, makes a contract with a frighteningly bewitching devil he meets at a crossroads at midnight. The devil entices him with magic bullets that always hit their mark and Wilhelm becomes addicted to the perfection they offer. As is so often the case in moralistic folk tales, the devil outsmarts his human prey by giving Wilhelm one cursed bullet with which he pays for fleeting success by unintentionally shooting his fiancée in the heart and forfeiting his sanity.

Weber's *Der Freischütz* is based on the same story but, as was typical of an 1820s opera, gives it a happy ending, unlike *The Black Rider*, which returns to the fatal design of the original. *Rider* thus carefully keeps its distance from *Freischütz*, despite (or because of) the latter's renown, especially in Germany. It changes the characters' names and borrows no tunes from Weber's "landmark work," which occupies a privileged position in the German operatic pantheon and is "frequently regarded as the German national opera *par excellence*."[127] Almost an anti-*Freischütz*, Waits's score is determinedly eclectic, capitalizing on his experience as "a leader in grit, poetry, freak shows, and romantic richness."[128] It draws on an array of styles, including European and US-American folk traditions, parlor tunes, operetta, the blues, burlesque, cabaret, Tin Pan Alley, Lutheran hymns, and horror movie music and sound effects. Its musical pastiche and English lyrics, moreover, create a sense of Euro-American worldliness (and world-weariness) on which the piece capitalizes. Wilson's hard-edged, hallucinatory mise en scène, which includes a surfeit of special effects, underscores the magical, uncanny aspects of the story and turns *The Black Rider* into a Gothic, surrealist, expressionist, vaudeville, pop opera, a.k.a. "a new kind of hybrid stage work."[129]

In fact, this new kind of stage work would increasingly become the rule on German stages. The name used most frequently to describe it is *Regietheater* (director's theatre), for decades the subject of analysis and debate. The term remains controversial, since any definition (as with the label "musical") also represents a value judgment. In brief, *Regietheater* denotes a mode of theatre-making as well as a production over which the director rules, either staging a preexistent text or dominating the work of her collaborators, be they playwrights, composers, or designers. Ulrich Müller sums it up thus: "On the one hand, *Regietheater* generally implies that *Regie* [direction] is as important as the text and the music; on the other, there is an understanding of the term reserved primarily for provocative or disparaging purposes: a type of *Regie* that seeks to dominate the drama, to deconstruct it, to question it, even to transform the story and/or interpret it in a new way."[130] It is often used derogatorily, especially in the Anglophone and opera worlds, where it is sometimes taken to be synonymous with "avant-garde" or "postdramatic"—or simply defamed as "Eurotrash." *Regietheater* in the German-speaking world is, in fact, the result of the convergence of theatrical, literary, and aesthetic traditions, many of them profoundly different from those which obtain in the United States or the UK. It is also unimaginable without the enormous system of state-subsidized theatrical and musical performances in Germany,

Austria, and Switzerland. To compare *Regietheater* with Anglo-American theatre is no more instructive than comparing the work of contemporaries such as Arnold Schoenberg and Ralph Vaughan Williams.

In German critical discourse, *Regietheater* is implicitly opposed to *Werktreue*, or fidelity, which, Müller emphasizes, is "essentially impossible" since first, exact archival reproduction is impossible, and second, to be intelligible and communicate with its audience, every performance must, if only implicitly, speak the language of its time and place.[131] Marvin Carlson and Matt Cornish wisely avoid employing the term *Regietheater* in their monographs on German theatre, as will I since it is too vague and freighted with value judgments to be analytically precise. But suffice it to say that all the work on which I am focusing in the remainder of this book could be considered *Regietheater*, of which Robert Wilson is an acknowledged pioneer and master. Even though his first New York performances date back to the mid-1960s, he began working abroad in 1971 and has directed and designed dozens of original pieces as well as countless productions of plays and operas on European stages, especially in France and Germany. Given the scenic and conceptual enormity of his work, subsidized theatres and opera houses have been far more welcoming and hospitable than US venues, and as a result he is far better known in Europe than in his homeland.

Robert Wilson used *The Black Rider* to reinvent musical theatre, just as, from the very beginning of his career, he used large-scale collaborations with Philip Glass, Lucinda Childs, Jessye Norman, and many others to reinvent what he calls opera. To fashion the musical, Wilson opted for two world-famous, true-blue, US-American collaborators (from different generations) with little experience making musical theatre. They chose an English title that references another trailblazing musical theatre spectacle (and adaptation of *Der Freischütz*), *The Black Crook* (1866), which is repeatedly described in histories as the first musical. Honoring its forebear, *The Black Rider* does indeed take up many of the conventions associated with the musical, including the central love plot, a carefully calculated oscillation between spoken dialogue and song (or progressive and repetitive temporalities), and use of distinctly different kinds of songs. Although *The Black Rider*'s narrative is laid out clearly and boldly, it is no ordinary musical, in part because the theatrical self-consciousness of every song brings them closer to Bertolt Brecht than Rodgers and Hart. As in many rock musicals, almost all the music disrupts and comments on the action rather than furthering the plot or developing character, although none takes up Brecht's leftist political program.

144   GERMANY

The thumbprints of Tom Waits and William Burroughs on *The Black Rider* are as strong as their voices are weather-beaten and raspy. Indeed, the renowned cragginess (and off-kilter machismo) of these collaborators helps give the piece what is coded as authenticity: an experimental edge and demented angularity that is linked to each artist's long association with an art (and lifestyle) branded bohemian, countercultural, alternative, or aesthetically revolutionary. The songs are vintage Tom Waits, and as Corinne Kessel notes, the score "embodies the torturous laments and regrets of broken souls with the rhythm of a skeletal drum, the dissonant melodies of piercing shrieks, and the slippery seductive sheen of the devil."[132] *The Black Rider* exploits a musical and existential darkness to give it an impeccably avant-gardist character that earned it a thirty-minute standing ovation at its premiere in one of Germany's most prestigious theatres and, on a world tour, inspired unanimous rave reviews. Its pedigree, however, was not quite impeccable enough to prevent an anonymous critic for *Der Spiegel* from slamming the piece as "'Cats' for intellectuals and snobs."[133]

Despite *Der Spiegel*'s flippant comparison, *The Black Rider* does share with *Cats* its unprecedented scale, success, and portability. Both recycle and refashion musical theatre conventions for the global box office, applying musical styles to well-known source materials that move them far from their sources. A more apt comparison, however, might be Andrew Lloyd Webber's *The Phantom of the Opera* (1986), with its Gothic subject matter and aborted wedding finale. Of the three, *The Black Rider* is the most obviously avant-gardist, based on a variation on the quintessential German folk tale, *Faust*, performed by a Hamburg-based crew of actors and musicians using US-American musical theatrical idioms. Robert Wilson's patented theatre of images combines their writers' virtuoso talents with literary and musical forms that are as deeply rooted in US conventions as the English-language song lyrics. The plot sticks closely to the "Freischütz" source material (the book was translated into German by Udo Breger und Wolfgang Wiens), but *Die Tageszeitung* correctly notes its parallels with stories of the mythologized Old West and "Lonesome American Cowboy" who lives and dies by the gun.[134] The musical even includes a spoken narrative about the myth that the quintessentially US-American Ernest Hemingway sold his soul to the devil in Hollywood. Many of the songs perform, in Stephen Holden's words, a "German Expressionist gloss of American vernacular music,"[135] using old-fashioned stanzaic forms and walking a stylistic tightrope between a demented Weimar cabaret style and US-American vaudeville. *Rider* also powerfully exploits Burroughs's own history, as junkie (it inveighs against marijuana and heroin) and more important, as the killer of Joan Vollmer, his second wife, in 1951. Burroughs famously declared that he shot her accidentally in a drunken game of "William Tell," and *The Black Rider* reiterates the narrative of the murder in a different register. According to Burroughs, his "drunken prank," like Wilhelm's capitulation to the devil, represented "a case of possession with tragic consequences." Burroughs's narrative of the event, however, gives the "case" a redemptive ending that *Rider* lacks:

> I am forced to the appalling conclusion that I would never have become a writer but for Joan's death, and to a realization of the extent to which this event has motivated and formulated my writing. I live with the constant threat of possession, and a constant need to escape from possession, from Control. So the death of Joan brought me in contact with the invader, the Ugly Spirit, and maneuvered me into a lifelong struggle, in which I have had no choice except to write my way out.[136]

Burroughs attempted to write his way out of hell by turning to the "cut up," an aleatoric literary technique that allowed his writing to bypass conscious control. Wilhelm (Stefan Kurt), however, is not so lucky and his attempt at shooting his way out of a rendezvous with destiny leads him straight to hell. Wilhelm's catastrophe is personified by the charismatic Ugly Spirit, Stelzfuß (Pegleg, Dominique Horwitz), who also plays a master of ceremonies whom Holden rightly identifies as a "fiendish descendant" of Joel Grey in *Cabaret* (Figure 4.3). Like an even more smilingly malevolent, vampiric version of Kander and Ebb's Emcee, or Nosferatu, Pegleg enters from a big black coffin, followed one by one by the grinning, ghoulish performers, and welcomes the audience with a vaudevillian refrain:

> Come on along with the Black Rider
> We'll have a gay old time
> Lay down in the web of the black spider
> I'll drink your blood like wine

Like a Broadway opening number with a chorus line of ghouls, the song repeatedly promises, "We'll have a gay old time."[137]

Pegleg's tease in "The Black Rider," "I'll drop you off in Harlem," signals that the tour he offers of US-American amusements is strongly inflected by

Figure 4.3 Pegleg, right (Dominique Horwitz) with company, *The Black Rider*, Thalia Theater, 1990. Photo by Martin Eberle.

African American vernaculars, especially the blues, which figure prominently in Waits's earlier work. In fact, however, only two songs in *Rider* bear an imprint of the blues, Pegleg's "Gospel Train" (which has a devil for its conductor), and at the piece's end, a snare drum–driven, bluesy striptease—or mad scene—with trumpet obbligato, performed by a flailing Wilhelm after he murders his bride. More important, *The Black Rider* draws on what is perhaps the classic and most notorious blues myth, that bluesman Robert Johnson, in exchange for his musical genius, sold his soul to the devil at a crossroads at midnight.[138] This myth is linked to Johnson's song "Crossroads" as well as his "Me and the Devil Blues" and "Hellhound on My Trail." It has been circulated in countless forms, and *The Black Rider* narrowly postdated the release of Walter Hill's film *Crossroads* in 1986 and the multi-platinum-selling CDs of *The Complete Recordings* of Johnson in 1990. The myth is also commemorated in the piece itself in the song "Crossroads," which, however, is not a version of the Johnson song or even a blues, but an accordion-accompanied beguine that tells a cautionary narrative about one Georg Schmid (George Smith in De Quincey), who, like Wilhelm, sold his soul to the devil.

The Black Rider's reimagining of the Broadway vernacular retains and distorts recognizable song types, which is in part a result of the musical

ENTER THE MUSICAL 147

synergy between Wilson and Waits, although Burroughs's abrasive fatalism is surely part of the equation. Waits's dark-hued score consists of two kinds of songs. The first comprises stanzaic, pseudo-*Volkslieder* (folk songs), most of them narrative, sparsely orchestrated, and reminiscent of sweetly melancholic ballads from the British Isles. These are linked to the love plot but each, like "The Briar and the Rose" and "I'll Shoot the Moon," has an ominous or violent subtext. The second is a diverse mix, consisting of more vaudevillian, if similarly menacing numbers, ranging from the blues to klezmer ("Russian Dance"), to Kander and Ebb/Weillian numbers, to Waits's death-obsessed, "stripped-down, heavily percussive 'bone' music."[139] All these songs, appropriately enough, are associated with Pegleg or other agents of the devil and all are performed presentationally, almost as provocations.

To understand why *The Black Rider* is a musical, one should compare the video recording of the Thalia production[140] with Waits's 1993 album of his own performances of songs from the show. The latter, lorded over by Waits's "scabrous guttural growl,"[141] is percussive and severe, while the theatre score (as arranged and orchestrated by Waits and jazz composer Greg Cohen) is richly and ingeniously colorful. As Kessel notes, the score revels "in the beauty of dissonance and the sour wheeze of a bizarre carnival orchestra,"[142] which includes glass harmonica, musical saw, and ondes Martenot (doubling Käthchen's screeching solos). Indeed, its eerie lushness puts it into a productive counterpoint with Burroughs's craggy prose and Wilson's "utterly seductive visual landscape aflame with saturated color, high-tech wizardry, mordant wit, distorted perspectives of line and gesture, and archetypal characterizations of our struggles with love, evil, and human folly."[143]

The most ambitious numbers in *The Black Rider* dramaturgically are three pseudo-folk ballads, "But He's Not Wilhelm," "Chase the Clouds Away," and "In the Morning," none of which made it onto Tom Waits's CD.[144] All three are memorable, or what *Die Tageszeitung* describes as "wonderfully kitschy earworm songs." But these three differ from the other songs insofar as each is presented in a scene that could have come from an operetta or a musical, in which spoken dialogue is punctuated by restatements of a refrain. The refrain (in English) is taken up by different characters, only to be interrupted by spoken dialogue (in German), and repeated. With each iteration, the number becomes more and more elaborately and exuberantly orchestrated, building to a musical and dramatic climax, complete with coda. Perhaps the most elaborate and ingenious of all is the seven-minute "Chase the Clouds Away," in which Käthchen, her parents, and Wilhelm plan her wedding day. It starts as if it was going to be the famous wedding march from Wagner's *Lohengrin* but immediately turns into a harmonium-accompanied chorale instead. An A-A-B refrain, it is sung through six times in the scene, its musical style and arrangement changing with each iteration. The tune has a deliberately antique quality to it, and it changes from Lutheran chorale, to *Volkslied*, to ardent duet, to quartet, which is broken off by a recitative-like soliloquy for the distraught Käthchen. Its next iteration provides a sound carpet for her mother's explosive performance of an abrasive descant (using extended vocal technique), as the song suddenly turns into 1920s-style, flapper jazz. The music inspires Wilhelm to pick up his rifle and execute military-like maneuvers that become an exuberant, syncopated dance, ending with a half-tempo kick line. But then, there is a surprise finale, when Pegleg pops up through the trap down center and declaims the last, sinister stanza to Wilhelm: "I'll wait here by the shady bush / And you'll be mine forever more."[145]

Despite its ambitious score, *The Black Rider* is first and foremost a piece by Robert Wilson, "the German theatre aficionado's favorite American wizard,"[146] which is most remarkable for its scenic magic and stark luxuriance. A tragedy played for laughs, *Rider* employs heavily made-up actors who look and move like silent-movie actors, dolls, life-size puppets, kabuki actors, or in the words of a more skeptical critic, "'The Munsters' reimagined by a *Vogue* photographer."[147] They all are given farcical turns, symphonies of shtick, that help the piece maintain "a pace that is closer to musical comedy than to opera."[148] The scene design, which combines hard-edged geometric forms, washes of color, and Wilson's signature, black-and-white chalky sketches, turns the piece into a dynamic succession of near tableaus, "challeng[ing] conventional notions of what is in fact conceivable within a proscenium."[149] Like most globally popular musicals, *The Black Rider* emphasizes images, movement, and song rather than text. As Waits has remarked, Wilson "doesn't really like words. I think he thinks of words as like tacks on the bedroom floor in the middle of the night when you're trying to make it to the bathroom."[150] The subordinate role played by language was a crucial factor in making the Thalia production "[w]ildly popular," allowing it to tour six European capitals, New York, and Hong Kong (with English titles). Picked up by other directors, *The Black Rider* was promptly mounted by theatres "all over Europe, with more than 30 productions in seven different languages."[151] In 2004, Wilson remounted it in English with an Anglophone cast, performing it in London, San Francisco, Los Angeles, and

Sydney. Since the Thalia premiere, it has been produced countless times all over the German-speaking world, including seven productions alone during the 2018–2019 season. Most important, *The Black Rider* is symptomatic of a new artistic settlement that has become especially widespread since around 2010. As David Roesner notes, music has become "omnipresent in German theatre – hardly any production does not credit a composer, music curator, sound designer, DJ, voice artist, or other musical contributor."[152]

The Black Rider's global success was by no means accidental but was planned from the beginning. Because the production, according to *Der Spiegel*, cost about 4 million Deutsche Marks (equivalent to 3.9 million euros in 2021), or 15 percent of the theatre's annual budget, the Thalia, in a first for a German state-subsidized theatre, invited private investors to "enter the culture business" in the hope of securing "a big profit." A leaflet declared, "you can finally become an entrepreneur when it comes to culture" and encouraged patrons to invest in a limited partnership (called Take 12) that was underwriting the production. It noted enticingly that, for example, a 6,000 DM investment would reap both economic and symbolic capital, since out of that sum, 4,000 DM would qualify as a tax-deductible donation while 2,000 DM would be invested in the limited partnership. Although *Der Spiegel*'s anonymous reporter seems somewhat ill at ease with this proposition, the article emphasizes that the arrangement is still small-scale in comparison with the purely commercial (and highly successful) runs of *Cats* in Hamburg and *Starlight Express* in Bochum.[153]

Although the state-subsidized/commercial model has by no means become commonplace since *The Black Rider*, cuts in government funding for the arts (especially during the consolidation of institutions and venues from East and West following reunification) have encouraged theatres and opera houses to program more popular music theatre. In Germany and Austria, innovative music theatre of all kinds has become an increasingly prominent part of season calendars. In the final chapter I will consider some of the most provocative and thoughtful reinventions of musical theatre classics in state-subsidized houses. In the next and penultimate chapter, however, I want to analyze the less well-studied descendants of the theatrical formula for which *The Black Rider* provided a prototype: the magnificent offspring born from the mating of avant-gardist stagecraft with the conventions of the Broadway-style musical. Since German reunification, no new piece has matched *Rider*'s global reach and boundary-breaking success. But a number of celebrated directors have come forward who have crafted innovative music theatre that mixes the conventions of avant-gardist performance, operetta, opera, variety show, and musical. This mixing has produced a huge field of work, but to my eyes and ears, a large part of its theatrical and musical allure is derived from its ingenious refashioning of the conventions of Broadway-style musical theatre.

5

Musical Comedy Recalibrated

The Black Rider is emblematic of a new German-language music theatre that mixes genres, styles, and conventions. Shying away from the operatic, this kind of work is usually performed by actors trained in spoken rather than musical theatre and is presented in state-subsidized *Schauspielhäuser* rather than opera or operetta houses. Typically, it features live diegetic music, and often song, with the musicians performing both as music makers and actors. Most important, this new musical theatre uses popular idioms, exploits the crackle of difference between speech and live music (including song), and celebrates the theatre as a place of enchantment and revelation. In the development of this work, the composer or musical director is normally part of the directorial team, participating in and sometimes driving the rehearsal process. Musicians are thus co-creators on equal footing with the stage director and the writer of the text. The actors, too, are crucially important players, often given break-out moments in which they step forward, grab a microphone, and belt out a pop or rock song or launch into a dance, monologue, or comic routine.

The range of examples of this new music theatre is staggeringly wide. Consider, for example, *Der Einzige und sein Eigentum* (The self and its own, 2022), directed by Sebastian Hartmann with an original score by PC Nackt and choreography by Ronni Maciel, based on the 1844 book of the same title by the German philosopher Max Stirner, an anarchist and drinking buddy of Marx and Engels. The piece, which features infectious, minimalist-influenced pop songs, a soft shoe, and a big Broadway-style finale, not only uses conventions associated with the musical, but also takes up one of its most pervasive themes, individual versus community.[1] Or the quirky, retro, jukebox musicals of Barbara Bürk and Clemens Sienknecht, such as *Ballroom Schmitz* (2018), which, in David Roesner's words, "transport their iconic source texts into a 1970s radio studio cum living room creating a genre mix of literature recitation, audio book, radio play, and DJ set," punctuated by "a highly eclectic mix" of pop songs.[2] Or the through-composed realization of

Sarah Kane's *4.48 Psychosis* (2020) fashioned by director Ulrich Rasche and composer Nico van Wersch, a three-hour endurance test for nine virtuoso actors on treadmills declaiming Kane's harrowing text with percussion-propelled precision. Or director Herbert Fritsch's anarchic farces and reworkings of classics that incorporate comic sketches and routines, songs, dramatic scenes, and synchronized dance. Fritsch's frequent collaborator is composer Ingo Günther, whose live performance is always a part of the dramatic action and whose musical score for their adaptation of *Amphitryon* (2019), for example, turns Molière's play into screwball musical comedy.

This new musical theatre is so diverse and draws on so many antecedents that any genealogy will be incomplete. I have already singled out *The Black Rider* as foundational but I would like to append to it the work of director Christoph Marthaler, whose theatre, like Wilson's, mines popular traditions and exploits the crackle of difference between speech and song. David Roesner argues, in fact, that Marthaler is the key figure in the manufacture of this new musical theatre genre, "revolutioniz[ing] the role of music and musical thinking for the German '*Sprechtheater*'" (spoken theatre).[3] Marthaler's original pieces, dating back to the early 1990s, are always musically inflected, and spoken dialogue is repeatedly interrupted by live performances of pre-existing, diegetic songs that are usually intoned chorally by the actors. These songs include an assortment of lieder, madrigals, cabaret, hymns, anthems, folk songs, sentimental ballads, and *Schlager*. Marthaler's plays, set in drab, decrepit, naturalistic, office-like spaces (designed by Anna Viebrock), could be waiting rooms, asylums, train stations, institutional dining rooms, or any other modern purgatory. The actors drift in a kind of suspended animation, the content of their exchanges abstract, incongruous, and cryptic. Although Marthaler's music theatre, like Herbert Fritsch's, has all the trappings of farce, it unfolds in a melancholic slow motion that puts it at a remove both from traditional comedy and from the various musical idioms that Marthaler plunders. Trained as a musician, he employs song, no matter how rarefied its arrangement, to evoke historical associations and events. He can thus, as he puts it, "suddenly replay 80 years of history" by having his actors sweetly intone "The Pilgrim's Chorus" from Wagner's *Tannhäuser* or the Nazi anthem, "Horst-Wessel-Lied."[4] Marthaler's plays are also driven by textual and gestural repetition, which Guido Hiß describes as "an absurd ballet that runs with clockwork perfection" from which there is "no escape, at most brief derailments."[5] Marthaler's pieces elicit audience laughter, but it is a nervous laughter at "the constant and often provocative recurrence of the same material" that disrupts the pensive, stagnant atmosphere.[6]

David Roesner is one of the few German scholars to recognize that since Wilson's and Marthaler's work of the early 1990s, "theatre music has been one of the key drivers of theatrical invention, innovation, and style." As he explains, "For many innovative theatre makers in Germany today, music is a key element" not only in their finished products, but also "in the gestation of their artistic profile, during the conception of a new production, in the creation and rehearsal process, in the performances themselves, and even in their marketing."[7] Music or song, interpolated into a play, "asserts itself," in Roesner's words, "as an equal with or against dramatic figures, texts, images, light and space."[8] Roesner and Matthias Rebstock call this hybridized practice composed theatre, which for them stretches back to Richard Wagner. Although their analytical frame is indispensable for studying theatre as musical composition, their 2012 book is very particular about what is included in the category.[9] Focusing on Euro-American avant-gardist traditions, "'high art' practices of canonical composers and their notated works,"[10] they construct a genealogy that leads from composers Richard Wagner, Arnold Schoenberg, and John Cage to directors such as Robert Wilson and Christoph Marthaler with secure high art credentials.

Because I am intent on opening up the category of musical theatre, I am focusing in this chapter not on makers of elite culture like Marthaler but on directors whose work repurposes *Unterhaltungsmusik* (entertainment music) and low comedy. Herbert Fritsch, whose many farcical, song-punctuated plays I would describe as a recalibration or reinvention of musical comedy, uses popular musical idioms and looks back unapologetically to traditional German low comedy, from the early modern clown Hanswurst to the silent film comic Karl Valentin. Fritsch's directorial work includes off-the-wall remountings of classic plays, operas, operettas, and musicals, as well as original plays with music that toss low comedy and avant-gardism into a blender and turn it to "high." I choose Fritsch as my primary example in this chapter because his work illuminates so many facets of German comedy and avant-gardist practice, the penchant of German directors to stage and choreograph freewheeling adaptations of classics with original musical scores, the geography of the theatre landscape in the German-speaking world, and the discomfort and prejudice that continues to stigmatize popular musical theatre in the land of Bach, Beethoven, and Brahms.

Pure Mayhem

Conventional wisdom has it that Germans are not funny. Brooding, tragic, melancholy, yes; but comic? It is little wonder then that director Herbert Fritsch polarizes critics and audiences by turning everything he touches into absurdly entertaining farce. Although he stages many different kinds of work in Germany, Austria, and Switzerland and has acquired a large crowd of admirers, his method has on occasion provoked as many boos as cheers.[11] His *Spamalot*-inspired production of Henry Purcell's semi-opera *King Arthur* (2016) at the Zurich Opera goaded one spectator during the performance to yell out from the balcony, "What happened to good taste?" (*Geht's auch mit Niveau?*). When an interviewer questioned Fritsch about the incident, he explained, "an aura of well-rehearsed, ritualized reverence hangs over opera, even more than drama. The art is celebrated with a holy seriousness that—let's be honest—sometimes covers up a certain routine."[12] Although most German directors work to de-routinize performance, none does so with more gusto than Fritsch. As the audience interjection in Zurich suggests, this de-routinization mixes farce and high seriousness in a way that sometimes inspires indignation. Fritsch's next production at the Zurich Opera, Weber's *Der Freischütz* (2016), the opera on which Wilson's *The Black Rider* is based, was more positively received than *King Arthur*, perhaps because it did not perform major surgery on "the German national opera."[13] Musically a complete rendering of Weber's folkloric, romantic *Singspiel*, it turned it, however, into a hallucinatory, lederhosen-and-dirndl kitsch explosion, in bright neon colors, complete with a psychedelic, flower-wallpapered forester's hut. Fritsch cast the acrobatic Florian Anders as the evil Samiel, a non-singing role who in this production became a red-suited, long-tailed devil who monitors all the comings and goings on stage and has the deplorable habit of climbing up church walls and disappearing under women's skirts.

Star directors usually shoot to fame in their twenties, so it was noteworthy when Herbert Fritsch became one of the hottest directors in the German-speaking world at age sixty. His ascendance capped a long career as petty thief, junkie, theatre student, solo performer, and leading actor at Berlin's Volksbühne am Rosa-Luxemburg-Platz under the directorship of Frank Castorf. Castorf, the most important and influential director during the first two decades after reunification, is celebrated not only for his revolutionary productions, but also for his artistic directorship of the Volksbühne, which he saved from oblivion and turned into the leading theatre in Germany.

Fritsch was a member of the ensemble between 1993 and 2007, starring in over a dozen Volksbühne productions, in which he was repeatedly described as an extreme-actor—a wild, exhibitionistic ham and scene-stealer, "revered by some, despised by others."[14] But in 2007, he and Castorf had a falling out and Fritsch turned to directing. In 2011, two Fritsch productions, Ibsen's *A Doll's House* and Gerhart Hauptmann's comedy *The Beaver Coat*, were selected for the most prestigious theatre festival in the German-speaking world, the Berliner Theatertreffen. Ibsen's domestic drama was transformed into a Gothic horror-comedy-thriller-melodrama while the Hauptmann became an "over-the-top . . . declaration of war against Naturalism and authorities of all kinds."[15] That same year, Castorf invited Fritsch back to the Volksbühne where, able to stage whatever he wanted, Fritsch opted to design and direct a 1913 boulevard comedy that deliberately challenged the political vernacular for which that theatre had become famous. He set *Die (s)panische Fliege* (The Spanish Fly),[16] a throwaway sex farce by Franz Arnold und Ernst Bach, on a giant, undulating Persian rug that covered the Volksbühne's huge stage (Figure 5.1). A trampoline, hidden among the rug's upstage folds,

Figure 5.1 The mustard tycoon and his family, from left: Bastian Reiber, Wolfram Koch, Harald Warmbrunn, Hans Schenker, Sophie Rois. In Arnold and Bach's *Die (s)panische Fliege*, directed by Herbert Fritsch, Volksbühne am Rosa-Luxemburg-Platz, 2011. Photo by Thomas Aurin.

would cause the characters on their entrances to bound headlong onto the stage. The play centers on a rich mustard tycoon, his puritanical wife, and his panic at the likelihood that a Spanish dancer (the title character), with whom he had a one-night stand years earlier, will show up on his doorstep. (Like Godot, she never appears.)

In Fritsch's hands, the performance of that quintessentially bourgeois mode of deception, sweeping things under the rug (a cliché in both German and English), was literalized. The production's overwrought theatricality, extravagant costumes, gravity-defying pratfalls, frenzied mugging, gargantuan wigs, and silly walks hilariously—if violently—unmasked narrow-mindedness and hypocrisy.

The four succeeding pieces Fritsch created for the Volksbühne employed far more music than *Die (s)panische Fliege* and, like that production, were all invited to the Theatertreffen. He has staged a wide range of opera and plays by Molière, Goldoni, Shakespeare, Feydeau, and many other playwrights all over the German-speaking world, into which he interpolates comic routines and elaborate musical numbers. His original pieces are innovative and iconoclastic comic exercises that veer sharply from text-based theatre, mixing gorgeously dissimilar scenic, gestural, and musical vocabularies. All feature Fritsch's own scene design and several are based on writings, songs, and performances of twentieth-century experimental artists who, like him, defy categorization. Yet for those well acquainted with Castorf's Volksbühne, Fritsch's very rebellion against its norms ironically marks the legitimacy of his claim to an oversize piece of the theatre's legacy. For what are Fritsch's comic routines if not a hyper-theatrical variation on what Matt Cornish describes as Castorf's political *lazzi*, the "pratfalls, wordplay, and practical jokes" that satirize "the ruling elite"?[17]

In the post-Castorf theatre landscape, Fritsch, despite—or more likely, because of—his popularity, and the unbridled pleasure his work produces, makes some critics nervous.[18] Or he is dismissed by those who, embarrassed by his actors' over-the-top performances, brand him, in his own words, nothing more than "an animal trainer."[19] These negative evaluations of Fritsch's work are, I believe, a result of his sometimes unnerving conversion of farce into tragedy, tragedy into farce, surface into depth, sorrow into joy. Most important, they signal critics' reluctance to value Fritsch's scandalous habit of joyfully deconstructing the binary opposition between art and entertainment.

Despite the prominence of social satire in Fritsch's work, he steers clear of both the impulsively political theatre that was the rule at the Volksbühne and the more recent turn in Germany to a literalist, sober, confrontational theatre, which Christopher Balme describes as post-fictional.[20] This documentary theatre, as exemplified by the work of Thomas Ostermeier, Rimini Protokoll, Lola Arias, and Milo Rau, is committed to a renunciation of exuberance and spectacle in favor of history, simulacra, and facticity. Because Ostermeier and Rau are the only major German directors whose work has been shown in New York since 2015, most New York theatregoers have no idea that there is a profusion of head-turning, fiercely contemporary new music theatre being made in the German-speaking world that is much more closely related to US musical theatre idioms than the rarefied post-fictional work of Ostermeier and company. It remains a mystery to me why none of this innovative musical theatre has been imported to New York. Instead of Fritsch and Marthaler, New York gets Broadway musicals and classics in "well-upholstered revivals,"[21] directed by British directors, which are decidedly old-fashioned and doggedly refuse to bring these works into conversation with contemporary politics and culture.

Given Anglophone readers' likely unfamiliarity with Fritsch's music theatre, I want to dive into it and splash around, following the lead of the performers in his farewell to the Volksbühne, *Pfusch* (2016). In the final scene of that piece (which spreads eleven battered upright pianos across the orchestra pit), a large swimming pool materializes center stage, complete with diving board, which the actors fill with blue, grapefruit-sized styrofoam "ice" cubes, and into which they repeatedly dive. The piece, whose title means botch or bungle, represents a perverse thank you to Claus Peymann, then artistic director of the Berliner Ensemble, who, after seeing *The Beaver Coat* in 2011, was quoted as saying, "Fritsch is a great actor. He's funny and cheeky, but that [production] was bellowed, amateurish folly. It's stupid, loud and silly. It was frightful, pure mayhem."[22] Fritschian mayhem is precisely the wondrous domain I am mapping, starting with a wide-angle view of the sights and disquieting sounds and then moving in for close-ups of three music theatre pieces that progress along a trajectory from more or less conventional to explosively unconventional. The first is a musical comedy, *Der schwarze Hecht* (The black pike, 2014); the second an iconoclastic jukebox musical, *Wer hat Angst vor Hugo Wolf?* (Who's afraid of Hugo Wolf?, 2016); and the third a wholly original play with music, *Zelt* (Tent, 2019), that employs an almost neo-classical structure to breach the frontier between sense and non-sense.

The Fritschian Cocktail

Herbert Fritsch was born in 1951 into a working-class Bavarian household in Augsburg, Bertolt Brecht's hometown, and as a young man was "programmed to crash."[23] Hanging out in Munich bars with US servicemen during the 1960s, he became a petty thief, vagabond, and junkie who, attempting one night to break into a pharmacy, was finally nabbed by the police. Pitied by a sympathetic judge, he enrolled in theatre school in Munich to avoid a prison sentence and started acting professionally in 1980 in Heidelberg. But he was frustrated because, in his words, "they always told me, 'you have to be real, you have to be really Herbert.' I said, 'What? I don't know who I am.'"[24] Fritsch developed his signature comedic style during the early 1980s in his self-produced *Null-Shows* (zero shows), in which he "did everything that was not allowed at the theatre," walking out on stage for ninety minutes with "no preparation, no rehearsals, no consideration beforehand about what I was going to do and no articulate language—just sounds." Despite his lanky frame and expressive and graceful manner off-stage, his solo performance, he recalls, became "a real high-frequency grimace show."[25] In 1989, he teamed up for the first time with Frank Castorf, the "first director who really appreciated" his style of performance.[26] For his debut with Castorf, he played a masturbating Mellefont in Castorf's controversial production of the first German bourgeois tragedy, Lessing's *Miss Sara Sampson* (1989), which used the Beatles' "Why Don't We Do It in the Road?" as a leitmotif and was the first Castorf production invited to the Theatertreffen.[27] After Castorf was appointed artistic director of the Volksbühne in 1992, Fritsch followed him to Berlin and remained a leading actor there until 2007.

It is challenging to translate or explicate writings about Fritsch's work as actor and director because critics, and Fritsch himself, employ odd, whimsical colloquialisms and untranslatable compound words. This untranslatability, however, does not disguise the fact that the work itself is unusually international in its sources of inspiration and often speaks a kind of gestural and affective Esperanto. Although comedy is typically more socially contingent, topical, and local in its references than serious drama, Fritsch's influences and points of reference—the Marx Brothers, Jacques Tati, Laurel and Hardy, Charlie Chaplin, Karl Valentin, Jerry Lewis, Loriot, Peter Sellers, and Monty Python—represent an unusually cosmopolitan crew. To these sources of inspiration must be added the historical avant-garde, both the early twentieth-century and post–World War II avant-gardes. Like the performances associated with Dada, surrealism, abstract expressionism, Fluxus, and the Vienna Actionists, Fritsch's pieces trespass borders and defy generic categories. Because he has trained a group of virtuoso, scenery-chewing actors (including Wolfram Koch, Bastian Reiber, Carol Schuler, and Florian Anders) who are uniquely capable of co-creating Fritschian slapstick. Fritsch sees his work as "a liberation from directing. It is the work of actors who develop a piece together. The confrontations among themselves, the electricity and the tension they generate, those are the decisive points.... That makes for a strong feeling for life."[28] That passionate feeling for life guarantees that Fritsch's work, like a bloody mary or screwdriver, produces a vertiginous light-headedness that makes even staid audiences giddy.

Although I cannot quite unmix the Fritschian cocktail, I will try to itemize the recipe by detailing several of its ingredients: scene design, costumes, and music. When Fritsch plans a production, he starts with the scenic and spatial concept, sometimes even before he knows which play he will be directing. As he explains, "the first thing I think: 'empty space.' With nothing, show everything."[29] Typically, his designs feature a dynamic play of deeply saturated colors, geometric forms, shiny or shimmering surfaces, washes of brightly colored light, sliding wings, concealed trampolines, flying equipment, and gigantic, out-of-scale props and pieces of furniture. Some of his works, such as *Murmel Murmel* (Volksbühne, 2012), use dynamic scenic elements to re-imagine a traditional wing-and-drop set as a funhouse of brightly colored frames constantly closing in and moving out. *Der die mann* (Volksbühne, 2015) features a giant yellow gramophone horn and a set of bright red stairs, rotating on the Volksbühne's shiny, sky-blue turntable. His realization of Dürrenmatt's *The Physicists* (Schauspielhaus Zurich, 2013) makes the entire stage into an enormous, padded cell with bile green walls and floor in which the three titular, deluded, homicidal scientists are locked.

Fritsch's ability to construct surrealist stage pictures is facilitated by Victoria Behr's larger-than-life costumes that magnify period details to the point of absurdity, installing a bird cage (with stuffed bird!) in the oversize woman's Louis XVI–style wig sported by the manservant Alain (*School for Wives*, 2014), or dressing 1960s-style Mad Men in brightly colored rubber suits, shiny transparent masks, and lacquered hair (*der die mann*). Her candy-colored costumes and wigs are often so elaborate and gargantuan, so overloaded with frilly details, that they make the actors look like grimacing scarecrows encased in ruffled sarcophagi. These oversize costumes almost demand that the resulting awkwardness and artificiality of their movement be transformed into lumpy, looney, slithery choreography.

The ceaseless dance of Fritsch's performers is ceaselessly attended by a sound carpet, that is, musical underscoring that runs in counterpoint with the action onstage and erupts into songs or sometimes even into a sound volcano. Fritsch has long been adamant that the term "spoken theatre" (*Sprechtheater*) is odious and that music theatre is a tautology. All theatre, he points out, is music theatre because language, with its rhythm and melody, is always music, just as all "acting is singing and dancing."[30] Because Fritsch has always loved "the extreme gestures of opera and ballet," he told his *Doll's House*'s cast that even without singing, they should "make it an opera."[31] Despite this directive, his work is invested less in reinventing opera than in musicalizing speech and enwrapping it in music in unpredictable ways to create "a new culture of using speech onstage." This style is intensely musicalized but "not recitative," and he points to Chinese opera as a prototype for "this singing-speaking."[32] His production of Thomas Bernhard's *Die Jagdgesellschaft* (The hunting party, 2022) follows through with this by featuring two actors dressed in Chinese opera–style costumes and make-up who impersonate and intone the lines of the Prince and Princess in pseudo-Chinese style.

In many of Fritsch's pieces, a more direct point of comparison than Chinese opera might be the musical. His version of Molière's *Amphitryon*, for example, has an elaborate score by Ingo Günther, composer, musical director, and keyboardist, which ingeniously multiplies the doppelgängers in this comedy of mistaken identities. Just as Jupiter and Mercury become the doubles of the men whose wives they covet, the live music juxtaposes two not-quite doubles, a piano and vibraphone, on either side of the stage, whose teasing, antiphonal counterpoint echoes Molière's. The climactic scene in the first part of the play, the explosive re-meeting of Alcmene with the real Amphitryon, is staged as if it were a Broadway-style, Act 1 finale in which the comedic misery of the confrontation between wife and husband is turned into elaborate song and dance. Starting as a pseudo-blues for Alcmene, the number is quickly picked up by Amphitryon and echoed by their comic servants, who make it a spirited quartet whose descending minor-mode refrain becomes an increasingly impassioned, if parodic, cri de coeur.

Ingo Günther has been Fritsch's most frequent musical collaborator, whose sometimes pungent, sometimes noisily percussive scores are clearly inspired by musical minimalism, while maintaining a jazz-inflected pop sensibility. Although Günther has written numerous discrete numbers for Fritsch plays, he also puts together elaborate set-pieces whose musical idiom and form are more difficult to parse. The most uninhibited is a twelve-minute percussive interlude for eleven upright pianos in *Pfusch* that requires actors to hammer away rhythmically at the keyboards, producing slowly changing harmonies that suggest a maddening, infernal, fortissimo, partly aleatoric reimagining of a Steve Reich piece crossed with Stravinsky's *Le Sacre du printemps*.[33] Günther's musical minimalism is always in sync with Fritsch's physical comedy, converting humans to machine-like creatures, a conversion that is as unnerving as it is droll. Most Fritsch productions feature extended comic routines of repeated twitches, winces, shudders, contortions, and double takes that become extended, minimalist themes and variations. Because Fritsch's gestural rhapsodies are only intermittently pantomimic, they become a kind of pure performance poetry entwined with musical scoring that refuses to play the subordinate, illustrative role usually given to incidental music.

Fritsch's production of the human as not-quite machine (as refracted by Günther's minimalist scores) is evident not only in the gestural rhapsodies he engineers but also in his habitual multiplication of near clones (Figure 5.2). All his original pieces feature multiple versions of selves, such as the seven Beatle-lookalikes in *der die mann*, the eleven ballerinas in *Murmel Murmel*, the thirteen swimmers in *Pfusch*, or the twenty-three janitors in *Zelt*. The uniform identity of Fritsch's packs of selves is often redoubled by his use of highly reflective stage surfaces that turn floors into mirrors. This replication of clones is emphasized by the near-identical costumes that sometimes suppress gender difference. The suppression is especially noticeable because it both emphasizes and undermines the unambiguous gender identity of the Beatle or ballerina being modeled. Most important, these packs of selves seem both conscious of and slightly uncomfortable with their doppelgängers. As a result, each is always making a noticeable effort to blend, to be one of the crowd, which requires that they forget their theatricalized attire and mode of behavior.

The proliferation of doubles also problematizes collective action, revealing the social and personal anxiety that troubles the romance of community, which historically has long been a central theme in musical theatre.

Figure 5.2 The ensemble as identical Vegas crooners in *Wer hat Angst vor Hugo Wolf?*, directed by Herbert Fritsch, Schauspielhaus, Zürich, 2016. Photo by Matthias Horn.

Reluctant or unable to conform, a performer will often, seemingly involuntarily, step forward to take stage and launch into a song or comic routine—or cadenza—only to be scolded by the others for the failure, or refusal, to disappear into the pack. These packs pay perverse homage to the unnervingly cheery uniformity of the chorus line in musical theatre, as epitomized by the mechanical precision of the Busby Berkeley chorus girls.

Although my description of Fritsch's music theatre might make it seem dauntingly esoteric, Fritsch is one of the few acclaimed German directors unafraid to be called an entertainer (*Unterhaltungskünstler*).[34] Indeed, he prides himself on making "full-steam-ahead theatre," which is "radically artificial, slapstick, [and] anarchic," and shamelessly embraces popular music.[35] In addition to underscoring, song is always foregrounded in Fritsch's productions, as if he were taking the conventions of operetta and musical theatre and overlaying them on absurdist drama. Indeed, his comic routines are really arias or set pieces, even if no vocalization is involved. Unlike Marthaler, with his rarefied mix of esoteric and popular, Fritsch is sometimes distrusted by the guardians of German high culture who gatekeep far more assiduously than their US-American counterparts. Indeed, the raucous laughter

Fritsch's work generates leads some people, he points out, to accuse him of "extreme superficiality."[36] Despite the long history of farce, going back to Aristophanes, as political and social critique and its more recent reinvention, in the hands of Samuel Beckett, as tragedy, critics and scholars almost invariably disparage comedy and laughter as trivial. In Germany, in particular, the disdain displayed by both theatre scholars and musicologists toward the lighter muse is linked, as Susan McClary points out, to the failure on the part of "the Fathers of Aesthetic Theory ... to recognize the Hilarious among their types, thus condemning us to unrelieved earnestness in the arts." As a result, work by directors like Fritsch, as well as entire genres, notably musicals and operettas, get "consigned to the trash heap."[37]

Fritsch's work makes the maintenance of cultural hierarchy almost impossible. Like a fun-house reflection of the Broadway musical, it turns classic source materials (plays, stories, songs, or other texts) into fodder for entertainment by soaking them in music and visuals that have a direct, if complex affective force. Perhaps Fritsch's most extravagant transformation of a classic into a song-and-dance fest is his production of Carlo Goldoni's *Trilogie der Sommerfrische* (usually translated as *The Holiday Trilogy*, 2014), which he made into a jukebox musical, with Carsten Meyer at the keyboard, based on the songs of the 1960s Italian pop singer-songwriter Gino Paoli. Fritsch's biting realization of Goldoni's elaborately plotted social satire unleashes grotesquely posturing, platinum-wigged, lobster-red sunburnt bodies on Paoli's infectious tunes almost like a diabolical version of *Mamma Mia!* The jet setters, gyrating in front of vibrating, psychedelic Kenneth Noland or Gerhard Richter–like striped backdrops, try to live *la dolce vita*, but instead betray the pervasive greed, lust, and corruption that make their class tick. In other words, the emptiness that is all too palpable behind their gloriously musical shenanigans exemplifies the horror and "despair" that underlie Fritsch's comedy.[38]

To realize the complex musicality of his work, Fritsch exploits one of the great benefits of the German state-subsidized system by mixing performers from different institutional realms. His Zurich *King Arthur* cast the prominent actor Wolfram Koch in the title role, while his original works performed in theatres showcase trained opera singers and stalwarts of the Fritschian universe, notably Ruth Rosenfeld and Hubert Wild. These mixtures of personnel underline the difficulty of classifying so much of his work. Perhaps a work such as his *King Arthur* is best understood as musical comedy run amok, a celebration of a hydra-headed theatricality that delights in disjoining genres and showcasing both its own performative excess and the dedicated actor/singers who make the piece live.

Avant-Gardist Mythmaking

Fritsch's weakness for clowns, as well as his campaign against reason, representational art, and generic differences, links him to a long tradition of German low comedy, from the clown Hanswurst and Viennese nineteenth-century farceur Johann Nestroy to Karl Valentin (1882–1948), the Bavarian comedian, clown, film and cabaret performer, and "celebrator . . . of illogic, subversion and chaos."[39] In *Valentin* (2017), Fritsch collaborated with jazz fusion composer Michael Wertmüller on one of his most elaborate through-composed pieces. Putting Valentin's routines through a theatrical food mill, Fritsch's spectacle employs an austere yet mobile wing-and-drop set composed of huge sheets of brown packing paper. The piece represents a homage to the same Valentin whom Bertolt Brecht hailed as "the man he learned most from" and with whom he collaborated in the early 1920s. Brecht especially prized Valentin's performance of "short sketches in which he played recalcitrant employees, orchestral musicians or photographers, who hated their employers and made them look ridiculous."[40] According to one of Brecht's associates, Valentin's performances, which aimed "to jolt his audience out of the past," made Brecht "shriek . . . with laughter"[41] and were decisive in helping Brecht develop his theory of *Verfremdung* (estrangement).[42] Fritsch's *Valentin*, which features eleven actors and a fifteen-piece, mostly brass ensemble has an extremely eclectic score that mixes progressive jazz, operetta, Bach chorale, and *Schlager*. Its last ten minutes suggests that the piece is at heart an elegy for Valentin's heyday, the Weimar Republic, as the brown paper borders rise and fall dramatically like storm clouds in a baroque theatre while the actors and band, seemingly oblivious to the coming tempest, march to Robert Stolz's rousing "Adieu, mein kleiner Gardeoffizier" (Goodbye, my little guardsman, 1930).

Valentin's transformation of articulate speech into a Dada sound poem is not the exception but the rule in Fritsch's own pieces. Language does not evaporate, but is used more for its music than its sense. Of all his pieces, *Murmel Murmel* (which followed *Die (s)panische Fliege* at the Volksbühne) is perhaps the most extreme, a play whose text consists solely of one German word, "Murmel," meaning a toy marble, the verb murmur, an abbreviation of *Murmeltier* (marmot), the trench coat–wearing private-eye dog Murmel in *The Mumbly Cartoon Show* (1976–1977), or more colloquially, a testicle. Over the course of the piece's eighty minutes, the word is intoned, screamed, whispered, sung, stretched, chewed, swallowed, burped, and spit out. Fritsch's mise en scène ensures that the audience's focus is not on the word's meaning but the innumerable ways of turning it into a verbal gesture, routine, or showstopper. Unlike most musicals, *Murmel Murmel* does not have a plot. It is, rather, the realization of a piece of concrete poetry by the German-Swiss artist Dieter Roth (1930–1998). Associated with Fluxus and the Vienna Actionists, the "chameleonlike" Roth produced a "torrent of work" in countless media but was best known for his artist's books, such as his 1961 "Literature Sausage," a framed, chopped book pressed into the shape of a sausage.[43] His "most notorious show in the United States" was the 1970 "Steeple Cheese (A Race)" that consisted of thirty-seven suitcases of cheese that were left in a Los Angeles gallery to decompose "over the duration of the show." In this and other still lifes, Roth "brought 'dead nature' perversely back to life"[44] and all his works stage a dark, anarchic, compulsive energy. They also blur the boundaries between installation and performance, organic and inorganic, art and garbage.

Dieter Roth's 1974 book, *Murmel*, is composed of 176 pages filled with the obsessive repetition of a single word, "murmel." But it is typeset to resemble a conventional play, complete with characters and speeches—except that the only "character" is named Murmel and the only "speech" is represented by columns and columns of "murmel." Fritsch met Roth during the 1980s and promised to stage the play, a promise he fulfilled by doubling Roth's title and turning his poetry into a "very strict composition" of "acoustic wallpaper patterns." Fritsch points out that "the graphic arrangement of Dieter Roth's text creates a certain rhythmic structure" that is emphasized by the pulse of Ingo Günther's quasi-minimalist, eclectic musical score.[45] Rather than superimpose a plot onto Roth's poem, Fritsch uses the text to make "extreme emotional and physical demands" of his eleven actors. "We cannot make beautiful scenes of dialogue out of it, which would betray the 'murmel' structure." "Scenes inevitably arise," he notes, "but the idea is to attempt not only the anti-psychological but also the anti-scenic."[46]

Murmel Murmel is far more entertaining than one might expect from perusing Roth's granitic text. It is also the most widely traveled of Fritsch's pieces, having toured across Europe and played at the Edinburgh Festival. But it has never been imported to the United States. An exercise in theatrical virtuosity requiring athletic, hyper-kinetic performers, *Murmel Murmel* is in three parts, with costume changes between each part. Fritsch's kaleidoscopic set is fashioned of variously colored, horizontal and vertical sliding panels that at times approximate a proscenium stage; at others, a set of nested frames or boxes; at others, a collection of sliding screens. Given its many possible configurations, it sometimes evokes an animated, three-dimensional version of a Josef Albers or Kenneth Noland painting and makes use of both artists' bright color palettes. In Part 1, the actors are dressed like 1960s trendsetters whose louche poses call to mind cool jazz "swingers." The action and music alternate between solos, pastiches of super-hip quasi-pop songs, and tutti, the actors relishing the physical contortions, poses, and mugging. Most memorably, they repeatedly stumble and fall into the orchestra pit, onto a hidden trampoline, bouncing up or crawling back on stage to continue the show, their nonchalance undisturbed (Figure 5.3). In Part 2, they enter as mock ballerinas in tutus but soon shed their tutus and don neutral masks to become the mimes who annoy tourists in city parks and then parodic versions of the balletic dancers populating pretentious companies like Pilobolus or Momix. In Part 3, they reappear as near clones in black pants with skinny

Figure 5.3 Simon Jensen falls into the abyss. *Murmel Murmel*, directed by Herbert Fritsch, Volksbühne am Rosa-Luxemburg-Platz, 2012. Photo by Thomas Aurin.

ties, bald-pate wigs, and glasses, each singing and playing a melodica (or blow-organ, a wind instrument with a keyboard). Lined up across the stage, they become a super-syncopated, Marx Brothers version of the Comedian Harmonists, the German, all-male, close-harmony vocal ensemble that was internationally renowned in the late 1920s and early 1930s. *Murmel Murmel* ends with an elaborately staged curtain call that, like Dieter Roth's own work, represents a carnival of creativity and reinvention.

A Zombie Musical

Unlike *Valentin* and *Murmel Murmel*, which fashion their own unique musical theatre hybrids, Fritsch's production of *Der schwarze Hecht* by Paul Burkhard is a bona fide musical comedy. Although it is not exactly a repertory staple even in its native Switzerland, this *musikalische Komödie* did produce the first Swiss global hit and make its composer world famous.[47] To celebrate its seventy-fifth birthday, Herbert Fritsch was invited in 2014 to direct it at the Schauspielhaus Zurich, the house in which it premiered in 1939. The musical, written in Swiss German dialect with book and lyrics by Jürg Amstein, is based on a 1927 dialect comedy, *De sächzgischt Giburtstag* (The sixtieth birthday) by Emil Sautter. Its claim to international renown, however, dates back to 1950 when it was adapted into High German by Robert Gilbert and Erik Charell, who, as producer and director, had acquired hands-on knowledge of Broadway musical comedy during his emigration to the United States during the Third Reich. The adaptation became a hit in Munich as *Das Feuerwerk* (Fireworks) and was produced shortly thereafter in Paris and London. Although it is sometimes referenced as the last German-language operetta to become part of the standard repertoire,[48] it is now commonly called a musical comedy.[49] It was filmed in 1954 (as *Feuerwerk*), with Romy Schneider and Lilli Palmer in the starring roles, but it owes its celebrity to its bittersweet theme song "O mein Papa," which became a German hit for the Swiss singer Lys Assia in 1950 and then a number one worldwide hit for Eddie Fisher in 1954 as "Oh! My Papa." Given Burkhard's gifts as musical dramatist, songwriter, and orchestrator, there is far more of interest in the piece than its hit song.

Der schwarze Hecht is a more craggy, less sentimental piece than *Feuerwerk*, which tames, romanticizes, and domesticates the Swiss original. In all versions, however, the piece thematizes the conflict between high and low, stuffy bourgeois mores and the freedom and creativity of an artistic life. Its plot centers on Anna, the daughter of the rich, conservative industrialist Albert Oberholzer, who is celebrating his sixtieth birthday with a feast of roasted pike, freshly hooked by a young fisherman, to which celebration he has invited his bumptious brothers and their affected wives. Just as they sit down to dinner, Albert's renegade brother Alois, the black sheep of the family, accompanied by his exotic Eastern European wife Iduna, returns after an absence of thirty years to offer birthday greetings. Going by the name Ringmaster Obolski, he and the captivating Iduna run a traveling circus, which the family shuns as tasteless and vulgar, blind to the fact that the entertainers are in fact the most cultured and attractive figures in the piece (Figure 5.4). They are so seductive that the men gather like flies around Iduna while Alois completely charms the young Anna with the prospect of a glamorous circus life. At the end of the Act 1, she falls asleep and imagines what might happen if she ran away to join the circus. Act 2 is her dream—or nightmare—in which her relatives rematerialize as circus animals and clowns. When she wakes, to a smoking, charred, blackened pike that the

Figure 5.4 Hubert Wild, center right, as circus Ringmaster Obolski and Ruth Rosenfeld, upper left, as his wife Iduna. Paul Burkhard's *Der schwarze Hecht* (The black pike, 1939), directed by Herbert Fritsch, Schauspielhaus, Zürich, 2014. Photo by Matthias Horn.

distracted cook left too long on the fire, she reluctantly decides to remain at home, settling for a tame domestic life with the young fisherman.

Like many other musicals from the 1930s and 1940s, *Der schwarze Hecht* (as well as *Das Feuerwerk*) features extensive dream sequences that become the theatrical highlights of the piece. Like the late Rodgers and Hart musicals, *Oklahoma!*, *Carousel*, and *Lady in the Dark*, *Der schwarze Hecht* uses the dream as a pretext to stage a spectacle of de-repression that allows a character to acknowledge and wrestle with fantasies, forgotten memories, and disavowed desires. While the Rodgers musicals typically offer the dream as a ballet, *Der schwarze Hecht* devotes an entire act to Anna's fantasies. Most important, the dream in all these works is more than just a character's private vision; it is also an opportunity for the creators to turn the world upside down, to exploit the extravagance and resources of the musical theatre, and the joys (and terrors) of de-repression, on both individual and societal levels. As a plot device, the dream sequence engineers a break with continuity and logic, rationality and sobriety, and allows the flights of musical and theatrical fantasy that historically have been crucial in making the musical so alluring.

Lady in the Dark, opening a year and a half after *Der schwarze Hecht*, makes an especially instructive point of comparison. With its extravagant second act "Circus Dream," *Lady* embraces its Freudian framework by using dreams to work through repressed memories. Although *Der schwarze Hecht* does not attempt the same catharsis, its opening night program observes that through the piece, "psychoanalytical theory lightheartedly and innocently enters the world of the old magic opera."[50] Its entrance, however, is less innocent than the writer supposes. Rather than Freud, Freud's erstwhile student Carl Jung makes a more apposite interlocutor. Like Burkhard and Sautter, Jung lived and worked in Zurich and *Der schwarze Hecht* teems with Jungian archetypes and masks. The gist of the musical is the recasting, through theatrical prestidigitation, of the insufferable relatives as clowns and circus animals, the men clothed in "glittering harlequin costumes instead of dusty frock coats," the women in corsets and short skirts "instead of expansive crinolines."[51] Fritsch highlights this transposition, illustrating Jung's "shadow," which, Jung argues, hides behind the socially acceptable mask and represents "the primitive and inferior man with his desires and emotions." In *Psychology and Religion* (1938), Jung notes that "the less [the shadow] is embodied in the individual's conscious life, the blacker and denser it is." In other words, the more deeply repressed, the more dangerous, "liable to burst forth in a moment of unawareness." Importantly, however, the shadow is not only dangerous; its very "childish or primitive qualities" could "in a way vitalize and embellish human existence." But, Jung adds ruefully, "'it is not done.'"[52] Anna's dream provides precisely the occasion to do what is not done in polite society, licensing an orgy of farcical terror, the kind in which Herbert Fritsch has long specialized.

Although Fritsch repeatedly satirizes the haute bourgeoisie in his work, his portrait of the Oberholzers is particularly vicious. Taking his cue from circus and horror movies, he turns the celebration into a "zombie birthday party"[53] by transmuting Albert's sixtieth birthday into his 101st. Albert's superannuation permits him to wander around the stage like a senile ghost, and suggests to one critic that Fritsch's comedy is in fact a portrait of "a society on the verge of dementia,"[54] from which not even Obolski and Iduna can escape. Yet Fritsch judiciously retains the piece's wonderfully inventive and tuneful score, in Roman Vinuesa's arrangement for two pianos, accordion, clarinet, and cello, "which magically brings [it] to life."[55] The sweetly infectious songs give the production its hinge, as it swings back and forth between nostalgic fantasy and dark, satiric comedy. The songs for the family members and Kattri, the cook, are delivered in a throaty, full-blooded style, as if they had been borrowed from *The Threepenny Opera*. But once Ringmaster Obolski and Iduna enter, everything changes. Looking like a fairy-tale or operetta prince and princess, they are musical virtuosos as well as acrobats of the ring. Obolski (Hubert Wild) is a baritone who can easily soar into falsetto range while Iduna (Ruth Rosenfeld) is a legitimate soprano with seductive vocal skills. The agility and sheer beauty of their voices provide an operetta-style antidote to the ongoing horror show while Iduna's "O mein Papa" mesmerizes the party guests. Like a snake-charmer or lion-tamer, she sings her moving tribute to her father—"who was a wonderful clown, . . . a great artist"—so beautifully that the partygoers have no choice but to join her in the refrain. Just before the end of the first act, Anna gets so carried away by the dream of circus magic that she goes into a trance, lights on to the trapeze, and the curtain falls.

Like a drunken excursion to the big top, the second act of Fritsch's *Der schwarze Hecht* turns the birthday party into "a dynamic orgy of colors and shapes" that "beguiles and stuns."[56] The original *Der schwarze Hecht* ends with the departure of the circus, the end of carnival, and Anna's return, however reluctantly, to normality. Like most every other theatrical dream (going back to *A Midsummer Night's Dream*), it ends with an awakening. But Fritsch's production awakens from the nightmare only reluctantly and never fully restores the status quo, thereby "elegantly bypass[ing] the moralizing conclusion of the original."[57] Instead, the fisherman Marinello, who at the beginning had wrestled the oversize pike as if it were an alligator, returns in Act 2 costumed as Iduna's prized black circus pony. When Anna's dream reaches its harrowing climax, and Alois and Iduna are about to saw her in half, the pony screams to stop them—and save her. Thus begins a musical comedy finale turned inside out. The pony silently strips off his costume to disclose a gold-glittered body and, like a mute Prince Charming (or ominous deus ex machina), walks over to Anna, kisses her, and vacantly takes her hand. She then sweetly sings to him the poignant, melancholy ballad, "Anna's Love Song," "Es wird mir heiß und kalt" (I get hot and cold), which is less a celebration of coupledom than an expression of continued yearning, while the firelight flickers on the rest of the cast, standing upstage immobilized with the blackened fish. At the song's conclusion, the pair skip away a little too merrily and stand in the bright red glow of the fake fire over which the pike had been roasting, looking as if they had taken a detour to hell. The musical ends with the coughing revelers carrying the smoking, scorched fish, while the ingeniously negligent cook, Kattri, sings the title song. There is a blinding flash of light, which cues the characters to disappear behind a moving wallpaper flat as the now white-lit stage returns us to mundane reality.

The surrealistic circus in *Der schwarze Hecht* is unique in Fritsch's work, a show-within-a-show that suggests that the real subject of Fritsch's musical is the theatre itself as a site of creative destruction, a place of fantasy, music, and de-inhibition. In that sense, *Hecht* is one of Fritsch's most self-reflexive works, and the program note by dramaturg Sabrina Zwach emphasizes the parallels between the actual circus and the "Fritschian circus" or "artist-family," made up of costumers, actors, singers, musicians, and dramaturgs. Both circuses evince an "artificiality" that is predicated on exaggeration, acrobatics, and diegetic song. Both demand artists who are magicians, clowns, and contortionists, and honor the dictum that "no idea can be too stupid as long as it is funny." Intriguingly, Zwach also stresses the danger that underpins both "systems," the fact that Fritsch "in his productions always draws his bow string back dangerously far" while withdrawing the safety net, for both actors and audiences.[58] In its zeal to create and destroy, moreover, Fritsch's *Hecht* also perversely references and reflects upon the founding monument of modern music theatre, *The Ring of the Nibelungs*. Like *Das Rheingold*, it begins with the creation of the world, a four-minute-long, arpeggiated E-flat major chord, as the characters slowly materialize in shimmering, deep blue light, and it ends with what looks like a funeral pyre for the central couple who represent the throbbing hearts of both works. In Fritsch's *Ring*, however, Brünnhilde is a mean girl, Siegfried a mannequin, Wotan a doddering, senile patriarch, and the food of the gods an immolated fish.

Liederabend or Jukebox Musical?

If *Der schwarze Hecht* turns musical comedy into a circus nightmare, *Wer hat Angst vor Hugo Wolf?* takes a hatchet to the songbook of one of the most innovative and challenging composers of classic German lieder. Indeed, Hugo Wolf (1860–1903) is the only composer whose work Herbert Fritsch has used as the basis for a wholly original piece. It has musical direction and arrangements by Ruth Rosenfeld (also one of the singing actors) and Carsten Meyer (also at the keyboard), impersonating an impossible combination of John Cage, Elvis Presley, Frank Zappa, Burt Bacharach, and Elton John. The piece turns the epigrammatic Wolf into the cool dude of the German lied while demonstrating a perverse understanding of and respect for the composer's unique modus operandi. Staged liederabends have become increasingly fashionable among classically trained singers attempting to brand themselves theatrical and adventurous, yet *Wer hat Angst vor Hugo Wolf?* is very atypical. The arrangements are often startlingly different from Wolf's own, with a liberal use of formulas associated with popular rather than classical music (dance rhythms, syncopated vamps, added tone chords), as well as bossa nova, cha-cha-cha, and boogie-woogie. However, because, as Eric Sams writes, Wolf's "melodic lines are rarely complex" and his "music is notable for its concord," his songs arguably lend themselves more readily to musical popularization than those of most other lieder composers.[59] The seven female vocalists and male pianist also at times transform into a band, playing ukulele, recorders, do-it-yourself percussion, and using extended piano techniques. If Wolf's songs were better known, I would claim that the piece's eclecticism and inventive use of popular styles make it a jukebox musical, but audiences are unlikely to exit the theatre humming the tunes.

Hugo Wolf, whose "songs are more often praised than sung,"[60] was the most esoteric and eccentric of classic lieder composers. Even his most sympathetic critics, like Susan Youens, admit that his music is "a 'hard sell'" both to performers and audiences "who might prefer less taxing strains."[61] Sams maintains that "music-lovers" are by no means "unanimous about whether it is enjoyable" and that Wolf's songs in fact "seem nicely calculated to put people off."[62] Thus Fritsch and company have good reason to ask: who's afraid of Hugo Wolf? Rather than bluntly answer the question, they at once amplify "Wölfie's own howl"[63] while wrapping it in popular styles. A master of concision, Wolf wrote a corpus of songs that is complex, contradictory, and elusive, and after his death he became known, Youens explains, "as 'the Poet's Composer,' someone who cared more about poetry, served it more faithfully, delved into it more deeply than other lieder composers."[64] His songs, moreover, use finely tuned harmonies, Lawrence Kramer notes, "not so much [to] 'express' the text as scrutinize it," enveloping the voice, on "the model of Wagnerian music-drama," in "extratextual non-vocal music that may incorporate, but always transcends, the point of view embodied in that voice."[65] This critical distance made Wolf uniquely skilled at writing *Rollenlieder* (role songs), sung by characters, as well as comic songs whose wit is dramatized by weird harmonic shifts and surprising accompaniments. During a period when humor "was to be found primarily in operettas, waltz songs, or children's songs," Wolf gave his comic songs "a psychological slant,"[66] lightness, and complex play of irony that makes those of his contemporaries, Mahler and Strauss, sound labored by comparison. Fritsch and company (not surprisingly) focus on these comic songs, foregrounding the words and sometimes even stripping poems of their music (including texts by Goethe and Lenau not set by Wolf) and presenting them as monologues or prologues to songs. This formula repeats Wolf's own practice in recital of pointing up "the interrelationship of music and poetry by prefacing the performance of each of his lieder with a recitation of its text," thereby staging "the lied as a reproduction of meaning and figuratively re-enact[ing] its composition."[67]

Wer hat Angst vor Hugo Wolf? echoes the reflexivity of Wolf's own performances by theatricalizing every song. With the exception of Ruth Rosenfeld, all the vocalists are known primarily as actors and their style of vocal production is decidedly non-operatic, exemplifying the "singing-speaking" that Fritsch so values. More daringly, the piece underscores the violence at the heart of the lied that Wolf himself articulated in an 1896 letter: "There is something cruel in the intimate amalgamation of poetry and music, although actually only the latter plays the cruel role. There is definitely something vampiric about the music."[68] Fritsch's liederabend takes the composer at his word by emphasizing the Gothic elements, which, when combined with occasional howling on the part of the actors, reminds audiences that the composer's surname also describes the *Canis lupus*, the feral, carnivorous relative of man's best friend. Even the *Frankfurter*

Allgemeine could not resist multiplying wolf references by punningly observing that Fritsch's "synesthetic nonsense-music theatre" puts "Hugo Wolf's heartfelt ballads through the meat grinder" (*Fleischwolf*).[69] The violence that *Wer hat Angst vor Hugo Wolf?* wreaks on the classic liederabend, however, is partially assuaged by the piece's "breathtaking craftmanship"[70] and musicality. It is also aestheticized by the piece's simple scenic concept, which teasingly references Barnett Newman's cycle of four paintings, "Who's Afraid of Red, Yellow and Blue" (1966–1970), whose title in turn teasingly references Edward Albee's 1962 play, *Who's Afraid of Virginia Woolf?* Fritsch's scene design, with its rotating, lacquered slabs of red, yellow, and blue on the Schauspielhaus' large turntable, reimagines Newman's paintings in three (or four) dimensions, while at the same time restoring a Wo(o)lf to the title. Newman's large canvases with their vertical stripes are usually considered his late masterpieces and epitomize his turn from surrealism to an abstract, "exalted," sublime art, "freed of the impediments of memory, association, nostalgia, legend, myth."[71]

Wer hat Angst vor Hugo Wolf?'s prototypical musical reference is of course the song "Who's Afraid of the Big, Bad Wolf?" (by Frank Churchill and Ann Ronell) from the classic 1933 Walt Disney cartoon, *Three Little Pigs*. But the piece never quotes the song and the closest it gets to musical doggerel is "Chopsticks." Nor does it adopt the moralizing stance of the cartoon, or even Albee's play. Rather, all the rotating, shiny pieces—colored slabs, grand piano, and turntable—give the piece a kaleidoscopic look that is matched by a startling range of musical styles and modes of delivery. Alternating among song, spoken text, and musical interludes, it crackles with difference and, like most musicals and liederabends, breaks into two parts (in this case, without intermission). The first part resembles a revue, with several costume changes; the second is more serious, the actors clothed in differently colored pseudo-Chanel suits, with heels, which lend the proceedings a mock-seriousness.

The piece is bookended by two contrasting arrangements of "Gesang Weylas" (Weylas's song) by Eduard Mörike, the nineteenth-century poet who wrote the texts for many of Wolf's most acclaimed songs. The initial "Gesang Weylas" is "less a song than an incantation"[72] and its a cappella performance provides an austere introduction. For that song and the piece's first few numbers, the seven female actors sing and dance in boyish drag as tuxedoed gigolos from 1920s Berlin—or 1960s Las Vegas—and swing Hugo Wolf as if he were Burt Bacharach. These numbers are followed by a whimsical interlude for four actors as elaborately dressed geishas, complete with large-print kimonos, creative headdresses, and fake Japanese dancing. The second part of the piece is more episodic and sets pianist Carsten Meyer both in concert with and in opposition to the singers. Costumed as a cross between late Elvis Presley and early Elton John, he engineers two percussive interludes featuring on-the-string playing that turns the piano into a spectral harp. Given his gender, Meyer might be a stand-in for Hugo Wolf but if so, he is Wolf as glitter-flecked trickster. The piece's second part, which he introduces with a spasmodic stomping foot dance, functions like the second act of most musicals, spotlighting the more serious songs while ending with a spirited finale.

Unlike most jukebox musicals, *Wer hat Angst vor Hugo Wolf?* is not based on the composer's biography and avoids reducing Wolf's songs to exemplars of what Kramer calls "the Wolf legend": "the tale of the moody, sensitive, but aesthetically disciplined artist" who wrote uniquely tortured songs, was tragically afflicted with neurosyphilis, and institutionalized for the last years of his life.[73] The piece resists that narrative, instead juxtaposing farce and tragedy, as Fritsch does in so much of his work. The emotionally fraught climax of the second part is a performance of one of Wolf's last songs, his "strange and terrifying" setting of Michelangelo's portentous "Alles endet, was entstehet" (All that is created ends), a poem that speaks "the language of the dead."[74] It is performed first as hyper-dramatic spoken text, building, as the speaker climbs onto the piano, to a hysterical climax, or what one critic calls a "scream-orgy."[75] But that recitation is only the prelude to an even more impassioned sung performance gradually picked up by all the actors, their hands shaking rhythmically (in fear?) while the song's repeated descending minor scale sounds a death knell. At its end, the accompaniment and stage lighting suddenly change and the music morphs into "Twist and Shout," which forms a bridge to a swinging rock 'n' roll version of one of Wolf's most playful erotic songs, "Ich hab in Penna" (I have in Penna). Death is not defeated, but momentarily overruled.

A contrary glance into an utterly different kind of death is provided by the finale of the first part, Wolf's most pornographic song, "Erstes Liebeslied eines Mädchens" (First love song of a maiden), to a text by Mörike. Composed as "an antidote to the sexual hypocrisies [Wolf] decried in his own time and place,"[76] the song charts a young woman's first-person narrative of an attack by "a sweet eel," a "snake" that "slithers to my breast" and "plunges down to my heart" (Figure 5.5). Although the maiden fears this delectable, frightful creature will prove "the death of me," she ends shuddering with terror and

Figure 5.5 Eel fishing with Carol Schuler, left, and Ruth Rosenfeld, right. "Erstes Liebeslied eines Mädchens" (First Love Song of a Maiden). *Wer hat Angst vor Hugo Wolf?*, directed by Herbert Fritsch, Schauspielhaus, Zürich, 2016. Photo by Matthias Horn.

delight.[77] *Wer hat Angst vor Hugo Wolf?* turns this "waltz on speed"[78] into a slow, sexy, 4/4 ballad duet for Ruth Rosenfeld and Carol Schuler, dressed as black-outfitted women, complete with white-haired fright wigs. Their surreal, retro outfits make the couple suggest an alternative cabaret duo and specifically, Marlene Dietrich and Margo Lion in their celebrated 1928 lesbian duet, "Wenn die beste Freundin" (When the best friend), by Mischa Spoliansky and Marcellus Schiffer.

Wolf's breathless narration of sexual conquest is turned into a not-so-innocent dialogue in which, though nearly immobilized, the two describe an extremely pleasurable interlude, sexual passion turned into seductive play. It is not exactly a love duet, but rather a breathy—à la Donna Summer—coolly sexualized sharing.

The sexy entente cordiale that ends the first part is echoed at the end of the piece by an exhilarating, musical comedy–style finale composed of pop rearrangements of two of Wolf's best-known songs. The first, "Er ist's" (It's him!), is a joyful welcome to spring, the second, a reprise of "Gesang Weylas," Mörike's apostrophe to a faraway fantasy land. Fritsch and company slow down the lively "Er ist's," turning this "splendid *tour de force*"[79] into a deliberate march, the actors in a V-formation, playing a merrily chirping obbligato on soprano recorders. Meyer gives the accompaniment a bolero rhythm, while the actors march in place enthusiastically, led by Rosenfeld, who also conducts. The coda repeats the final line, "Spring, you are come!," seven times, all the while modulating up, until the actors make a false exit, stopped by the blue slab. Instead of marching off, they slowly turn as the piano launches into a 1970s-style ballad vamp and they line up across the stage to sing a reprise of Wolf's utopian salutation, "Gesang Weylas." This final song is a paean to "the fictive island-kingdom of Orplid," created by the young Eduard Mörike and "populated by rustic mortals, elves, fairies, a cursed king, and a goddess named Weyla."[80] Turning Wolf's harp-like chords into the soulful piano stylings of 1970s singer-songwriters like Carole King or Roberta Flack, the arrangement updates Wolf, coaxing "these romantic fantasies" into reality, if only in the imagination.[81] The simple arrangement and the singers' gentle counterpoint function to make the song an understated, quietly consoling echo of all the musical theatre finales that envision and transport performers and audiences alike to a promised land—be it Oklahoma, Brigadoon, or the end of Finian's rainbow. Who could possibly be afraid of this munificent Hugo Wolf?

In Defense of Comedy

Since bursting onto the scene as a director in 2011, Herbert Fritsch has taken advantage of the decentralized state-subsidized system, directing work at prestigious *Schauspielhäuser* and opera houses in over a dozen cities in Germany, Austria, and Switzerland. He even served as "mis-director" (*Verirrter*) for a rambunctious, elaborately staged, multimedia performance entitled "Nonsense in Residence" by violinist Patricia Kopatchinskaja and members of the Berlin Philharmonic, playing—and enacting—pieces by Kurt Schwitters, John Cage, György Ligeti, and others.[82] Despite Fritsch's commitment to avant-gardism, he has been able to maintain his distance from the politically engaged work that fills so many stages. He argues that the latter has become ineffectual, a fig-leaf, as he puts it, for politicians and audiences alike, an art that compels people to acquiesce instead of impelling them to work for change.[83] "There is a lot of consternation about politics in the theatre," Fritsch said in 2014. "We audience down here, you actors up there, always with the same catchphrases. In the auditorium, the audience sits and nods and says, 'Yes, yes, it's all so terrible.' And the journalists celebrate the grand gestures of honesty, which, after all, are all rehearsed." The theatrical prodigality of his own work seems to mock the self-effacing performance styles coded as profound. "When an actor speaks very quietly and is so self-absorbed," Fritsch says, sarcastically, "then he must be feeling it very deeply."[84]

Veering sharply away from sober self-absorption, Fritsch champions a species of broad comedy that, he emphasizes, was destroyed by the Nazis. Although West German cultural policy used theatre "to work out the guilt" of Nazism and World War II, postwar Germany—ironically and tragically— "forgot to change," maintaining Nazi norms and neglecting to commemorate and restore what had been lost. (The maintenance of prewar styles afflicted operetta even more disastrously than *Schauspiel*.)[85] He notes ruefully that when directing in Berlin, "some people at the Volksbühne said to me that I am doing this Nazi theatre, because it's funny." He points out, however, that these same people then fail to ask the key question, "What did the Nazis kill? The Nazis killed humor. The Nazis killed the clowns ... in the twenties.... [T]hey killed comedians who were Jews and comedians who were not Jews because they were comedians and writers. And this was German culture!" His mission, on the contrary, is to breathe new life into Weimar comedy and cabaret, "to continue with this prewar culture, where it was cut off. ... And this, for me, is political: to give a new way of life, to give another way of life. This is wonderful!"[86]

It may seem very un-Fritschian to use the director's suspicion of political theatre as a jumping-off point for a more general consideration of the politics of performance, a subject that is ubiquitous in theatre scholarship. But I feel compelled to do so to defend the kind of musical theatre that is often considered mere entertainment. The more I reflect on musical theatre's knack for providing pleasure, the more I am drawn back to a theorist who was no friend of popular performance and who might well have hated Fritsch's work, Theodor W. Adorno. In "Commitment" (1962), Adorno famously attacks Brecht and Sartre as exemplars of the ineffectiveness and bad faith inherent in the well-intentioned work of engaged, but ultimately naïve leftists. Adorno's objections are twofold. The more obvious one concerns his antipathy to what he considers the redundant didacticism of committed art, for which he borrows "the American phrase 'preaching to the converted.'" As he wrote sixty years ago (pre-echoing Fritsch), "[i]n Germany, commitment often means bleating what everyone is already saying or at least secretly wants to hear."[87] Adorno's second and more complex objection concerns the always already compromised status of committed art. "Works of art which by their existence take the side of the victims of a rationality that subjugates nature," that is, works that advocate for the oppressed, "are even in their protest constitutively implicated in the process of rationalization itself."[88] The stricter the moralizing, the more lethally it is contradicted by the vehicle that communicates it. "The notion of a 'message' in art, even when politically radical, already contains an accommodation to the world: the stance of the lecturer conceals a clandestine entente with the listeners."[89] In other words, what Adorno labels politically radical art requires both "lecturer" and listener to disavow their knowledge of the contract that enables its articulation in the first place, thereby disabling its effectivity.

In contradistinction to committed art, Adorno endorses autonomous art, especially the decidedly unpolemical works of Franz Kafka and Samuel Beckett, which for Adorno testify to the migration of "politics . . . into autonomous art." The political force of such artworks lies not in their subject matter or message, "the totality of their effects, but their own inherent structure" as "nonconceptual objects,"[90] their articulation of what Adorno calls "the unspeakable."[91] For Adorno, Beckett is the master of the unspeakable, whose "incomprehensibility," obliteration of meaning, and skill at murmuring the "name of disaster . . . silently" make him unique.[92] Beckett reappears in

Adorno's unfinished *Aesthetic Theory* (1970), in which Adorno takes up the question of utopia more directly than in his earlier work. He there concedes that utopia can be enunciated only through "the absolute negativity of collapse" or catastrophe. Because utopia "is blocked by the real functional order," it can be conceived only negatively. To imagine utopia positively, in concrete terms, is to "betray it by providing semblance and consolation."[93] Importantly, this negative utopia is not a delusion but "the true consciousness of an age in which the real possibility of utopia—that given the level of productive forces the earth could here and now be paradise—converges with the possibility of total catastrophe."[94] Writing in the late 1960s, Adorno was doubtlessly thinking catastrophe via nuclear apocalypse, which remains a persistent possibility sixty years on. In the twenty-first century, however, this threat must be multiplied by the reality of climate change, which gives Adorno's doomsaying new currency.

Although I know that applying (i.e., instrumentalizing) Adorno represents a betrayal, I cannot help calling him as a character witness for Herbert Fritsch, whose work, I believe, could be read as a fantasy recreation of Beckett as a writer of a musical comedy. I am arguing here not that Fritsch copies Beckett, but that he translates Beckett into a different language. While Beckett's silent articulation of the name of disaster is effected through writing, Fritsch's medium, theatrical performance, is much less permanent. However, for Fritsch, like Beckett, hilarity opens the gate to a paradise that is always already lost. Catastrophe is sidesplitting. In other words, like the great comedians who inspire him (or the joyful musical comedies of the 1920s and 1930s), Fritsch uses the theatre to luxuriate in absurdity. Of course, Beckett too was a comic writer whose *Waiting for Godot* (1953) deliberately calls up the ghosts of Laurel and Hardy, Abbott and Costello, and other immortal comic duos. Beckett's works are littered with the debris of classic comedy, and his *Film* (1965) even stars Buster Keaton, one of the silent film greats. Although in my reading of *Der schwarze Hecht*, I show how Fritsch turns the romantic content of musical comedy inside out, I want here to analyze a different mode of upending of convention by examining a play that offers up a musical theatre camping trip—on acid.

Tenting Tonight

Herbert Fritsch premiered *Zelt* (2019), a valedictory, apocalyptic music theatre piece at Vienna's Burgtheater at the end of the artistic directorship of

Karin Bergmann. *Zelt*, a collaboration with composer/conductor/electric violinist Matthias Jakisic, is speechless—its only text consists of two lines from the recognition scene of Richard Strauss's *Elektra* (1909) sung in a refulgent falsetto by Hubert Wild a few minutes into the piece. Although *Zelt*'s ninety-five-minute action involves the preparation for and aftermath of two performances, one human, the other non-human, its real subject is the theatre itself as a site of work, play, fantasy, machinery, and dreams. With a cast of twenty-three people, sixteen tents, as well as Jakisic, *Zelt* is set on an empty stage with a shiny, mirror-like, blue-green polished floor. It is unique among Fritsch's original pieces because although the actors exploit comic rhythms and gestures and incorporate comic routines, most of *Zelt* is oddly unfunny, as if the humor had been deliberately drained out of it. The performance unfolds at a glacial pace, but it has a more clearly recognizable plot than Fritsch's other original pieces and is structured symmetrically, like a three-act play, plus prologue and epilogue. It tells the story of a camping trip, with what I might call an Austrian-style hootenanny at its center, that finally ends up in hell—or is it paradise? It is narrated not only through the activities of people and tents, but also through the constantly changing, evocative, and sometimes poisonously garish lighting (designed by Friedrich Rom). To answer the question, "why tents?," I might reference the tent as a temporary sanctuary, a flimsy remedy for homelessness, or a portable shelter available to countless travelers, from Arctic explorers to refugees escaping war-torn and impoverished parts of the world.

Zelt's seventeen-minute prologue consists of a silent, slow-motion, ritual mopping of the stage by the full cast, dressed as a cleaning crew in bright green uniforms, yellow rubber gloves, and red shoes, caps, and bandanas (costumes by Bettina Helmi). Synchronized, they spread out around the space, sweep, congregate, march, mop, and move in formation like a squadron. As is usual with Fritsch, however, one of the actors is always slightly out of step with the others, the performer whose individualism both threatens and fortifies the community. At their exit, Jakisic enters as conductor and proceeds to accompany and direct the rest of the performance from his perch in front of the stage. What I am calling Act 1 begins with the entrance of Hermann Scheidleder in traditional Austrian dress who slowly, painstakingly builds a trekking tent. Then, the rest of the cast emerges from the tent, like a swarm of little people tumbling out of a Volkswagen, sporting loudly colored, pseudo-folkloristic Austrian costumes, with white painted faces and pink cheeks. They proceed to assemble fifteen more trekking tents (in red, orange, yellow, blue, green, and violet; Figure 5.6). Their work finished, Act 2 begins as the lights dim (as if evening were falling on the campground) and all twenty-three actors sling a guitar or accordion over their shoulders and, huddled together at the lip of the stage, they perform a riotous, twenty-minute concert around an invisible campfire before being quickly dispersed by a sudden rainstorm. As Act 3 opens, the actors disappear into the tents and, presumably, bed. The tents begin to glow like beautifully colored Japanese lanterns and, because they have been secured to the fly system with lift lines, they fly gently into the air, dancing up and down in a graceful, magical, unaccompanied five-minute ballet. The sky brightens and the tents slowly descend to earth, as if to offer an escape hatch for the human performers who seem to—but could not possibly—be sleeping in the flying tents. After a pause, the epilogue begins as the tents ascend one last time. In their wake, seventeen detached heads are seen scattered across the empty stage, wearing white fright wigs and make-up, floating on what looks like a smooth-as-glass, Caribbean-blue sea that stretches to infinity. Their eyes dart about in alarm as a searchlight illuminates them one by one and the curtains slowly close.

Figure 5.6 The ensemble displaying their handiwork. *Zelt*, directed by Herbert Fritsch, Burgtheater, 2019. Photo Copyright: Reinhard Werner, Archiv Burghtheater.

Zelt's final tableau acts as a kind of negative deus ex machina that causes one to rethink everything that has gone before. In this case, the gods do not descend but rather are left behind in a panic as their empty vehicles rise back up into the heavens. This devastating, five-minute tableau is crushingly beautiful and horrifying or, to borrow Adorno's lexicon, an enunciation of both paradise and catastrophe. It stands in mute contrast to the rest of the piece, which, except for the concert, is more about rehearsal than performance, more about preparation than actuality, misadventure than achievement. And while theatre has long been used both to produce and problematize the audience as collective, *Zelt*'s synchronization of a large cast of nameless figures shows that onstage labor too is inextricably entwined with the conundrum of individual and group, soloist and team, uniqueness and anonymity. As Michael Laages notes, "this is pure overwhelming theatre, . . . no joke, but rather a limitless fantasy about the collective and about all collectives in the theatre."[95]

The interpretation of a textless, mostly abstract theatre piece is always an iffy business. Yet I feel compelled to marshal a reading of *Zelt* because when I saw it in April 2019, I felt as if I'd been knocked for a loop. Other great performances I'd seen had from the beginning signaled their momentousness, but *Zelt* caught me unawares. Its almost offhanded prologue is a highly aestheticized translation of the tedious, backbreaking labor required to keep the shimmering stage floor spotless. The succeeding three-act play presents a protracted series of quasi-mishaps during the performers' construction and occupation of their temporary shelters. The musical performance that interrupts the action is a strangely wonky affair. After overcrowding the stage with a throng of guitars and accordions, the campers, in concert—but not in concert—raise their instruments and batter away at them rhythmically, like a jam session in hell (Figure 5.7). The problem is that they don't know how to play them, or at least don't play them as they were designed to be played. As if inhabiting an alternate musical universe, the guitarists pluck wildly at their dampered strings, turning them into percussion instruments, while the accordions wheeze voicelessly, the players punching away at the bass buttons and running their fingernails up and down the keyboards. As conducted by the passionately gesticulating Jakisic, this musical interlude is structured around a succession of hypnotically repetitive rhythmic riffs, building to a sonic hurricane that climaxes in wild, flamenco-like foot stomping.

It is, in effect, a minimalist percussion concerto grosso for non-percussion instruments, complete with mini-cadenzas for each of the players in its final

Figure 5.7 An Austrian-style hootenanny. *Zelt*, directed by Herbert Fritsch, Burgtheater, 2019. Photo Copyright: Reinhard Werner, Archiv Burgtheater.

section. Were the dynamics not so carefully shaped, the impromptu might have devolved into a spectacle of virtuosic ineptitude. But the music is as maddeningly infectious as the players' rock-star moves are dazzling. It ends precipitously, as if a rainstorm erupted out of nowhere, the ensemble fracturing into chaos and the players running into their tents for shelter. Peace descends and the show's real headliners, who are not the human actors but the multicolored tents, lift off and slowly dance in midair, the protagonists in a dream ballet. These exquisitely graceful non-human actors return to earth at the break of day, their enchanted interlude concluded, like spaceships visiting from a distant galaxy. Then suddenly, they ascend into the flies, leaving behind seventeen wild-looking, seemingly decapitated heads, alone together, afloat on a crystalline sea, nightmare versions of Nagg and Nell from Beckett's *Endgame* or Winnie from *Happy Days*.

Trying to understand *Zelt*, I want to enlist Adorno's aid one last time. As he wrote in reference to *Endgame*: "Understanding it can mean nothing other than understanding its incomprehensibility," a task that proceeds from "concretely reconstructing [the piece's] meaning structure—that it has none."[96] Exiting through the Burgtheater's sumptuously neo-baroque foyer into a crystalline spring night in Vienna,[97] I felt that *Zelt*'s meaninglessness occasioned my own (re)discovery of catastrophe in this Austrian paradise, a rediscovery compressed, or encapsulated in its final tableau. In light of that tableau, I could not help seeing the piece, like the Burgtheater's impossibly grand public spaces, as a fabulous anachronism, an imperial hallucination, a reflection on Aristotelian dramaturgy long after its expiration date. In other words, *Zelt* both preserves and cancels what Adorno describes (in relation to *Endgame*) as "[d]ramatic components reappear[ing] after their demise. Exposition, complication, plot, peripeteia, and catastrophe return as decomposed elements in a post-mortem examination."[98] Indeed, *Zelt* is almost neo-classical in its anti-logical embrace of the three unities. But because *Zelt*'s post-mortem turns the tragic protagonist into a mob of clowns, it leaves me wondering how to explain the awe generated by a tragedy masquerading as a clown show.

Despite the precision of Adorno's scalpel, he pays little attention to pleasure, which, along with notions like "fun" and "enjoyment," retains for him an "infantile quality" that renders them deceitful and dangerously suspect, in large part because of their association with the culture industry, that is, entertainment.[99] Yet even Adorno acknowledges that "if the last traces of pleasure were extirpated, the question of what artworks are for would be an embarrassment."[100] So how do I theorize the pleasure generated by a comedy that stretches comic form and musical conventions to their breaking point?

Consider one of Adorno's few affirmative references to comedy in *Dialectic of Enlightenment* (1944), his denunciation of the culture industry co-written with Max Horkheimer. Despite their perpetually aggravated tone, Adorno and Horkheimer manage to look back affectionately and nostalgically at the subversive power of popular Hollywood comedies, which, after all, were favorites of the working classes. Adorno and Horkheimer note that "a legitimate part of popular art up to Chaplin and the Marx [B]rothers" was "pure nonsense ... as buffoonery and clowning" that ridiculed the high and mighty. To justify their affection, they cite "[c]artoon and stunt films" that "were once exponents of fantasy against rationalism" because "they allowed justice to be done to the animals and things electrified by their technology, by granting the mutilated beings a second life."[101] Are not the conventions of silent-film comedy granted "a second life" by their protégé Herbert Fritsch, who stages their "fantas[ies] against rationalism" even more boldly than Chaplin?

Fritsch's anti-rationalist derring-do reminds me that pleasure can never be completely expunged from musical theatre because, like the Road Runner in the eponymous cartoon, it keeps popping back up, even, or especially, when it seems finally to have been snuffed out. In a world in perpetual crisis, the giddiness and exhilaration generated by an insane musical impromptu and comic gestural rhapsodies may not threaten the scaffolding of post-industrial capitalism, but they do offer an antidote to hopelessness and despair.

Fritsch's aversion to the most fashionable elements of German theatre—politics, nudity, and stage blood—does not mean that his works abjure transgression. On the contrary, he could easily take his place in the tradition that dates back to Aristophanes, Cervantes, commedia dell'arte, the Gershwins, and Cole Porter, comedy that ridicules and punctures the pretenses of the tyrannical, arrogant, and self-important. Interestingly, Fritsch dates his love of transgression back not to art but to his own brief life of crime: "The feeling I had when I first slipped through a broken window has stayed with me all my life: you stand in a room you have conquered." And he acknowledges that because he derives a similar transgressive joy from every performance, he endeavors to give his actors, if not criminal energy, then at least "the willingness to take risks and break rules."[102]

Curtain Call

I would be remiss if I did not elaborate on one of the great pleasures of every Fritsch production, the curtain call, which invariably is as elaborately choreographed and full of surprises as the play that precedes it. Curtain calls in Germany are always much lengthier than those that follow plays in the United States and typically last as long as the audience will keep clapping. In the United States, only Broadway musicals, at least since *Mamma Mia!*, regularly exploit curtain calls as an opportunity for an encore or celebratory epilogue. But Fritsch's curtain calls, which shamelessly milk applause, are the most extended and ornate I have seen on the German stage. Moreover, because curtain calls do not require complicated sound and light cues, they remain more improvisatory—that is, immediately responsive to the audience—than any other part of the show. Rather than simply staying in character, or dropping character, the actors are granted full power as stage acrobats to juggle both. As a result, the Fritsch curtain call prolongs, recapitulates, and extinguishes the play it follows, becoming both coda and epilogue. It is often impossible to know where the play ends and the curtain call begins, because both mobilize the same conventions.

Because *Zelt* has a more lethal final cadence than any other Fritsch play, its curtain call functions as a temporary resurrection. It starts when the actors crawl back up on the stage through traps, wriggling their way on their bellies down to the front, and one by one, like a wave of synchronized chorus girls, raise their heads to grin and acknowledge the applause. Then they jump back into the traps, only to pop up a moment later gesticulating frantically like jacks-in-the-box. After finally exiting into the wings, they return with their musical instruments and line up again across the lip of the stage as if they were going to play an encore, but instead suddenly scatter, sowing musical and choreographic pandemonium. And so it goes.

Zelt's curtain call serves as a reminder that both *Spiel* in German and "play," its English translation, designate a theatre piece as well as ludic activity or practice. It is thus an opportunity for actors and audience to frolic and bask in the glow of the intense, if transient, pleasure the production unleashes. Yet it also serves to divert attention away from the fact that a performance must finally die and that its makers have limited power to determine how long its memory will endure. A performance may be as mortal as the workers laboring on- and off-stage, but a curtain call that goes on and on as if it was never going to end is a reminder that theatre can still serve as a place of wonder, a temporary shelter (like a tent!) from debility and death. I have several times seen a Fritsch curtain call continue even after the house lights came up, the actors skipping hand in hand around the stage until the crew started to strike the set. The disinclination to end makes me recall that although the conventions of Greek tragedy are the stuff of legend, the stage even today retains a trace of its mythic, ritual identity as a sanctuary, a place where people cannot die. Or as Fritsch puts it: "The only safe place in the world for me is the stage. Offstage, my life is a mess. Onstage, everything is clear."[103]

6

Celebrating the Great Tralala

Although Broadway classics like *West Side Story* and *Fiddler on the Roof* are still considered laughable by many German intellectuals,[1] indistinguishable from commercial fare like *Cats* and *The Lion King*, a number of well-known and -respected directors in Germany have labored to rethink these classics and reassess the status of musicals in state-subsidized theatres. Among those aiming to legitimize popular music theatre, none has a higher profile than Barrie Kosky, Intendant of the Komische Oper Berlin from 2012 until 2022. Kosky reframed the mission of the smallest of the three major, state-subsidized Berlin opera houses by returning to the modus operandi of Walter Felsenstein, who re-founded the house in East Berlin in 1947 and remained Intendant until his death in 1975. By the 1970s, Felsenstein had succeeded in making it, in the words of the *New York Times*, the home of "music theater of unsurpassed sophistication" that was able to reach "nearly all levels of the city's population."[2] Kosky, who admires his illustrious predecessor for "radically changing everything we know about opera,"[3] follows Felsenstein's lead and eschews Wagner, Strauss, and the heavier Verdi works in favor of operas and operettas that often use spoken dialogue instead of recitative. (The house had been named after the Opéra Comique in Paris.) Understanding the need to compete with its two larger, "relatively stuffy" siblings,[4] Kosky succeeded in giving the Komische Oper a witty, exciting, and provocative new identity, rebranding it as truly *komisch*, meaning both comical and strange—and very Berlin. Although the *New York Times* has sometimes seemed discomfited by Kosky's audacity, it acknowledges that he is "a showman through and through, who operates with a young idealist's belief in the power of theater and a brazen disregard for divisions between so-called high and low art."[5]

Barrie Kosky's most high-profile innovation was to produce full productions of a series of nearly forgotten operettas by Jewish composers. He directed lavish stagings of Paul Abraham's *Ball im Savoy* (2013), Oscar Straus's *Eine Frau, die weiss, was sie will!* (A woman who knows what she wants!, 2015) and *Die Perlen der Cleopatra* (The pearls of Cleopatra, 2016), and Jaromir Weinberger's *Frühlingsstürme* (Spring storms, 2020), while handing the reins to others for other works by Paul Abraham, Mischa Spoliansky, and Nico Dostal. Although all the operettas Kosky directed had been premiered on the eve of the Nazi takeover, he insists that they be performed not as acts of mourning but as restitutions for contemporary audiences of the "fantasy jazz world" of the early 1930s that Berlin operetta created and celebrated.[6]

In addition to modifying the Komische Oper's repertoire, Barrie Kosky saw to it that more work was performed in the original language and made sure his productions, many of them exuberantly choreographed by Otto Pichler, exuded a wild, sexy, populist glow. Adding Broadway musicals to his seasons, he also directed acclaimed productions of *Kiss Me, Kate* (2008), *West Side Story* (2013), *Anatevka* (*Fiddler on the Roof*, 2017), and *Candide* (2018). In this chapter, I analyze all four productions, which for me were revelations, far more creative, thoughtful, and emotionally overwhelming than these same musicals' recent Broadway revivals. Most important, all four productions bring these mid-twentieth-century classics into the present, not through a clichéd updating of the stories but by forcefully placing the musicals in dialogue with urgent twenty-first-century social and political issues. It is no wonder that Kosky's ingenious contemporizations, his provocative mixtures of high and low, art and glitz, have made the Komische Oper "wildly popular with a wide variety of visitors" and a magnet for music theatre lovers from all over Europe and the United States.[7] Shortly into Kosky's reign as Intendant, the *New York Times* anointed him "a feted star" in the Berlin arts scene and, citing a local critic, declared that Kosky "has brought something of the glamour of Broadway to Berlin."[8]

By the end of Kosky's tenure as Intendant, he was universally acclaimed. But even after his first season, the Komische Oper was named Opera House of the Year (in 2013) by *Opernwelt* magazine, while Kosky himself was named Best Director at the 2014 Opera Awards.[9] By 2019, the *Times* was ready to concede that he "may be the most interesting opera director of the past decade."[10] Kosky succeeded in establishing what the press calls the house's sexy, new "brand"; lowered the audience's age; and increased attendance from 64 to 87 percent of capacity.[11] The Komische Oper, according to the *Tagesspiegel*, "was suddenly a place for daring *Regietheater*, for provocative productions."[12] His operetta performances always sold out and even his production of Jean-Philippe Rameau's *Castor et Pollux* attracted a 95 percent capacity crowd.[13] Kosky's very success, however, has made some German cultural critics nervous. In *Die Welt*, the often acerbic Manuel Brug describes him as a gate-crasher, a "Mister Entertainment" in the capital's "high culture jungle," where "U and E" are still filed in separate drawers. Although, Brug writes, Kosky was hired as a "flashy, dirty, satirical" artist who would not indulge in the "brooding, heavy *Regietheater*" that fills so many of Berlin's other state-subsidized stages, he has, Brug concedes, "matured" into an "internationally sought-after," "serious" director.[14]

Kosky's maturity is evinced less by the seriousness of his work than by his skill at subverting the clear distinctions between different kinds of musical theatre. He insists that operetta is not an inferior subgenre of opera and he bridles at the presumption that it is "almost a dirty word in German high culture."[15] To dismiss operetta, he notes, as "banal and stupid . . . gives you a very narrow definition of what musical theatre is—and what life is." Kosky points out that Berlin operetta was loved by eminent conductors such as Bruno Walter and Otto Klemperer and he prefers to describe musical theatre not as "opulent" or "spectacular," but "sensual."[16] Kosky's success at championing operetta, musicals, and avant-gardist opera simultaneously in a high-profile house is also a sign of a thoroughgoing disruption of the cultural hierarchy taking place in Germany. Or as Kosky puts it, "What I'm doing fits into the *Zeitgeist* of what is actually changing within the German cultural landscape. . . . If I had been doing this fifteen or twenty years earlier I don't think it would be successful, because everyone would say, 'What's this?'"[17] Above all, Kosky declares his passion for the "great Tralala" that is a necessary ingredient in the musical theatre recipe. "You have to celebrate the Tralala."[18]

By eagerly embracing his passion for musicals, Kosky is also having an impact on other theatres. Two dedicated operetta houses, the Staatsoperette Dresden and Wiener Volksoper, have markedly enhanced the quality of their productions since 2015. They are thus following Kosky's lead and effectively transforming an increasing number of operettas into musicals, while nimbly avoiding the stigmatizing label. The hybridization of musical theatre categories in Germany is especially apparent in productions of work by the most genre-bending of composers, Kurt Weill and Leonard Bernstein. In the United States, George Gershwin and, increasingly, Stephen Sondheim, are the two composers whose work has been most readily accommodated to the crossover category on recordings and in live performance. Gershwin's music, especially *Rhapsody in Blue*, is used ad nauseam in the United States to emblematize both the spirit of urban life and the catholicity of musical cultures in the United States. But in Germany and Austria, Bernstein and Weill are the key figures whose work most dramatically challenges the distinction between *U-* and *E-*.[19] They are also the two composers whose music theatre dominates the rest of this chapter. After brief studies of Barrie Kosky's *Anatevka* (*Fiddler on the Roof*) and *Kiss Me, Kate*, I offer more detailed analyses of his Komische Oper productions of *West Side Story* and *Candide*. In the final section, I survey five Kurt Weill musicals performed during the 2021–2022 season, among them Barrie Kosky's *Die Dreigroschenoper* and *Aufstieg und Fall der Stadt Mahagonny*. Although my emphasis throughout is on how musicals are contemporized, the Weill section also focuses on metatheatricality, that is, how directors use the pieces to reflect on theatre as a mode of artistic and social practice. Why is the work of Kurt Weill so valuable for directors who aim to exploit musical theatre as a way to think about what theatre is and can do?

Barrie Kosky's ability to undermine the cultural hierarchy is increasingly being matched by that of other directors, especially the visionary Berlin theatre-maker Ersan Mondtag, who has directed (and designed) a number of surreal musical theatre collaborations, including a dreamlike, gender-reversed *Baal* (2019), Brecht's first play, at the Berliner Ensemble (with Weimar-inspired songs by Eva Jantschitsch); original dance theatre pieces; and Sibylle Berg's wicked satire of bourgeois complacency, *Hass-Triptychon— Wege aus der Krise* (Hatred trilogy—ways out of the crisis, 2019, with a pop-rock score by Beni Brachtel) at Berlin's Maxim Gorki Theater. He has also staged a number of non-canonical operas, including a deconstruction of Kurt Weill's *Der Silbersee* (in German, English, and Dutch, 2021) at Opera Ballet Vlaanderen in Antwerp, which I analyze at the end of the chapter. Another innovative director is Christian Weise, whose *Im weissen Rößl* (Schauspiel Düsseldorf, 2013) wallows in Austrian kitsch. He has staged revue-operettas (a.k.a. musicals) by Mischa Spoliansky, including, most memorably, a gloriously artful and artificial *Alles Schwindel* (Everything's a swindle, 2017) at the Gorki Theater. Also at the Gorki, Yael Ronen continues her series of collaboratively developed pieces about hot-button issues (the European refugee crisis, the war in the former Yugoslavia, Roma and Sinti, #MeToo, and cancel culture), several of which feature songs that unambiguously bring Broadway to mind. Indeed, her piece about cancel culture, *Slippery Slope* (2021), is even given the subtitle, *Almost a Musical*, and is performed entirely in English, the "universal language of musicals" (*Musical-Weltsprache Englisch*).[20] But the piece's unwillingness to embrace the label, even when it so obviously *is* a musical, is also symptomatic of the continuing anxiety among German artists and intellectuals about the production of the genre called musicals in elite state-subsidized houses.

Despite my love for the work of these other directors, I choose Barrie Kosky as the focus of this chapter because he is arguably the pioneer, the one whose success has helped pave the way for these and other directors to take on more musicals, or almost musicals. Kosky is also distinguished by his high international profile, prolific and varied output, and flair for theorizing his work. At the same time, I bring up these other directors to point out that Kosky's achievements must be put in the context of a recent blossoming of a wide range of popular music theatre. Kosky could be speaking for any of the above when he argues that comedy is as philosophical as tragedy and that music theatre by definition represents a mutable admixture of "text, music, choreography, masks, symbolism, [and] ritual" that makes unique demands on singing actors.[21] As a director totally committed to collaboration and process, he insists, "Theatre is a verb, not a noun."[22] In his rehearsals of both operettas and musicals, performers

> must do two things: with the left eye you must be deadly serious; treat your characters seriously; treat the situation seriously. With the right eye you must be completely objective and outside the action and winking to the audience saying, "Isn't this fantastic? Isn't this ridiculous? Isn't life a joke?" So you have to have this combination of "objective–subjective," of "serious but ironic," of "I am treating the situation and characters very seriously, but I'm also laughing at the whole ridiculousness of life."[23]

To separate out and devalue operettas and musicals in favor of opera and experimental music theatre is completely to misunderstand the history of music theatre in the German-speaking world. Kosky points out that Felsenstein's "great invention of modern music theatre" was predicated on the fact that "he saw no difference" between opera and operetta. And Max Reinhardt, Kosky continues, "was the most anti-snob of all anti-snobs, because he loved cabaret, he loved circus, he loved epic spectacle."[24] The most ambitious of Kosky's productions, such as *Candide* (2018), interweave high and low, tragedy and farce so deftly and powerfully that they bring to mind the provocative defense of kitsch enunciated by the controversial Austrian critic, journalist, and political activist Günther Nenning: "If you don't love kitsch, you don't understand anything about art." And while Nenning's declaration focuses on the conventions of operetta, he could just as well be writing about musicals as reimagined by contemporary German directors:

> Anyone who really believes that people . . . believe in operetta-style happiness does not understand anything about kitsch. And whoever believes that people don't believe in operetta-style tragedy doesn't understand anything about art. The superiority of kitsch over art and operetta over other art forms is based on the simplest co-existence of happiness and tragedy. Only those who love kitsch understand life.[25]

Like the best German directors of musicals and operettas, Nenning knew that the road to tragedy is littered with banana peels.

Fiddler on the (Other Side of the) Wall

Among Barrie Kosky's musicals at the Komische Oper, the one that puts him most palpably and literally in touch with tradition is his production of Jerry Bock and Sheldon Harnick's *Anatevka*, whose very opening number (in both English and German) is titled "Tradition." His realization of the musical hearkens back to Walter Felsenstein's most popular and long-running success. Titled *Der Fiedler auf dem Dach* in East Berlin, it opened in January 1971 and continued in the Komische Oper's repertoire until 1988, racking up a total of 506 performances.[26] Barrie Kosky's remounting of *Anatevka*, plus his emphasis on the drama of music theatre, are among the ways he honors the memory of Walter Felsenstein and the history of the house. Indeed, his illustrious predecessor was hailed for decades as a pioneer of refashioning postwar music theatre as a kind of updated *Gesamtkunstwerk* in which all elements are subordinated to "an integrated conception . . . in which the music and drama are as one."[27] As Intendant of a generously bankrolled East German opera house, Felsenstein enjoyed an artistic carte blanche that would be impossible to replicate today, even in Germany's richly subsidized system. He had the luxury of rehearsing productions for months, which usually translated into 300 to 450 hours per piece, "simply to work on dramatic problems with his singing actors before opening night." In 1971, this timeframe was estimated to be about ten times as long as that given most "[o]pera directors elsewhere."[28] Although Felsenstein was famously tyrannical and contemptuous of singers who put beauty of tone before dramatic values, the *New York Times* noted that his greatest gift was "to be able to invest almost anything he directs with an enormous freight of new meanings and resonances," praise that decades later would be echoed in the most astute reviews of Kosky's work. Like Kosky,

Felsenstein brought many rarities to the stage, including "lightweight and/or obscure pieces that he [could] elevate into something uniquely his own."[29] The king of opera in a country that weaponized its performing arts for the Cold War blitz, Felsenstein turned the Komische Oper (on the western edge of the "grim, totalitarian austerity of East Berlin"[30]) into a cultural beacon that, like the Leipzig Gewandhaus Orchestra or the Dresden Staatskapelle, showcased the artistic excellence of East German culture while, at least in the *Times*'s estimation, eschewing politics.[31]

Despite the almost fifty years separating Felsenstein's and Kosky's *Fiddler on the Roof*, international critics uncannily reiterated each other's patronizing astonishment that each director had succeeded in turning one of the most popular musicals into "something beyond kitsch."[32] If Felsenstein made the piece feel "very different from New York: sadder, more introverted, more serious,"[33] Kosky managed to eliminate "much of the stereotypical schlock"[34] and give the routinely "sentimentalized" songs new "weight and take on deep meaning."[35] *Der Fiedler auf dem Dach* was the only musical Felsenstein ever directed, and his production marked the East German premiere of a piece whose West German premiere had been in Hamburg in 1968. Felsenstein had seen *Fiddler* in New York in 1967 and hoped to bring Jerome Robbins to East Berlin to restage his worldwide hit. In the event, Robbins backed out and Felsenstein staged it himself, "rethink[ing] the piece from scratch," with a new translation by his son Johannes.[36] Obtaining the rights, however, was a complicated procedure. With an Austrian passport and house in West Berlin, Felsenstein repeatedly had to perform a "kind of political highwire act"[37] with the East German authorities, who not surprisingly were reluctant to approve the production of a work about the "Russian oppression of a Jewish community." This balancing act was compounded by several years of "delicate" negotiations for the performance rights with *Fiddler*'s US-American creators, which required Felsenstein to travel to New York to finalize the deal.[38] Kosky, honoring the work of his predecessor, understands that Felsenstein's direction of the piece required "unbelievable courage," both because of the its politically critical stance and Felsenstein's "radical" choice to perform a Broadway musical in an East Berlin opera house.[39] Felsenstein's *Fiedler*, which he rehearsed for three and a half months, kept closely to the original text and score and was the first production not obliged to reproduce Robbins's choreography and mise en scène. *Fiedler*, Felsenstein declared, "shows great poetical truth," despite the fact that its book, he claimed, "is much better than the music." Accordingly, he did not change "much in the play, except to put more accent on the dialogue" and interpolate six "old Yiddish folk songs," each of which related to the preceding scene, played and sung in German by one of the orchestra's violinists who was turned into a character.[40]

Given *Fiddler*'s negative portrayal of Russians as virulent anti-Semites, Felsenstein seems to have appeased a "jittery Ministry of Culture"[41] by playing down anti-Semitism and emphasizing the "agony of the czarist regime" and the class-based "burdens and humiliations" suffered by "Tevje, the milkman"—and working-class hero.[42] The production omitted the word "pogrom"[43] while foregrounding the fact that the action takes place in "1905, on the eve of the revolutionary period."[44] The Komische Oper program, which had been much revised to placate government censors, quotes a 1917 lecture by Lenin in which he decries the "butchery" by the "blood-stained," "hated czarist regime" of the Jews, understood less as a persecuted religious sect than as representatives of the "socialist working class, the proletariat."[45] The production itself, meanwhile, seems to have spotlighted the heroic mien of Perchik, the revolutionary student, played "in a committed and convincing way" by Felsenstein's younger son Christoph.[46]

Although Barrie Kosky never saw Felsenstein's *Fiedler* live on stage, his *Anatevka* displays striking parallels with its predecessor. Both foreground the fiddler by turning him into a prominent if non-speaking character, Felsenstein by giving him Yiddish songs, Kosky by casting the role with a boy who is also the sole modern-dressed figure in the musical. Wearing a green hoodie, sporting headphones, and entering on a scooter at the top of the show, the boy takes out his fiddle and begins to play. He pauses for a moment when he hears a knock coming from the wardrobe door center stage that punctures the stark upstage wall, a giant, Gerhard Richter–like, grainy, washed-out, black-and-white photo of snowy woods (setting by Rufus Didwiszus). When he opens the wardrobe door, Tevye enters, as if being called back from the dead, and begins telling the boy the story of Anatevka and its people, a story much better known to German audiences in 2017 than in 1971. Kosky's Tevye, "the milkman who quarrels with God," is Max Hopp, a lanky, lyrical protagonist who loses three daughters, and whose performance deliberately cuts against the grain of the traditional shtick to become in Kosky's words, "a cross between Job, Mother Courage, King Lear, and Charlie Chaplin."[47]

The narrative framing of Kosky's *Anatevka* continues for the entire piece, since the boy, who acts as a surrogate for the audience, shows up regularly to

Figure 6.1 Ensemble at "Sabbath Prayer," *Anatevka* (*Fiddler on the Roof*), directed by Barrie Kosky, Komische Oper Berlin, 2017. Photo by Iko Freese.

hear more of the saga of Russian Jewry. Kosky explains that, in his mind's eye, the boy is Tevye's great-great-grandson, although he looks like almost any other blond German adolescent. As the boy plays what Kosky identifies as his father's violin, "the shtetl suddenly pours out of the wardrobe," brought back to life by melody.[48] In order to avoid what Kosky calls "kitsch shtetl romanticism,"[49] the town is represented not by quaint houses or rooms (even in the expressionist-cubist style of Felsenstein's production) but rather takes its cue from the lyric to the final song, "Anatevka": "A little bit of this, A little bit of that, A pot, A pan, A broom, A hat."[50] The first act setting is a jumble of containers—wardrobes, cupboards, and closets—a giant collage, fragments of a home, a way of life, that fills the turntable, which revolves almost magically, bringing different perspectives and possibilities into view. Kosky compares this scene with his own memories of crawling around as a child in his parents' closet, between the fur coats, and the entire first act becomes in effect a child's rediscovery of a lost way of life. By the second act, the jumble is gone, and only one small cupboard remains in the cold, snowy wilderness. The possibilities have shrunk, reduced to a single piece of furniture, which also resembles nothing as much as a gravestone. At the end, Tevye pulls the cart, carrying his wife, two remaining daughters, and all his possessions, a Mother Courage who disappears into an uncertain future.

For Barrie Kosky, *Anatevka* is first and foremost a play about exile, wandering, and waiting for the messiah. Hence the importance of tradition, the "'cultural DNA of the Jewish experience,'" as a performative link with, continuation, and fictionalization of the past. Tradition, like the Broadway musical itself, is a constantly evolving trope that "must change in order to survive."[51] Kosky's conception of *Anatevka* as exilic narrative also links it with two other pieces of music theatre he has directed at the Komische Oper, Arnold Schoenberg's *Moses and Aron* (in 2015) and Kurt Weill and Bertolt Brecht's *Rise and Fall of the City of Mahagonny* (in 2021). In fact, Kosky sees *Anatevka* as the third part of a Jewish trilogy, beginning with the Schoenberg, that allegorizes the ceaseless wandering of the Jews through the desert. All three pieces foreground the chorus, end ambivalently with characters on the move, and focus on the violent conflict between the protagonist and the society of which he is a part. For Kosky, the expulsion of the Jews from Anatevka is emblematic of other exilic migrations, not least of all the mass emigration of Jews from Europe in the 1930s. But he also sees it in relation to the ongoing refugee crises that have been transforming Germany—and the world. Kosky recognizes a tragic irony in the fact that *Anatevka* would gain an "electrifying relevance" today by being reset in the West Bank. The words,

Figure 6.2 Tevye (Max Hopp) prepares to take his leave of his home, *Anatevka* (*Fiddler on the Roof*), directed by Barrie Kosky, Komische Oper Berlin, 2017. Photo by Iko Freese.

"'You must leave your home!,' are heard by thousands of Palestinian Tevyes and Goldes every day—that is a terrible irony."[52]

As the most explicitly Jewish of the musicals Kosky has directed, *Anatevka*, according to German-Israeli historian Cilly Kugelmann, has a deliberately Talmudic quality. For her, that means recognizing Kosky's penchant for staging ambiguity and contradiction, which Kugelmann sees as analogous to the polyvocality of the Talmud, which embraces opposite points of view in order to translate "revealed doctrine" into "eternal and timeless truth."[53] Kosky himself understands this Talmudic quality as the performance of "contradictory arguments,"[54] a procedure he transposes "to the interpretation of theatre and opera." Most important, performance for him always represents contemporization, "working out the inherent meaning of a piece to make it plausible"—and relevant—"for a contemporary audience."[55] Kosky's passion for both historicity and contemporaneity means, Kugelmann notes, that he takes sources "more seriously than is often demanded by *Werktreue* [fidelity to the original], which is nothing more than a solicitation"—and excuse—"for ritualized repetitions."[56]

For his finale as Intendant at the Komische Oper, Barrie Kosky staged a glittering farewell that could almost serve as a companion to *Anatevka*. Working with music director Adam Benzwi, he put together *Barrie Kosky's All-Singing, All-Dancing Yiddish Revue* (2022), a tribute to US Borscht Belt entertainers of the 1950s and 1960s: the same years *Fiddler on the Roof* was being conceived and written. This metatheatrical extravaganza was designed as a lavish showcase for the great singing actors with whom Kosky has worked in Berlin and is sung primarily in Yiddish, with some English and German texts. An elaborate variety show featuring candy-colored costumes and Yiddish and US pop songs, it is performed by the Komische Oper's full orchestra, chorus, soloists, and corps de ballet—complete with showers of confetti and ten (male and female) Elvis impersonators gyrating to a Herb Alpert medley. Although all the personages in the *Revue* are fictitious, most are based on real Jewish stars of the era, such as the singing Barry Sisters and the comedian Micky Katz. The piece is far more celebratory than *Anatevka* and serves as a reminder that Kosky traces the Komische Oper's history back long before Felsenstein, all the way to 1892, when the very building on Behrenstraße in which the company is housed was constructed as the Metropol-Theater. The Metropol became one of the most celebrated revue and operetta house in Berlin until the Nazis came to power in 1933, and it was home to the Weimar era's most celebrated (and mostly Jewish) operetta stars: singing actors such as Fritzi

Massary and Richard Tauber and composers such as Friedrich Hollaender and Paul Abraham.

Barrie Kosky's All-Singing, All-Dancing Yiddish Revue performs a fascinating series of contradictions. On the one hand, it's like a sequel to *Anatevka* that answers the question: what would the Americanized grandchildren of Tevye have enjoyed if in the postwar decades, they, like countless other middle-class Jews, had frequented the Jewish resorts in the Catskill Mountains? In answering that question, the *Revue* simultaneously (and paradoxically) serves as a kind of a "prequel" to *Anatekva* that celebrates the musical and theatrical traditions (primarily operetta and Yiddish vaudeville) out of which *Fiddler on the Roof* sprang. It also pays homage to the Borscht Belt, where both Bock and Harnick worked during the 1950s.[57] At the same time, *Barrie Kosky's All-Singing, All-Dancing Yiddish Revue* asks a tantalizingly counterfactual question: what if the Nazis had never come to pass and Germany had an unbroken tradition of Jewish-inflected popular musical theatre? It accordingly adopts a strategy exactly counter to that of Fritzi Massary, who converted to Protestantism in 1917 to further her career, by turning Kosky's stars, Max Hopp, Helmut Baumann, and Dagmar Manzel, into the Jews they never were: Max Hoppelsteiner, Herschel Baumann, and one of the singing Bagelman Sisters. What if, the piece asks, the living cultures of central European Jews had not been destroyed? By proposing such a refulgent answer to these unanswerable questions, *Barrie Kosky's Yiddish Revue* offers a profoundly utopian reflection on the glories of a history that never happened.

The Gayest Show in Town

Barrie Kosky, the very public face of the Komische Oper for ten years, is (in his own words) a "Jewish, gay kangaroo,"[58] an Australian, gay, polyglot Jew with Polish and Hungarian roots who has long maintained that he feels completely "at home" in Berlin: "Berlin has always been and is still a city of gypsies and travelers. It is a city for displaced dreamers and lost souls."[59] As a self-declared outsider, he does not carry the same baggage that a German director does, and in the tradition of the Metropol-Theater, delights in careening between camp and seriousness, high culture and kitsch.

None of Kosky's Broadway musicals is as indebted to the Metropol tradition as Cole Porter's *Kiss Me, Kate*, a free adaptation of Shakespeare's *The*

Taming of the Shrew that was a first-wave musical import to Germany and is the oldest of the few Broadway musicals that are a staple of state-subsidized theatres. For his debut musical at the Komische Oper in 2008, Kosky reconceptualized the piece from the ground up so it would speak directly to contemporary Berlin residents (and tourists) for whom the city was the "poor but sexy" metropolis, a quickly gentrifying but scruffy, lewd, art-filled town that still bore the scars of the divided city.[60] With his in-yer-face, camp version of *Kate*,[61] Kosky presented his credentials as an out gay director who, as a non-US-American Anglophone, understands, loves, and knows how to translate Broadway conventions transnationally. Breaking with Felsenstein's tradition in order to revel in the glitz, glamour, and pathos of musical comedy, Kosky used the production to declare his deep love of theatricality and keen awareness of the historical provenance of the 1948 Broadway hit that revived Cole Porter's career and won the first Tony Award for Best Musical. Kosky's production emphasizes the piece's metatheatricality with his signature, over-the-top style, which underscores the polychrome opulence of both Porter's pastiche of *The Taming of the Shrew* and the Broadway musical as a genre. Few musicals are as tuneful or lyrically profligate as *Kiss Me, Kate*, and the brilliance and infectiousness of the score conceal Porter's experimental audacity and skill at writing extremely divergent song types, from ballads to comic specialty numbers, operetta waltzes to pseudo-blues. Kosky, moreover, caricatures the US-American-ness of the piece by turning this backstage musical into a hyper-theatricalized reflection on US-American musical comedy. He exaggerates the not always flattering stereotypes that Germans have of US culture in general and the Broadway musical in particular. Kosky joked that the costumes commandeered every last sequin in Berlin,[62] and indeed, Bianca's suitors and the large chorus are costumed in glittering, sequined, brightly colored cowboy outfits, a deliberately nonsensical choice considering there are no cowboys in either *Kate* or *Shrew*. And by turning all the chorus boys gay, Kosky emphasizes the gay subcultural links to the musical, Porter's own homosexuality, and Germany's clichéd but not inaccurate view of the Broadway musical as the most emblematically gay US-American performance genre.[63]

It was apposite that Kosky's first musical at the Komische Oper should be *Kiss Me, Kate*, since that piece thematizes and performs precisely the collision of high culture with popular culture that he loves, juxtaposing Shakespeare against vaudevillian musical comedy, which has long been considered the lightest, most topical, and most disposable of musical theatre genres. (Kosky's first production at the house in 2003 had been György Ligeti's *Le Grand Macabre*, an opera that also thematizes the collision of high and low.) *Kiss Me, Kate*, a backstage musical about a touring company's performance of a musicalization of *Shrew*, overlays three different plots and theatrical idioms: the original Shakespeare story; the tempestuous relationship between an egotistical director, Fred Graham, and his star and ex-wife, Lilli Vanessi; and juxtaposed against both, an intrigue with gangsters as well as the backstage chaos of a show on the road when the weather is simply "Too Darn Hot."[64] Although Kosky brings out the farce in all three plots, he recognizes that the backstage love story is the most seriously musicalized, the one that explicitly references operetta and in which most is at stake. But even this plot he sees as a collision of high and low, describing it as a combination of George and Martha from Edward Albee's *Who's Afraid of Virginia Woolf* and Kermit and Miss Piggy from *The Muppet Show*.[65]

The key to understanding the particular cocktail of *U-* and *E-* that Kosky mixes up in *Kiss Me, Kate*, and in most of his operetta productions, is the idea of camp, which is commonplace in the United States but quite foreign to German culture, especially a prestigious state-subsidized opera house. The *Kiss Me, Kate* program includes lengthy excerpts from Susan Sontag's pathbreaking "Notes on 'Camp,'" originally published in 1964, plus an essay by Christoph Dompke about Cole Porter's virtuosic use of innuendo as well as the sexual (mainly homosexual) connotations and resonances of classic musicals and their importance in US gay male culture both before and after Stonewall. Kosky's production exploits the play of irony, sentimentality, parody, and nostalgia that constitutes camp while celebrating what Sontag calls its "theatricalization of experience," its way of transforming *being* into *playing*.[66] The backstage setting of *Kiss Me, Kate* makes the piece especially suitable for being turned into a multiply metatheatrical piece and in Kosky's production, the orchestra is seated on risers stage left while the space around it alternates between stage, dressing room, and wings. This spatial arrangement is linked to a temporal scheme that shifts between rehearsal and performance, pre-show and post-show, allowing Kosky to make almost every number into a diegetic, elaborately choreographed, self-consciously theatrical performance. Only Lilli's "So in Love" and Fred's gentle second act reprise of the song seem to be non-diegetic and provide moments of stillness and inwardness. And while there are other bittersweet images, including the unexplained appearance of two elderly chorus girls applying make-up who haunt Lilli's dressing room like ghosts (in a likely echo of Sondheim's *Follies*), most of the production represents a manic, hyper-theatrical fantasy of the Broadway musical.

The elements that make Kosky's *Kiss Me, Kate* (and most of his subsequent productions) camp are primarily the costumes and choreography, which are extravagant, flamboyant, and highly sexualized. Otto Pichler's athletic, hyper-kinetic, hip-centered choreography, the likes of which, Kosky notes, had never been seen in a state-subsidized theatre before,[67] accentuates the chorus's emphatically erotic ways while undermining traditional gender roles. The male dance chorus is as flamboyantly sexual as the female is ardent and vigorous. This choreographic subversion of the gender binary is crucial in camping the production (and most of their later collaborations) and tying it in with the long histories of theatrical cross-dressing and gay drag. Kosky explains that the costumes (by Alfred Mayerhofer) were decisively influenced by the Cockettes, "a totally crazy artist's collective from San Francisco." Founded in 1969, during the first heady days of gay liberation, the Cockettes were a group of gender-bending, gender-fluid people who lived and performed together and embodied the hippie avant-gardist dream of turning life into art and art into life. Kosky references their "totally crazy, gay drag happenings" in which they parodied Broadway musicals and sang their own bizarre versions of pop songs. "All were on LSD and wore crazy masks, had green and orange beards, fur costumes, and sequins."[68] *Kiss Me, Kate* virtually copies some of the Cockettes' costumes and uses Cole Porter's score to resuscitate their hallucinatory, utopian spectacles.

The audacity of Kosky's style, public voice, and mise en scène have earned him a sizable following among Berlin's large and very public LGBTQ+ communities. As he realizes, however, his "radical queer reading" of canonical works is not always to the liking of critics, who sometimes censure his highly homosexualized work in pieces like *Kiss Me, Kate* and *Die schöne Helena*.[69] A subheading in a *Tagesspiegel* article about Kosky, "Not only the gay community of Berlin is delighted," implies that some Berliners are less than delighted and see his work as coterie art for a niche audience.[70] Kosky himself maintains that his queer readings "confront the audience." "If," he contends, "I was a heterosexual director" who put "dancing girls" onstage "like you see at the Friedrichstadtpalast [Berlin's premier, over-sequined revue house], they wouldn't say, 'That's *so* heterosexual!'"[71] On the other hand, in an interview with the gay press, when asked how gay [*schwul*] *Die schöne Helena* is, he responds: "Must we say gay? This actually is too narrow for me.... It's not only camp and funny when it comes to sex or the body, because I want to achieve more, . . . to call into question the categories of taste, while having great fun."[72] His hedging on this question is a sign that he understands how fraught these issues are in Germany, where heteronormativity has been the rule in large and medium-sized state-subsidized theatres and camp is equated with kitsch.

Although Kosky is familiar with German and US scholarship that highlights the long association of opera, operetta, and musicals with gay and lesbian subcultures, this work remains marginalized in Germany, where identity politics–driven cultural theory and artistic practice have not gained the kind of traction they have in the Anglophone world. The suspicion that identity politics is retrogressive and divisive is related in part to the genocidal consequences during the Third Reich of the pseudo-scientific racism formulated in Germany during the late nineteenth century, as well as the classification and pathologization of sexual practices and identities. Although racist pseudo-science was nearly ubiquitous before World War I, two of the leading and most influential sexologists, Richard von Krafft-Ebing and Magnus Hirschfeld, were German, and their work, for better or worse, remains a cornerstone in the study of minoritized and stigmatized

Figure 6.3 Petruchio (Roger Smeets) held aloft by the Cockettes, *Kiss Me, Kate*, directed by Barrie Kosky, Komische Oper Berlin, 2008. Photo by Monika Rittershaus.

sexual identities. Homosexuality remained criminalized in both Germanys until the late 1960s, and the persecution and incarceration of gay men was especially widespread in West Germany. Although registered partnerships became available in 2001, same-sex marriage was not legalized until 2017.[73] To their credit, German theatre practitioners, administrators, and scholars since around 2010 have become far more outspoken about the need for *Diversität*, but it is almost always code for *Migrationshintergrund* (migration background) or gender, not sexuality. Among academics, questions of sexuality are rarely raised in either theatre studies or musicology, which remain much more determinedly heterosexist preserves than in the Anglophone world. German theatregoers, as well, are more wary of identity politics than their US-American and British cousins, who are more conversant with the long and important histories of Anglophone gay and lesbian playwriting, performance, and spectatorship. As Kosky puts it, "I think that Germans have no sense in the mainstream of queer culture. I think what we take for granted in the English-speaking theatre has been so influenced by gay aesthetics."[74] As he recognizes, his queer theatre practices provide a link to Anglo-American theatrical traditions, in which queer conventions and tropes are far more pervasive. In Germany, on the other hand, *schwule Kultur* (gay or queer culture) is much more closely associated with entertainment (cabaret, variety, television, and stand-up comedy) than art. But change may be in the air. In February 2021, a lead article in the *Süddeutsche Zeitung* featured headshots of 185 actors who chose to out themselves as LGBTQ+ to protest homo- and transphobia in the theatre and film industries, a surprising development in Germany that suggests that queer is now being normalized far more actively than in 2012 when Barrie Kosky became Intendant at the Komische Oper.[75]

At the turn of the twenty-first century, there was little in the state-subsidized theatres to distinguish the work of lesbian and gay directors such as Andrea Breth and Robert Wilson from that of their straight colleagues. But beginning in the 2010s, Kosky must be numbered as one of a small group of high-profile directors working to give elite German theatre a more queer mien, among them Falk Richter, Jette Steckel, Christian Weise, and Ersan Mondtag.[76] Mondtag is the only one who, like Kosky, directs opera and other large-scale works, and he is one of the few directors who shares Kosky's taste for excess, especially in his collaborations with the riotously flamboyant actor Benny Claessens. Stylistically, Mondtag's work is more concept-driven than that of most German directors (he designs his own maximalist sets), and his frequent pastiche of expressionism and/or surrealism, along with his fascination with horror and historical trauma, gives it a menacing quality that Kosky's lacks. Yet little of the work of these directors is likely to appear especially queer to Anglophone theatregoers used to *Angels in America*, Jeanine Tesori and Lisa Kron's *Fun Home* (2013), or Paula Vogel's *Indecent* (2015).

Barrie Kosky, working with Otto Pichler, has been a pacesetter in playing fast and loose with gender and sexuality in musicals, operettas, and opera, especially in dance. Indeed, one of the most recognizable features of most of Kosky's work has been both the spectacularization of dancers' bodies, particularly male dancers, and the gender fluidity of singing and dancing choruses. In 2014, his *Die schöne Helena* raised eyebrows when, instead of the predictable scantily clad chorus girls, he substituted, in *Die Welt*'s words, "six shirtless, snazzy [*schmucke*] gentlemen of the ballet who, wearing Bavarian leather trousers, offer a porthole view of their naked asses."[77] In most of Kosky and Pichler's work, both male and female dancers perform as chorus "girls" and "boys," a convention that was used to great effect in *Kiss Me, Kate*, as well as in their Paul Abraham, Jacques Offenbach, and Oscar Straus collaborations. This strategy contrasts sharply with the work of "so many German directors" who, in Kosky's words, use "cross-dressing or transvestites as a symbol onstage of decadence or perversion,"[78] as one is likely to see in productions of Alban Berg's *Lulu*. On the contrary, Kosky and Pichler celebrate the flesh and the plasticity of gender—let's call it genderfuck—to suggest that identity is always drag, a costume, a mask that can be put on or taken off at will. This queer masquerade can be seen as an elaboration of the breeches or trousers roles in opera, but Kosky has taken the trope far beyond its use in Handel and Strauss and made it a new law of musical theatre. In his hands, the application of this law is so frankly sexy that it is being picked up by many German theatres that perform operettas and musicals, including dedicated operetta houses such as the Wiener Volksoper and the Staatsoperette Dresden. At the same time, Kosky is insistent that the queering of popular music theatre that he practices, like *RuPaul's Drag Race*, reaches beyond LGBTQ+ communities and delights the Komische Oper's large heterosexual audience.[79] The diverse groups of opera and musical theatre lovers that now visit the Komische Oper, especially from other parts of Europe, are also spreading these glad tidings beyond the German-speaking world. Against all odds, genderfuck is becoming fabulously commonplace.

"Lemme tell it to the world!"

One of Barrie Kosky's most resounding critical and popular successes at the Komische Oper was the first Broadway musical he directed as Intendant, *West Side Story*. Co-directed with choreographer Otto Pichler in 2013, it earned unanimous rave reviews and was a runaway hit in Berlin, playing in repertoire until 2019. Kosky and Pichler chose to localize the musical and at the same time, through that localization, universalize it as a plea for tolerance and understanding. Their *West Side Story*, in other words, represents a visionary updating of the piece that adapts it, without changing the score, for a country in which there are very few immigrants, or children of immigrants, from the Caribbean or Latin America. In Germany, the people with a migration background (*Migrationshintergrund*) as a rule come instead from Turkey, the Balkans, Eastern Europe, and the Middle East (in Berlin in 2014, 28.6% of the population so described themselves).[80] Accordingly, Kosky and Pichler presented the piece in implicit dialogue with what in Germany in the 2010s was widely called postmigrant theatre, a counterhegemonic theatre by and/or about Germans with a migration background. At the same time, they staged it in a far more abstract and contemporary way than most US-American productions, while retaining and celebrating *West Side Story*'s wealth of Latin-inspired music. Their production not only de-Hispanicizes the Sharks but also more generally de-ethnicizes it, turning the Jets and the Sharks into mirror images of each other. Kosky understands that the US "in the 20th century was a great metaphor for immigration" and he sees the piece as dramatizing less particular social crises of the 1950s than an ongoing, recurrent global struggle between old immigrants and new immigrants. Puerto Rico he argues, "is just a synonym for the 'other' country, . . . 'the new.'"[81]

Kosky's interpretive strategy of universalizing *West Side Story* is at odds with that taken in recent US-American realizations of one of the most controversial canonical musicals. Accusations of racism have dogged it from the very beginning, and Arthur Laurents's 2009 revival, Ivo van Hove's 2020 revival, as well as Steven Spielberg's 2021 film all attempt to alleviate the piece's alleged racism by including far more Spanish and giving more facticity, particularity, and depth to the Puerto Rican characters and situations. Although Leonard Bernstein had a long and serious engagement with Latin American cultures and musical styles (and his wife, Felicia Montealegre, was Latin American), Stephen Sondheim later confessed that he "never even met a Puerto Rican" before writing the lyrics.[82] And it is clear from the piece's lengthy development process that its concern with Puerto Rican immigration was, as Brian Herrera points out, "an expeditious afterthought, motivated neither by explicit antipathy toward nor active interest in the lived experience of Puerto Ricans in New York City."[83] Unlike Spielberg and van Hove, who attempt diligently to particularize the Puerto Rican characters, Kosky and Pichler deliberately strip *West Side Story* down to "a ritual of music and dance," globalizing its themes of migration, diaspora, and exile.[84] Instead of accentuating the racialized cliches, Kosky and Pichler free the piece, one German critic notes, "from the stereotypes that we so often see in musicals."[85]

Kosky and Pichler were granted permission by the Jerome Robbins estate to stage the play without Robbins's choreography and they chose not to try to repair what Kosky argues is a "radically minimalist" piece, but "blow away the dust."[86] Their production was staged on a vast, empty, black stage, with a thin white line slicing the space into two, into which a few set pieces (vegetable stand, bed, thicket of mirrored disco balls) are rolled on or flown in as needed. By forgoing realistic and culturally specific scenic elements, Kosky and Pichler dispense with the geographic and cultural particularity of New York City, or of Berlin, for that matter, in favor of "any city at the beginning of the 21st century."[87] Rather than opt for a facile and "banal" topicality and turn the conflict between the Anglo Jets and the Puerto Rican Sharks into a battle between German skinheads and Turkish immigrants, the spare, up-to-date costumes and the intense, raw, and highly sexualized embodied presence of the characters (and performers) insinuate a gritty contemporaneity.[88]

Unlike Kosky's *Kiss Me, Kate*, which extravagantly and surrealistically accentuates the musical's campy comedy, his *West Side Story* plays it absolutely straight and makes a case for the piece as one of the tragic masterpieces of US music theatre.

When *West Side Story* opened on Broadway in 1957, it received mixed reviews (and lost the Tony Award for Best Musical to *The Music Man*) and only in 1961, with the release of the film, did it begin to achieve the classic status it has since enjoyed in much of the world. In Germany and Austria, on the other hand, it was initially attacked and dismissed and only gradually has it acquired cultural legitimacy. The same year the film was released, an English-language, Broadway touring company performed *West Side Story* in Munich where it was condemned, except for Robbins's choreography, as "banal" and "musically thin"[89]—a "catastrophe of taste."[90] "All spontaneity, all freedom, all honest feeling, all real toughness are banned," *Theater heute* wrote, "no operetta can be more kitschy, no film more untrue, no pamphlet, no advertisement more over-calculated."[91] The turning point in *West Side Story*'s reception, however, proved to be its first German-language production at the Wiener Volksoper in 1968, where it starred the young, soon-to-be opera star Julia Migenes (who also had created the role of Hodel in *Fiddler on the Roof* on Broadway). Although it received mixed reviews, Leonard Bernstein, who was conducting Richard Strauss's *Der Rosenkavalier* at the nearby Wiener Staatsoper, was being hailed as a hero and his musical was appreciated for its skill, in Raymond Knapp's words, in "merg[ing] the popular with the difficult" and providing "no easy answers."[92] Viennese critics recognized *West Side Story*'s adeptness in "blend[ing] the tonal qualities of large symphonic and jazz orchestras"[93] and its instrumentality in abolishing the "'class conflict' between high and low art" and "democratizing world literature."[94] Wolfgang Jansen argues, however, that the change in reception between 1961 and 1968 was due primarily to a new openness to socially critical art.[95] Viennese critics could not help but recognize in the piece's "'hard' style a ruthless confrontation with the problems of social reality" and in its critique of "racist oppression in the shadow of the Statue of Liberty" a reference to "the youth riots" then taking place in West Berlin.[96]

West Side Story's aesthetic daring and its social criticism have been decisive in its gradual acceptance into the German musical theatre canon. Shortly after reunification, its popularity peaked with more than 400 performances of twenty-two different productions, drawing 320,000 spectators.[97] Among first-wave musicals, it is the only one that pointedly takes up racial politics and, indeed, agitates for a new world that would be free of prejudice and hatred. It is the musical that most decisively juxtaposes high modernist and popular styles, both musically and choreographically. It is, moreover, the only first-wave musical to feature a working-class dramatis personae, Latin American musical vernaculars, and a tragic plot, the latter borrowed from its Shakespearean model, *Romeo and Juliet*. Unlike the van Hove and Spielberg realizations of *West Side Story*, Kosky and Pichler's production attempts—and against all odds, succeeds—at reframing the debates about race and representation. It thereby provides a provocative answer to the question of how to adapt politically charged and highly particularized material for an audience that is very different from the one for which the work was conceived.

The work of four avowedly liberal, gay Jews, *West Side Story* was seen as topical and daring in 1957 because of its success at taking on burning issues: racism, Puerto Rican immigration to New York City, and juvenile delinquency. Given Leonard Bernstein's musical pedigree and aspirations, it

Figure 6.4 The dying Tony (Tansel Akzeybek) in the arms of Maria (Julia Giebel), Act 2 of *West Side Story*, directed by Barrie Kosky, Komische Oper Berlin, 2013. Photo by Iko Freese.

was also the most musically adventurous show of the decade, referencing not operetta but opera. It maintains, Raymond Knapp emphasizes, a "consistency of . . . musical fabric" and "very high degree of musical integration that creates the affective logic of the piece,"[98] not least of all because it is constructed on the interval of the tritone, the augmented fourth, or *diabolus in musica*. Bernstein uses this unstable interval to generate both Wagnerian leitmotifs and "[Anton] Webern-like manipulations of basic cells" which, Knapp notes, "locate the show on the intractably mean streets of the modern city,"[99] or in Kosky's words, "in a 20th-century metropolis."[100] In the cautionary song "Cool," Bernstein even manages to incorporate a twelve-tone fugue that, rather than being sung, is danced to Jerome Robbins's revolutionary choreography and helps to give the musical an important measure of high-culture legitimacy.

A central issue in the controversies surrounding *West Side Story* has been the very different musical and choreographic styles Bernstein and Robbins developed for the rival gangs. The score brashly juxtaposes a dissonant, heavily syncopated, "hard-edged jazz-blues idiom for the Jets" against "a rhythmically charged but generalized 'Latin' style for the immigrant Sharks."[101] While the cool, urban jazz reaches back to the bebop of the 1940s, the "Latin" style has a longer and more complex pedigree. Latin American music had been one of the principal ingredients in the development of jazz at the beginning of the twentieth century, but between the 1920s and late 1950s, it became fully "assimilated into mainstream American music."[102] Dances such as the tango, rumba, and merengue became increasingly popular as both musical and dance styles, culminating in the mambo and cha-cha-cha crazes of the 1950s, which in fact reached far beyond the United States. Cuban band leader Pérez Prado was famous globally as "King of the Mambo" and enjoyed hits in West Germany as early as 1955.[103] As Elizabeth A. Wells notes, "the mambo itself was not an overtly lascivious dance, [but] its association with the sensual lent it much of its glamour."[104] So when *West Side Story* premiered at the height of the mambo craze, incorporating different kinds of Latin music, it struck sympathetic chords with a public that had already been captivated by Latin song and dance.

Bernstein's use of Latin music is especially important because he was also drawing on a tradition of Spanish-style music that, from the middle of the nineteenth century, had been an important ingredient in European art music. Although it was only one of several kinds of exotic music used by European composers, it produced the largest body of concert works that are still part of the standard repertoire. Russian composers (Glinka and Rimsky-Korsakov) were among the first to exploit it, but the orientalized Spanish idiom was especially important for the French, from Lalo to Debussy and Ravel, and its locus classicus is undoubtedly Bizet's *Carmen*, which, Kosky notes, provides the model for *West Side Story* as "tragic opéra comique."[105] During the 1930s, this idiom was picked up by modernist US composers, most notably Bernstein's mentor, Aaron Copland, in the turn to a more populist idiom. By the 1950s, the Latin musical style had become the only one that carried both lowbrow sex-appeal and highbrow, modernist prestige, and thus was perfectly suited for a work that aimed to elevate the Broadway musical.

West Side Story's use of Latin music has long generated criticism because it is seen as the most exotic element in a musical that, despite its critique of racism, has often and correctly been criticized, especially the song "America," for exploiting racist stereotypes. In the 1950s, the musical quickly became established, Brian Herrera notes, "as the template for all things Puerto Rican in US popular performance,"[106] despite the fact that among its most "Puerto Rican" numbers, "Mambo" is Cuban while "America" "combines the indigenous Mexican form, the *huapango*, with the Puerto Rican genre of the *seis*."[107] An orientalizing project that portrays its Puerto Rican characters as more colorful, sexualized, and hot-blooded than its Anglos, *West Side Story* was initially believed by many to be a "sociologically authentic representation of—or even solution to—New York City's social problems."[108] The Jets are individualized and almost entirely male, while the Shark men are barely differentiated and relegated to the background in favor of the Puerto Rican women who perform two of the show's most celebrated songs, "America" and "A Boy like That"/"I Have a Love." (Like many orientalizing operas, *West Side Story* gives much of its most memorable music to its exoticized characters.) Although Arthur Laurents tried to correct this asymmetry in his 2009 Broadway revival by having the Puerto Ricans' numbers translated into Spanish, this asymmetry is so musically and dramatically generative that it cannot be substantially changed without completely undermining the musical.

The challenge facing Kosky and Pichler, in being allowed to jettison Robbins's choreography, was the imperative of making a widely performed musical speak to a contemporary Berlin audience. Pichler devised dance that is more aggressive and street-based than the original while they re-imagined this drama of migration and assimilation for a Germany that for centuries has experienced wave after wave of migrants and refugees. Yet not until 2015 did then-Chancellor Angela Merkel first refer to Germany as a "nation of immigrants."[109] Kosky explains that it would have been easy to turn *West Side Story* into a ripped-from-the-headlines-style turf war between "neo-Nazis or right-wing thugs" and Turkish Germans, along with the hackneyed choice of making Tony a "reformed neo-Nazi who works in a shop,"[110] which is an exact analogue to the cliché Spielberg later opted for. But he also knew that kind of updating would render parts of the piece nonsensical. Inspired instead by images and videos of the Arab Spring, in which "you didn't know" by the clothes "who was on one side, who on the other, or who was Shiite, who Sunni," he chose nearly identical dress for the Jets and the Sharks, so that "the costuming doesn't give away who's who," and let the performers speak with their own many different dialects.[111] The fact that the Shark men are more heavily tattooed than the Jets exoticizes and eroticizes them, but that practice elaborates on the orientalization already built into the piece. Kosky also resisted a facile updating by casting Julia Giebel, a blond German born in Cologne, as the Puerto Rican Maria, and Tansel Akzeybek, a black-haired Turkish German born in Berlin, as her Polish American Tony.[112]

Contemporizing *West Side Story*, "stripping the piece bare of all the clichés,"[113] removing geographical markers (principally the fire escapes that are habitually used in other productions), and erasing the visual signs of racial and ethnic difference, Kosky and Pichler transpose the musical to what one critic describes as a "globalized everywhere."[114] By so abstracting the space, creating the "world of the city . . . solely by light and the human body," they allow "the real questions to come into the foreground: Who owns the land? To whom does the city belong? Who came first?"[115] This abstraction, which also makes the score paramount and song and dance the primary vehicles for conveying the piece's intense emotionality, is totally opposed to the ornamentalized approaches taken by the recent Hollywood and Broadway realizations of the piece. It is, on the one hand, absolutely inimical to the over-particularized, computer-generated, shameless nostalgia of Spielberg's film. On the other hand, Kosky and Pichler's simple trust in the performers—and the score—on a bare stage also reveals the shallowness of van Hove's conception and its overreliance on huge video projections that dwarf the actors and the piece, and lead audiences to fear, in Ben Brantley's words, that they have mistakenly "stumbled into a casting call for a Calvin Klein fragrance ad."[116] In both cases, Spielberg and van Hove seem unwilling to trust the piece and instead rely on gimmicks that ultimately undermine the musical's impact.

Nothing illustrates Kosky and Pichler's performer-centered approach and understanding of the music's emotional arc as clearly as their use of the large stage turntable at two pivotal moments, "The Dance at the Gym" and "Somewhere." The setting for "The Dance at the Gym" is created simply by lowering dozens of outsized disco balls from the flies that create a magical, other-worldly space of shadows and light as the stage below them is filled with the many bodies of the large singing chorus and dancing chorus, performing the mock-stately "Promenade" and the wild, impassioned "Mambo." At the end of the Mambo comes the sudden, magical modulation to the "Cha-Cha," as Tony and Maria spot each other and, as they later sing, "I saw you and the world went away."[117] Kosky and Pichler understand that this disappearance of the world is at the very heart of the musical and they stage it by freezing the chorus on the rotating turntable, while Tony and Maria stare and slowly approach each other. This is exactly the opposite of Spielberg's strategy of rendering this moment as doggedly literally as possible, sacrificing the very public nature of their encounter and resetting their meeting under the bleachers. That choice negates the very essence of the piece, which lies in the clash between an otherworldly, impossible, utopian "somewhere" and the all too real hatred and death that fill the mean city streets. Kosky and Pichler understand that the power of this contradiction depends spatially on the simultaneity of two non-places, and they sharpen the contradiction in their staging of "Somewhere" by substituting for the single offstage soprano the entire community, that is, the full chorus standing on the circumference of the turntable, circling a no man's land. In the ballet that follows, Tony and Maria are joined by their older doubles, dancing, while they picture themselves together decades later in a future they will not live to see. Although Spielberg includes the ballet, his choice for the musical's final scene banalizes it by choosing to rescind the glimmer of transcendence that Bernstein and Sondheim offer to Maria and the dying Tony in the aching melody and lyric of "Somewhere."

Filling an empty space with bodies and light, Kosky and Pichler's *West Side Story* exploits the theatre at its most elemental. Nonetheless, their abstraction of the piece (as well as its casting) places it in conversation with critical discourses about postmigrant theatre, a term that began to be used by Shermin Langhoff while she was artistic director of Berlin's Ballhaus Naunynstraße between 2008 and 2013. Appointed Intendantin of the Maxim Gorki Theater in 2013 (the same year that the Komische Oper premiered *West Side Story*), Langhoff turned the Gorki into a center for a postmigrant theatre that would "incorporate the bodies and stories of immigrants into German history, as well as . . . promote new forms of hyphenated, even hybrid, German identity."[118] In the early and mid-2010s, "postmigrant" was often applied by Langhoff and others to the work of first-, second-, or third-generation Turkish Germans, many of them descended from the postwar *Gastarbeiter* (guest workers). But it was also being given a wider meaning and application as part of what Azadeh Sharifi calls a "migratory aesthetics." According to Sharifi, postmigrant theatre is "a decolonising strategy," rooted in the histories and experiences of migration, diaspora, and exile, and references far more than Germans of Turkish descent.[119] Postmigrant, which can also be a mode of self-description, points less to identity than to histories of border crossings, both elected and forced, and the "stories and perspectives of those who themselves have not migrated but who have this migration background as part of their personal knowledge and collective memory."[120] Although in the 2020s, the term "postmigrant" is considered dated and has been superseded by different terminology (*Migrationshintergrund, Diversität, Rassismus, Antirassismus*), its importance stems in part from the fact that, like "queer," it cuts across identity categories and is linked to an activism that militates for and generates a more diverse culture.

Kosky and Pichler's globalized *West Side Story* must also be seen in relation to major institutional changes at the Komische Oper. Even before Barrie Kosky's arrival, the house made a commitment to social and cultural activism with its multipronged and ongoing initiative, "Selam Opera!" Its purpose is to alter preconceptions about opera and develop an "appreciation of musical theatre among audiences of Turkish origin." An "intercultural project" launched by the self-styled "opera house for all," Selam Opera! aims to modify modes of production, distribution, and reception and turn the house into a center for "cultural diversity." Begun during the 2010–2011 season under the name "Türkisch—Oper kann das!" ("Opera can speak Turkish!"), it expanded under Kosky's directorship and has included hiring new staff members to establish personal and professional contacts with Berlin's Turkish community, setting up workshops as well as educational and media outreach programs, and adding Turkish translations to the subtitling system. Selam Opera!'s most mobile component is the Operndolmuş (opera minibus) that carries two singers, three instrumentalists, and one dramaturg to "community centres, old people's homes, migrant organizations and educational establishments in city districts with a notably high proportion of people from different cultural areas." Aiming to "build bridges from [these sites] to the world of opera," the initiative attempts to redress the inequities of the German educational system, given that "40% of primary school pupils in Berlin have a language of origin other than German."[121] Beginning in 2013, the Komische Oper commissioned several bilingual Turkish-German children's operas and the next year organized a symposium and published a 176-page book, *Selam Opera!*, that includes essays by activists, scholars, community leaders, practitioners, and arts administrators from across the globe that explain the project and detail the histories of postmigrant theatre, Turkish music, and intercultural performance. Its cover image (like the cover image of this book) is a photograph of the electrifying "The Dance at the Gym" from *West Side Story*, the Komische Oper's production that is most actively engaged with questions of migration, diversity, and racism.[122] Selam Opera! proves, in other words, that the Komische Oper has put its money where its mouth is.

Candide as Existential Vaudeville

Imagine a world that persistently rewards the rich and powerful while immiserating the masses. Imagine an international cartel that scapegoats minorities and immigrants, while treating women like chattel to be bought, coddled, and dumped. Voltaire did so in his 1759 novella *Candide* by simply observing—and ruthlessly satirizing—the world around him. Leonard Bernstein and his collaborators did so two centuries later in their notorious flop. Sixty years on, Barrie Kosky followed suit and succeeded rapturously in resurrecting *Candide* by underscoring both its historicity and its urgent contemporaneity.

Bernstein's *Candide* (1956) is a puzzling piece. Its Broadway premiere, with a dazzlingly inventive score by Bernstein and heavy-handed libretto by Lillian Hellman, garnered famously mixed reviews, and conventional wisdom has it that its failings are obvious, although no two critics are agreed on what they are. Its overture has become a concert hall favorite and despite the firmament of starry names associated with it over the years, it has been radically revised more often than any other musical. [123] Its plot is as impudently peripatetic as its protagonists, and its wildly eclectic score ranges in style from bubbling, musical comedy charm song to coloratura aria, Spanish dance to operatic cri de coeur. At least seven different libretti follow in the wake of Hellman's much-disparaged original, and only once has it enjoyed a long run in the theatre, in Harold Prince's 1973 musically stripped down, environmental staging for which Hugh Wheeler wrote a frothy new book. Hellman, who considered Wheeler "a hack," was very unhappy with his revision and withdrew the performance rights to her script.[124] The 1973 libretto does indeed turn the piece into a brittle comedy, which has been criticized by conductor John Mauceri as being "one long joke" from which the "heart, the tears, and the faith" were stripped.[125] Yet by necessity, Wheeler's rewrite has become the jumping-off point for all subsequent revivals and adaptations, which as a rule keep moving the piece closer and closer back to Voltaire's original. Although by the 1980s, six lyricists were credited on the title page, the lion's share is by Richard Wilbur, former US poet laureate and twice winner of the Pulitzer Prize.

Harold Prince's Broadway production, like many others, streamlined *Candide*'s emotional and musical scale and emphasized its farcical elements at the expense of Voltaire's penchant (in Bernstein's words) for "throw[ing] light on all the dark places."[126] Bernstein and Hellman were drawn to the novella for its caustic satire of Leibnizian (and, in their view, Eisenhowerian) optimism, and of Spanish Inquisition–style tyranny, which they saw as being analogous to McCarthyism. Their *Candide*, like Voltaire's, thus depicts anything but the best of all possible worlds. Bernstein and Hellman were committed leftists who had been bullied and threatened during the anti-communist witch hunt of the early 1950s, and both were intent on using *Candide* as artistic revenge. Although Hellman was taken to task for "wield[ing] the text as too blunt an instrument of social critique,"[127] hers and every subsequent version of the musical mount a satirical attack on political tyranny, militarism, ideological straitjacketing, materialism, and colonialism.

Despite Bernstein's championing of "American musical comedy" during the 1950s,[128] *Candide* is plainly a satire of European operetta, which, dating back to the nineteenth century, has always been the most satirical and topical of musical theatre genres. But it is also undeniably an eclectic, Broadway-style operetta whose inventive, ambitious score places it in line with the other genre-stretching musicals of the 1950s.[129] With its considerable musical and vocal demands, *Candide* is usually encountered these days in opera houses. And given the density of opera houses in the German-speaking world, one is much more likely to see it there than elsewhere (it was premiered in German in Vienna in 1976 and has since established itself on the edges of the standard repertoire). *Candide*'s first act, whose action is more or less the same in all the post-Hellman versions, follows the characters from Westphalia to their embarkation for the New World and has a straightforward narrative that plays well in the theatre. In contrast, *Candide*'s second act varies substantially from version to version and is usually seen as scattershot and digressive, an odyssey without an Ithaca, resolving only belatedly and provisionally in its radiant finale, "Make Our Garden Grow."

The theatrical challenges of performing *Candide* vary from version to version. Even Hellman scholars consider her original script "something of a 'black sheep' among the playwright's works," and she is credited in revised versions only as writer of "additional lyrics."[130] In the twenty-first century, the two editions that remain the most widely performed are the 1988 Scottish Opera version adapted by John Wells and John Mauceri and approved by Leonard Bernstein, and the 1999 Royal National Theatre version adapted by John Caird. The former is the standard opera house version and uses the original orchestrations by Bernstein and Hershy Kay. The latter, reorchestrated by Bruce Coughlin, is more picaresque, fast-paced, and closer in style to an absurdist musical comedy.

In every version of *Candide*, its theatrical dynamism lies in the violent clash between the ravishing beauty, sweep, and wit of its music and lyrics and the relentless succession of horrors that comprises its plot. (Stephen Sondheim considers it to have "the most scintillating set of songs yet written for the musical theater.")[131] This clash, however, is not a flaw; on the contrary, it is the crux of the piece's unique brilliance and power. I quote at length Raymond Knapp's description of the "parade of human misery" that Voltaire's *Candide* flaunts to emphasize the musical's uniquely schizophrenic logic. These realities include

> devastating natural disasters (earthquakes, fires, storms at sea, and the like), the plague, syphilis, war (including forced conscription, multiple rape, dismemberment, and other brutalities), slavery (including multiple rape, punitive dismemberment, and other brutalities), piracy (including rape, dismemberment, and other brutalities), partial cannibalism, . . . public torture and execution, . . . religious conflict and persecution, racial conflict and persecution, class-based exploitation, political corruption, prostitution and other more direct forms of sexual slavery, . . . power lust, blackmail and extortion, . . . and everyday cruelties such as poverty, hunger, the repayment of kindness with betrayal, and a general lack of human charity toward those who suffer.[132]

How is a director to stage the contradiction between such a jarringly "unpleasant" plot and such a dazzling score? A realistic production being unthinkable, most directors choose to emphasize the farcical, fantastical, cartoon-like character of *Candide*'s brutalities and the two-dimensionality of its protagonists. Barrie Kosky does as well, but by radicalizing the clash between the sublime and the ridiculous, he turns it into an "existential vaudeville" that takes *Candide*'s sparkling comedy seriously by mining it for tragedy.[133] For all its silliness, Kosky's *Candide* disproves Leibnizian optimism by depicting the realest of all possible worlds as a merry-go-round of exploitation, greed, and slaughter. By underscoring this message, Kosky's staging (based on John Caird's 1999 version, but using the Bernstein-Kay orchestrations) exploits the intriguing parallels between Bernstein's operetta and two plays that took the world by storm during the decade of *Candide*'s launch, Samuel Beckett's *Waiting for Godot* (1952) and *Endgame* (1957). Like Beckett's plays, Kosky's production spotlights and honors *Candide*'s absurdist logic as the inexorable law of a ruthlessly arbitrary and devastatingly unjust world. Like them, it employs classic vaudeville turns while reframing and ironizing them. (In 2020, Kosky directed Beckett's *Not I* and *Rockaby* at the Komische Oper on a triple bill with Schoenberg's *Pierrot Lunaire*, while the next year, the program for his *Don Giovanni* at the Wiener Staatsoper featured excerpts from *Waiting for Godot* and an interview with him titled "Waiting for the Commendatore.")[134] In recognizing *Candide*'s kinship with its absurdist contemporaries, Kosky's production exposes the philosophical fatalism that underlay the post–World War II boom years and simultaneously illuminates the darkest corners of our own world.

Despite the existential gloom into which Kosky's protagonists sink, his mise en scène is anything but solemn. Rather, his strategy reminds me of Bert States's description of *Waiting for Godot*, which, according to States "offers a collision of the essentially pure energies of comedy and tragedy."[135] Delighting in the piece's "musical schizophrenia,"[136] Kosky stages it as a rowdy, carnivalesque vaudeville (performed in Martin G. Berger's new German translation). Using only movable set pieces (designed by Rebecca Ringst) and flashy costumes (by Klaus Bruns) that run the gamut from faux eighteenth century to Las Vegas showgirl, kitschy folkloric to contemporary street dress, Kosky's spectacle is at once gaudy and stark. The stage is lit by Alessandro Carletti, whose sharp beams of white light pierce the often smoke-filled space, and the surreal choreography is by Otto Pichler. The dancers work overtime while Cunegonde's coloratura tour de force, "Glitter and Be Gay," is staged as a flashy pole dance in a Paris dive in which Cunegonde is surrounded by six wriggling women dancers.

Perhaps the score's most elaborate number dramatically is the Lisbon "Auto-da-fé," in which the chorus's merry celebration is intermittently interrupted by a series of summary trials and executions.

> What a day, what a day
> For an auto-da-fé!
> It's a lovely day for drinking
> And for watching people fry![137]

In Kosky's staging, the auto-da-fé is an unmistakably contemporary media event, complete with cameras and boom microphones, that climaxes in the hanging of Pangloss and the flogging of Candide. The throngs of merrymakers are joined by a chorus line of leggy, wildly can-canning, female and male show "girls" in Vegas-style bright blue and white one-pieces, with oversize feather headdresses and trains. The trial and punishment of Pangloss and Candide is preceded by two others, the first of three cartoonish

Figure 6.5 A puzzled Candide (Allan Clayton) surrounded by the ensemble during the Venice scene, Act 2 of *Candide*, directed by Barrie Kosky, Komische Oper Berlin, 2018. Photo by Monika Rittershaus.

Orthodox Jews and the second of a refugee couple carrying plastic tote bags (the woman wears a hijab). Both pairs are nonchalantly condemned and machine-gunned, then hastily dragged off-stage by the dancing "girls." The clangorous dissonance between the giddy song and dance and the gruesome interruptions intensifies Bernstein's musical contrast between the chorus's *allegro giocoso* and the Inquisitors' dirge-like chant. Kosky's "Auto-da-fé" is such a tour de force because it (like the Bernstein original) is a shocking indictment of the bourgeois entertainment machine that ignores, while profiting from, genocidal violence.

Kosky's transformation of the main characters into unmistakably contemporary refugees is but one of many examples of the renewed relevance that his *Candide* contrives. The first act closes with Candide and company (along with the chorus) en route to the New World paddling for their lives in three large rubber dinghies, which unmistakably evoke the leaky, makeshift barks in which refugees flee between North Africa and Europe. In the second act, in Surinam, Candide's servant Martin, "the most wretched, pessimistic person [Candide] could find,"[138] is re-gendered as a woman-played-by-a-man street-sweeper in the tradition of the scene-stealing travesty roles of Monteverdi or Cavalli. Martin's carnivalesque drag (as working-class executor of feminized labor) gives his misanthropy a grotesquely good-natured twist. Indeed, the fastidiously measured delivery by Martin (Tom Erik Lie) of the spoken invective against an insidious God, and the wretched planet he created, becomes one of the highlights of the show:

> When I look at this globe—or globule rather—I can't help thinking that God has abandoned it to *some* malignant force. I've never seen a town that didn't desire the destruction of its neighbour—nor a family that didn't want to kill another family. The poor hate the rich, but they creep and they cringe to them. The rich treat the poor like so many sheep, flogging their wool and their flesh for money....
>
> But has Mankind always been like this? Have they always been liars, cheats and frauds, traitors, thieves, ingrates and brigands? Will they always be cowardly, envious, vain, ambitious, feeble, fickle, gluttonous, drunken, lecherous, greedy, miserly, bloodthirsty, slanderous, debauched, fanatical, cruel, hypocritical and stupid?[139]

Although amusing, this tirade (closely modeled on Voltaire) by the arch-pessimist in the piece provides a much more accurate characterization of the world onstage (and off!) than Pangloss's fraudulent platitudes.

The second act of Kosky's *Candide* bears witness to the slow unraveling of optimism and hope. Martin's remarkable disquisition on misery is one of three moments in the staging that bring the existentialist subtext to the surface. As narrator, Voltaire/Pangloss sets the scene, and throughout the second act, his litany of new locales—Paraguay, Surinam, Marseilles, Venice—is each time greeted by Candide's befuddled question, "*Warum* [why the next venue on his seemingly arbitrary itinerary]?" Voltaire's reply is always, "*Warum nicht?*" (why not?). His first answer is affable, but with each iteration, Voltaire becomes more and more exasperated. His final "*Warum nicht?*" is almost spit out, sounding less the innocent reply to a rhetorical question than the sadistic threat of the merciless creator of the worst of all possible worlds, a.k.a. God.

For all Candide's trials and tribulations, it is questionable whether Voltaire's protagonist ends his journey an enlightened man. Beginning with the 1988 Scottish Opera version, however, Bernstein's hero is given a moment of illumination, the elegiac aria "Nothing More than This" that follows his ridiculously overdue acknowledgment of Cunegonde's venality. In Kosky's production, Candide's performance of this complaint (with lyrics by Bernstein) reaches far beyond Cunegonde's betrayal to become a bitter rejection of Pangloss's irresponsible optimism and a tragic acknowledgment of the precarity and evanescence of earthly things.

Following Voltaire and Bernstein, Kosky does not let *Candide* end in disgust and despair. Rather, for the final number, "Make Our Garden Grow," he stages the entire social collective—the world—and brings the full cast on stage. In this luminous finale, Kosky also brings the action unmistakably into the contemporary world of which we are all citizens. This world, in fact, had been represented literally in Kosky's production by the repeated appearance of characters carrying small globes (including the five penitent kings and queens in the Venice sequence singing the haunting "King's Barcarolle"). When Voltaire is revealed at the top of the show, wearing a gargantuan wig, he is carrying a globe. During the opening scene in the Westphalian schoolhouse, a large colored map of the world hangs on the back wall bearing the legend: DIE ERDE, KLIMAZONEN (the earth, climate zones, most of them an alarming red, orange, or yellow). Just before the final number, a giant-sized inflated globe appears upstage and slowly rolls toward the audience, only to be intercepted by Candide and Cunegonde and then hoisted aloft and given to members of the chorus, clad in contemporary dress, who begin slowly to spin this fragile blue and green orb. The presence of this grandiose, miniature earth gives a new meaning and urgency to one of the most resplendent and moving finales in all music theatre. "This is our world," it seems to say, "now threatened by man-made apocalypse. Its fate is in our hands. Guard it, protect it, heal it, make our garden grow."

Preferring a gently admonitory finale to a happily romantic one, Kosky recognizes that when Candide and Cunegonde finally confront each other at the end of their travels, "they are one thing to each other above all else: alien" (*fremd*).[140] The meaning of this sentence is complicated by the fact that the German word *fremd* has no equivalent in English. It means alien, strange, unfamiliar, unknowable; but it also means foreign. And it is precisely this foreignness in which Kosky's *Candide* basks: the foreignness of Bernstein's utterly Americanized operetta in the genre's homeland; the foreignness of Voltaire's stinging skepticism in a Broadway musical; and the foreignness of this production's glitzy, Las Vegas–style turns in a state-subsidized opera house.

In a favorable review of *Candide* in the *Frankfurter Allgemeine Zeitung*, a bastion of German high culture, Christiane Tewinkel notes the surprising incongruity of Kosky's *Candide* at the Komische Oper. She ends by remarking that "rarely has one seen the spirit of the Friedrichstadtpalast enter an opera house with such verve."[141] Referencing Berlin's temple to overstuffed, Las Vegas–style musical shows, Tewinkel betrays, I believe, a certain uneasiness regarding Kosky's wildly lavish production of Bernstein's politically charged masterpiece. Such splendor, Broadway-style extravagance, and creativity are indeed uncommon in the high-pressure (but well-funded) world of German opera. What was perhaps less apparent to her (and other German critics) was the ingenious way that Kosky translates a quintessentially US-American Cold War liberal protest against tyranny into an emotionally overpowering reflection on the contemporary state of the planet and the human species, which, some sixty-odd years after *Candide*'s premiere, has become far more precarious and endangered than Bernstein could have imagined.

Kurt Weill 2022

The challenges in staging the category-defying music theatre works of Leonard Bernstein are dwarfed in comparison with those facing contemporary directors of the works of Kurt Weill, a composer whose stature in the German-speaking world has only grown since the end of World War II. Not surprisingly, productions of his German works far eclipse his

Broadway canon, which is more challenging for German directors, actors, and audiences unfamiliar with the Broadway idiom of the 1940s. This is true despite the fact that *Lady in the Dark*, *Street Scene* (1946), and *Love Life* (1948) challenge the conventions and expand the horizons of musical theatre as radically as any of his German works.[142] During the 2021–2022 season, I was able to see five very differently tailored productions in different-sized theatres of five Kurt Weill works that together provide a revealing panorama of musical theatre in the German-speaking world. I provide a brief analysis of the first two, more traditional productions. For the remaining three, more ambitious interpretations, I detail how the works are used as vehicles for thinking about the political potential of music theatre in 2022.

Sebastian Sommer's *Happy End*, the smallest in scale of the productions in consideration, premiered in May 2022 at the Renaissance Theater, a 548-seat private theatre in the heart of former West Berlin. Next is Matthias Davids's production of *Lady in the Dark*, which opened in December 2021 at the Wiener Volksoper, a richly subsidized 1,261-seat house with a wide-ranging repertoire and a specialization in operetta. Third is Barrie Kosky's *Die Dreigroschenoper*, which premiered in August 2021 at the Berliner Ensemble, the theatre founded by Bertolt Brecht in East Berlin in 1949 and housed in the 660-seat Theater am Schiffbauerdamm. Fourth is Kosky's *Aufstieg und Fall der Stadt Mahagonny*, which opened at the Komische Oper's own 1,190-seat theatre in October 2021. Finally, I consider Ersan Mondtag's hallucinatory *Der Silbersee*, which premiered in September 2021 at Opera Ballet Vlaanderen's 1,008-seat theatre in Ghent, Belgium.[143]

Although these five productions represent only a fraction of the eighteen new productions of Kurt Weill pieces in continental Europe during the 2021–2022 season, the large majority were of his most performed piece, *Die Dreigroschenoper*. Of the five Weill productions I saw, four were performed more or less intact, while only one, Mondtag's *Der Silbersee*, completely reconceived the original by rewriting much of the libretto and turning the piece into a play-within-a-play. Nonetheless, all five productions performed the scores as written and brought the work to life by metatheatricalizing pieces that are already centrally concerned with questions of art and performance. Each piece features diegetic song, while using music self-consciously to reflect on its own employment of the conventions of musical theatre. This is perhaps clearest in the case of *Lady in the Dark*, whose plot is centered on Liza's forgetting and subsequent remembrance of her childhood theme song, "My Ship." But all the pieces knowingly deploy the conventions of popular song, operetta, or opera to foreground the power of musical theatre as a culinary art form (to borrow Bertolt Brecht's terminology), which is to say, "a means of pleasure" or enjoyment whose seductive power can also be used as social leverage.[144]

Although Brecht was Kurt Weill's most famous collaborator and the writer who most memorably theorized theatre as a mode of defamiliarization (*Verfremdungseffekt*), all of Weill's musical theatre works, even those written before Brecht, employ some mode of ironic distancing. Most commonly, this is a result of Weill's noticeable manipulation of musical idioms, especially evident in *Happy End*, which, Stephen Hinton points out, "is a play *about* music."[145] Music is not only integral to the action, the score is "all 'diegetic' in that it involves actual performance of one kind or another"[146] to dramatize the conflict between the criminal underworld and the Salvation Army. This plays out in the piece in the collision between infectious jazz- or dance-inspired songs and maudlin or militant (and slightly ridiculous) hymns and anthems.

Sebastian Sommer's *Happy End* manages to rescue a famously challenging play whose Berlin 1929 premiere sharply divided audiences and was attacked by critics who complained both of the plot's triviality and of what they took to be a clumsy agitprop harangue tacked on to the piece's dubiously happy ending. With music by Kurt Weill, book by Elisabeth Hauptmann, and lyrics by Bertolt Brecht, the libretto was originally attributed to the pseudonymous Dorothy Lane and not published until 1977. Set, like several later Brecht plays, in a Chicago overrun by criminals, *Happy End* is patently "Hollywoodish,"[147] inspired by gangster films, and an attempt by the three creators to capitalize on the unexpected, runaway success of their first musical about criminals, *Die Dreigroschenoper*. *Happy End*, however, sticks more closely to musical comedy formula with a clearly delineated gangster hero, Bill Cracker, and a not-quite-saintly heroine, Sister Lilian Holiday. In contrast to its predecessor, the plot is clearly centered on the unlikely romance between hero and heroine. Like *Dreigroschenoper*, it employs a satirical deus ex machina, but the piece comes much closer to delivering the happy ending promised by its title, complete with two loving couples. The real surprise in the final scene is thus not the resolution of the romantic plot but the unexpectedly pointed political message that accompanies it.

Sommer recognizes that the musical comedy structure of *Happy End* requires a light touch and he never tries to overload the satire, while managing to take the turn to didacticism at the end absolutely seriously. The

Renaissance Theater is a relatively intimate space, built in 1902 as a proto–Art Deco style theatre, with a dark wooden interior, and the production more than fills its small stage. Center stage is an utterly contemporary looking rectangular shelter, with wide, shiny, white sidewalls, inlaid with LED strips, that functions like a false proscenium. The production thereby stages the musical as both the period piece it is and as a contemporary intervention. This is made especially clear by the costuming. Although the sometimes stylized movement and make-up of the actors evoke German expressionism, the brightly colored, angular costumes give it a contemporary look. Most important, however, is the speech of the Fly, the female leader of the gang and wife of Hannibal, the amnesiac Salvation Army lieutenant. This speech culminates in a well-known series of questions that Brecht later purloined for Macheath in his revised *Die Dreigroschenoper*: "What is a crowbar compared with a stock certificate? What is the robbing of a bank compared with the founding of a bank? What is the murder of a man compared with the employment of man?"[148] The Fly's performance of these questions manages to cut through the musical comedy cheer and matches the pungency of Weill's score. Her speech is capped off, in Stephen Hinton's words, by a chorus commemorating "the canonization of the saints of capitalism, Morgan, Ford, and Rockefeller, as the local gangsters join forces with the street peddlers of religion."[149] In this production, the Fly's big speech and the final chorus are both addressed pointedly to the Renaissance Theater audience, as if to remind us that one of the largest branches of Deutsche Bank sits across the street from the theatre.

At the opposite pole from the intimate Renaissance Theater is the Wiener Volksoper, a grandiose, late nineteenth-century opera and operetta house that may be less prestigious (and smaller) than the Wiener Staatsoper but has a history of producing the Austrian premieres of Broadway musicals dating back to *Kiss Me, Kate* in 1956. Its 2021 *Lady in the Dark* did not mark the Austrian premiere (which took place forty years before), but it was a lavish revisioning of a masterpiece that is famously challenging in the theatre. Making fierce musical and dramatic demands of its lead actors, chorus, corps de ballet, and orchestra, and taking place in both real and imaginary locations, the piece is a sophisticated, complex spoken drama into which are inserted three or, more properly, four one-act operas. Taking psychoanalysis as its subject and dramaturgical method, it puts its heroine, Liza Elliott, editor of the fashion magazine *Allure*, in the throes of career burnout, through the Freudian wringer. With its traditionally gendered conflict between career and romance, the piece is often considered hopelessly dated and sexist.

But as directed by one of the most experienced directors of musicals in the German-speaking world, Matthias Davids, it proves the stage worthiness of what is arguably the first concept musical and, along with *Love Life*, Weill's most ambitious US-American work. It also demonstrates, for those insistent on trying to bifurcate and hierarchize Weill's career, that the Broadway Weill is as innovative and skilled as the Berlin Weill.

Matthias Davids has staged dozens of canonical and non-canonical musicals since the beginning of his career in the 1990s and has been the artistic director of the musicals division at Landestheater Linz since 2012. He first directed *Lady in the Dark* in 2011 at the Staatsoper Hannover in one of the first productions of a classic musical I had seen in Germany that made me aware of the tremendous resources of the state-subsidized theatres. Ten years later, working in Freud's hometown, Davids takes character psychology utterly seriously and manages to make the notoriously problematic book by Moss Hart work as the cohesive, affecting play it demonstrably is. Like Barrie Kosky in his *West Side Story*, Davids proves that you don't need to rewrite the book, or try to correct the play's politics by turning the psychoanalyst Dr. Brooks into a woman (as is sometimes done in the United States), but to stage the piece as both a 1941 period piece and a contemporary fable. Most important, Davids and his team understand that the way to give *Lady in the Dark* the emotional heft for which its creators were aiming is to allow the musicalized dream sequences fully to realize their seductive, hallucinatory beauty. The scene design (by Hans Kudlich) and costumes (by Susanne Hubrich) are thus calculatedly over-the-top.

In directing the first musical about psychoanalysis in a handsomely subsidized theatre, Davids is able to render each of the dream sequences in extraordinary detail. Each springs out of the memories, desires, and fears that are unleashed by Liza's hours on the psychiatrist's couch, which in this production is a giant, Persian-rug upholstered amalgam of couch and bed, which neatly infantilizes Liza but also gives her space to remember and dream. Above it is a huge, angled mirror that, in the best Freudian (or Lacanian) fashion, reflects Liza's image back to her—and to the audience. The scene design for the *Allure* office is contemporary, but Liza's dreams are cartoon-like wonders: the Glamour Dream an elegant, deep blue, haute couture fantasy scape; the Wedding Dream, a picture-book graduation followed by a marriage ceremony that goes terribly awry; and the Circus Dream, the Greatest Show on Earth bursting through the confines of the proscenium arch. Watching all three dreams, I was reminded that *Lady in the Dark* opened only three years after Disney's first full-length, animated musical fantasy, *Snow White and the Seven Dwarfs*, based on the Grimm Brothers' fairy tale. Like cartoon fantasies, the Wedding Dream's "The Princess of Pure Delight" turns the dancers into broken dolls or puppets, with oversize, cracked heads, and the Circus Dream into a riot of multicolored dancers, acrobats, and contortionists. Lording over the Circus Dream is a giant, bikinied drawing mannequin that almost makes the stage look as if it were a maquette. Resembling a skewed and twisted animated film, the Vienna *Lady in the Dark* illustrates with great clarity Liza's desperate—and unsuccessful—attempt to internalize the pretty little fairy tale princess that her parents, and the culture around her, want her to become. It is thus as haunted by the Brothers Grimm as by Walt Disney, a Freudian nightmare that reminds us that the original "Snow White," which ends with the wicked Queen dancing herself to death in a pair of red-hot, iron slippers, is far more disquieting than any Hollywood cartoon.

By dramatizing Liza's confrontation with her larger-than-life demons, *Lady in the Dark* lets its heroine heal. But the 1941 resolution also presents a serious challenge for modern audiences. Thanks to psychoanalysis, Liza has tamed her inner demons, remembered the lyric to her childhood theme song, "My Ship," and made peace with Charley, her feisty opponent. But the script does not deliver the romantic happy ending promised by most mid-century musicals. In the original, Liza is ready to hand over the reins of *Allure* to Charley, but post-#MeToo, Davids and company opt for a more creditable solution: power sharing. Most intriguingly, the production provides more than a hint that Charley is gay and as a result, the question of romance becomes moot. Instead, a warm, affable working partnership develops that puts a savvy twist on the ending, eliminating Liza's subjugation and (possibly and productively) displacing Hart's own homosexuality onto the stylish, charming Charley, who, it turns out, is haunted by the same "My Ship" that Liza is. Despite its concluding position in the musical, however, "My Ship" also does not provide a fairy tale ending. Liza's ship never quite comes in, remaining to the end in the conditional mood: three of the last seven lines of the lyric begin with the word "if." Musically that mood is conveyed by the song's vacillation between F major and D minor and its choice to end with the major tonic plus an added sixth, carefully prepared by voice leading, making it both major and minor. This non-resolution is echoed by the final conversation between Liza and Charley, a discussion about the layout of the magazine, which also breaks off without reaching a conclusion. *Lady in the*

Dark, in other words, ends with a debate about the value, meaning, and effectivity of art.

Lady in the Dark's interrogation of the power of art allows the musical to take its place next to Kurt Weill's German works, most of which are similarly "art about art,"[150] music about music, theatre about theatre. This reflexivity is especially intriguing in Weill's most widely performed pieces, *Die Dreigroschenoper* and *Aufstieg und Fall der Stadt Mahagonny*, both of which received new productions directed by Barrie Kosky that premiered a few months after theatres reopened following the Covid-19 lockdowns. Kosky mounted *Mahagonny* at the Komische Oper, while he used *Dreigroschenoper* to make his debut with the legendary Berliner Ensemble, in whose house, Theater am Schiffbauerdamm, the play premiered in 1928. Because Kosky's *Dreigroschenoper* was only the Berliner Ensemble's third production of the piece (following Erich Engel's in 1960 and Robert Wilson's in 2007), he was under some pressure to produce a distinguished realization of this classic. Directing two of the most revered pieces of music theatre in the wake of Covid, Kosky opted for strikingly stripped-down productions of great scenic refinement and ingenuity. As with his *West Side Story*, both pieces look, sound, and feel as if they had been re-engineered to speak directly to contemporary audiences. Having worked his way through so many operettas by Kurt Weill's contemporaries, Kosky understands Weill's musical dramaturgy and emphasizes the importance of text while rejecting what he characterizes as the regrettably widespread mode of delivering Brecht's songs: park, bark, snark. Whether working with opera singers or actors, Kosky has little patience with abrasive performances and the accusatory and arrogant posturing, that is, the snark, of too many actors in Brecht productions, in Germany and elsewhere.[151] His collaboration at the Berliner Ensemble with music director Adam Benzwi, an expert conductor of operettas and musicals, is especially felicitous because Benzwi knows how to propel the songs while honoring the musical subtleties and spicy Weillian counterpoint. Both Kosky and Benzwi understand that *Dreigroschenoper* was premiered not in an opera house but in a *Schauspielhaus*, and that the score's many "culinary" songs, which are deliberately designed to seduce, demand a certain vocal allure.

Like almost all Kosky's work, his *Dreigroschenoper* and *Mahagonny* adopt modern dress and manners. Re-envisioning their male protagonists as thugs who wield their switchblades casually and lethally, Kosky ushers both pieces into the age of gangster capitalism, a world of extortion, murder, and sadistic paybacks, all driven by the seductive and lethal power of money, and even more, the lack thereof. *Dreigroschenoper* is set among the rich and glamorous in a fantasy London while *Mahagonny* envisions the opera's imaginary metropolis as a boozed-up, sex-charged, anarchic, working-class paradise that is gradually transformed into hell. Although the mise en scène of the former piece shrinks the size of both the gang and the police, the latter floods the stage with crowds, reminding audiences (even in the time of Covid) that cities, as Weill notes, emerge "from people's needs" and are made up more of human bodies than bricks and mortar.[152] Notably, however, both productions nearly empty the stage for the final scenes, leaving only stark, desolate tableaus, missives from a devastated world. Even *Dreigroschenoper*'s Mounted Messenger is purely formulaic, and no hint of jubilation greets Macheath's eleventh-hour reprieve. On the contrary, his rescue from the gallows merely releases him into the cutthroat, capitalist jungle over which he seems hell-bent to lord. The finale of *Mahagonny* is even bleaker, the production ending not with marching groups of demonstrators but an offstage chorus whose protests from the wings seem to mock Jim Mahoney's bloodied corpse, an image that evokes the arbitrary yet systematic fatality of Kranz Kafka's *The Trial* or Shirley Jackson's "The Lottery." In both productions, Kosky's refusal to provide catharsis gives an apocalyptic echo to Weill's chilling cadences, which seems all too apropos for a world ravaged by pandemics, poverty, climate change, and neo-fascist bullies. If each piece, Stephen Hinton notes, was first presented as a "warning against barbarism,"[153] Kosky's productions seem to announce: the barbarians have arrived.

Die Dreigroschenoper uses a very simple setting (designed by Rebecca Ringst) composed of a huge, mobile, three-story, jungle gym–like structure, which is meant to suggest prison and playground, a vast nighttime underground city of cops and robbers, and "a labyrinthine rat's burrow" of pipes and sewers. Behind it sparkle glitter curtains, like "the fabric of dreams," that give the stage a Broadway luminescence. As Ringst explains, these elements together comprise a "hard, cold world that shimmers back and forth in the light—between grandiosity and shithole."[154] The monochrome black-and-white set and costumes is periodically punctuated by the lustrously colored dresses of the three women whom Mackie seduces, Polly, Jenny, and Lucy, and most of all by the shock of red stage blood on the unidentified man whom Mackie viciously knifes just before the "Second Threepenny Finale."

In this jungle, the Peachums are elegantly coutured racketeers, reeking of elitist self-satisfaction, who remind audiences that "a connection to high culture, . . . however ironic," is part of the piece's "style."[155] Mrs. Peachum is a predator in a black sable coat (evoking Maria Callas in her 1970 Blackglama ad) and Mr. Peachum a smoking-jacketed ruffian. Polly is tough-as-nails, while Jenny is hard-edged yet wistful and melancholic. The center of the piece, however, is Macheath, played by Nico Holonics, a Dionysian emcee who weaponizes his leading-man good looks and charm. His curly pompadour and almost exaggeratedly beautiful croon clash startlingly with his voracious appetite and homicidal ruthlessness, reminding one that Macheath was originally played by an operetta star, Harald Paulsen. Kosky has intriguingly cast the LGBTQ-identified Kathrin Wehlisch as Tiger Brown,[156] which she plays as part breeches role, part drag king, part transman, a sexually indeterminate character whom Kosky describes as the most faithful (and lonely) of Macheath's lovers.[157] This undecidability licenses a sexual intimacy between Brown and Macheath that begins with a disconcertingly seductive "Cannon Song" and ends with Brown attempting to feed the blindfolded Macheath his last meal of limp, hollandaise-dripping, phallic asparagus.

In the third act, the blindfolded, unredeemable Macheath is denied even the astute social commentary provided by the farewell speech that Brecht later pinched from *Happy End* to sharpen *Dreigroschenoper*'s political message. Instead, he is attached to wires and a noose and hanged high above the empty stage until his putative rescue. Although the cast lines up across the lip of the stage as they hearken to the arrival of the invisible Mounted Messenger, they soon disappear behind the glitter curtain. Their disappearance puts a very dark spin on Weill's parody of an operatic deus ex machina. The production ends, like *Mahagonny*, with the actors singing the final Bach-like chorale not on-stage but off-, as Macheath is quickly reclothed in a modern business suit, a cutthroat ready to disappear into the urban crowds. "[W]e're giving you a happy ending," Kosky sniggers, "Is that what you want?"[158] At the very end, a giant-lettered LED sign is lowered from the flies that spells out the hero's narcissistic credo, "LOVE ME," which is nothing more than a recipe for tyranny, rot, exploitation, and despair.

If Kosky's *Dreigroschenoper* was the well-deserved hit of the 2021–2022 Berlin theatre season, his *Mahagonny* is decidedly less user-friendly. The production is more idea-driven, observing "almost an Old Testament ban on the image" and at times becomes virtually a piece of conceptual art. The nearly empty stage is dominated in the first act by a huge black drop with a metallic grid that evokes both Brecht's "city of nets" and a barbed-wire enclosed camp. "It is very important," Kosky notes, "not to illustrate or to stage what they're singing and talking about."[159] The backdrop is supplemented and then superseded by two giant, mirrored, V-shaped walls as well as rolling wardrobe-sized mirrors into which the citizens of Mahagonny stare distractedly, their images become life-size, mirror-bound selfies. Although these animated selfies, which Kosky describes as a "breathtakingly terrible form of narcissism,"[160] bring the piece decidedly into the age of TikTok, they also serve at its end to multiply Jim Mahoney's mangled body to infinity. The theatre's turntable is dotted with traps that serve as entrances and exits but in reality resemble nothing as much as graves. In this production, they become the crypts for a lost utopia as well as the dumping ground for both elite culture and kitsch, the canonical operas that Weill references (works by Mozart, Beethoven, and Wagner)[161] as well as the two insufferably sentimental numbers the piece quotes, "A Maiden's Prayer" by Tekla Bądarzewska-Baranowska and "Des Seemanns Los" by H. W. Petrie-Martell.

Because Kosky sees *Mahagonny* as the second part of his Jewish trilogy, and a companion to Schoenberg's *Moses und Aron*, his production emphasizes the biblical and mythical character of the narrative. The piece begins, he explains, in an Old Testament wilderness and ends with the passion and death of the not exactly Christlike hero, Jim Mahoney, whose second-act aria, "Nur die Nacht" (only the night) Kosky regards as an analog to Jesus' prayer in the Garden of Gethsemane.[162] Fatty the Bookie and Trinity Moses are introduced as Jewish and Christian clergymen, while in the penultimate scene God does indeed come to Mahagonny, but in the figure of a "fake *deus ex machina*," a "God-Machine" or mechanical Golem which, Kosky explains, constitutes "a deeply satirical take on the idea of God coming to save people when it's already over."[163] The robotic ape-like monster rides in a mini gocart on which is written in Hebrew characters "emet" (truth), which hastily drops a letter and turns into "met" (death), proving, in Kosky's words, the slippage between the two terms.[164] The ritualistic quality of the action is underlined by Moses's savage blinding of Jim with his own knife, which, like the blinding of Oedipus in *Oedipus the King* or Gloucester in *King Lear*, turns Jim into an emblem of tragic man, whose emotional and spiritual sightlessness is rewarded by the gouging out of his eyes. His execution is then viciously mechanized as a sadistic, scapegoating ritual in which the citizens of Mahagonny one by one stick Jim's switchblade into his prostrate body. Weill's caustic, militant funeral march that ends the piece finds the stage empty except for Jim's blood-spattered corpse, reflected and multiplied to infinity in the on-stage mirrors, while the off-stage chorus mounts an unseen "huge demonstration," in Weill's words, "that heralds the city's demise."[165] Kosky's choice to end *Mahagonny* with this horrifying tableau instead of marching crowds sharpens the incongruity between what is seen and what is heard. In doing so, the production does what Kosky claims "all great theatre pieces" do, serving as

> a laboratory for contradictory ideas about human existence with no ready-made answers. And when it's over, I leave the theatre, go out into the street, and start thinking about my life—because I've had this experience. I don't go out and think: "Aha, yes, that's the way it is." I start to think: how was the music? How were those scenes? How was each element in the play on stage? How did all this affect me and what am I thinking now? I think that's the function of theatre.[166]

Epilogue to the Weimar Republic

Like Barrie Kosky, Ersan Mondtag contends that theatre begins when the audience files out of the house[167] and like Kosky, he uses Kurt Weill's works to interrogate musical theatre as a social practice. His reimagining of Weill's *Der Silbersee* is both looser and more topical than Kosky's *Mahagonny*, with an ending that is even more unresolved. Director Mondtag and dramaturg Till Briegleb transform *Der Silbersee* into a play-within-a-play supposedly being produced in 2033, the hundredth anniversary of the piece's February 1933 premiere, nineteen days after Hitler was appointed Chancellor. With a libretto and lyrics by Georg Kaiser, and the subtitle, *Ein Wintermärchen* (a Winter's Tale), the piece references Shakespeare's romance as well as Heinrich Heine's acerbic poem, "Deutschland: Ein Wintermärchen," which he wrote in exile in Paris. The last of Kurt Weill's German works, this hybrid *Schauspiel-Oper* (play-opera) combines elements of spoken drama, opera, operetta, and revue and is the Weill piece that most pointedly references contemporary politics. Nazi stormtroopers protested the Leipzig premiere, which was well-reviewed despite the demonstrations, but the Nazis canceled all performances as of March 4, 1933. Hans Rothe, a journalist, translator of Shakespeare, and dramaturg under Max Reinhardt later remembered:

> At the Leipzig premiere of *Der Silbersee*, everyone who counted in the German theater met together for the last time. And everyone knew this.

> The atmosphere there can hardly be described. It was the last day of the greatest decade of German culture in the twentieth century.[168]

Although many had feared the Nazi takeover, the end was precipitous and all of *Silbersee*'s creators ended up fleeing Germany. As Stephen Hinton describes it, this final flowering of the Weimar Republic begs for "human sympathy," but it also suggests that sympathy is "hardly a sufficient condition for the peace and well-being of the community." The following thirteen years of terror proved all too tragically that as well-intentioned as art may be, "action must necessarily take place outside of the theater."[169]

Ersan Mondtag's reimagining of this valedictory, allegorical fairy tale is an intricately layered affair, superimposing "the current social climate" onto *Silbersee*'s nightmare realm. It thus responds to and tries to intervene in the contemporary world in which "radicalisation, polarization and intolerance are once again driving politics," social inequality is growing, and "freedom of expression is once again under pressure."[170] The plot of this new *Silbersee*, however, hews closely to the 1933 original, which is a kind of fractured fairy tale in which the immiserated hero, Severin, unemployed and starving, is shot in the leg by the policeman Olim while trying to steal a pineapple. The remorseful Olim miraculously wins a castle in a lottery and endeavors to become Severin's "good fairy" and rescue him from indigence. But Severin wants only to wreak vengeance on his unknown assailant, whom the guileless wayfarer Fennimore, arriving at the castle in the second act, inadvertently aids him in recognizing. After an explosion of rage, Severin finally makes peace with Olim, who is swindled of his castle and riches by Fennimore's aunt, the "wicked witch," Frau von Luber, "a loathsome fascist" who consigns both men "to a hopeless fate."[171] In the final, snow-swept winter scene, they flee to Silbersee prepared to drown only to discover that Spring has magically descended upon the shining, frozen lake, over which they are able to make a wondrous escape.

This plot synopsis, however, does not even begin to describe the plot's baroque logic and its fantastic (and almost Symbolist) concoction of reverie and nightmare, utopia and dystopia. In accordance with the allegorical, fairy tale plot, the characters are more black-and-white than in Weill's earlier works, and the piece's complexity is less to be found in the dialogue per se than in the many strange, allusive occurrences that punctuate the action and whose meaning is not easily deduced. It is also concentrated in the score, which is one of Weill's richest, requiring a thirty-piece orchestra, operatically trained singers, and virtuoso actors able to zigzag between Kaiser's conversational prose, melodrama, and Weill's "irrational, revelatory music."[172] The eclectic score, "the kind of music the Nazis hated,"[173] includes a tango, nostalgic waltz, protest song, melodrama, Bachian pastiche, Verdian revenge aria, militaristic march, and an incandescent, otherworldly final chorus.

Mondtag, the youngest of the directors discussed in this chapter, is anything but conventional, and all his works (plays, operas, dances, and performance pieces) are intended as aesthetic and political provocations. He designs most of his own extremely elaborate sets and, as with Fritsch, his directorial concept is usually a consequence of his scenic design. He is a self-declared "maximalist" who sets different visual styles and conventions against each other in apparently illogical ways. As he explains,

> We live in a time of fragments, leftovers, a rubbish of impressions and splinters, and we long to put them all together like the fragments of antique statues. . . . I want to bring about a visual experience that dissects the everyday rhythm, robs everyday arrangements of their innocence, allows a new self-observation because it forces the eye to turn to things it would

Figure 6.6 The hall of Olim's castle. From left: Hanne Roos, Daniel Arnaldos, Benny Claessens, and Marjan De Schutter in Act 2 of *Der Silbersee*, directed by Ersan Mondtag, Opera Ballet Vlaanderen, 2021. Photo by Annemie Augustijns.

otherwise overlook. I want to make sightless seeing possible. And then work on what happens when something so new, so literally foreign occurs that our orderly everyday lives can no longer absorb it and the encounter exposes the supposedly stable world to be an unstable mirage. At that moment something begins to break down. A horror becomes visible that has been there all along but hidden under the veneer of habit.[174]

Lush, violent, and extravagant, Mondtag's mode of defamiliarization can make opera, historically the most "culinary" of the performing arts, an uncomfortable experience. His mise en scène, like Barrie Kosky's, is rooted in both a recognition of the historicity of a work and an urgent desire to stage its contemporary relevance. Like Kosky, he understands that a straightforward updating impoverishes a piece of musical theatre by "lead[ing] to very flat analogies."[175] Mondtag's work, especially in opera houses, is thus calculatedly contradictory and processual, "a rubbish of impressions and splinters" that disorients and disquiets.

The mode of disorientation that Mondtag rehearses represents a development of the work of revolutionary artists with whom he apprenticed in the 2010s, Frank Castorf and the directing/designing team, Vegard Vinge and Ida Müller, visionaries who remain little known to most opera lovers and music critics (despite the fact that Castorf directed a controversial *Ring der Nibelungen* at Bayreuth in 2013).[176] Opera critics' lack of familiarity with the traditions into which Mondtag taps makes it sometimes difficult for them to understand and appreciate his theatrical strategies. From Castorf, Mondtag learned the principles of bricolage and the incorporation of the rehearsal process, with all its seemingly arbitrary detours and intrusions, into the mise en scène. From Vinge/Müller he learned maximalism, visual overkill, painterly extravagance, the many possibilities offered by masks and bodysuits, a grotesque and often gory literalism, and a mode of stripping classics to their mythic essence. Like theirs, Mondtag's work, despite its willfulness, is rooted in a visceral understanding of opera's musical dramaturgy, which was buttressed in *Der Silbersee* by the inspired, idiomatic conducting of Karel Deseure, which ensured that Weill's score was able to anchor the "unstable mirage" of Mondtag's mise en scène.

Mondtag's *Der Silbersee* superimposes two politically charged narratives: the story of the piece's stormy premiere and an attempt to stage a revival in 2033, retitled *Silbersee 33*, in a country threatened by a neo-fascist putsch. The theatre management stops the show shortly into the run-through because of threats from the (fictional) Iron Front. This new scene consists of dialogue taken from the recollections of *Silbersee*'s creators, coupled with excerpts from original reviews, incendiary articles, and Nazi correspondence. In performance, the scene appears not as a historical reconstruction but as a frighteningly contemporary interpolation. The director of *Silbersee 33*, always on the lookout for a concept, is played by Benny Claessens, a performer whose campy, deranged extravagance evokes no one as much as the great Divine, the legendary drag-queen star of the early films of John Waters, the "king of filth." Exasperated, the director takes over the role of Olim and turns the plot into what Claessens describes as an "incredibly queer"[177] love story between Olim and Severin, for which the costumes and mise en scène riff repeatedly on Pierre et Gilles, Pier Paolo Pasolini, *Star Wars*, *Aida*, and *Turandot*. But even this love story is subject to wild codeswitching as a result of the proliferation, in Kevin Clarke's words, of "bad ideas" on the part of the fictional director.[178]

The lumpenproletariat of *Silbersee 33*'s opening scene, living on the shore of the polluted lake, are wildly misshapen mutants with extra limbs, eyes, and digits, who hark back to the "poor and disenfranchised" of 1933 and conjure a chilling premonition of what 2033 could hold. The replacement director wants to reset the action as a conflict between Palestinians and Israelis, but management pulls the plug on that and substitutes "a Biblical interpretation" in which Frau von Luber, costumed in a Klimt-like, printed robe, becomes an "Israelite slave" who plans and executes bloodless "a coup d'état."[179] Or maybe the director intends the piece to be a reimagining of *Aida* in which Fennimore gets to play the captured Ethiopian princess and von Luber a vengeful Amneris. Or a *Turandot*, in which Fennimore is cast as the self-sacrificial Liù and von Luber as the merciless empress. Olim and Severin, meanwhile, suffering from the "delusion that proletarians can be pharaohs," are vanquished by von Luber and transformed into gay martyrs, a half-naked Jesus (Olim) and Saint Sebastian (Severin), who are summarily expelled from the castle. For the final scenes, Frau von Luber and her confederate Baron Laur are reclothed as villains from Chinese opera, in reference to their similarity to the authoritarian Xi Jinping, whose government persecutes, imprisons, and attempts the cultural erasure of Uyghur Muslims.[180] Just before the final scene, however, the piece screeches to a halt when it is reported that an angry right-wing mob has begun throwing projectiles through the theatre's windows, presumably in response the piece's anti-fascist, anti-homophobic content. But the performers, citing the Belgian Revolution of 1830 that began after a Brussels performance of Auber's *La muette de Portici*, decide the show must go on. In the final scene, the lovers Olim and Severin begin their last walk toward death, even though they know that death is not their real goal.

Der Silbersee's metatheatricality is insistently foregrounded in the scenes in which characters (or actors?) heatedly debate how to stage *Silbersee 33*. It is also evident in the production's interrogation of the conventions of opera. Thus, for example, the production deftly satirizes one of contemporary opera's more inelegant practices, the sometime double casting of roles by singers and actors. In *Silbersee*, this plays out in the Fennimore of two performers of utterly different miens, the skilled soprano Hanne Roos and equally skilled comic actor Marjan De Schutter, the former singing her heart out in "The Ballad of Caesar's Death" while the latter passionately, if distractedly, strums away at her fake harp. The metatheatricality is also emphasized by a tripartite set, sitting on the theatre's turntable behind a false proscenium, composed of three utterly different locales, one for each act. The first act setting is a Magritte-like room, with a small platform, made up entirely of a blue painted sky flecked with distant white clouds. The second is a full-size Egyptian temple gone mad, with colossal female and male caryatids resembling characters from *Turandot*, Christian mythology, and cartoons. The third is the two-story, dark wood-paneled, neo-Gothic hall of the castle won in the lottery, whose walls are covered with an eclectic array of paintings. Despite the hyper-realism of all three designs, the second and third act sets are cunningly lit so that no matter how much one squints, one cannot quite make out the identity of the mutant caryatids. This unstable combination of legible and illegible, obvious and obscure, serious and parodic repeatedly pries open what Mondtag calls the "hermetically sealed framework in which a middle-class audience sits and pays for a finished product."[181]

Der Silbersee's superimposition of historical crises is centered on the theatre as a site of protest and resistance. Although some of the crises it evokes are (all too) real and some fictional (but all too plausible), the piece finally becomes a meditation on "the predicament of art within repressive systems."[182] Riffing on the historical position of the 1933 original, it asks: how can one use the stage to make a political intervention without being censored, closed down, exiled, or exterminated? Mondtag's production adds to that a second question: how can one use a performance of music theatre in a generously subsidized house (like Opera Ballet Vlaanderen) in an ostensibly democratic society to launch a social and political critique that makes a difference?

This last question is the one for which, even though I have reached the end of this chapter, I do not have an answer. All the productions I analyze here launch an explicit or implicit critique of the societies in which they are being performed, targeting sexism, homophobia, racism, elitism, xenophobia, fascism, and/or greed. When I began writing this chapter, I knew I needed to end with *Silbersee* because of its daring leap into the future and its skill not at providing answers but asking the right questions. For me, this production zeroes in on the most important question: why and how do you produce resistant art in an actively repressive society? This question becomes especially challenging when one remembers Audre Lorde's admonition, which Olim/the director/Benny quotes just before the final scene: "your silence will not protect you." In the 1933 *Der Silbersee*, Weill and Kaiser refrain from answering the question about the effectivity of art, even in the face of German fascism, delivering instead one of the most mysteriously utopian endings in all musical theatre. Olim and Severin are borne aloft by the miracle of Silbersee and the luminous voices of Fennimore and the chorus sing a stirring refrain that ends, however, like so much of Weill's music, without resolution to the tonic (on the melodic leading tone instead).

In Mondtag's staging of the finale, the turntable keeps revolving through the three different sets as the two lovers wander through the environments in which they have lived, finally taking their places in the blue, Magritte-like dream space. In the next revolution of the stage, they are discovered again in the blue, but now lying dead with the other mutants. In the next revolution, they are magically and impossibly alive again, laughing. In other words, like the 1933 original, the production depicts both the nightmare of fascist genocide and the belief that something else is possible. But Weill and Kaiser knew that this something else must be fought for and forged outside the theatre. Within its walls, Olim and Severin can search only for a more provisional answer. Just before their trek to the lakeshore, Severin turns to his lover and asks, "Why to Silbersee?" In reply, Olim (or is it the director? or Benny?) enunciates what remains the great promise and the great mystery of musical theatre, "Because I want to get swept off my feet!"

Afterword

One cold December evening a few years ago, I was dining with my friend Daniel Gundlach at a Swabian restaurant in the Viktoria-Luise-Platz in the heart of Schöneberg, one of Berlin's gay neighborhoods. Seated at a table near us were two young men, deeply interested in each other, speaking a language we did not immediately recognize. One seemed from his inflections to be Spanish, the other Polish. As we listened, we realized they were actually speaking English, albeit an idiosyncratic and heavily accented version. Watching their body language, we could see they were communicating quite successfully even though their patois was unlike any I had ever heard. Their faulty English, in short, allowed them to cross the heavily armed border between Romance and Slavic languages and cultures.

As I pondered a conclusion for this book, I remembered that dinner. Like the English spoken by that couple, the Broadway-style musical, I have argued, functions globally as a lingua franca[1] that is decipherable cross-culturally even though it represents an entwinement of clashing musical and theatrical vernaculars. This lingua franca, however, is not one language but a compilation of as many idiolects as there are subcultures and ethnicities. Like the English of our dinner companions, it is a mode of seduction with its own eccentric vocabulary, syntax, and idioms, and will be different each time it is extemporized. It still manages, however, to communicate not only information but also a rich tapestry of emotions.

I became absolutely convinced of the musical's status as lingua franca in 2017 when I attended a performance of *Seopyeonje* in Seoul. Preparing to see the musical, I had watched snippets of the film on YouTube and read a plot synopsis. Because I had seen *pansori* and *changgeuk* several years previously, I had some understanding of the performance traditions the musical references. But I knew nothing about *pansori*'s elaborate training process, nor did I understand how endangered it had become during the waves of industrialization that swept South Korea in the postwar years. Shortly after the performance began, however, it became clear to me that *Seopyeonje* was speaking a musical theatre language I could understand, and I became fascinated by the way the piece was using different kinds of music and different theatrical conventions to tell an extremely complex and ultimately horrifying story. By the second act, I felt I was following every line, every gesture, every musical phrase. I was riveted by the musical's skill at setting antagonistic musical styles at war with each other while retaining dramatic comprehensibility. During the final sequence, Song-hwa and Dong-ho's performance of *Simcheong*, I felt overwhelmed by the tragic scene being played out before me between estranged siblings. It was as if *Seopyeonje* had plumbed my dreams and was giving me great clarity about the way that love and resentment within families can become so inextricably and devastatingly interwoven.

When I returned from Seoul, Ji Hyon (Kayla) Yuh loaned me her recording of *Seopyeonje* and Hansol Oh generously agreed to translate the lyrics for me. Listening to it and following the English text, I realized that I had indeed understood the piece, even though I speak very little Korean. I had long known that music could span cultural divides, but that experience proved to me that the best musical theatre has a piercing lucidity and emotional heft that allow it to reach people who may have limited knowledge of the spoken language, as well as the musical and theatrical styles on which it draws. I am not saying that musicals' lingua franca represents a universal language. On the contrary, understanding a musical requires at least some familiarity with the musical, theatrical, and narrative idioms it speaks. Nonetheless, the musical, alongside Shakespeare, is the only form of theatre that is widely performed around the world. It is the closest we get to global theatre.

As renowned as Shakespeare is, his plays are rarely taken to task for being aesthetically and politically inconsequential. *Othello*, *The Merchant of Venice*, and *The Tempest* pose serious challenges regarding race, religion, and indigeneity, which contemporary productions are forced to deal with, like it or not. Most of the comedies and tragedies can be customized to be performed by eight actors or eighty. And they are routinely updated: translated, adapted, and staged in ways that put them into conversation with local or global concerns. In performance, they can be tailored to charm or unsettle, to moralize or not, and to forge community or problematize it. But musicals can be more demanding because they usually require more elaborate institutional machinery and the participation of actors, singers, musicians, and often dancers. Moreover, because Shakespeare has been constructed as one of the keystones of Western high culture, his plays are assumed to be important. Musicals, on the other hand, are often deemed trivial, mere entertainment, a diversion akin to soccer or rock concerts. But because musical theatre audiences are as a rule less rowdily engaged in the live event than soccer fans, they may seem in contrast passive and unengaged. But the fact that the performance of a musical has not, to my knowledge, sparked rampaging hooligans does not mean that musical theatre audiences are not passionate and engrossed.

This active engagement is proven by the testimony of countless fans and by the wild proliferation of theatre pieces all over the world that call themselves musicals. One Chinese fan, Yilun (Della) Wu, writes that she became captivated by the genre because she was so surprised that her "emotions would be that much affected by [a] show" in which "every element on the stage created a make-believe but compelling space for audiences."[2] *The Routledge Companion to Musical Theatre*, in which her remarks appear, edited by Laura MacDonald and Ryan Donovan with William A. Everett and published in 2023, is the first collection of essays to make a compelling case for musical theatre as a truly global art.[3] It proves the enormity of the field and testifies to the many ways that the musical has impacted cultures around the world and will, I hope, lead to more and more groundbreaking scholarship.

As my final example of musical theatre's power as a lingua franca, let me transport you back to the hot, dry German summer of 2022. My friend Kevin Clarke suggested we go on a field trip to the small town of Bad Freienwalde (population 12,000), east of Berlin near the Polish border, to attend a performance of *La Cage aux Folles* at the German equivalent of summer stock. Although I had seen several productions of the musical in Germany and Austria and had grown extremely weary and wary of its old-fashioned, homonormative plea for tolerance, I took the commuter train with Kevin and Daniel out to this picturesque town only about an hour from Berlin. An hour by train, but light years from Berlin's queer subcultures. The performance was being given in the town's small Hof-Theater, directed by the summer theatre's Intendant, Matthias S. Raupach, who played Georges, to the Albin of his real-life partner, Andreas Renee Swoboda. The production was clearly put together on the cheap and sported clever projections and a pre-recorded orchestral track—as well as heartfelt performances. The crowd was mixed in age but very straight, and because it was a Sunday matinee there was a preponderance of well-mannered spectators who most likely grew up in the former GDR and remained there even after reunification. One such denizen sat in front of us: a white-haired man who looked less like a local theatre buff than a retired farmer. When Georges and Albin kiss for the first time during the reprise of "Song in the Sand," he winced in disgust and I had a "Toto, I've-a-feeling-we're-not-in-Berlin-anymore" moment. But later in the second act, when Georges sang tenderly to his son, "Look over There," pointing to Albin, that same man could be seen wiping away a tear. By the time we got to the Finale, when Georges and Albin sang an encore of "The Best of Times," took their bows, and kissed passionately one last time, he applauded and cheered heartily. What more could one ask of any kind of theatre?

Notes

Preface

1. Leonard Bernstein and Stephen Sondheim, "Dear Officer Krupke," *West Side Story*, vocal score (New York: Schirmer & Chappell, 1957), 168.
2. See Yu-Sun Lee, „Das Seouler Selbstporträt Linie 1. Eine Bestandsaufnahme des Seouler Alltags in den 1990er Jahren," in *Deutschsprachige Literatur und Theater seit 1945 in den Metropolen Seoul, Tokio und Berlin: Studien zur urbanen Kulturentwicklung unter komparatistischen und rezeptionsgeschichtlichen Perspektiven*, ed. Iris Hermann, Soichiro Itoda, Ralf Schnell, and Hi-Young Song (Bamberg: University of Bamberg Press, 2015), 319–32.

Chapter 1

1. Michael Paulson, "How 'The Lion King' Got to Broadway and Ruled for 25 Years (So Far)," *New York Times*, November 16, 2022; Gordon Cox, "Broadway's "The Lion King" Becomes Top Grossing Title of All Time," *Variety*, September 22, 2014, accessed April 5, 2016, http://variety.com/2014/legit/news/broadways-lion-king-box-office-top-title-1201310676/.
2. Cited in Hyunjung Lee, "'Broadway' as the Superior 'Other': Situating South Korean Theater in the Era of Globalization," *Journal of Popular Culture 45*, no. 2 (2012): 325.
3. Richard Wilk, "The Local and the Global in the Political Economy of Beauty: From Miss Belize to Miss World," *Review of International Political Economy 2*, no. 1 (Winter 1995): 124. Italics in original.
4. See *History of AFRTS: The First 50 Years* (Alexandria, VA: American Forces Information Service and Armed Forces Radio and Television Service, 1993).
5. Cited in Marion Linhardt, "Local Contexts and Genre Construction in Early Continental Musical Theatre," in *Popular Musical Theatre in London and Berlin*, ed. Len Platt, Tobias Becker, *and* David Linton (Cambridge: Cambridge University Press, 2014), 45.
6. Peter Bailey, "'*Hullo, Ragtime!*': West End Revue and the Americanisation of Popular Culture in pre-1914 London," in Platt, Becker, and Linton, eds., *Popular Musical Theatre*, 139.
7. Scott McMillin, *The Musical as Drama* (Princeton, NJ: Princeton University Press, 2006), 2, 6–7.

8. Raymond Knapp, *The American Musical and the Formation of National Identity* (Princeton, NJ: Princeton University Press, 2005), 12.
9. Millie Taylor, *Musical Theatre, Realism and Entertainment* (Surrey, UK: Ashgate, 2012), 1.
10. Stephen Banfield, *Sondheim's Broadway Musicals* (Ann Arbor: University of Michigan Press, 1995), 6–7.
11. Millie Taylor, "'If I Sing': Voice, Singing and Song," *Studies in Musical Theatre* 6, no. 1 (2012): 4.
12. Brian D. Valencia, "A Method for Musical Theatre Dramaturgy," in *The Routledge Companion to Dramaturgy*, ed. Magda Romanska (Abingdon: Routledge, 2015), 342–43.
13. See Lehman Engel, *The Making of a Musical* (New York: Macmillan, 1977).
14. Kenneth Burke, *Counter-Statement* (Berkeley: University of California Press, 1968), 31.
15. Moss Hart, Ira Gershwin, and Kurt Weill, *Lady in the Dark: Musical Play*, vocal score (New York: Chappell, 1941), 129.
16. See bruce d. mcclung, *Lady in the Dark: Biography of a Musical* (New York: Oxford University Press, 2007), 99.
17. Burke, *Counter-Statement*, 123–38.
18. Carolin Stahrenberg and Nils Grosch, "The Transculturality of Stage, Song and Other Media: Intermediality in Popular Musical Theatre," in Platt, Becker, and Linton, eds., *Popular Musical Theatre*, 190.
19. Katherine Leigh Axtell, "*Maiden Voyage: The Genesis and Reception of Show Boat, 1926-1932*" (PhD diss., University of Rochester, 2009), 334.
20. Len Platt and Tobias Becker, "Popular Musical Theatre, Cultural Transfer, Modernities: London/Berlin, 1890–1930," *Theatre Journal* 65, no. 1 (March 2013): 17–18.
21. Richard C. Norton and Kevin Clarke, "'*Baedecker gone-mad. An experience not to be missed*': The International Success of *Im weissen Rössl/White Horse Inn*," liner notes to *Selections from* White Horse Inn, Sepia Records 1141, n.p. Souvenir Program, *White Horse Inn*, Center Theatre, New York, 1936, n.p.
22. Len Platt and Tobias Becker, "'A happy man can live in the past': Musical Theatre Transfer in the 1920s and 1930s," in Platt, Becker, and Linton, eds., *Popular Musical Theatre*, 128–29.
23. See Olaf Jubin, "Horses for Courses oder Mehr als ‚Zuschau'n Kann I Net': *White Horse Inn* als anglifzierte bzw. amerikanisierte Version von *Im weißen Rößl*," in „*Im weißen Rößl*": *Kulturgeschichtliche Perspektiven*, ed. Nils Grosch and Carolin Stahrenberg (Münster: Waxmann, 2016), 157–77.
24. See Nils Grosch, "*Im weißen Rößl* Gattungen und Subgattungen im populären Musiktheater," in Grosch and Stahrenberg, eds., „*Im weißen Rößl*," 31–32.
25. Although the phrase "Golden Age" is common among musical theatre specialists, I use it reluctantly in part because most specialists link it to an extremely problematic concept, the so-called integrated musical, and use it to denote the period from *Oklahoma!* (1943) until the late 1960s, when the rock musical began to supplant the

Rodgers and Hammerstein formula. Because of my skepticism about the viability of the concept of the integrated musical, I would prefer to theorize the Golden Age more in musical terms, beginning in the early 1920s with the appearance of jazz-inflected musicals like *Shuffle Along* (1921) and *Lady, Be Good* (1924) and ending with the triumph of rock in the late 1960s.

26. It is categorized as an operetta in the comprehensive catalogue, Deutscher Bühnenverein, *Wer spielte was?: 2018/19 Werkstatistik* (Würzburg: Verlag Königshausen & Neumann, 2020).
27. See A. J. Goldmann, "Review: 'Hamilton' in German? It's a Thrill," *New York Times*, October 7, 2022, accessed October 13, 2022, https://www.nytimes.com/2022/10/07/theater/hamilton-review-hamburg-germany.html.
28. See Alter.com, accessed June 1, 2022, https://alter.com/trademarks/live-broadway-75221198.
29. See Ralf Ptak, "Neoliberalism in Germany: Revisiting the Ordoliberal Foundations of the Social Market Economy," in *The Road from Mont Pèlerin: The Making of the Neoliberal Thought Collective*, ed. Philip Mirowski and Dieter Plehwe (Cambridge, MA: Harvard University Press, 2006).
30. See Samuel S. Kim, ed., *Korea's Globalization* (Cambridge: Cambridge University Press, 2000).
31. See Patrick Healy, "Yo, Adrian! I'm Singin'!" *New York Times*, December 5, 2012, accessed December 15, 2012, http://www.nytimes.com/2012/12/09/theater/a-hit-in-germany-a-rocky-musical-aims-at-broadway.html?ref=theater. See also Stage Entertainment on IBDB, accessed May 26, 2022, https://www.ibdb.com/broadway-cast-staff/joop-van-den-ende-22679.
32. Choe Sang-Hun, "For 'Dreamgirls,' Pacific Overtures," *New York Times*, March 13, 2009, accessed June 4, 2009, http://www.nytimes.com/2009/03/14/theater/14drea.html.
33. Cited in Gordon Cox, "A Twist in Tuner's Next Turn," *Variety*, November 23–29, 2009.
34. Sang-Hun, "For 'Dreamgirls,' Pacific Overtures."
35. Ma Jin, "Broadway's Dreamgirls, Korean Style," Dynamic-Korea.com, accessed May 7, 2009, http://dynamic-korea.com/print.php?tbl=Etc&uid=200800041702.
36. Cox, "A Twist in Tuner's Next Turn."
37. Sang-Hun, "For 'Dreamgirls,' Pacific Overtures."
38. Alan Wasser, American Theatre Wing, *"Beyond Broadway: International Theatre,"* Videotaped October 2009, accessed October 23, 2011, http://americantheatrewing.org/wit/detail/beyond_broadway_10_09.
39. Sang-Hun, "For 'Dreamgirls,' Pacific Overtures."
40. Michael Riedel, "Eastern 'Dreamgirls,'" *New York Post,* March 28, 2008, accessed May 7, 2009, http://www.nypost.com/f/print/entertainment/theater/item_Cg1dvulJ4dE5iYmBl6LrOK.
41. Cited in Kwon Mee-yoo, "Don Quixote Eager to Enter Broadway," *Korea Times*, June 6, 2011, accessed June 1, 2022, https://m.koreatimes.co.kr/pages/article.asp?newsIdx=88409.

246   NOTES

42. See Allen Woll, *Black Musical Theatre: From Coontown to Dreamgirls* (Baton Rouge: Louisiana State University Press, 1989).
43. Cited in Ji Hyon (Kayla) Yuh and Emilio Méndez, "Translating Race in Musical Theatre," in *The Routledge Companion to Musical Theatre*, ed. Laura MacDonald and Ryan Donovan with William A. Everett (Abingdon: Routledge, 2023), 544–45.
44. Ji Hyon (Kayla) Yuh, "'Are they supposed to be *heugin*?': Negotiating Race, Nation, and Representation in Korean Musical Theatre" (PhD diss., The Graduate Center CUNY, 2018), 175, 180.
45. Choe Sang-Hun, "For 'Dreamgirls,' Pacific Overtures."
46. Cox, "A Twist in Tuner's Next Turn."
47. Yuh and Méndez, "Translating Race in Musical Theatre," 545.
48. Adam Hetrick, "*Dreamgirls* National Tour to Premiere at Apollo Theater in 2009," *Playbill.com*, November 18, 2008, accessed October 16, 2009, http://www.playbill.com/news/article/123465-Dreamgirls_National_Tour_to_Premiere_at_Apollo_Theater_in_2009. For clips of the Korean production, see http://www.youtube.com/watch?v=sS9AmIia4t0&feature=related, http://www.youtube.com/watch?v=EXT_uU4ViwI&feature=related, and http://www.youtube.com/watch?v=ryCvei_g-sY&feature=related (accessed October 17, 2009).
49. Ben Brantley, "Hopeful Divas Back Where It All Began," *New York Times*, November 23, 2009, C1.
50. Kyung Hyun Kim, *Hegemonic Mimicry: Korean Popular Culture of the Twenty-First Century* (Durham, NC: Duke University Press, 2021), 18, 13, 11.
51. Cox, "A Twist in Tuner's Next Turn."
52. Stage Entertainment, accessed May 27, 2022, https://www.stage-entertainment.com/about-us.
53. Stage Entertainment Deutschland, accessed May 22, 2022, https://www.stage-entertainment.de/ueber-uns/wer-wir-sind.
54. Stage Entertainment Deutschland, http://www.stage-entertainment.de/unternehmen/index.html; Stage Entertainment Corporate Website, accessed October 25, 2012, http://www.stage-entertainment.com/companies_vision.htm.
55. Healy, "Yo, Adrian! I'm Singin'!"
56. Healy, "Broadway on the Elbe," *New York Times,* December 9, 2012, accessed May 27, 2022, https://www.nytimes.com/2012/12/10/theater/tarzan-and-lion-king-make-hamburg-a-theater-city.html.
57. Stage Entertainment, http://www.stage-entertainment.de/unternehmen/index.html.
58. "Gefeierte Premiere für 'Rocky'-Musical," accessed December 14, 2012, http://www.fr-online.de/kultur/rocky-als-musical-gefeierte-premiere-fuer--rocky--musical,1472786,20906458.html.
59. "Rocky Musical Knocks Out Critics in Hamburg," *The Guardian*, November 20, 2012, accessed December 14, 2012, http://www.guardian.co.uk/stage/2012/nov/20/rocky-das-musical-hamburg. Of the creative principals, only Steven Hoggett, the British fight choreographer, is not US-based.
60. This pastiche is similar to the interpolation of "I'm a Believer" into *Shrek the Musical* and "The Addams Family" television theme song into the musical of the same name.

In all these cases, the expensive rights to these songs doubtlessly added considerably to production budgets.
61. Unlike *Dreamgirls, Rocky* did not save its producers any money by being first produced abroad.
62. "Premiere in Hamburg: 'Rocky' als Musical-Star Gefeiert," *Stern*, November 18, 2012, accessed December 14, 2012, http://www.stern.de/kultur/premiere-in-hamburg-rocky-als-musical-star-gefeiert-1928227.html.
63. "Erster deutscher Musical—Export an den Broadway," accessed May 20, 2013, http://www.stage-entertainment.de/musicals-shows/rocky-das-musical-hamburg/news/rocky-das-musical-geht-an-den-broadway.html?ref=3391&nodevice=x&et_cid=100&et_lid=195.
64. Johannes Mock-O'Hara, cited in "Erster deutscher Musical—Export an den Broadway."
65. "Premiere in Hamburg," *Stern*.
66. Cited in "Premiere in Hamburg," *Stern*.
67. Chris Jones, "Broadway 'Rocky' Offers the Thrill of a Fight," *Chicago Tribune,* March 13, 2014, accessed March 14, 2014, http://articles.chicagotribune.com/2014-03-13/entertainment/ct-rocky-broadway-review_1_rocky-balboa-margo-seibert-thrill.
68. Ben Brantley, "'Rocky,' the Musical, Brings Songs to a Film Story," *New York Times*, March 13, 2014, accessed March 14, 2014, http://www.nytimes.com/2014/03/14/theater/rocky-the-musical-brings-songs-to-a-film-story.html.
69. Healy, "Broadway on the Elbe," C1.
70. Jonathan Matusitz, "Disneyland Paris: A Case Analysis Demonstrating How Glocalization Works," *Journal of Strategic Marketing 18*, no. 3 (June 2010): 233.
71. Barbara Kisseler, cited in Matusitz, "Disneyland Paris."
72. Sean MacBride Commission, *Many Voices, One World: Towards a New, More Just and More Efficient World Information and Communication Order* (London: Kogan Page, 1980), 163–64.
73. Laura MacDonald, "Rising in the East: Disney Rehearses Chinese Consumers at a Glocalized Shanghai Disneyland," in *Performance and the Disney Theme Park Experience: The Tourist as Actor*, ed. Jennifer A. Kokai and Tom Robson (London: Palgrave Macmillan, 2019), 128, 129, 141.
74. Jonathan Burston, "Enter, Stage Right: Neoconservatism, English Canada and the Megamusical," *Soundings 5* (Spring 1997): 180; Jonathan Burston, "Recombinant Broadway," *Continuum: Journal of Media & Cultural Studies 23*, no. 2 (April 2009): 159–69; Dan Rebellato, *Theatre & Globalization* (Houndmills: Palgrave Macmillan, 2009), 46. See also Jessica Sternfeld and Elizabeth L. Wollman, "After the 'Golden Age," in *The Oxford Handbook of the American Musical*, ed. Raymond Knapp, Mitchell Morris, and Stacy Wolf (New York: Oxford University Press, 2012), 111–24; and Jessica Brater, Jessica Del Vecchio, Andrew Friedman, Bethany Holmstrom, Eero Laine, Donald Levit, Hillary Miller, David Savran, Carly Griffin Smith, Kenn Watt, Catherine Young, and Peter Zazzali, "'Let Our Freak Flags Fly': *Shrek the Musical* and the Branding of Diversity," *Theatre Journal 62*, no. 2 (May 2010): 151–72.

75. See, e.g., Philip Zapkin, *Hellenic Common: Greek Drama and Cultural Cosmopolitanism in the Neoliberal Era* (Abingdon: Routledge, 2022), 6–7.
76. Robin Leidner, cited in George Ritzer, *The McDonaldization of Society: An Investigation into the Changing Character of Contemporary Social Life* (Thousand Oaks, CA: Pine Forge Press, 1993), 10.
77. Ien Ang, "Global Media/Local Meaning," in Ang, *Living Room Wars: Rethinking Media Audiences for a Postmodern World* (New York: Routledge, 1996), 153.
78. Elihu Katz and Tamar Liebes, "Interacting with 'Dallas': Cross Cultural Readings of American TV," *Canadian Journal of Communication 15*, no. 1 (1990): 48.
79. Katz and Liebes, "Interacting with 'Dallas,'" 59–60.
80. Ben Brantley, "Tarzan Arrives on Broadway, Airborne," *New York Times*, May 11, 2006, accessed November 1, 2012, http://theater2.nytimes.com/2006/05/11/theater/reviews/11tarz.html.
81. *Die Welt*, quoted in MusicalONE, Pressestimmen zum Musical Tarzan in Hamburg, accessed May 30, 2022, https://www.musicalone.de/tarzan-musical/pressestimmen-zum-musical-tarzan-in-hamburg.html.
82. Thomas Schumacher, cited in Healy, "Broadway on the Elbe."
83. primadonna 76, accessed July 5, 2013, http://www.musicalfreunde.de/musical/hamburg/tarzan.
84. Sabrina89, June 1, 2013, and Pentragon, June 3, 2013, both accessed August 2, 2013, http://www.musicalfreunde.de/musical/hamburg/tarzan.
85. Adrian97, "Gänsehaut," June 16, 2013, accessed August 2, 2013, http://www.musicalfreunde.de/musical/hamburg/tarzan. See also Yilun (Della) Wu, "Introduction: Into the Theatre," in *The Routledge Companion to Musical Theatre*, ed. Laura MacDonald and Ryan Donovan with William A. Everett (Abingdon: Routledge, 2023), 481–85.
86. Rebellato, *Theatre & Globalization*, 49.
87. Sternfeld, *The Megamusical*, 73.
88. Mark Grant, *The Rise and Fall of the Broadway Musical* (Boston: Northeastern University Press, 2004), 309.
89. Stuart Ostrow, cited in Grant, *The Rise and Fall of the Broadway Musical*, 207.
90. Jacques Attali, *Noise: The Political Economy of Music*, trans. Brian Massumi (Minneapolis: University of Minnesota Press, 1985), 85.
91. Luc Boltanski and Eve Chiapello, trans. Gregory Elliott, *The New Spirit of Capitalism* (London: Verso, 2005), 445.
92. Mark Gobé, *Brandjam: Humanizing Brands through Emotional Design* (New York: Allworth, 2007), 290; see also B. Joseph Pine II and James H. Gilmore, *The Experience Economy: Work Is Theater & Every Business a Stage* (Boston: Harvard Business School Press, 1999), for their concept of "mass customization."
93. Volker Ludwig, in Wolfgang Prosinger and Julia Prosinger, „Grips-Chef Volker Ludwig wird 80: ‚Sie nannten mich Stalinist, Maoist und Kinderschänder,'" *Tagesspiegel*, June 13, 2017, accessed October 13, 2022, https://www.tagesspiegel.de/gesellschaft/sie-nannten-mich-stalinist-maoist-und-kinderschander-3716050.html.

94. GRIPS Team, "LINIE 1—Eine kurze Chronik der Höhepunkte," November 10, 2021, accessed October 14, 2022, https://grips.online/linie-1-eine-kurze-chronik-der-hoehepunkte.
95. Erin Glover, "The 1964 New York World's Fair—A New Disney Technology Is Born," accessed October 25, 2013, http://disneyparks.disney.go.com/blog/2011/04/the-1964-new-york-worlds-fair-a-new-disney-technology-is-born/.
96. "The Story behind the Song," Disneyworld attractions, accessed October 13, 2013, https://disneyworld.disney.go.com/attractions/magic-kingdom/its-a-small-world/. "It's a Small World" boat rides are at Disney theme parks in California, Florida, Tokyo, Paris, and Hong Kong.
97. Disney Musicals Around the World, accessed October 16, 2009, http://disney.go.com/theatre/aroundtheworld/#/home/.
98. Robert B. Sherman and Richard M. Sherman, "It's a Small World (After All)," accessed October 13, 2013, http://www.songlyrics.com/disney/its-a-small-world-lyrics/.
99. Hyunjung Lee, "'Broadway' as the Superior 'Other,'" 321.
100. See "Wie gehen wir mit dem Anderssein um?," Dramaturg Sarah Grahneis in conversation with director Sebastian Welker, program for *Hairspray*, Staatstheater Braunschweig, 2017, 8–10.
101. Paul Zollo, "Behind the Song: 'It's a Small World' by Richard & Robert Sherman," American Songwriter, accessed June 8, 2022, https://americansongwriter.com/behind-the-song-its-a-small-world-by-richard-robert-sherman/.
102. Richard Corliss, "Is *This* the Most Played Song in Music History?," *Time*, April 30, 2014, accessed June 8, 2022, https://time.com/82493/its-a-small-world-50th-anniversary/.
103. Marc Shaiman and Scott Wittman, "Can't Stop the Beat," *Hairspray*, music by Marc Shaiman and lyrics by Marc Shaiman and Scott Wittman, with a book by Mark O'Donnell and Thomas Meehan (New York: MTI, 2002), 98.

Chapter 2

1. See Daniel Tudor, *Korea: The Impossible Country* (Tokyo: Tuttle, 2012), 281.
2. Heon Joo Jung, "The Rise and Fall of Anti-American Sentiment in South Korea: Deconstructing Hegemonic Ideas and Threat Perception," *Asian Survey 50*, no. 5 (September/October 2010): 949.
3. Kyung Hyun Kim, *Hegemonic Mimicry: Korean Popular Culture of the Twenty-First Century* (Durham, NC: Duke University Press, 2021), 11.
4. Patrick Healy, "Musicals Couldn't Be Hotter Off Broadway (by 7,000 Miles)," *New York Times*, December 7, 2013, accessed December 9, 2013, http://www.nytimes.com/2013/12/08/theater/musicals-couldnt-be-hotter-off-broadway-by-7000-miles.html.
5. Hyunjung Lee, "'Broadway' as the Superior 'Other': Situating South Korean Theater in the Era of Globalization," *Journal of Popular Culture 45*, no. 2 (2012): 325.

6. Choon Mee Kim, *Harmonia Koreana: A Short History of 20th-Century Korean Music* (Seoul: Hollym, 2011), 10, 12.
7. Choi Yu-jun, "Modernity as Postcolonial Encounter in Korean Music," in *Decentering Musical Modernity: Perspectives on East Asian and European Music History*, ed. Tobias Janz and Chien-Chang Yang (Bielefeld, Germany: transcript Verlag, 2019), 44.
8. Dipesh Chakrabarty, *Provincializing Europe: Postcolonial Thought and Historical Difference* (Princeton, NJ: Princeton University Press, 2008), 5, 7, xiii.
9. Andrew Killick, *In Search of Korean Traditional Opera: Discourses of Changguk* (Honolulu: University of Hawai'i Press, 2010), xx.
10. Richard Nichols, "Introduction," in *Modern Korean Drama: An Anthology*, ed. Richard Nichols (New York: Columbia University Press, 2009), 1.
11. Andrew Killick, "Korean Ch'anggu'k Opera: Its Origins and Its Origin Myth," *Asian Music 33*, no. 2 (Spring/Summer 2002): 60, 43. See also Andrew P. Killick, "Jockeying for Tradition: The Checkered History of Korean Ch'anggŭk Opera," *Asian Theatre Journal 20*, no. 1 (Spring 2003): 43–70.
12. Killick, "Jockeying for Tradition," 43–44.
13. Nichols, "Introduction," 3–4.
14. See Tu-hyon Yi, "Ancient-1945: A History of Korean Drama," and Sok-ki Yo, "1946–1970: Korean Drama," in *Korean Performing Arts: Drama, Dance & Music Theatre*, ed. Hye-suk Yang (Seoul: Jipmoondang Publishing, 1997), 24, 39.
15. Andrew Killick, "Changgeuk," in *Pansori*, ed. National Center for Korean Traditional Performing Arts (Seoul: National Center for Korean Traditional Performing Arts, 2008), 105.
16. Okkyoung Baek, Jihyung Cho, Dongju Ham, Byungjoon Jung, Hyunsook Lee, and Jungsook Sohn, *Understanding Korean History* (Seoul: Jimoondang, 2011), 213.
17. Quoted by Tobias Janz and Yang Chien-Chang, "Introduction: Musicology, Musical Modernity, and the Challenges of Entangled History," in Janz and Yang, *Decentering Musical Modernity*, 23–24.
18. Kim, *Harmonia Koreana*, 22.
19. Chang Nam Kim, *K-Pop: Roots and Blossoming of Korean Popular Music* (Seoul: Hollym, 2012), 16; Kim Chi-young, "The Awakening of Women: Light and Shadow," *Koreana: Korean Arts and Culture 33* (Spring 2019): 26–27.
20. Dohyun (Gracia) Shin, email to author, October 7, 2022.
21. Kim, *K-Pop*, 16–17.
22. Chang Yu-jeong, "Pop Music Blooms in the Depths of Despair," *Koreana: Korean Arts and Culture 33* (Spring 2019): 29.
23. Chang, "Pop Music Blooms in the Depths of Despair," 29.
24. See Kim, *Harmonia Koreana*, 31, and "Ahn Eak-tai," *New World Encyclopedia*, accessed November 29, 2020, https://www.newworldencyclopedia.org/entry/Ahn_Eak-tai.
25. Choi, "Modernity as Postcolonial Encounter in Korean Music," 43.
26. Kim, *K-Pop*, 20.
27. John Lie, "What Is the K in K-pop?: South Korean Popular Music, the Culture Industry, and National Identity," *Korea Observer 43*, no. 3 (Autumn 2012): 343.

28. Chaibong, "Anti-Americanism, Korean Style," in *Korean Attitudes toward the United States*, ed. Steinberg, 228.
29. See Robinson, *Korea's Twentieth-Century Odyssey*, 27–31.
30. Keith Howard, "Korean Folk Songs & Folk Bands," *Koreana: A Quarterly on Korean Culture & Arts 8*, no. 3 (Autumn 1994): 20.
31. Ah-young Chung, "'Arirang' Makes It to UNESCO Heritage," *Korea Times*, June 12, 2012, accessed September 15, 2012, http://www.koreatimes.co.kr/www/news/culture/2014/07/317_126329.html; Howard, "Korean Folk Songs & Folk Bands," 20.
32. Chung, "'Arirang' Makes It to UNESCO Heritage."
33. Baek et al., *Understanding Korean History*, 271.
34. Kim, *Harmonia Koreana*, 40.
35. Kim, *K-Pop*, 23.
36. Ibid., 23–24.
37. Lee Kee-woong, "Before K-Pop: Popular Music since the Korean War: Eighth U.S. Army Shows and Korean Pop Music," *Koreana: Korean Culture & Arts 34*, no. 2 (Summer 2020): 10, accessed December 6, 2020, https://koreana.or.kr/user/0018/nd71906.do?View&boardNo=00003048&zineInfoNo=0018&pubYear=2020&pubMonth=SUMMER&pubLang=English.
38. Kim, Hegemonic Mimicry, 3, 19.
39. Lee, "Before K-Pop," 10.
40. Kim, Hegemonic Mimicry, 2.
41. Lee, "Before K-Pop," 13.
42. Kim, *K-Pop*, 23–24, 27, 28.
43. Zhang Eu-jeong, "The Kim Sisters Wow Las Vegas," *Koreana: Korean Culture & Arts 34*, no. 2 (Summer 2020), accessed December 6, 2020, https://koreana.or.kr/user/0018/nd71906.do?View&boardNo=00003048&zineInfoNo=0018&pubYear=2020&pubMonth=SUMMER&pubLang=English.
44. Danielle Seid, "60 Years before BTS, the Kim Sisters Were America's Original K-pop Stars," *The World*, May 9, 2019, accessed December 1, 2020, https://www.pri.org/stories/2019-05-09/60-years-bts-kim-sisters-were-americas-original-k-pop-stars. See also David Teszar, "From Seoul to Las Vegas: Story of the Kim Sisters," *Korea Times*, September 21, 2011, accessed November 30, 2020, http://www.koreatimes.co.kr/www/news/special/2011/09/178_95166.html.
45. Kim, *Harmonia Koreana*, 43.
46. Park Chan-seok, cited in ibid., 56.
47. WorldData.info, accessed October 29, 2022, https://www.worlddata.info/asia/south-korea/economy.php#:~:text=Worldwide%20gross%20domestic%20product%20in,is%20currently%20at%20rank%2010.
48. Evan S. Medeiros, Keith Crane, Eric Heginbotham, Norman D. Levin, Julia F. Lowell, Angel Rabasa, and Somi Seong, *Pacific Currents: The Responses of U.S. Allies and Security Partners in East Asia to China's Rise* (Santa Monica, CA: Rand Corporation, 2008), 63; Trading Economics, South Korea GDP per capita, accessed October 29, 2022, https://tradingeconomics.com/south-korea/gdp-per-capita.

49. Michael E. Robinson, *Korea's Twentieth-Century Odyssey* (Honolulu: University of Hawai'i Press, 2007), 130, 129.
50. Kim, *K-Pop*, 44.
51. Ingyu Oh and Hyo-Jung Lee, "K-pop in Korea: How the Pop Music Industry Is Changing a Post-Developmental Society," *Cross-Currents: East Asian History and Culture Review*, no. 9 (December 2013): 106.
52. Kim, *K-Pop*, 40.
53. Ibid., 48, 50, 45.
54. Robinson, *Korea's Twentieth-Century Odyssey*, 144.
55. William M. Drennan, "The Tipping Point: Kwangju, May 1980," in *Korean Attitudes toward the United States: Changing Dynamics*, ed. David I. Steinberg (Armonk, NY: M. E. Sharpe, 2005), 297.
56. See Kim, *Harmonia Koreana*, 59–65.
57. Howard, "Korean Folk Songs & Folk Bands," 21.
58. Youna Kim, "Introduction: Korean Media in a Digital Cosmopolitan World," in Kim, *The Korean Wave: Korean Media Go Global* (London: Routledge, 2013), 3; Kim, *K-Pop*, 65.
59. Chin A. Lee, *Daehangno: Theater District in Seoul* (Seoul: Hollym, 2011), 72–73.
60. Lie, "What Is the K in K-pop?," 352.
61. "Hallyu, yeah!: A 'Korean Wave' Washes Warmly over Asia," *The Economist*, January 25, 2010, accessed July 28, 2014, http://www.economist.com/node/15385735; Ji-sook Bae, "Hallyu Seeks Sustainability," *Chosun Ilbo*, February 12, 2013, accessed July 28, 2014, http://www.webcitation.org/6FHqPkNDz; Jimmyn Park, "The Direct Economic Contribution of Hallyu—The 'Korean Wave' of Popular Culture—Is Small, but the Benefits to Korea Can Extend Well beyond the Culture Industry, Writes Jimmyn Parc," *Asialink*, August 9, 2022, accessed October 28, 2022, https://asialink.unimelb.edu.au/insights/koreas-cultural-exports-and-soft-power-understanding-the-true-scale-of-this-trend.
62. Youjeong Oh, *Pop City: Korean Popular Culture and the Selling of Place* (Ithaca, NY: Cornell University Press, 2018), 2–3.
63. Won Jong-won, "Korean Musicals Branch Out onto the Global Stage," *Koreana*, Summer 2022, accessed October 27, 2022, https://www.koreana.or.kr/koreana/na/ntt/selectNttInfo.do?nttSn=111598&bbsId=1113.
64. Ibid.
65. Joseph Kim and Seung-Ho Kwon, "K-Pop's Global Success and Its Innovative Production System," *Sustainability* 14 (2022): 11101, accessed October 26, 2022, https://doi.org/10.3390/su141711101.
66. Hee-sun Kim, "Appropriating *Gugak* and Negotiating K-Heritage: K-Pop's Reconstruction of Korean Aesthetics in the Age of Digital Globalization," *ESPES: The Slovak Journal of Aesthetics 11*, no. 1 (2022): 28.
67. Hyunjoon Shin, "K-pop the Sound of Subaltern Cosmopolitanism?," *Routledge Handbook of East Asian Popular Culture*, ed. Koichi Iwabuchi, Eva Tsai, and Chris Berry (London: Routledge, 2017), 118–19.

NOTES   253

68. Youjeong Oh, *Pop City*, 106–8. Oh presents an extremely detailed account of the production system.
69. Shin, "K-pop the Sound of Subaltern Cosmopolitanism?," 117.
70. Youjeong Oh, *Pop City*, 108.
71. Lie, "What Is the K in K-pop?," 356, 360.
72. Youna Kim, "Introduction," 17.
73. Ibid., 15.
74. Kim, "Appropriating *Gugak* and Negotiating K-Heritage," 27, 29, 36.
75. Kent A. Ono and Jungmin Kwon, "Re-Worlding Culture?: YouTube as a K-pop Interlocutor," in Kim, *The Korean Wave*, 199.
76. See Hugh McIntyre, "At 2 Billion Views, 'Gangnam Style' Has Made Psy a Very Rich Man," *Forbes*, June 16, 2014, accessed August 27, 2014, http://www.forbes.com/sites/hughmcintyre/2014/06/16/at-2-billion-views-gangnam-style-has-made-psy-a-very-rich-man/.
77. See, e.g., "Rattle that Cage," accessed August 17, 2014, http://www.dorjeshugden.com/forum/index.php?topic=2761.0.
78. Kim, Hegemonic Mimicry, 54–55.
79. Choi, "Modernity as Postcolonial Encounter in Korean Music," 50.
80. Kim, "Introduction," 3, 14–15; Youna Kim, "Korean Wave Pop Culture in the Global Internet Age," in Kim, *The Korean Wave*, 87.
81. Anandam Kavoori, "The Korean Wave as a Cultural Epistemic," in Kim, *The Korean Wave*, 217.
82. Jeong Duk Yi, "Globalization and Recent Changes to Daily Life in the Republic of Korea," in *Korea and Globalization: Politics, Economics and Culture*, ed. James Lewis and Amadu Sesay (Abingdon: Routledge Curzon, 2002), 11.
83. President Kim Young Sam, *Korea's Reform and Globalization*, cited in Gi-Wook Shin, *Ethnic Nationalism in Korea: Genealogy, Politics, and Legacy* (Stanford, CA: Stanford University Press, 2006), 215.
84. Shin, *Ethnic Nationalism in Korea*, 208.
85. Kim, "South Korean Cultural Diplomacy," 127.
86. "Nationaloper Korea gibt erstmals Gastspiel in Westeuropa," NMZ LIZ Kulturinformationszentrum, January 18, 2006, accessed October 4, 2014, http://www.nmz.de/kiz/nachrichten/181-oper-und-konzert-aktuell-oper-und-konzert.
87. Seung-hye Yim, "'Soul Mate' Aims to Give Hope after Sewol," *Korea Joongang Daily*, May 19, 2014, accessed September 26, 2104, http://koreajoongangdaily.joins.com/news/article/article.aspx?aid=2989312.
88. Corrie Tan, "Trojan Women: The Greek Tragedy That Became a Queer Korean Opera," *The Guardian*, May 16, 2018, accessed October 29, 2022, https://www.theguardian.com/stage/2018/may/16/trojan-women-ong-keng-sen-euripedes-korea-southbank-centre.
89. Kim, "Searchers and Planners," 155.
90. Youna Kim, "Korean Wave Pop Culture in the Global Internet Age," in Kim, *The Korean Wave*, 80.

91. Meredith Woo-Cumings, "Unilateralism and Its Discontents: The Passing of the Cold War Alliance and Changing Public Opinion in the Republic of Korea," in *Korean Attitudes toward the United States: Changing Dynamics*, ed. David I. Steinberg (Armonk, NY: M. E. Sharpe, 2005), 65.

92. Ronald Meinardus, "Anti-Americanism in Korea and Germany," in Steinberg, ed., *Korean Attitudes toward the United States*, 86.

93. Wayne Arnold of Lowe Profero, cited in Leong, "How Korea Became the World's Coolest Brand."

94. Ibid.; Euny Hong, "Excerpt: The Concerted Effort to Build a Pop-Culture Juggernaut, from 'The Birth of Korean Cool' by Euny Hong," *National Post*, August 2, 2014, accessed September 7, 2014, http://arts.nationalpost.com/2014/08/02/excerpt-the-concerted-effort-to-build-a-pop-culture-juggernaut-from-the-birth-of-korean-cool-by-euny-hong/.

95. Won, "Korean Musicals Branch Out Onto the Global Stage."

96. Patrick Healy, "Musicals Couldn't Be Hotter Off Broadway (by 7,000 Miles)," *New York Times*, December 7, 2013, accessed December 9, 2013, http://www.nytimes.com/2013/12/08/theater/musicals-couldnt-be-hotter-off-broadway-by-7000-miles.html.

97. Won, "Korean Musicals Branch Out Onto the Global Stage."

98. Healy, "Musicals Couldn't Be Hotter Off Broadway (by 7,000 Miles)."

99. "Korean Musicals Catch on Overseas," *Arirang News*, January 7, 2014, accessed August 17, 2014, http://www.arirang.co.kr/News/News_View.asp?nSeq=164771; "Arts & Culture—Korea's Musical Theater Boom," *Arirang News*, December 16, 2013, accessed August 17, 2014, http://www.arirang.co.kr/News/News_View.asp?nSeq=154630.

100. See Interpark Tickets, accessed September 12, 2014, http://ticket.interpark.com/global/.

101. The Broadway League, "The Demographics of the Broadway Audience 2018–2019," accessed July 31, 2022, https://www.broadwayleague.com/research/research-reports/#:~:text=The%20average%20age%20of%20the,record%20high%20of%203.8%20million; United States Census, Income and Poverty in the United States: 2019, accessed July 31, 2023, https://www.census.gov/library/publications/2020/demo/p60-270.html.

102. Broadway League, "The Demographics of the Broadway Audience 2012–2013," accessed August 18, 2014, http://www.broadwayleague.com/index.php?url_identifier=the-demographics-of-the-broadway-audience; "Arts & Culture—Korea's Musical Theater Boom."

103. Sang-man Yi, "1946–1970: Korean Opera," in Yang, ed., *Korean Performing Arts*, 192–95.

104. Ji Hyon (Kayla) Yuh, "'Are They Supposed to Be Heugin?': Negotiating Race, Nation, and Representation in Korean Musical Theatre," PhD diss., The Graduate Center, City University of New York, 2018, 7, 32, 49, 55. See also Sissi Liu and Rina Tanaka, "The Broadway-Style Musical in/and Global Asias: 1920–2019," in *The Routledge

Companion to Musical Theatre, ed. Laura MacDonald and Ryan Donovan with William A. Everett (Abingdon: Routledge, 2023), 418–35.
105. Min-young Yoo, "Development of the Modern Musical in Korea," *Koreana: A Quarterly on Korean Culture & Arts 95*, no. 1 (Autumn 2001): 10–13. Yoo's article provides an excellent English-language survey of the history of musical theatre in Korea up to 2001.
106. Yuh, "'Are They Supposed to Be Heugin?,'" 63.
107. Yoo, "Development of the Modern Musical in Korea," 10–17.
108. Ho-kun Mun, "1971–1997: Music Theater in Korea Today," in Yang, ed., *Korean Performing Arts*, 207.
109. See Yu-Sun Lee, „Das Seouler Selbstporträt Linie 1. Eine Bestandsaufnahme des Seouler Alltags in den 1990er Jahren," in *Deutschsprachige Literatur und Theater seit 1945 in den Metropolen Seoul, Tokio und Berlin: Studien zur urbanen Kulturentwicklung unter komparatistischen und rezeptionsgeschichtlichen Perspektiven*, ed. Iris Hermann, Soichiro Itoda, Ralf Schnell, and Hi-Young Song (Bamberg: University of Bamberg Press, 2015), 321.
110. Lee Ji-Young and Haley Yang, "50 Years On, Korea's Most Iconic Protest Song Gets a Modern Makeover," *Korea JoongAng Daily*, June 10, 2021, accessed October 9, 2022, https://koreajoongangdaily.joins.com/2021/06/10/entertainment/kpop/Kim-Mingi-Kim-Mingi-Morning-Dew-Achim-Isul/20210610163200407.html.
111. Hyunjung Lee, *Performing the Nation in Global Korea: Transnational Theatre* (Basingstoke: Palgrave Macmillan, 2015), 74.
112. See Lee, *Daehangno*, 66; Yoo, "Development of the Modern Musical in Korea," 17.
113. Healy, "Musicals Couldn't Be Hotter Off Broadway."
114. Woo-Cumings, "Unilateralism and Its Discontents," 58.
115. See Steinberg, ed., *Korean Attitudes toward the United States*.
116. List of U.S. Military Installations in South Korea, accessed September 8, 2014, http://www.lifeinkorea.com/Communities2/military.
117. Heon Joo Jung, "The Rise and Fall of Anti-American Sentiment in South Korea: Deconstructing Hegemonic Ideas and Threat Perception," *Asian Survey 50*, no. 5 (September/October 2010): 950.
118. Chang Hun Oh and Celeste Arrington, "Democratization and Changing Anti-American Sentiments in South Korea," *Asian Survey 47*, no. 2 (March/April 2007): 347.
119. "South Korean Students in America," Asia Matters for America, accessed September 6, 2014, http://www.asiamattersforamerica.org/southkorea/data/students/koreansinamerica; "Number of International Students Studying in the United States in 2018/19, by Country of Origin," *Statista*, accessed November 8, 2020, https://www.statista.com/statistics/233880/international-students-in-the-us-by-country-of-origin/.
120. See Seoho Lee, "South Korea's Film Rules Need a Reboot," *Foreign Policy*, July 10, 2022, accessed November 3, 2022, https://foreignpolicy.com/2022/07/10/south-korea-film-movie-industry-screen-quota-protectionism-free-trade-covid/.

121. Patrick Healy, "Korean Cash Takes Broadway Bows," *New York Times*, December 31, 2013, accessed August 17, 2014, http://www.nytimes.com/2014/01/01/theater/korean-cash-takes-broadway-bows.html.
122. Healy, "Musicals Couldn't Be Hotter Off Broadway."
123. Cited in ibid.
124. Patrick Healy, "Korean Cash Takes Broadway Bows," *New York Times*, December 31, 2013, accessed November 8, 2020, https://www.nytimes.com/2014/01/01/theater/korean-cash-takes-broadway-bows.html.
125. OD Musical Company website, accessed October 23, 2012, http://www.odmusical.com/english/company/overview.html.
126. Healy, "Korean Cash Takes Broadway Bows."
127. Simone Genatt, American Theatre Wing, "Beyond Broadway: International Theatre," *videotaped* October 2009, accessed October 23, 2011, http://americantheatrewing.org/wit/detail/beyond_broadway_10_09.
128. Cited in Healy, "Musicals Couldn't Be Hotter Off Broadway."
129. Dohyun (Gracia) Shin, "Musical Theatre Industry in 2010s South Korea," November 17, 2020.
130. Ho Jin Yun, "Musical The Last Empress, A Delicious Dish Savored by Many for Fifteen Years," Koreabrand.net, accessed August 20, 2014, http://www.koreabrand.net/en/know/know_view.do?CATE_CD=0013&SEQ=1654. This error is repeated by Yoo, "Development of the Modern Musical in Korea," 16.
131. Lee, "'Broadway' as the Superior 'Other,'" 320–21.
132. *Korea Joongang Daily*, cited in souvenir program for *Hero: The Musical* during its visit to Lincoln Center, n.p.
133. Kolleen Park, cited in Kirk, "'Last Empress.'"
134. Jason Zinoman, "*Body Blows and Slapstick, with a Side of Ham*," *New York Times*, October 8, 2007.
135. Ricardo Saludo, "Making of an Asian Hit," *Asia Week*, December 18, 1998, accessed August 24, 2014, http://www-cgi.cnn.com/ASIANOW/asiaweek/98/1218/feat3.html.
136. Ho Jin Yun, cited in Don Kirk, "'Last Empress,' Musical Echo of Korea's History," *New York Times*, March 27, 1998, accessed September 1, 2013, http://www.nytimes.com/1998/03/27/style/27iht-last.t.html.
137. Lee, *Global Fetishism*, 52.
138. "Performing Arts: Musical 'Hero,'" Korean Cultural Service New York, accessed August 31, 2014, http://www.koreanculture.org/?document_srl=11928; Ho Jin Yun, cited in Mee-yoo Kwon, "Yun Takes Musical 'Hero' to New York," *Korea Times*, accessed July 12, 2012, https://www.koreatimes.co.kr/www/news/art/2012/10/145_92515.html. The performances were not sold out and the producers ended up distributing many free tickets.
139. "'Hero: The Musical,' First Korean Musical Produced Overseas Debuts at Lincoln Center," *Huffington Post*, August 26, 2011, accessed July 14, 2012, http://www.huffingtonpost.com/2011/08/26/hero-the-musical-lincoln-center_n_938465.html.

140. Robert L. Daniels, "Review: 'The Last Empress,'" *Variety*, August 25, 1997, accessed August 23, 2014, http://variety.com/1997/film/reviews/the-last-empress-2-1200450 617. For information on the Shamanic Rite, see Lee, "'Broadway' as the Superior 'Other,'" 324–27.

141. Lewis Segal, "Theater Review: Korea's Evita," *Los Angeles Times*, September 15, 1998, accessed August 23, 2014, http://articles.latimes.com/1998/sep/15/entertainment/ca-22807.

142. Ho Jin Yun, cited in Don Kirk, "'Last Empress,' Musical Echo of Korea's History," *New York Times*, March 27, 1998, accessed September 1, 2013, http://www.nytimes.com/1998/03/27/style/27iht-last.t.html.

143. Lee, "'Broadway' as the Superior 'Other,'" 322.

144. Ho Jin Yun, cited in ibid., 325.

145. Yongha Shin, "An Chunggun's Political Philosophy as seen in 'Peace in East Asia'"; National Institute of Korean History, "Background," in *Hero* souvenir program, n.p.

146. Ho Jin Yun, cited in Lee, "'Broadway' as the Superior 'Other,'" 325.

147. "Characters," in *Hero* souvenir program, n.p.

148. English supertitles from Lincoln Center performances of *Hero: The Musical*, August 2011.

149. *Segye Ilbo* and *Korea Joongang Daily*, cited in "Reviews," *Hero* souvenir program, n.p.

150. Biography of Ho Jin Yun, in *Hero* souvenir program, n.p.

151. "'Hero: The Musical,' First Korean Musical Produced Overseas Debuts at Lincoln Center," *Huffington Post*, August 26, 2011, accessed May 29, 2012, http://www.huffingtonpost.com/2011/08/26/hero-the-musical-lincoln-center_n_938465.html.

152. Kelsey Blair, "Since the 1980s: The Global Musical Theatre Ecology," in *The Routledge Companion to Musical Theatre*, ed. Laura MacDonald et al., 159.

153. Rachel Saltz, "Politics, History and All That Jazz: Good vs. Evil in 34 Songs," *New York Times*, August 29, 2011; Ho Jin Yun, quoted in Lee, "'Broadway' as the Superior 'Other,'" 325.

154. Jessica Sternfeld, *The Megamusical* (Bloomington: Indiana University Press, 2006), 94. Unlike the megamusical, the new transnational musical is usually not through-composed.

155. Elizabeth L. Wollman, *The Theater Will Rock: A History of the Rock Musical, from "Hair" to "Hedwig"* (Ann Arbor: University of Michigan Press, 2009), 128.

156. Gregory Bernard, "Off Broadway Theater Review: HERO—THE MUSICAL," *Theater-New York*, August 28, 2011, accessed January 20, 2012, http://www.stageandcinema.com/2011/08/28/hero.

157. Kyung Hyun Kim, *Hegemonic Mimicry*, 11.

158. See, e.g., Elisabeth Vincentelli, "Seoul-ful, Tuneful Korean 'Hero' Welcome," *New York Post*, August 26, 2011, accessed August 13, 2013, http://www.nypost.com/p/entertainment/theater/seoul_ful_tuneful_korean_hero_welcome_bpZFwIec3IQH9HbOLjsoUO.

159. Kim, Harmonia Koreana, 81.

160. "Costume Design," in *Hero* souvenir program, n.p.

161. "The Life of An Chunggun," in *Hero* souvenir program, n.p.

162. "Synopsis," *Hero* souvenir program, n.p.
163. Youngseok Moon, "Sociological Implications of the Roman Catholic Conversion Boom in Korea," *Korea Journal 51*, no. 1 (Spring 2011): 149.
164. "Why South Korea Is So Distinctively Christian," *The Economist*, April 12, 2014, accessed August 30, 2014, http://www.economist.com/blogs/economist-explains/2014/08/economist-explains-6.
165. Moon, "Sociological Implications of the Roman Catholic Conversion Boom in Korea," 148, 169.
166. Chaibong, "Anti-Americanism, Korean Style," 222.
167. Shin, *Ethnic Nationalism in Korea*, 31.
168. Cited in Hyun-jung Lee, "Haunting the Empress: Representations of Empress Myungsung in Contemporary South Korean Cultural Products," *Situations 2* (Fall 2008): 98.
169. English supertitles from Lincoln Center performances of *Hero: The Musical*.
170. See "Lessons from K-pop's Global Success," Korea-marketing.com, accessed September 14, 2014, http://www.korea-marketing.com/lessons-from-k-pops-global-success/.
171. Kwon, "Yun takes musical 'Hero' to New York."
172. Elisabeth Vincentelli, "For 'KPOP,' a Broadway Transfer Is More like a Reinvention," *New York Times*, November 4, 2022, 19.
173. Jason Kim, Helen Park, and Max Vernon, *KPOP*, Broadway script, Circle in the Square, New York, NY, November 27, 2022, 5.
174. Youjeong Oh, *Pop City*, 114.
175. Kim, *Hegemonic Mimicry*, 235.
176. Ibid., 235.

Chapter 3

1. Choi Yu-jun, "Modernity as Postcolonial Encounter in Korean Music," in *Decentering Musical Modernity: Perspectives on East Asian and European Music History*, ed. Tobias Janz and Chien-Chang Yang (Bielefeld, Germany: transcript Verlag, 2019), 47–48.
2. D. Bannon, "Unique Korean Cultural Concepts in Interpersonal Relations," *Translation Journal 12*, no. 1 (January 2008), accessed March 21, 2018, http://translationjournal.net/journal/43korean.htm.
3. Tudor, *Korea*, 121.
4. Sandra So Hee Chi Kim, "Korean *Han* and the Postcolonial Afterlives of 'The Beauty of Sorrow,'" *Korean Studies 41* (2017): 257.
5. Chang-Hee Son, *Haan of Minjung Theology and Han of Han Philosophy: In the Paradigm of Process Philosophy and Metaphysics of Relatedness* (Lanham, MD: University Press of America, 2000), 15. Note that Son transliterates the word as *haan*.
6. Choi, "Modernity as Postcolonial Encounter in Korean Music," 50.

7. "Homegrown Musicals the Next Wave in Hallyu?" Arirang News, accessed September 18, 2014, http://www.arirang.co.kr/News/News_View.asp?nSeq=160612.
8. Jong-won Won, quoted in "Musical 'Frankenstein,'" *KBS World Radio*, April 22, 2014, accessed September 20, 2014, http://world.kbs.co.kr/english/program/program_trendkorea_detail.htm?No=1001471.
9. "Musical 'Frankenstein,'" KBS World Radio, April 22, 2014, accessed December 14, 2020, http://world.kbs.co.kr/service/contents_view.htm?lang=e&menu_cate=culture&id=&board_seq=13009&page=3&board_code=trendkorea.
10. Musicals in Seoul, "The Musical Frankenstein Review," May 12, 2014, accessed December 14, 2020, https://musihsoo.tumblr.com/post/85506790758/the-musical-review.
11. Julie Jackson, "'Frankenstein' Musical Grim, but Totally Worth It," *Korea Herald*, December 13, 2015, accessed December 14, 2020, http://www.koreaherald.com/view.php?ud=20151213000391.
12. "Musical 'Frankenstein,'" KBS World Radio, April 22, 2014, accessed December 14, 2020, http://world.kbs.co.kr/service/contents_view.htm?lang=e&menu_cate=culture&id=&board_seq=13009&page=3&board_code=trendkorea.
13. "Homegrown Musicals the Next Wave in Hallyu?" Arirang News.
14. Jimin Lee, "BWW Review: *Frankenstein* at Blue Square Interpark Hall, the Revenge Awaits," June 28, 2018, accessed November 28, 2020, https://www.broadwayworld.com/south-korea/article/BWW-Review-FRANKENSTEIN-at-Blue-Square-Interpark-Hall-The-Revenge-Awaits-20180628.
15. "Musical 'Frankenstein,'" KBS World Radio.
16. Binge-watch 'Frankenstein' Highlight Numbers (Press Call Act 1 ver.) [Stay at Home Theatre], accessed December 17, 2020, https://www.youtube.com/watch?v=n8E6PUlGtfw.
17. "Wounded," translated by Hansol Oh, accessed December 18, 2020, https://www.youtube.com/watch?v=LMNE7xMwruY.
18. "Musical 'Frankenstein,' the Monster That Dominated Korean Theaters," *HAFS Harbinger*, March 8, 2016, accessed December 12, 2020, https://hafsharbinger.wordpress.com/2016/03/08/musical-frankenstein-the-monster-that-dominated-korean-theaters/.
19. "Musical 'Frankenstein,'" KBS World Radio.
20. Hee-chul Kim, quoted in "Musical 'Frankenstein,'" KBS World Radio; "Homegrown Musicals the Next Wave in Hallyu?" Arirang News. In London and New York, *Les Misérables* was also a collaboration between commercial producers and a state-supported theatre, the Royal Shakespeare Company, which continues to collect substantial royalties. See Michelle Dean, "Without Public Arts Funding, We Wouldn't Have 'Les Misérables,'" *Nation*, January 7, 2013, accessed October 2, 2014, http://www.thenation.com/blog/172039/without-public-arts-funding-we-wouldnt-have-les-miserables#.
21. Hee-chul Kim, quoted in "Musical 'Frankenstein,'" KBS World Radio; "Homegrown Musicals the Next Wave in Hallyu?" Arirang News.

22. Patrick Healy, "Heartthrobs Rule the Korean Stage," *New York Times*, December 26, 2013, accessed September 19, 2014, http://www.nytimes.com/2013/12/29/theater/k-pop-stars-selling-stage-musicals-in-korea.html?ref=theater.
23. Cited in "Musical 'Frankenstein,'" KBS World Radio. In fact, the lead actors were celebrated and popular musical theatre stars.
24. In relation to female spectatorship, I want to note the preponderance of musicals in Korea that not only spotlight attractive young men but also employ barely concealed homoerotic subtexts. These include *Thrill Me* and even *Frankenstein*, in which the most popular and inspirational song, "In Your Dream," is really a love song between two men, Victor and Henry. See https://www.youtube.com/watch?v=ZQZb6Lg3XRE (accessed December 25, 2020).
25. Thierry Loreau, cited in Dana Hwang, "Korean Music Mystery Revealed," Korea.net, May 30, 2012, accessed September 19, 2014, http://www.korea.net/NewsFocus/Culture/view?articleId=100556.
26. Jungyun Kwon, "Spotlight on Korea's Classical Musicians," Korea.net, accessed September 19, 2014, http://www.korea.net/NewsFocus/Culture/view?articleId=103971. The competition rotates in three-year cycles, alternating among voice, violin, and piano.
27. Cited in Dana Hwang, "Korean Music Mystery Revealed," Korea.net, May 30, 2012, accessed September 19, 2014, http://www.korea.net/NewsFocus/Culture/view?articleId=100556. The only country that can compare with Korea in its production of so many highly skilled classical musicians is Finland, which, however, has a much longer history of Western musical training. See Richard B. Woodward, "After Sibelius, Finland's Rich Bounty of Musicians," *New York Times*, June 12, 2005.
28. The Korean production is directed by Laurence Connor and James Powell, with musical staging by Michael Ashcroft.
29. Jonathan Burston, "Recombinant Broadway," *Continuum: Journal of Media & Cultural Studies* 23, no. 2 (April 2009): 168.
30. For Chung's bio, see *Hero* souvenir program, n.p.
31. Chung's performance of the number at the Korea Musical Awards can be watched on YouTube at http://www.youtube.com/watch?v=0rF14UPXADU (accessed September 21, 2014).
32. Richard Wagner, cited in V. A. Howard, *Charm and Speed: Virtuosity in the Performing Arts* (New York: Peter Lang, 2008), 3.
33. David L. Palmer, "Virtuosity as Rhetoric: Agency and Transformation in Paganini's Mastery of the Violin," *Quarterly Journal of Speech* 84 (1998): 345, 352.
34. Cherkell, "Musical 'The Days.'"
35. Choi, "Modernity as Postcolonial Encounter in Korean Music," 43.
36. See National Gugak Center, History, accessed December 7, 2020, http://www.gugak.go.kr/site/homepage/menu/viewMenu?menuid=001005003&lang=en.
37. National Gugak Center, Contemporary Gugak Orchestra, accessed December 7, 2020, http://www.gugak.go.kr/site/homepage/menu/viewMenu?menuid=001005005005001.

38. National Gugak Center, Major Business & Vision, accessed December 7, 2020, http://www.gugak.go.kr/site/homepage/menu/viewMenu?menuid=001005002&lang=en.
39. See National Gugak Center, Publications, accessed December 7, 2020, http://www.gugak.go.kr/site/program/board/basicboard/list?boardtypeid=24&menuid=001003002005&lang=en.
40. Choi, "Modernity as Postcolonial Encounter in Korean Music," 57. See "Traditional Music: Remixed for the Global Stage," *Koreana*, Spring 2022.
41. Cited in Heather Willoughby, "The Sound of *Han*: *P'ansori*, Timbre and a Korean Ethos of Pain and Suffering," *Yearbook for Traditional Music 32* (2000): 18.
42. Heather Alane Willoughby, "*The Sound of Han: P'ansori, Timbre, and a South Korean Discourse of Sorrow and Lament*" (PhD diss., Columbia University, 2002), 89.
43. Kim, "Korean Wave Pop Culture in the Global Internet Age," 85.
44. Nam-dong Suh, "Toward a Theology of Han," quoted in Boo Woong Yoo, *Korean Pentecostalism: Its History and Theology* (New York: Peter Lang, 1987), 222.
45. Tudor, *Korea*, 122.
46. Kyung Hyun Kim, *Hegemonic Mimicry: Korean Popular Culture of the Twenty-First Century* (Durham, NC: Duke University Press, 2021), 221.
47. Kim, "Korean *Han* and the Postcolonial Afterlives of 'The Beauty of Sorrow,' " 258, 259, 264, 266, 273.
48. See Kim, "Korean *Han* and the Postcolonial Afterlives of 'The Beauty of Sorrow,' " 271; Mark Slobin, *Fiddler on the Move: Exploring the Klezmer World* (New York: Oxford University Press, 2000), 99; Kyung Hyun Kim, *Hegemonic Mimicry*, 227.
49. Lim Jae-hae, cited in Tudor, *Korea*, 124.
50. Tudor, *Korea*, 124.
51. My thanks to Doh-yun (Gracia) Shin for this insight.
52. "Emptying nostalgia's vault," *Korea Times*, accessed September 26, 2014, https://www.koreatimes.co.kr/www/common/printpreview.asp?categoryCode=143&newsIdx=130877.
53. See Cherkell, "Musical 'The Days': An Overview," Scotch and Asparagus, April 8, 2013, accessed September 26, 2014, https://scotchandasparagus.wordpress.com/2013/04/08/musical-the-days-an-overview/#more-6689.
54. See Sotaro Suzuki, "South Korean Singer's Death Cast in Mystery," *Nikkei Asia*, October 14, 2017, accessed November 19, 2020, https://asia.nikkei.com/Location/East-Asia/South-Korea/South-Korean-singer-s-death-cast-in-mystery.
55. "AAK! Music: Around Thirty by Kim Gwang-Seok (1994)," Ask a Korean, February 3, 2010, accessed September 24, 2014, http://askakorean.blogspot.de/2010/02/aak-music-around-thirty-by-kim-gwang.html.
56. Kwon Mee-yoo, "The Rise of Kim Kwang-seok's Posthumous Career," accessed September 26, 2014, http://121.78.129.108/www/common/printpreview.asp?categoryCode=143&newsIdx=150069.
57. See Die Orsons—"Kim Kwang Seok" (Official Video), YouTube, accessed November 20, 2020, https://www.youtube.com/watch?v=kRxDuRLC8d4&list=RDkRxDuRLC8d4&start_radio=1.
58. "AAK! Music: Around Thirty by Kim Gwang-Seok (1994)."

59. English plot synopsis, souvenir program for *The Days*, 2013.
60. This latter links its function to that of the Wagnerian leitmotif.
61. Kim Duk-muk, "Bukhansan Keeps Alive Shaman Traditions," *Koreana: Korean Art & Culture 18*, no. 1 (Spring 2004): 10, accessed November 16, 2020, https://issuu.com/the_korea_foundation/docs/2004_01_e_b_a.
62. See "Grievance Cleansing Ritual," *Encyclopedia of Korea Folk Culture*, accessed November 21, 2020, https://folkency.nfm.go.kr/en/topic/detail/1863.
63. Kim Chang Nam, *K-Pop*, 50.
64. See 김광석 슈퍼콘서트 풀버전 Kim Kwangseok Super Concert Full Version, YouTube, accessed October 4, 2014, http://www.youtube.com/watch?v=zxTLz5Z7dPA.
65. It is worth noting that sequences of descending fifths are not uncommon in pop music as well as classical, as Gloria Gaynor's "I Will Survive" proves.
66. Cherkell, "Musical 'The Days.'"
67. "Emptying nostalgia's vault."
68. See Elizabeth L. Wollman, *The Theater Will Rock: A History of the Rock Musical, from "Hair" to "Hedwig"* (Ann Arbor: University of Michigan Press, 2009).
69. Seo Bo-bin, quoted in "Creative Musicals in Korea: Reminiscing about Kim Kwang," *Arirang*, April 11, 2019, accessed November 15, 2020, http://www.arirang.com/news/News_View.asp?nseq=235095&sys_lang=Kor.
70. canisarangyou, "김광석—사랑했지만 Kim Kwang Seok—Though I Loved You," kmusiclyrics, KMusic English Translations, October 13, 2011, accessed October 3, 2014, http://kmusiclyrics.wordpress.com/2011/10/13/%EA%B9%80%EA%B4%91%EC%84%9D-%EC%82%AC%EB%9E%91%ED%96%88%EC%A7%80%EB%A7%8C-kim-kwang-seok-though-i-loved-you/.
71. See Ji Chang-wook's performance on the 2013 Musical Awards, accessed October 3, 2014, http://www.youtube.com/watch?v=7zAoaN4fjfc.
72. Kim Hakjoon, "The Establishment of South Korean–Chinese Diplomatic Relations: A South Korean Perspective," *Journal of Northeast Asian Studies 13* (1994): 31.
73. Hakjoon, "The Establishment of South Korean–Chinese Diplomatic Relations," 41, 31, 44.
74. "Sopyonje (1993)," accessed November 23, 2017, http://www.koreanfilm.org/kfilm90-95.html#sopyonje.
75. David E. James, "Preface," in *Im Kwon-Taek: The Making of a Korean National Cinema*, ed. David E. James and Kyung Hyun Kim (Detroit: Wayne State University Press, 2002), 14.
76. Chungmoo Choi, "The Politics of Gender, Aestheticism, and Cultural Nationalism in *Sopyonje* and *The Genealogy*," in James and Ki, eds., *Im Kwon-Taek*, 110.
77. The exact family relationships vary among the different versions. In the stories, Yu-bong is the biological father of Song-hwa (who is the younger of the children), but not Dong-ho. In the film, Yu-bong is the biological father of neither child and Dong-ho is the elder of the children. In the musical, Yu-bong is the biological father of neither child, but Dong-ho is the younger of the children. What remains consistent from version to version is the fact that Yu-bong is constructed as a kind of adopted father to both brother and sister, who are not however biologically related. The stories and film

take place between the late 1930s and the 1960s, while the musical is set about twenty years later. The musical also spotlights the ghost of Dong-ho's biological mother (and lover of Yu-bong), so constructing a quartet of leading characters.

78. Chan E. Park, *Voices from the Straw Mat: Toward an Ethnography of Korean Story Singing* (Honolulu: University of Hawai'i Press, 2003), 159, 158.
79. Choi, "The Politics of Gender, Aestheticism, and Cultural Nationalism in *Sopyonje* and *The Genealogy*," 116, 131.
80. In the stories and film, Dong-ho is a collector of medicinal herbs for a pharmaceutical company.
81. Andrew Killick, *In Search of Korean Traditional Opera: Discourses of Changguk* (Honolulu: University of Hawai'i Press, 2010), 41.
82. Robert Koehler and Byeon Ji-yeon, *Traditional Music: Sounds in Harmony with Nature* (Seoul: The Korea Foundation, 2011), 51.
83. Killick, *In Search of Korean Traditional Opera*, 41.
84. Francisca Cho, "Korean Religion," in *Encyclopedia.com*, August 2, 2020, https://www.encyclopedia.com/environment/encyclopedias-almanacs-transcripts-and-maps/korean-religion.
85. See Dong Kyu Kim, "Looping Effects between Images and Realities: Understanding the Plurality of Korean Shamanism" (PhD diss., University of British Columbia, 2012), 77–90. Kim also prefers to see Korean shamanism as a set of cultural practices rather than a religion and he argues it that became categorized as a religion only under the Japanese occupation.
86. *Seopyeonje*, 7.
87. Kim, "Looping Effects," 91–98.
88. Koehler and Byeon, *Traditional Music*, 52.
89. National Center for Korean Traditional Performing Arts, quoted in Nicholas Harkness, *Songs of Seoul: An Ethnography of Voice and Voicing in Christian South Korea* (Berkeley: University of California Press, 2013), 97.
90. Harkness, Songs of Seoul, 98, 100.
91. Ch'e Su-chong, cited in Willoughby, "The Sound of *Han*: P'ansori, Timbre, and a South Korean Discourse of Sorrow and Lament," 103.
92. Jacopo Peri's *Euridice* (1600) and Claudio Monteverdi's *Orfeo* (1607).
93. In his detailed ethnographic analysis of Korean vocal production, Nicholas Harkness argues that Western-style bel canto singing (as exemplified by Korean Christian singing) and *p'ansori* singing are absolutely antithetical anatomically, culturally, and theologically. Although his argument is convincing as far as it goes, his failure even to mention the two most popular modes of singing in Korea, K-pop and musical theatre performance, and to position them in his rigidly bipolar scheme, considerably limits its applicability. See Harkness, *Songs of Seoul*.
94. *Seopyeonje*, as directed by Jo Gwang-hwa, was premiered in 2010 and remains in the rotating repertoire of commercial theatres; the version I saw in Seoul in 2017 was substantially the same as the original.
95. Park, *Voices from the Straw Mat*, 3.

96. "Paper Money," in *Encyclopedia of Korean Folk Culture*, accessed July 31, 2020, https://folkency.nfm.go.kr/en/topic/detail/2848.
97. "Grievance Cleansing Ritual," in *Encyclopedia of Korean Folk Culture*, accessed July 31, 2020, https://folkency.nfm.go.kr/en/topic/detail/1863.
98. Consider the title character in *Oedipus the King* and Gloucester in *King Lear*.
99. The Seopyeonje story in all its variants indisputably represents a kind of Freudian nightmare, as disturbing in its way as Sophocles' *Oedipus the King*.
100. Killick, *In Search of Korean Traditional Opera*, 43.
101. David E. James, "Im Kwon-Taek: Korean National Cinema and Buddhism," in James and Kim, eds., *Im Kwon-Taek*, 52.
102. English translations by Hansol Oh.
103. English translations by Hansol Oh.
104. Pyeon Jang-wan, quoted in Julian Stringer, "*Sopyonje* and the Inner Domain of National Culture," in James and Kim, eds., *Im Kwon-Taek*, 165.
105. D. A. Miller, *Place for Us [Essay on the Broadway Musical]* (Cambridge, MA: Harvard University Press, 1998), 71.
106. Choi, "Modernity in Korean Music," 51.
107. Susan McClary, *Feminine Endings: Music, Gender, and Sexuality* (Minneapolis: University of Minnesota Press), 81.
108. Choi, "The Politics of Gender, Aestheticism, and Cultural Nationalism in *Sopyonje* and *The Genealogy*," 116.
109. Choi notes that the character of Song-hwa in the film "does not develop much and remains essentially flat"; "The Politics of Gender, Aestheticism, and Cultural Nationalism," 121.
110. Stacy Wolf, "Keeping Company with Sondheim's Women," in *The Oxford Handbook of Sondheim Studies*, ed. Robert Gordon (New York: Oxford University Press, 2014), 365. See also Stacy Wolf, *Changed for Good: A Feminist History of the Broadway Musical* (New York: Oxford University Press, 2011).
111. You can see Lee Jaram's performance on YouTube with English titles, https://www.youtube.com/watch?v=bgug3vBytRw (accessed May 21, 2018).
112. Stringer, "*Sopyonje* and the Inner Domain of National Culture," 166.
113. Stringer, "*Sopyonje* and the Inner Domain of National Culture," 167.
114. Text of the Convention for the Safeguarding of the Intangible Cultural Heritage, UNESCO, accessed May 28, 2018, https://ich.unesco.org/en/convention.
115. Stephen Banfield, *Sondheim's Broadway Musicals* (Ann Arbor: University of Michigan Press, 1995), 6–7.
116. Choi, "Modernity as Postcolonial Encounter in Korean Music," 59.
117. Michael Billington, "The Last Empress," *The Guardian*, February 4, 2002, accessed May 20, 2015, http://www.theguardian.com/stage/2002/feb/05/theatre.artsfeatures2.
118. Choi, "Modernity as Postcolonial Encounter in Korean Music," 59.

Chapter 4

1. Three other, smaller genres included in the book are puppet theatre, revue, and intermedial performance (Project/Mehrspartenproject/Performance). See Deutscher Bühnenverein, *Wer spielte was?: 2018/19 Werkstatistik* (Würzburg: Verlag Königshausen & Neumann, 2020).
2. Deutscher Bühnenverein, press release, December 11, 2020, accessed May 7, 2021, https://www.buehnenverein.de/de/presse/pressemeldungen.html?det=597. Although the Bühnenverein includes statistics for Austria and Switzerland, they are more exhaustively complete for Germany than for the other two countries.
3. Deutsches Musikinformations Zentrum, Einnahmen der öffentlich finanzierten Theater 2019 (Musik- und Sprechtheater), accessed November 9, 2022, https://miz.org/de/statistiken/einnahmen-der-oeffentlich-finanzierten-theater-musik-und-sprechtheater.
4. Deutscher Bühnenverein, *Theaterstatistik 2018–2019* (Cologne: Deutscher Bühnenverein, 2020), 274, 289.
5. Deutscher Bühnenverein, *Wer spielte was?: 2018/19 Werkstatistik* (Würzburg: Verlag Königshausen & Neumann, 2020), 387. These numbers include Germany, Austria, and Switzerland.
6. Attendance at Broadway shows in New York from 2006 to 2019, by category, Statista.com, accessed May 7, 2012, https://www.statista.com/statistics/197638/attendance-at-broadway-shows-since-2006/.
7. Although the Bühnenverein's theatre statistics are more complete for Germany, their catalogue of performances and repertoire, *Wer spielte was?*, gives equal weight to Germany, Austria, and Switzerland, distinguishing between number of performances in Germany, on the one hand, and the German-speaking world, on the other.
8. Deutscher Bühnenverein, *Wer spielte was?*, 75–83.
9. See Stephen Hinton, *Weill's Musical Theater: Stages of Reform* (Berkeley: University of California Press, 2012), 93.
10. Christiane Lutz and Alexander Menden, "Musicals in der Krise: Les Misérables," *Süddeutsche Zeitung*, May 6, 2021, accessed July 17, 2021, https://www.sueddeutsche.de/kultur/musicalbranche-coronakrise-probleme-1.5286169.
11. Ramona Fülfe, *Kulturmarketing: Impulse für eine zielgruppengerechte Ansprache im Bereich E-Musik* (Hamburg: Diplomica Verlag, 2011), 6.
12. Mandy Risch and Andreas Kerst, *Eventrecht kompakt: Ein Lehr- und Praxisbuch mit Beispielen aus dem Konzert- und Kulturbetrieb* (Heidelberg: Springer, 2009), 293.
13. Moritz Eggert, "Schüler fragen nach U und E," blog, *Neue Musikzeitung*, accessed June 27, 2022, https://blogs.nmz.de/badblog/2021/04/13/schueler-fragen-nach-u-und-e/.
14. Barrie Kosky, "What the f***?!?" in *Breaking Free: Die wunderbare Welt des LGBTQ-Musicals*, ed. Kevin Clarke (Berlin: Querverlag, 2022), 9–17.
15. Marianne Wellershoff, "Taaata-ta-ta-ta-taa," *Kultur Spiegel* (September 2014), accessed March 15, 2015, http://www.spiegel.de/spiegel/kulturspiegel/d-128809892.html.

16. "Die Kleingedruckten," *Kultur Spiegel* (September 2014), accessed March 15, 2015, http://www.spiegel.de/spiegel/kulturspiegel/d-128809890.html.
17. See Nils Grosch, "Zwischen Ignoranz und Kulturkritik: Das Musical in der Rezeption durch die deutschsprachigen Wissenschaften," in *Die Rezeption des Broadwaymusicals in Deutschland*, ed. Nils Grosch and Elmar Juchem (Münster: Waxmann, 2012), 11–12.
18. Hans-Thies Lehmann, trans. Karen Jürs-Munby, *Postdramatic Theatre* (London: Routledge, 2006), 180.
19. *Das Feuerwerk* is in fact a translation into High German and adaptation of Burkhard's Swiss-German dialect operetta, *Der schwarze Hecht* (the black pike), first performed at the Zurich Schauspielhaus in 1939.
20. Volker Klotz, *Operette: Porträt und Handbuch einer unerhörten Kunst* (Kassel: Bärenreiter, 2004), 20.
21. Micaela Baranello, *The Operetta Empire: Music Theater in Early Twentieth-Century Vienna* (Berkeley: University of California Press, 2021), 2.
22. Baranello, *The Operetta Empire*, 17.
23. David Savran, "Middlebrow Anxiety," in *A Queer Sort of Materialism: Recontextualizing American Theater* (Ann Arbor: University of Michigan Press, 2003), 15.
24. Thomas Siedhoff, *Handbuch des Musicals: Die wichtigsten Titel von A bis Z* (Mainz: Schott, 2007), 401.
25. Thomas Siedhoff, "Aufstieg, Fall und Emanzipation des deutschen Musicals," in *Die Rezeption des Broadwaymusicals in Deutschland*, ed. Nils Grosch and Elmar Juchem (Münster: Waxmann, 2012), 44.
26. Uta G. Poiger, *Jazz, Rock, and Rebels: Cold War Politics and American Culture in a Divided Germany* (Berkeley: University of California Press, 2000), 3.
27. Quoted in Wolfgang Jansen, *Musicals: Geschichte und Interpretation* (Münster: Waxmann, 2020), 223.
28. See Poiger, *Jazz, Rock, and Rebels*.
29. Jansen, *Musicals*, 47.
30. Horst Koegler, cited in Jansen, *Musicals*, 57.
31. Elmar Juchem, "Zur Wahrnehmung von Rodgers & Hammerstein in Deutschland," in Nils Grosch and Elmar Juchem, eds., *Die Rezeption des Broadwaymusicals in Deutschland*, 70–72.
32. Heinz Ritter, "Wild-West mit Lebensmut," *Telegraf*, September 14, 1951.
33. K g l., "Operetta ohne Bart," *Tag*, September 7, 1951.
34. Friedrich Luft, "Broadway Gastspiel 'Oklahoma' in Titania-Palast," *Neue Zeitung*, September 14, 1951.
35. Hans Preuß, *Berliner Zeitung*, September 20, 1951.
36. Juchem, "Zur Wahrnehmung von Rodgers & Hammerstein in Deutschland," 73.
37. See Juchem, "Zur Wahrnehmung von Rodgers & Hammerstein in Deutschland."
38. Juchem, "Zur Wahrnehmung von Rodgers & Hammerstein in Deutschland," 74–75.
39. Wolfgang Jansen, "Von der Operette zum Musical: Zur Entwicklung des unterhaltenden Musiktheaters nach 1945," in *Welt der Operette: Glamour, Stars*

and *Showbusiness*, ed. Marie-Theres Arnbom, Kevin Clarke, and Thomas Trabitsch (Vienna: Brandstätter Verlag, 2011), 251.
40. Jansen, *Musicals*, 65.
41. Jansen, "Von der Operette zum Musical," 255.
42. Friedrich Luft, cited in Jansen, *Musicals*, 195.
43. Hellmut Kotschenreuther, "Ein Wort zum Thema 'Musical,'" program for *My Fair Lady*, Theater des Westens, Berlin, 1962, 1.
44. "Elizas Triumphzug um die Welt," souvenir program for *My Fair Lady*, Deutsches Theater, Munich, 1962, n.p.
45. Rudolf Brendemühl, cited in Jansen, *Musicals*, 228.
46. Jansen, *Musicals*, 228.
47. Jansen, *Musicals*, 230–31.
48. Cited in Jansen, *Musicals*, 231.
49. See Katrin Stöck, "'Don't laugh and forget the world, (but) recognize it and yourself with laughter': Operetta and Light Music Theatre in the GDR," in *Popular Music Theatre under Socialism: Operettas and Musicals in the Eastern European States 1945 to 1990* (Münster: Waxmann, 2020), 110.
50. Siedhoff, *Handbuch des Musicals*, 388.
51. Joachim Brügge, "By George, she's got it! Elizas 'Jargon' in ausgesuchten deutschsprachigen Übersetzungen—die Wiener Inszenierung von 1969 und andere Mundartversionen von My Fair Lady," in Grosch and Juchem, eds., *Die Rezeption des Broadwaymusicals in Deutschland*, 78.
52. Arthur Maria Rabenalt, cited in Baranello, *The Operetta Empire*, 6.
53. See Dominic McHugh, *Loverly: The Life and Times of My Fair Lady* (New York: Oxford University Press, 2012), 199–209.
54. A Korean adaptation of *Linie 1* premiered in 1994 that became more popular than the German original and was even invited back to Berlin in 1998 to be performed in its birthplace. Lee Chin A, *Daehangno: Theater District in Seoul* (Seoul: Hollym, 2011), 66.
55. See Matthias Weigel, "Im Beat der Finsternis," *nachtkritik*, November 24, 2012, accessed June 6, 2021, https://www.nachtkritik.de/index.php?option=com_content&view=article&id=7491:the-black-rider-friederike-heller-und-kante-bitten-an-der-berliner-schaubuehne-zum-teufelspakt-musical&catid=34:schaubuehne-berlin&Itemid=100476. According to *Wer spielte was?*, *The Black Rider*, a musical, received eight new productions in 2018–2019, seen by 23,162 theatregoers. Deutscher Bühnenverein, *Wer spielte was?*, 66.
56. Rainer Luhn, interview with Kevin Clarke and the author, Berlin, June 27, 2021.
57. Jessica Sternfeld and Elizabeth L. Wollman, "After the 'Golden Age,'" in *The Oxford Handbook of The American Musical*, ed. Raymond Knapp, Mitchell Morris, and Stacy Wolf (New York: Oxford University Press, 2011), 112.
58. Wolfgang Jansen, "'Bringt es uns weiter?': Zur Rezeption des Musicals in der DDR," in Grosch and Juchem, eds., *Die Rezeption des Broadwaymusicals in Deutschland*, 139.
59. Michael Stolle, *Der Komponist Gerd Natschinski: Der Meister von Musical, Filmmusik und Schlager in der DDR* (Hamburg: Tredition, 2018), 188.

60. Wolfgang Jansen, "From *Trembita* (1952) to *The King David Report* (1989): Operettas and Musicals from European Socialist Countries in the Repertoire of the GDR," in *Popular Music Theatre under Socialism: Operettas and Musicals in the Eastern European States 1945 to 1990*, ed. Wolfgang Jansen (Münster: Waxmann, 2020), 144.
61. Stöck, "'Don't laugh and forget the world,'" 110.
62. Stöck, "'Don't laugh and forget the world,'" 109.
63. Stöck, "'Don't laugh and forget the world,'" 110.
64. Stöck, "'Don't laugh and forget the world,'" 113.
65. Roland H. Dippel, "East and West Germany in the Light Music Theatre of the GDR before and after the Construction of the Berlin Wall in 1961," in Jansen, ed., *Popular Music Theatre under Socialism*, 132.
66. Dippel, "East and West Germany in the Light Music Theatre of the GDR," 135.
67. Roland Dippel, "Heiteres Musiktheater: Operette in der Deutschen Demokratischen Republik," in Arnbom, Clarke, and Trabitsch, eds., *Welt der Operette: Glamour, Stars and Showbusiness*, 238.
68. H. P. Hofmann, liner notes for Gerd Natschinski, Helmut Bez, and Jürgen Degenhardt, *Mein Freund Bunbury*, Nova Records 8 85 031 (VEB Deutsche Schallplatten Berlin), 1972.
69. Gerd Natschinski, quoted in Stolle, *Der Komponist Gerd Natschinski*, 186.
70. H.P. Hofmann, liner notes for Gerd Natschinski, Helmut Bez, and Jürgen Degenhardt, *Mein Freund Bunbury*.
71. Siedhoff, *Handbuch des Musicals*, 362.
72. H. P. Hofmann, liner notes for Gerd Natschinski, Helmut Bez, and Jürgen Degenhardt, *Mein Freund Bunbury*.
73. See Wolfgang Jansen, *Cats & Co.: Geschichte des Musicals im Deutschsprachigen Theater* (Berlin: Henschel, 2008), 67.
74. Critic Horst Koegler, cited in Stolle, *Der Komponist Gerd Natschinski*, 181.
75. See Stolle, *Der Komponist Gerd Natschinski*, 187.
76. Quoted in Stolle, *Der Komponist Gerd Natschinski*, 181.
77. Siedhoff, "Aufstieg, Fall und Emanzipation des deutschen Musicals," 56.
78. Peter Czerny, liner notes to Guido Masanetz, music, Otto Schneidereit and Maurycy Janowski, lyrics, *In Frisco ist der Teufel los*, Nova 8 85 016, 1971.
79. Roland Dippel, "Heiteres Musiktheater schwelgt in Nostalgie: 'In Frisco ist der Teufel los,'" Operetta Research Center, accessed June 17, 2021, http://operetta-research-center.org/heiteres-musiktheater-schwelgt-nostalgie-frisco-ist-der-teufel-los/.
80. Priscilla Layne, *White Rebels in Black: German Appropriation of Black Popular Culture* (Ann Arbor: University of Michigan Press, 2018), 79.
81. Franz Loeser, cited in Michael Rauhut, "The Voice of the Other America: African-American Music and Political Protest in the German Democratic Republic," in *Between the Avant-Garde and the Everyday: Subversive Politics in Europe from 1957 to the Present*, ed. Timothy Brown and Lorena Anton (New York: Berghahn Books, 2011), 98.
82. Layne, *White Rebels in Black*, 81.
83. Layne, *White Rebels in Black*, 79.

84. Layne, *White Rebels in Black*, 81.
85. Dippel, "Heiteres Musiktheater," 238.
86. Rainer Luhn, interview with Kevin Clarke and the author. Luhn used the English phrase.
87. Uwe Schütte, "Introduction—Pop Music as the Soundtrack of German Post-War History," in *German Pop Music: A Companion*, ed. Uwe Schütte (Berlin: De Gruyter, 2017), 8.
88. Schütte, "Introduction," 8.
89. Timothy Scott Brown, *West Germany and the Global Sixties: The Anti-Authoritarian Revolt, 1962–1978* (Cambridge: Cambridge University Press, 2013), 158.
90. Ralf Reinders, cited in Brown, *West Germany and the Global Sixties*, 161.
91. Brown, West Germany and the Global Sixties, 4.
92. Brown, *West Germany and the Global Sixties*, 6.
93. Schütte, "Introduction," 9.
94. David Robb, "The Protest Song of the Late 1960s and Early 1970s—Franz Josef Degenhardt and Ton Steine Scherben," in Schütte, ed., *German Pop Music: A Companion*, 43.
95. Robb, "The Protest Song of the Late 1960s and Early 1970s," 47.
96. Brown, *West Germany and the Global Sixties*, 168.
97. Brown, *West Germany and the Global Sixties*, 165. See also John Littlejohn, "Krautrock—The Development of a Movement," in Schütte, ed., *German Pop Music: A Companion*, 63–84.
98. Liner notes, Ton Steine Scherben, Hoffmanns Comic Teater, *Herr Fressack und die Bremer Stadtmusikanten*, LP, Rotbuch Verlag, 1973.
99. Timothy Scott Brown, "Culture, Class, and Communism: The Politics of Rock in the West German 1968," *Twentieth Century Communism*, no. 9 (2015): 77. See also Achim Müller, "Eisen erzieht," in *Scherben: Musik, Politik und Wirkung der Ton Steine Scherben*, ed. Wolfgang Seidel (Mainz: Vencil, 2006), 131–40.
100. Brown, *West Germany and the Global Sixties*, 189.
101. Günter Ehnert and Detlef Kinsler, *Rock in Deutschland: Lexikon deutscher Rock-Gruppen und Interpreten* (Hamburg: Taurus, 1984), 221–22. Several band members joined forces with Nina Hagen in 1977 to become the Nina Hagen Band, which released two classic albums.
102. Brown, *West Germany and the Global Sixties*, 167.
103. Gert Möbius, cited in Brown, *West Germany and the Global Sixties*, 173.
104. Robb, "The Protest Song of the Late 1960s and Early 1970s," 53.
105. Tabatha Erdman and Vivienne Meier, "Theater als Kampfplatz," *Überflieger* (June 2013), 25.
106. The Grimms' rooster, cat, dog, and donkey are turned in this version into Marina the hen, Susie the pig, Harry the dog, and Franz the donkey.
107. Kai Sichtermann, Jens Johler, and Christian Stahl, *Keine Macht für Niemand: Die Geschichte der Ton Steine Scherben* (Berlin: Schwartzkopf & Schwarzkopf, 2008), 154.

108. Ton Steine Scherben, Hoffmanns Comic Teater, "Ich will nicht mehr das arme Schwein sein," *Herr Fressack und die Bremer Stadtmusikanten*, accessed July 12, 2021, https://riolyrics.de/song/id:111.
109. See Elizabeth L. Wollman, *The Theater Will Rock: A History of the Rock Musical, from "Hair" to "Hedwig"* (Ann Arbor: University of Michigan Press, 2009).
110. Erika Hughes, "*Linie 1* and the GRIPS Theater: Traversing Divided and Reunified Berlin," in *Nationalism and Youth in Theatre and Performance*, ed. Victoria Pettersen Lantz and Angela Sweigart-Gallagher (London: Routledge, 2014), 21.
111. Volker Ludwig, "GRIPS Theatre: A Brief History 1969–2001," *Grips Theater Berlin*, Berlin, 2002, 6.
112. Ludwig, "GRIPS Theatre," 12.
113. Hughes, "*Linie 1* and the GRIPS Theater," 24.
114. Heinz Ritter, cited in "Linie 1," Musicallexikon.
115. Hellmut Kotschenreuther, cited in "Linie 1," Musicallexikon: populäres Musiktheater im deutschsprachigen Raum 1945 bis heute, herausgegeben von Wolfgang Jansen und Klaus Baberg in Verbindung mit dem Zentrum für Populäre Kultur und Musik der Albert-Ludwigs-Universität Freiburg, accessed July 6, 2021, www.musicallexikon.eu.
116. Volker Ludwig, Birger Heymann, and the band No Ticket, *Linie 1* (Berlin: Felix Bloch Erben, 2013), 39. "Carbon dioxide" is clearly a reference to the highly polluted city, encircled as it was by coal-burning East Germany.
117. Kotschenreuther, cited in "Linie 1," Musicallexikon: populäres Musiktheater im deutschsprachigen Raum 1945 bis heute.
118. Ludwig, Heymann, and the band No Ticket, *Linie 1*, 11–12.
119. Jansen, *Cats & Co.*, 165–66.
120. Volker Ludwig, Birger Heymann, and the band No Ticket, *Linie 1*, Polydor 831 219-2, 1986, liner notes, n.p. These lyrics are sung in English on the recording. See also *Linie 1: Eine musikalische Revue* (live performance 2006), Die Theater Edition DVD, 2016.
121. Alisa Solomon, "Coming to Grips," *Village Voice review* (August 2, 1988), reprinted in booklet for Ludwig, Heymann, and the band No Ticket, *Linie 1*, Die Theater Edition video (2006 performance), 2016, n.p.
122. Kotschenreuther, cited in "Linie 1," Musicallexikon: populäres Musiktheater im deutschsprachigen Raum 1945 bis heute.
123. Yu-Sun Lee, „Das Seouler Selbstporträt Linie 1. Eine Bestandsaufnahme des Seouler Alltags in den 1990er Jahren," in *Deutschsprachige Literatur und Theater seit 1945 in den Metropolen Seoul, Tokio und Berlin: Studien zur urbanen Kulturentwicklung unter komparatistischen und rezeptionsgeschichtlichen Perspektiven*, ed. Iris Hermann, Soichiro Itoda, Ralf Schnell, and Hi-Young Song (Bamberg: University of Bamberg Press, 2015), 332.
124. *Heiße Ecke—Das St. Pauli Musical*, accessed July 19, 2021, https://www.tivoli.de/programm-tickets/heisse-ecke/. St. Pauli is a riverside working-class and red-light district in Hamburg. See also Jansen, *Cats & Co.*, 270–72.
125. See Jansen, *Cats & Co.*, 267–69.

126. Stephen Holden, "Review/Theater: The Black Rider; When Tragedy Becomes the Food of Satire," *New York Times*, November 22, 1993.
127. Michael C. Tusa, "Cosmopolitanism and the National Opera: Weber's *Der Freischütz*," *Journal of Interdisciplinary History 36*, no. 3 (Winter 2006): 483.
128. Corinne Kessel, *The Words and Music of Tom Waits* (Westport, CT: Praeger, 2009), 60.
129. Jessica Werner, "An Introduction to the Unexpected: Robert Wilson's Theater of the Future," *The American Conservatory Theater performance program*, 2004, accessed July 16, 2021, https://www.tomwaitsfan.com/tom%20waits%20library/www.tomwaitslibrary.com/theblackrider-press.html.
130. Ulrich Müller, "Regietheater/Director's Theater," in *The Oxford Handbook of Opera*, ed. Helen M. Greenwald (Oxford: Oxford University Press, 2015), 2.
131. Müller, "Regietheater/Director's Theater," 11.
132. Corinne Kessel, *The Words and Music of Tom Waits* (Westport, CT: Praeger, 2009), 35.
133. "Teufelspakt für Millionen," *Der Spiegel*, April 8, 1990, accessed July 18, 2021, https://www.spiegel.de/kultur/teufelspakt-fuer-millionen-a-2082ec4d-0002-0001-0000-000013498534.
134. Lore Kleinert, "Wir zeigen euch was," *TAZ*, April 8, 1990, accessed July 18, 2021, https://taz.de/Wir-zeigen-euch-was/!1773573/.
135. Holden, "Review/Theater: The Black Rider."
136. Cited in Ted Morgan, *Literary Outlaw: The Life and Times of William S. Burroughs* (New York: Avon, 1988), xxii.
137. Tom Waits, "The Black Rider," *The Black Rider*, Island CID 8021/518 559-2, 1993. This last line seems deliberately to evoke the last line of "The Flintstones" cartoon theme song.
138. See Adam Gussow, *Beyond the Crossroads: The Devil and the Blues Tradition* (Chapel Hill: University of North Carolina Press, 2017).
139. Kessel, *The Words and Music of Tom Waits*, 106.
140. Video of Wilson, Waits, Burroughs, *The Black Rider: The Casting of the Magic Bullets*, Wiener Festwochen, June 1990.
141. Kessel, *The Words and Music of Tom Waits*, 57.
142. Corinne Kessel, *The Words and Music of Tom Waits* (Westport, CT: Praeger, 2009), 34.
143. Werner, "An Introduction to the Unexpected."
144. See "Song by Song: A Podcast about Tom Waits," accessed July 21, 2021, http://www.songbysongpodcast.com/but-hes-not-willhelmchase-the-clouds-awayin-the-morningnews-from-the-duke.
145. Video of Wilson, Waits, Burroughs, *The Black Rider*.
146. "Teufelspakt für Millionen," *Der Spiegel*.
147. Anne Marie Welsh, "'Bullets' Ably Blends Visuals with Music," *San Diego Union Tribune*, May 2, 2006, accessed July 25, 2021, https://www.tomwaitsfan.com/tom%20waits%20library/www.tomwaitslibrary.com/theblackrider-press.html.
148. Holden, "Review/Theater: The Black Rider."

149. Werner, "An Introduction to the Unexpected."
150. Cited in Kessel, *The Words and Music of Tom Waits*, 60.
151. Kessel, *The Words and Music of Tom Waits*, 9.
152. David Roesner, "From the Spirit of Music—Dramaturgy and Play in Contemporary German Theatre," *TDR: The Drama Review 67*, no. 2: 119.
153. "Teufelspakt für Millionen," *Der Spiegel*.

Chapter 5

1. The piece had been announced in the Deutsches Theater's season as a "Musical" but at the last minute the designation was changed to "Musiktheater."
2. David Roesner, "From the Spirit of Music—Dramaturgy and Play in Contemporary German Theatre," *TDR 67*, no. 2: 113.
3. Roesner, "From the Spirit of Music," 106.
4. Christoph Marthaler, quoted in Guido Hiß, "Marthalers Musiktheater," in *Musiktheater als Herausforderung. Interdisziplinäre Facetten von Theater- und Musikwissenschaft*, ed. Hans-Peter Bayerdörfer (Tübingen: Niemeyer, 1999), 215.
5. Hiß, "Marthalers Musiktheater," 214–15.
6. Matthias Rebstock, "Composed Theatre: Mapping the Field," in *Composed Theatre: Aesthetics, Practices, Processes*, ed. Matthias Rebstock and David Roesner (Bristol, UK: Intellect, 2012), 47.
7. Roesner, "From the Spirit of Music," 106, 119.
8. David Roesner, "No More 'Unheard Melodies'—Zwölf Thesen zur Schauspielmusik im zeitgenössischen Theater," *etum: E-Journal for Theatre and Media 2* no. 2 (2015): 11.
9. See Matthias Rebstock and David Roesner, eds., *Composed* Theatre: Aesthetics, Practices, *Processes* (Bristol, UK: Intellect, 2012).
10. David Roesner, "'It is not about labelling, it's about understanding what we do': Composed Theatre as Discourse," in Rebstock and Roesner, eds., *Composed Theatre*, note *18*, 326.
11. See Tornbjörn Bergflödt, "'Der Freischütz' in Zürich—eine Oper wider den tierischen Ernst," *Suedkurier,* September 19, 2016, accessed July 27, 2021, http://www.suedkurier.de/nachrichten/kultur/Der-Freischuetz-in-Zuerich-eine-Oper-wider-den-tierischen-Ernst;art10399,8909594.
12. Herbert Fritsch, in "Aus dem einfachen erwächst die Magie," interview with Claus Spahn, *Der Freischütz* program, Opernhaus Zürich, 2016, 16. This question is very difficult to translate. Niveau literally means level, but its usage here turns it into an issue of taste and brow level. In this case, that the work is too lowbrow for an opera house.
13. Michael C. Tusa, "Cosmopolitanism and the National Opera: Weber's *Der Freischütz," Journal of Interdisciplinary History 36*, no. 3 (Winter 2006): 483.

14. Tobias Becker, "Regiestar Herbert Fritsch: Bühnen-Anarchist unter Volldampf," *Der Spiegel*, May 18, 2011, accessed July 30, 2015, http://www.spiegel.de/kultur/gesellschaft/regiestar-herbert-fritsch-buehnen-anarchist-unter-volldampf-a-763060.html.
15. Ellinor Landmann, "Das Einmaleins der Bösartigkeit," *Theatertreffen*, 2011, accessed April 27, 2021, https://www.berlinerfestspiele.de/de/berliner-festspiele/programm/bfs-gesamtprogramm/programmdetail_20448.html.
16. Fritsch's emendation of Arnold and Bach's title to *Die (s)panische Fliege* makes for a play on words that translates as both *The Spanish Fly* and *The (s)Panicked Fly*.
17. Matt Cornish, *Performing Unification: History and Nation in German Theater after 1989* (Ann Arbor: University of Michigan Press, 2017), 131.
18. Katrin Hildebrand, "Herbert Fritsch: 'Aktualität langweilt mich,'" *Merkur*, July 2, 2014, accessed July 30, 2015, https://www.merkur.de/kultur/goldoni-residenztheater-muenchen-herbert-fritsch-merkur-interview-3669608.html.
19. Herbert Fritsch, interview with author, Berlin, July 31, 2014.
20. Christopher Balme, "Post-fictional Theatre, Institutional Aesthetics, and the German Theatrical Public Sphere," *TDR 67*, no. 2 (2023): 14–31.
21. Ben Brantley, "Theater Review: Another Slice of Roast Boor, En Croute," *New York Times*, July 28, 2000.
22. Becker, "Regiestar Herbert Fritsch."
23. Ulrich Seidler, "Im Gesprach mit Herbert Fritsch: Kommt mal runter, Leute!" *Berliner Zeitung*, April 27, 2013, accessed July 30, 2015, http://www.berliner-zeitung.de/theatertreffen/im-gespraech-mit-herbert-fritsch--kommt-mal-runter--leute-,14999632,22644238.html.
24. Herbert Fritsch, interview with author, Berlin, July 31, 2014.
25. Matthias Heine, "Interview mit Herbert Fritsch: Murmel? Murmel!" *Berliner Morgenpost*, March 22, 2012, accessed July 31, 2015, http://www.morgenpost.de/printarchiv/kultur/article1934019/Murmel-Murmel.html.
26. Herbert Fritsch, interview with author, Berlin, July 31, 2014.
27. Marvin Carlson, *Theatre Is More Beautiful than War: German Stage Directing in the Late Twentieth Century* (Iowa City: University of Iowa Press, 2009), 98.
28. Michaela Ernst, "Der Letzte Akt: Hinter den Kulissen des Burgtheaters," *Oooom*, May 8, 2019, accessed February 27, 2021, https://www.ooom.com/digital/herbert-fritsch-der-letzte-akt/.
29. Herbert Fritsch, interview with author, Berlin, July 31, 2014.
30. Herbert Fritsch, interview with author, Berlin, July 31, 2014.
31. Stefan Kirschner, "Warum Paul Linckes 'Frau Luna' immer noch beliebt ist," *Berliner Morgenpost*, June 18, 2013, accessed July 30, 2015, http://www.morgenpost.de/kultur/article117252874/Warum-Paul-Linckes-Frau-Luna-immer-noch-beliebt-ist.html.
32. Herbert Fritsch, interview with author, Berlin, July 31, 2014.
33. Ingo Günther, "11 Pianos," *Herbert Fritsch—Theatermusik*, MP3, 2017.
34. Irene Bazinger, "Herbert Fritsch: Ein Clown fürs Leben," *Cicero*, December 22, 2012, accessed July 31, 2015, http://www.cicero.de//salon/herbert-fritsch-ein-clown-fuers-leben/52933.
35. Becker, "Regiestar Herbert Fritsch."

36. Hildebrand, "Herbert Fritsch: 'Aktualität langweilt mich.'"
37. Susan McClary, "The Lure of the Sublime: Revisiting the Modernist Project," in *Transformations of Musical Modernism*, ed. Erling E. Guldbrandsen and Julian Johnson (Cambridge: Cambridge University Press, 2015), 21–35.
38. Hildebrand, "Herbert Fritsch: 'Aktualität langweilt mich.'"
39. Oliver Double and Michael Wilson, "Karl Valentin's Illogical Subversion: Stand-up Comedy and Alienation Effect," *New Theatre Quarterly 20*, no. 3 (2004): 203–15.
40. Bertolt Brecht, *Brecht on Performance: Messingkauf and Modelbooks*, ed. Tom Kuhn, Steve Giles, and Marc Silberman (London: Bloomsbury, 2014), 59.
41. Denis Calandra, "Karl Valentin and Bertolt Brecht," *The Drama Review: TDR 18*, no. 1 (1974): 86–98
42. Robert Sackett, *Popular Entertainment, Class, and Politics in Munich, 1900–1923* (Cambridge, MA: Harvard University Press, 1982), 132.
43. John Paoletti, "Opus of Excess," *Art in America*, September 2004, 104–51.
44. Paoletti, "Opus of Excess."
45. Peter Laudenbach, "Interview mit dem heißesten Regisseur der Stadt: Herbert Fritsch," *Tip Berlin*, May 3, 2012, accessed June 20, 2013, http://www.tip-berlin.de/kultur-und-freizeit-theater-und-buehne/interview-mit-dem-heissesten-regisseur-der-stadt-herbert-frit.
46. Laudenbach, "Interview mit dem heißesten Regisseur der Stadt: Herbert Fritsch."
47. Barbara Villiger Heilig, "Tanz der Lemuren," *Neue Zürcher Zeitung*, September 26, 2014, accessed August 7, 2021, https://www.nzz.ch/feuilleton/buehne/tanz-der-lemuren-1.18391672.
48. See Jansen, *Cats & Co.*, 20.
49. See Christian Berzins, „Ein Silvesterkracher im September," *Tagblatt*, September 26, 2014, accessed August 8, 2021, HTTPS://WWW.TAGBLATT.CH/KULTUR/BUCH-BUEHNE-KUNST/EIN-SILVESTERKRACHER-IM-SEPTEMBER-LD.1645908.
50. Oskar Wälterlin, quoted in Philipp Flury and Peter Kaufmann, „O mein Papa . . . Paul Burkhard: Leben und Werk" (Zürich: Orell Füssli Verlag, 1979), 52.
51. Heilig, "Tanz der Lemuren." The recasting was preserved in *Das Feuerwerk* but eliminated from the film, in which the touring circus is entirely real.
52. Carl Jung, *Psychology and Religion: West and East* (Princeton, NJ: Princeton University Press, 1958), 93, 95.
53. Kläui, "'O mein Papa.'"
54. Alfred Ziltener, "Die Damen sind Giftspritzen, die Herren vertrottelt," *Südostschweiz*, September 26, 2014, accessed August 8, 2021, https://www.suedostschweiz.ch/zeitung/die-damen-sind-giftspritzen-die-herren-vertrottelt.
55. Heilig, "Tanz der Lemuren."
56. Heilig, "Tanz der Lemuren."
57. Ziltener, "Die Damen sind Giftspritzen, die Herren vertrottelt."
58. Sabrina Zwach, „Es ist nicht immer gut, wenn man viel spricht," program for Paul Burkhard, *Der schwarze Hecht*, Schauspielhaus Zürich, 2014, 17–19.
59. Eric Sams, *The Songs of Hugo Wolf* (London: Methuen, 1961), 3–4.

60. Lawrence Kramer, "Hugo Wolf: Subjectivity in the Fin-de-Siècle Lied," in *German Lieder in the Nineteenth Century*, ed. Rufus Hallmark (New York: Routledge, 2010), 239.
61. Susan Youens, "Tradition and Innovation: The Lieder of Hugo Wolf," in *The Cambridge Companion to the Lied*, ed. James Parsons (Cambridge: Cambridge University Press, 2004), 222.
62. Sams, The Songs of Hugo Wolf, 1.
63. See Youens, "Tradition and Innovation," 204.
64. Susan Youens, *Hugo Wolf and His Mörike Songs* (Cambridge: Cambridge University Press, 2000), x.
65. Kramer, "Hugo Wolf," 240–41.
66. Youens, "Tradition and Innovation," 211.
67. Kramer, "Hugo Wolf," 240.
68. Cited in Schauspielhaus Zürich, *Wer hat Angst vor Hugo Wolf?*, accessed September 6, 2021, http://archiv.schauspielhaus.ch/de/play/602-Wer-hat-angst-vor-Hugo-Wolf.
69. Martin Halter, *Frankfurter Allgemeine*, April 28, 2016, accessed September 6, 2021, cited in https://nachtkritik.de/index.php?option=com_content&view=article&id=12451:wer-hat-angst-vor-hugo-wolf-herbert-fritsch-schauspielhaus-zuerich&catid=38:die-nachtkritik-k&Itemid=40.
70. seniorweb.ch, cited on Schauspielhaus Zürich, *Wer hat Angst vor Hugo Wolf?*, http://archiv.schauspielhaus.ch/de/play/602-Wer-hat-Angst-vor-Hugo-Wolf.
71. Barnett Newman, "The Sublime Is Now," in *Reading Abstract Expressionism: Context and Critique*, ed. Ellen G. Landau (New Haven, CT: Yale University Press, 2005), 139.
72. Sams, The Songs of Hugo Wolf, 87.
73. Kramer, "Hugo Wolf," 239.
74. Sams, The Songs of Hugo Wolf, 260. For the text, see Youens, "Tradition and Innovation," 220.
75. theaterfischer.de, cited on Schauspielhaus Zürich, *Wer hat Angst vor Hugo Wolf?*
76. Youens, *Hugo Wolf and His Mörike Songs*, xi.
77. See "Erstes Liebeslied eines Mädchens," accessed September 9, 2021, https://www.oxfordlieder.co.uk/song/245.
78. Youens, *Hugo Wolf and His Mörike Songs*, 109.
79. Sams, *The Songs of Hugo Wolf*, 43.
80. Youens, "Tradition and Innovation," 209.
81. Sams, *The Songs of Hugo Wolf*, 87.
82. In the Kammermusiksaal, Philharmonie, January 22, 2022.
83. Kirschner, "Warum Paul Linckes 'Frau Luna' immer noch beliebt ist."
84. Hildebrand, "Herbert Fritsch: 'Aktualität langweilt mich.'"
85. See Kevin Clarke, "Big Bang Theory: Germany's Queer Operetta Revolution," *TDR* 67, no. 2 (2023): 161–82.
86. Herbert Fritsch, interview with author, Berlin, July 31, 2014.
87. Theodor W. Adorno, "Commitment," in *The Essential Frankfurt School Reader*, ed. Andrew Arato and Eike Gebhardt (New York: Urizen, 1977), 308, 317.
88. Adorno, "Commitment," 308, 315.

89. Adorno, "Commitment," 317.
90. Adorno, "Commitment," 318, 317.
91. Theodor W. Adorno, "Trying to Understand *Endgame*," in *The Adorno Reader*, ed. Brian O'Connor (Malden, MA: Blackwell, 2000), 324.
92. Adorno, "Trying to Understand *Endgame*," 320, 327.
93. Theodor W. Adorno, *Aesthetic Theory*, trans. Robert Hullot-Kentor (London: Continuum, 2002), 32.
94. Adorno, Aesthetic Theory, 33.
95. Michael Laages, "Das Theater schwebt," *Nachtkritik*, April 27, 2019, accessed February 27, 2021, https://www.nachtkritik.de/index.php?option=com_content&view=article&id=16697:zelt-burgtheater-wien-noch-ein-abschied-an-der-burg-mit-herbert-fritsch-laesst-das-ensemble-das-theater-schweben&catid=80&Itemid=100089.
96. Adorno, "Trying to Understand *Endgame*," 322.
97. Although the Burgtheater dates back to the eighteenth century, its neo-baroque home was built in 1888. It was largely destroyed in a bombing raid during World War II and was rebuilt in the 1950s.
98. Adorno, "Trying to Understand *Endgame*," 337.
99. Adorno, Aesthetic Theory, 14.
100. Adorno, Aesthetic Theory, 13.
101. Max Horkheimer and Theodor W. Adorno, *The Dialectic of Enlightenment: Philosophical Fragments*, trans. Edmund Jephcott (Stanford, CA: Stanford University Press, 2002), 109–10.
102. Ulrich Seidler, "Im Gesprach mit Herbert Fritsch: Kommt mal runter, Leute!" *Berliner Zeitung*, April 27, 2013, accessed July 30, 2015, http://www.berliner-zeitung.de/theatertreffen/im-gespraech-mit-herbert-fritsch--kommt-mal-runter--leute-,14999632,22644238.html.
103. Peter Laudenbach, "Interview mit dem heißesten Regisseur der Stadt: Herbert Fritsch," *Tip Berlin*, May 3, 2012, accessed June 20, 2013, http://www.tip-berlin.de/kultur-und-freizeit-theater-und-buehne/interview-mit-dem-heissesten-regisseur-der-stadt-herbert-frit.

Chapter 6

1. Manuel Brug, "Die glitzernde Revolution," *Die Welt*, 5 December 5, 2021.
2. John Rockwell, "East Berlin Cheers Comic Opera Eclat," *New York Times*, August 8, 1973, 22, accessed December 18, 2021, https://www.nytimes.com/1973/08/08/archives/east-berlin-cheers-comic-opera-eclat-potential-a-factor-few-changes.html.
3. Cited in Ben Miller, »Ich will nicht, dass die Leute eine Eintrittskarte kaufen, um eine ›entartete‹ Operette zu sehen,« interview with Barrie Kosky, *Van*, June 8, 2022, accessed July 5, 2022, https://van-magazin.de/mag/barrie-kosky-2022/.
4. Joshua Barone, "*After 10 Years, Barrie Kosky Leaves His Opera House Dancing*," *New York Times*, June 13, 2022.
5. Barone, "After 10 Years, Barrie Kosky Leaves His Opera House Dancing."

6. Cited in Miller, »Ich will nicht, dass die Leute eine Eintrittskarte kaufen, um eine ›entartete‹ Operette zu sehen.«
7. Manuel Brug, "Tischgespräch: Der Regisseur Barrie Kosky will Operette riechen," *Die Welt*, October 11, 2014, accessed April 9, 2015, http://www.welt.de/kultur/buehne-konzert/article133165563/Der-Regisseur-Barrie-Kosky-will-Operette-riechen.html.
8. Alison Smale, "Australian Director Barrie Kosky Carries On Innovative Operatic Tradition in Berlin," *New York Times*, April 21, 2015, accessed April 21, 2015, http://www.nytimes.com/2015/04/22/arts/international/australian-director-barrie-koskie-carries-on-innovative-operatic-tradition-in-berlin.html?_r=1. The *Times* quotes Wolfgang Prosinger of the *Tagesspiegel*.
9. The Opera Awards are given by the UK-based Opera Awards Foundation and *Opera Magazine*, accessed April 13, 2015, http://www.operaawards.org/.
10. Seth Colter Walls, "One of Opera's Great Directors, Binge-Worthy in Berlin," *New York Times*, October 28, 2019, accessed January 7, 2022, https://www.nytimes.com/2019/10/28/arts/music/barrie-kosky-komische-oper.html.
11. Brug, "Tischgespräch"; Volker Blech, "Barrie Kosky plant eine Operette auf Jiddisch in Berlin," *Berliner Morgenpost*, January 30, 2015, accessed April 9, 2015, http://www.morgenpost.de/kultur/berlin-kultur/article136935872/Barrie-Kosky-plant-eine-Operette-auf-Jiddisch-in-Berlin.html; Smale, "Australian Director Barrie Kosky Carries On Innovative Operatic Tradition in Berlin."
12. Prosinger, "Die Erfolgsstory des Barrie Kosky."
13. Blech, "Barrie Kosky plant eine Operette auf Jiddisch in Berlin."
14. Brug, "Tischgespräch."
15. "Comeback der Berliner Operette der Jahrhundertwende," interview with Herbert Fritsch and Barrie Kosky, *Tip Berlin*, June 3, 2013, accessed July 30, 2013, http://www.tip-berlin.de/kultur-und-freizeit-theater-und-buehne/comeback-der-berliner-operette-der-jahrhundertwende.
16. Cited in "Man muss das Tralala zelebrieren," *Süddeutsche Zeitung*.
17. Barrie Kosky, Interview with the author, November 12, 2014.
18. Cited in "Man muss das Tralala zelebrieren," *Süddeutsche Zeitung*.
19. Stephen Sondheim remains underrepresented on German stages, except for *Sweeney Todd*, in part because of the challenges of translating his work and finding German singing actors who understand the conventions of Sondheim performance.
20. Georg Kasch, „Am Tag, als der Shitstorm kam," *Nachtkritik*, November 7, 2021, accessed June 19, 2022, https://www.nachtkritik.de/index.php?option=com_content&view=article&id=20197:slippery-slope-maxim-gorki-theater-berlin&catid=52&Itemid=40.
21. Barrie Kosky, Interview with the author, November 12, 2014.
22. Barrie Kosky, quoted in Marion Brasch and Juri Sternburg, photographs by Jörg Brüggemann, *Die Dreigroschenoper. Making of: Barrie Kosky inszeniert Brecht / Weill am Berliner Ensemble* (Leipzig: Spector, 2021), 113.
23. Barrie Kosky and Ulrich Lenz, "Australian Director Barrie Kosky on the Subversiveness of a Predominantly Jewish Genre: An Interview by Ulrich Lenz,"

in *The Cambridge Companion to Operetta*, ed. Anastasia Belina and Derek B. Scott (Cambridge: Cambridge University Press, 2019), 289–90.
24. Barrie Kosky, Interview with the author, November 12, 2014.
25. Günther Nenning, „Die Kunst der Kanaille," in *Das Land des Glücks*: Österreich und seine Operetten, ed. Erik Adam and Willi Rainer (Klagenfurt: Hermagoras, 1997), 14–15.
26. Ovrtur, "*Fiedler auf dem Dach*, Komische Oper Production (1971)," accessed January 20, 2022, https://ovrtur.com/production/2899885.
27. Howard Taubman, "Felsenstein Makes No Artistic Compromise," *New York Times*, June 5, 1960, X9.
28. Donal Henahan, "Sing Along with Felsenstein?," *New York Times*, May 30, 1971, 13. Henahan reported that the government subsidy for the Komische Oper in 1971 amounted to $19.5 million in 2022 US dollars.
29. Rockwell, "East Berlin Cheers Comic Opera Eclat," 22.
30. Rockwell, "East Berlin Cheers Comic Opera Eclat," 22.
31. Taubman, "Felsenstein Makes No Artistic Compromise."
32. Rockwell, "East Berlin Cheers Comic Opera Eclat," 22.
33. Rockwell, "East Berlin Cheers Comic Opera Eclat," 22.
34. A. J. Goldman, "A Seven-Hour 'Les Misérables'? Fans of the Musical Should Stay Away," *New York Times*, December 7, 2017.
35. Swed, "Commentary: Critic's Notebook."
36. Rockwell, "East Berlin Cheers Comic Opera Eclat," 22.
37. Henahan, "Sing Along with Felsenstein?," 14.
38. Howard Taubman, "East Berlin to Get 'Fiddler' This Year," *New York Times*, February 5, 1970, 32.
39. Barrie Kosky, in "Der 'Milchmann-Prophet': Barrie Kosky über Tradition, kulturelle DNA und die Erfahrungen der Kindheit," *Anatevka* program, Komische Oper Berlin, 3 December 2017, 11.
40. Henahan, "Sing Along with Felsenstein?," 14.
41. James Helme Sutcliffe, "Germany (East): Felsenstein's 'Fiddler,'" *Opera*, May 1971, 406.
42. Stephan Stompor, "Ein Musical nach Scholem Alejchems Erzählung 'Tewje, der Milchmann,'" program to *Der Fiedler auf dem Dach*, Komische Oper Belin, May 15, 1973, n.p.
43. Sutcliffe, "Germany (East): Felsenstein's 'Fiddler,'" 406.
44. Joseph Stein, Jerry Bock, and Sheldon Harnick, *Fiddler on the Roof* (New York: Limelight Editions, 2004), vi.
45. In program for *Der Fiedler auf dem Dach*, n.p.
46. Sutcliffe, "Germany (East): Felsenstein's 'Fiddler,'" 406.
47. Kai Luehrs-Kaiser, „'Ein Nazi ist ein Nazi ist ein Nazi'—Gespräch mit Barrie Kosky," *tip Berlin*, December 1, 2017, accessed June 24, 2022, https://www.tip-berlin.de/konzerte-party/gespraech-mit-barrie-kosky/.
48. Kosky, in "Der 'Milchmann-Prophet,'" 5.
49. Kosky, in "Der 'Milchmann-Prophet,'" 4.
50. Stein et al., *Fiddler on the Roof*, 108.

51. Kosky, in "Der 'Milchmann-Prophet,'" 6, 7.
52. Kosky, in "Der 'Milchmann-Prophet,'" 7.
53. Cilly Kugelmann, „Ein Spaßmacher, dem es ernst ist: Wie es dem Regisseur Barrie Kosky gelingt, Talmud und Kabbala auf die Bühne zu bringen. Ein Gastbeitrag," *Tagespiegel*, October 27, 2021, accessed June 26, 2022, https://www.tagesspiegel.de/kultur/lobrede-auf-barrie-kosky-ein-spassmacher-dem-es-ernst-ist/27740186.html.
54. Cited in Miller, »Ich will nicht, dass die Leute eine Eintrittskarte kaufen, um eine ›entartete‹ Operette zu sehen.«
55. Cilly Kugelmann, „Ein Spaßmacher, dem es ernst ist: Wie es dem Regisseur Barrie Kosky gelingt, Talmud und Kabbala auf die Bühne zu bringen. Ein Gastbeitrag," *Tagespiegel*, October 27, 2021, accessed June 26, 2022, https://www.tagesspiegel.de/kultur/lobrede-auf-barrie-kosky-ein-spassmacher-dem-es-ernst-ist/27740186.html.
56. Kugelmann, „Ein Spaßmacher, dem es ernst ist."ge.
57. See Philip Lambert, *To Broadway, To Life! The Musical Theater of Bock and Harnick* (New York: Oxford University Press, 2010).
58. Manuel Brug, „Die zauberhafte Rettung einer jüdischen Tradition," *Die Welt*, June 18, 2022, accessed July 4, 2022, https://www.welt.de/kultur/article239396929/Intendant-Barrie-Kosky-Die-Rettung-einer-juedischen-Tradition.html.
59. Cited in Frederik Hanssen, "Seit 100 Tagen ist Barrie Kosky Intendant der Komischen Oper Berlin," *Der Tagespiegel*, December 20, 2012, June 4, 2013, http://www.tagesspiegel.de/kultur/interview-mit-barrie-kosky-wir-haben-die-magische-grenze-erreicht/7543928.html.
60. Klaus Wowereit, mayor of Berlin between 2001 and 2014, famously used the phrase in 2003 to describe the city.
61. Barrie Kosky, interview with Kevin Clarke adapted as "Vorwort," in *Breaking Free: Geschichte(n) des LGBT-Musicals* (Berlin: Querverlag, 2022).
62. „Barrie Kosky in Gespräch über *Kiss Me, Kate*," *Kiss Me, Kate* program, Komische Oper Berlin, 2008, 9.
63. See Kevin Clarke, ed., *Breaking Free: Geschichte(n) des LGBT-Musicals* (Berlin: Querverlag, 2022).
64. Cole Porter, book by Sam and Bella Spewack, *Kiss Me, Kate* (New York: Tams-Witmark Music Library, 1948), 2–1–1.
65. „Barrie Kosky in Gespräch über *Kiss Me, Kate*," *Kiss Me, Kate* program, Komische Oper Berlin, 2008, 9.
66. Susan Sontag, "Notes on 'Camp,'" in *Against Interpretation and Other Essays* (New York: Dell, 1966), 287.
67. Barrie Kosky, "What the f***?!?" in *Breaking Free: Die wunderbare Welt des LGBTQ-Musicals*, ed. Kevin Clarke (Berlin: Querverlag, 2022), 14.
68. „Barrie Kosky in Gespräch über *Kiss Me, Kate*," *Kiss Me, Kate* program, 9.
69. Paul Schultz, "Interview—Barrie Kosky bleibt bis 2022 an der Komischen Oper Berlin," *Blu*, October 2014, accessed May 12, 2015, http://www.blu.fm/subsites/detail.php?kat=B%C3%BChne&id=8655#.VIQ6-ct0zIU.
70. Prosinger, "Die Erfolgsstory des Barrie Kosky."
71. David Savran, Interview with Barrie Kosky, November 12, 2014.

72. Schultz, "Interview—Barrie Kosky bleibt bis 2022 an der Komischen Oper Berlin."
73. See Kevin Clarke, "Big Bang Theory: Germany's Queer Operetta Revolution," *TDR* 67, no. 2 (2023): 161–82.
74. Savran, Interview with Barrie Kosky, November 12, 2014.
75. Caroline Emcke and Lara Fritzsch, "Wir sind schon da," *Süddeutsche Zeitung Magazin 5*, February 4, 2021.
76. Interestingly, both Steckel and Weise used Shakespeare's *Othello* as coming-out pieces by turning Othello and Desdemona into same-sex couples, Steckel at the Deutsches Theater in 2009 and Weise at the Maxim Gorki Theater in 2016.
77. Brug, "Tischgespräch."
78. Savran, Interview with Barrie Kosky, November 12, 2014. His refusal to use transvestism as a sign of decadence is clear in the staging of Der Tanz um das goldene Kalb in Schoenberg's *Moses und Aron* in 2015, which was centered on a female dancer who was later joined by three male dancers.
79. See Kosky, "What the f***?!?" 9–17.
80. Matt Cornish, *Performing Unification: History and Nation in German Theater after 1989* (Ann Arbor: University of Michigan Press, 2017), 173.
81. „Nur Licht und Körper: Regisseur Barrie Kosky im Gespräch über jüdische Wurzeln, antike Tragödien und Momente der Sprachlosigkeit," *West Side Story* program, Komische Oper, 2013, 11.
82. See "The Great 'West Side Story' Debate," *New York Times*, December 1, 2021, accessed July 8, 2022, https://www.nytimes.com/2021/12/01/theater/west-side-story-steven-spielberg-movie.html?searchResultPosition=15.
83. Brian Eugenio Herrera, *Latin Numbers: Playing Latino in Twentieth-Century U.S. Popular Performance* (Ann Arbor: University of Michigan Press, 2015), 98.
84. „Nur Licht und Körper," 10.
85. Irina Grabowski, quoted in „Die West Side Story in der Komischen Oper," Kultur Radio, November 25, 2013, accessed July 7, 2014, http://www.inforadio.de/progr amm/schema/sendungen/kultur/201311/197181.html.
86. „Nur Licht und Körper," 10–11.
87. „Nur Licht und Körper," 12.
88. „Nur Licht und Körper," 12.
89. Joachim Kaiser: " 'Glänzend gemacht'—aber Kitsch, Jerome Robbins' 'West Side Story' in der Bundesrepublik gezeigt," in *Theater heute*, Nr 8, August 1961, Seite 3–6, quoted in Musical Lexicon, https://www.musicallexikon.eu/inhalte/West%20S ide%20Story%20Muenchen?searchterm=west+side+ (accessed 6 July 2022).
90. Cited in Wolfgang Jansen, *Musicals: Geschichte und Interpretation* (Münster: Waxmann, 2020), 115.
91. Kaiser, " 'Glänzend gemacht.' "
92. Raymond Knapp, *The American Musical and the Formation of National Identity* (Princeton, NJ: Princeton University Press, 2006), 215.
93. Rubin, "Big Theatre, Not Enough Music: The 'West Side Story' in the Volksoper," *Volksstimme*, March 1, 1968, Musical Lexicon, accessed July 6, 2022, https://www.

musicallexikon.eu/inhalte/West%20Side%20Story%20Wien?searchterm=west+side+.
94. Dominik Hartmann, cited in Jansen, *Musicals*, 127.
95. Jansen, *Musicals*, 124–25.
96. Marcel Rubin and Dominik Hartmann, quoted in Jansen, *Musicals*, 126–27.
97. Jansen, *Musicals*, 134.
98. Knapp, *The American Musical and the Formation of National Identity*, 208, 211.
99. Knapp, *The American Musical and the Formation of National Identity*, 211.
100. „Nur Licht und Körper," 11.
101. Knapp, *The American Musical and the Formation of National Identity*, 205.
102. Elizabeth A. Wells, *West Side Story: Cultural Perspectives on an American Musical* (Lanham, MD: Scarecrow Press, 2010), 103.
103. See Pérez Prado, chartsearcher.de, accessed July 9, 2022, https://www.chartsurfer.de/artist/p-rez-prado/songs-fvnre.html.
104. Wells, West Side Story, 107.
105. „Nur Licht und Körper," 9.
106. Herrera, Latin Numbers, 103.
107. Wells, *West Side Story*, 124.
108. Herrera, Latin Numbers, 101.
109. Cited in Cornish, *Performing Unification*, 174.
110. Savran, Interview with Barrie Kosky, 12 November 12, 2014.
111. Savran, Interview with Barrie Kosky, 12 November 12, 2014; „Nur Licht und Körper," 11.
112. "Turkish tenor Tansel Akzeybek: from İzmir to Berlin," *Today's Zaman*, February 28, 2015, accessed May 20, 2015, http://www.todayszaman.com/anasayfa_turkish-tenor-tansel-akzeybek-from-izmir-to-berlin_373791.html. The B-cast Maria, Alma Sadé, is an Israeli soprano while the Tony, Michael Pflumm, was born in Baden-Württemberg.
113. Savran, Interview with Barrie Kosky, November 12, 2014.
114. Asel, in Grabowski, "Die West Side Story."
115. „Nur Licht und Körper," 11, 12.
116. Ben Brantley, "'West Side Story' Review: Sharks vs. Jets vs. Video," *New York Times*, February 20, 2020.
117. *West Side Story* vocal score, 64.
118. Cornish, *Performing Unification*, 174.
119. Azadeh Sharifi, "Moments of Significance: Artists of Colour in European Theatre," in *The Culture of Migration: Politics, Aesthetics and Histories*, ed. Sten Pultz Moslund, Anne Ring Petersen, and Moritz Schramm (London: Bloomsbury 2015), 256.
120. Shermin Langhoff, Tuncay Kulaoglu, and Barbara Kastner, "Dialoge I: Migration dichten und deuten. Ein Gespräch," quoted in Azadeh Sharifi, "Theatre and Migration: Documentation, Influences and Perspectives in European Theatre," in *Independent Theatre in Contemporary Europe: Structures—Aesthetics—Cultural Policy*, ed. Manfred Brauneck and ITI Germany (Bielefeld: transcript, 2017), 327.

121. Anne-Kathrin Ostrop, "Interculturalism at the Komische Oper Berlin," "Selam Opera!" Komische Oper Berlin, accessed May 22, 2015, http://english.komische-oper-berlin.de/discover/selam-opera/. Also Anne-Kathrin Ostrop, "Interkultur an der Komische Oper Berlin," in Komische Oper Berlin, "*Selam Opera!: Interkultur im Kulturbetrieb*" (Leipzig: Henschel, 2014), 35–42.
122. Komische Oper Berlin, "*Selam Opera!*"
123. I make this claim with some trepidation, although the only other musical that would seem to be in serious running for this dubious honor is *Show Boat*, which has also been completely revised many times, although over many more years and for completely different reasons.
124. Quoted in John W. Baxindine, "*The Trouble with Candide: Analysis of an Operetta*" (senior thesis, Harvard University, 2000), 3.
125. John Mauceri, "*Candide* or No Exit," from the program of the 1988 Scottish Opera Production.
126. Leonard Bernstein, "Colloquy in Boston," *New York Times*, November 18, 1956, 133.
127. Elizabeth B. Crist, "The Best of All Possible Worlds: The Eldorado Episode in Leonard Bernstein's *Candide*," *Cambridge Opera Journal 19*, no. 3 (November 2007): 227.
128. Crist, "The Best of All Possible Worlds," 227.
129. I am thinking, for example, of Gian Carlo Menotti's *The Consul* (1950), Wright and Forrest's *Kismet* (1953), Jerome Moross's *The Golden Apple* (1954), Menotti's *The Saint of Bleecker Street* (1955), Frank Loesser's *The Most Happy Fella* (1956), Bernstein's own *West Side Story* (1957), and Marc Blitzstein's *Juno* (1959).
130. Baxindine, "*The Trouble with* Candide," 3–4.
131. Stephen Sondheim, *Finishing the Hat: Collected Lyrics (1954–1981) with Attendant Comments, Principles, Heresies, Grudges, Whines and Anecdotes* (New York: Knopf, 2010), 324.
132. Knapp, The American Musical and the Performance of Personal Identity, 318.
133. "Existentielles Vaudeville: Regisseur Barrie Kosky über musikalische Schizophrenie, Gartenarbeit und den Sinn des Leben" ("Existential Vaudeville: Director Barrie Kosky on Musical Schizophrenia, Gardening, and the Meaning of Life"), *Candide* Program, Komische Oper Berlin, 2018, 15.
134. "Warten auf den Commendatore: Nikolaus Stenitzer im Gespräch mit Barrie Kosky," *Don Giovanni* program, Wiener Staatsoper, 2021, 12–21.
135. Bert O. States, *The Shape of Paradox: An Essay on "Waiting for Godot"* (Berkeley: University of California Press, 1978), 61.
136. "Existentielles Vaudeville," 10.
137. Music by Leonard Bernstein, book by Hugh Wheeler, lyrics by Richard Wilbur, in a new version by John Caird, *Candide*, unpublished script, 36.
138. English Plot Summary, *Candide* Program, 39.
139. Music by Leonard Bernstein, book by Hugh Wheeler, lyrics by Richard Wilbur, in a new version by John Caird, *Candide*, unpublished script, 91. In German translation, the cadential fall on the word *dumm* (stupid) works more effectively than in

English, an effectivity accentuated by the molto ritardando that the actor playing Martin takes in the last words of the speech.
140. Und wenn sie am Ende wieder aufeinander treffen, sind sie sich vor allem eins: fremd, "Existentielles Vaudeville," 12.
141. Christiane Tewinkel, "*Candide* in Berlin: Weltverriss im Walzertakt" (Selten sah man den Geist des Friedrichstadtpalastes mit solcher Verve in ein Opernhaus einziehen), *Frankfurter Allgemeine Zeitung*, November 27, 2018, accessed January 10, 2019, https://www.faz.net/aktuell/feuilleton/buehne-und-konzert/bernsteins-candide-an-der-komischen-oper-in-berlin-15910560.html.
142. Among Weill's Broadway works, *Street Scene* is the most widely performed in the German-speaking world, but always in opera houses.
143. *Der Silbersee* was co-produced by Opera Ballet Vlaanderen and Opéra national de Lorraine and performed mainly in German, directed by a German director, and starring a Belgian-born actor who works primarily in Germany. Strictly speaking, Antwerp is not part of the German-speaking world, but in this case I think it is important to stretch that designation.
144. Bertolt Brecht, *Brecht on Theatre: The Development of an Aesthetic*, trans. John Willett (New York: Hill & Wang, 1964), 35.
145. Stephen Hinton, *Weill's Musical Theater: Stages of Reform* (Berkeley: University of California Press, 2012), 119.
146. Stephen Hinton, "Introduction," in *Happy End*, Kurt Weill Edition, Series I, Volume 6, 30.
147. Elisabeth Hauptmann, Music and Lyrics by Kurt Weill und Bertolt Brecht, *Happy End* (New York: Kurt Weill Foundation for Music, 2020), 1.
148. Hauptmann, Music and Lyrics by Kurt Weill und Bertolt Brecht, *Happy End*, 51.
149. Hinton, *Weill's Musical Theater*, 150.
150. Hinton, *Weill's Musical Theater*, 111.
151. Barrie Kosky, in Charlotte Pollex, *Honey and Nuts*, RBB Kultur film, 2021.
152. Weill, cited in Hinton, *Weill's Musical Theater*, 149.
153. Hinton, *Weill's Musical Theater*, 115.
154. Rebecca Ringst, quoted in Brasch and Sternburg, photographs by Brüggemann, *Die Dreigroschenoper. Making of*, 69.
155. Hinton, *Weill's Musical Theater*, 111.
156. See Emcke and Fritzsch, "Wir sind schon da."
157. Kosky, in Charlotte Pollex, *Honey and Nuts*.
158. "Double Your Premieres, Double Your Fun: An Interview with Barrie Kosky," *Kurt Weill Newsletter 39*, no. 2 (Fall 2021): 9.
159. "Double Your Premieres, Double Your Fun," 8.
160. "Menschliche Kaleidoskope: Regisseur Barrie Kosky über die Bibel, Selfies und den Sündenbock," program for *Aufstieg und Fall der Stadt Mahagonny*, program, Komische Oper Berlin, 2021, 11.
161. See Hinton, *Weill's Musical Theater*, 151.
162. "Menschliche Kaleidoskope," 11.
163. "Double Your Premieres, Double Your Fun," 9.

164. "Menschliche Kaleidoskope," 12.
165. Kurt Weill, cited in Hinton, *Weill's Musical Theater*, 149.
166. "Warten auf den Commendatore: Nikolaus Stenitzer im Gespräch mit Barrie Kosky," *Don Giovanni* program, Wiener Staatsoper, 2021, 20-1.
167. Ersan Mondtag, in conversation with the author, August 15, 2022.
168. Cited in *Der Silbersee: A Sourcebook*, ed. Joanna Lee, Edward Harsh, and Kim Kowalke (New York: Kurt Weill Foundation for Music, 2001), 13.
169. Hinton, *Weill's Musical Theater*, 137.
170. Jan Vandenhouwe, in program for *Der Silbersee*, Opera Ballet Vlaanderen, 2021, 4.
171. Ian Kemp, "Music as Metaphor: Aspects of *Der Silbersee*," in *A New Orpheus: Essays on Kurt Weill*, ed. Kim H. Kowalke (New Haven, CT: Yale University Press, 1986), 131.
172. Kemp, "Music as Metaphor," 131.
173. Piet De Volder, "Weill and Kaiser's Hybrid Winter's Fairy Tale," program of *Der Silbersee*, Opera Ballet Vlaanderen, 2021, 36.
174. Julian Zwingel, "'Migrationshintergrund zu haben.'—Interview mit Theaterregisseur Ersan Mondtag," Blog Rebellen, February 8, 2016, accessed July 23, 2022, https://www.blogrebellen.de/2016/02/08/ich-erinnere-mich-tatsaechlich-nicht-mehr-daran-einen-migrationshintergrund-zu-haben-interview-mit-theaterregisseur-ersan-mondtag/.
175. Till Briegleb, "Proletarians as Pharaohs," program for *Der Silbersee*, Opera Ballet Vlaanderen, 2021, 62.
176. See Christine Wahl, "Ich würde gern die Schaubühne übernehmen," *Tagspiegel*, May 6, 2017, accessed July 23, 2022, https://www.tagesspiegel.de/kultur/berliner-theaterregisseur-ersan-mondtag-bei-castorf-habe-ich-freiheit-gelernt-/19757608-2.html.
177. Cited in Kevin Clarke, "Ersan Mondtag's Over-the-Top Gay Production of 'Der Silbersee,'" Operetta Research Center, October 18, 2021, accessed July 24, 2022, http://operetta-research-center.org/ersan-mondtags-top-gay-production-der-silbersee/.
178. Clarke, "Ersan Mondtag's Over-the-Top Gay Production of 'Der Silbersee.'"
179. Briegleb, "Proletarians as Pharaohs," 63.
180. Briegleb, "Proletarians as Pharaohs," 63.
181. Gast Arbeiterin, "Meine Arbeit ist politisch weil ich selbst politisch bin," *Renk*, July 25, 2016, accessed July 23, 2022, https://renk-magazin.de/ersan-mondtag-meine-arbeit-ist-politisch-weil-ich-selbst-politisch-bin/.
182. Briegleb, "Proletarians as Pharaohs," 62.

Afterword

1. See Sissi Liu and Rina Tanaka, "The Broadway-Style Musical in/and Global Asias: 1920–2019," in *The Routledge Companion to Musical Theatre*, ed. Laura MacDonald and Ryan Donovan with William A. Everett (Abingdon: Routledge, 2023), 418–35.

2. Yilun (Della) Wu, "Introduction: Into the Theatre," in *The Routledge Companion to Musical Theatre*, ed. Laura MacDonald and Ryan Donovan with William A. Everett (Abingdon: Routledge, 2023), 482.
3. Laura MacDonald and Ryan Donovan with William A. Everett, eds., *The Routledge Companion to Musical Theatre* (Abingdon: Routledge, 2023).

Index

For the benefit of digital users, indexed terms that span two pages (e.g., 52–53) may, on occasion, appear on only one of those pages.

Figures are indicated by *f* following the page number

Abbott and Costello, 180
Abraham, Paul, 114, 188–89, 197–99, 205
abstract expressionism, 158–59
Academy Award, 22–23
ACOM International (Arts Communication International) (Korean production company), 58–59
Add4 (Korean rock group), 43
"Adieu, mein kleiner Gardeoffizier" (Stolz), 164
Adorno, Theodor W., 25–26, 111, 112–13, 179–80, 182–83, 184–85
"Aegukga" (South Korean national anthem), 40–41
Aesthetic Theory (Adorno), 179–80
Agitrock, 129–31, 132–33, 135–36
branches (*Liedermacher* and Krautrock), 130–31
Ahn Eak-tai, 40–41
"Aegukga" (South Korean national anthem), 40–41
Ahrens, Lynn, 21–22
Aida (Verdi), 236
"Air on the G String" (Bach), 85–86
Akzeybek, Tansel, 208*f*, 211–12
Albee, Edward, 173–74, 200–1
Albers, Josef, 165–67
"Alles endet, was entstehet" (Wolf), 175
Alles Schwindel (Spoliansky), 191
Weise production (Gorki Theater 2017), 191
Alpert, Herb, 197–99
"America" (*West Side Story*), 211
American Forces Korea Radio Network, 42–43

American Forces Network (AFN), 128–29
"Americanism," 12
musicals, in, 6–7
American Psycho (Sheik, Aguirre-Sacasa), 75
Amon Düül, 130–31
Amphitryon (Molière), 151–52, 160
Fritsch production (Berlin, Schaubühne 2019), 151–52, 160
Amstein, Jürg, 167
anarchism, 129–30, 132–33, 151–52, 164–65, 229
Anatevka (Bock, Harnick, trans. Merz, Hagen), 119–20
Kosky production (Komische Oper 2017), 189, 193–99, 196*f*, 198*f*, See also *Fiddler on the Roof*; *Fiedler auf dem Dach, Der*
An Chunggun, 61–62, 64, 66
Anders, Florian, 154, 158–59
Angels in America (Kushner), ix, 204–5
Animal Farm (Orwell), 133–34
Annie Get Your Gun (Berlin), 122–24
anti-capitalism, 126–27, 132–33
anticolonialism, 44–45, 65
anti-Semitism, 121
Apel, August, 141–42
Apollo Theater (Harlem), 19–21
Dreamgirls revival based on Seoul production, 18–21
Arias, Lola, 157
"Arirang" (Korean 'national folk song'), 41–42, 91, 98–99
Aristophanes, 186
Armed Forces Radio Service, x, 4–5
Armstrong, Louis, 42–43

Arnaldos, Daniel, 234*f*
Arnold, Franz, 154–56, 155*f*
artist, myth of the suffering, 40, 94–95, 100–2. *See also* Callas, Maria; Chatterton, Thomas; Holiday, Billie; Jeon Hye-rin; Joplin, Janis; Kim Kwang-seok; Kim U-jin; Orpheus; Piaf, Edith; *Seopyeonje*; *Sorrows of Young Werther, The*; van Gogh, Vincent; Yi Sang; Yun Sim-deok
ASCAP, 111–12
Assassins (Sondheim, Weidman), 75
Assia, Lys, 167
Attali, Jacques, 28
Aufstieg und Fall der Stadt Mahagonny (Weill, Brecht), 110, 126–27, 228–29
    Jenny (character), 126–27
    Jim Mahoney (character), 231–32
    Kosky production (Komische Oper 2021), 190–91, 197, 223, 228–29, 231–32
    "Nur die Nacht," 231–32
"Auto-da-fé" (*Candide*), 219–20
avant-gardism, 142–43, 144–45, 149–50, 153, 158–59, 178
Axtell, Katherine, 12

Baal (Brecht), 191
    Mondtag production (Berliner Ensemble 2019), 191
Bach, Ernst, 154–56, 155*f*
Bach, Johann Sebastian, 85–86, 164
Bacharach, Burt, 172, 174–75
Bądarzewska-Baranowska, Tekla, 231
Baez, Joan, 85–86, 130–31
Ball im Savoy (Abraham), 188–89
"Ballad of Caesar's Death, The" (*Der Silbersee*), 237
Ballhaus Naunynstraße, 213–14
Ballroom Schmitz (Bürk, Sienknecht), 151–52
Balme, Christopher, 157
Banfield, Stephen, 8–9, 102–3
Ban Ki-moon, 59
Bannon, D., 70–71
Baranello, Micaela, 113

Barré, Pierre, 77
Barrie Kosky's All-Singing, All-Dancing Yiddish Revue (Komische Oper 2022), 197–99
Barry Sisters (singing group), 197–99
Baumann, Helmut, 199
Bausch, Pina, 108–9
Beatles, the, 129–30, 132–33, 161
    Sgt. Pepper's Lonely Hearts Club Band, 132–33
    "Why Don't We Do It in the Road?," 158
Beaver Coat, The (Hauptmann)
    Fritsch production (Schwerin 2010), 154–56, 157–58
Becker, Tobias, 12–13
Beckett, Samuel, 162–63, 179–80, 217–18. *See also Endgame*; *Happy Days*; *Not I*; *Rockaby*; *Waiting for Godot*
"Becoming Dust" (*The Days*), 85–86
Beethoven, Ludwig Van, 114–15, 231
"Before the Crucifix" (*Hero: The Musical*), 64
Behr, Victoria, 159–60
Belgian Revolution (1830), 236–37
belting (vocal style), 77–78
Benanti, Laura, 77–78
Benatzky, Ralph, 12–13, 114
Ben-Hur (Lee, Wang), 72, 76
Ben-Hur: A Tale of the Christ (Wallace), 72
Bennett, Michael, ix, 18–19
Benzwi, Adam, 197–99, 228–29
Berg, Alban, 205
Berg, Sibylle, 191
Berger, Martin G., 218
Bergmann, Karin, 180–81
Berlin Airlift, 117–18
Berlin Blockade, 117–18
Berliner Ensemble, 157–58, 191, 223, 228–29
Berliner Theatertreffen, 154–56, 158
Berlin Philharmonic, 178
"Berlin Song" (*Linie 1*), 136–37
Berlin Wall, x–xi, 29–30, 114–15, 141
Bernard, Gregory, 62–63
Berne Convention, 52

Bernhard, Thomas, 160
Bernstein, Leonard, ix–x, 126, 190–91, 207–10, 217, 222–23. See also *Candide*; *Fancy Free*; *On the Town*; *West Side Story*
"Best of Times, The" (*La Cage aux Folles*), 243–44
Bieber, Justin, 48
Biermann, Wolf, 130–31
"Big Hunk o' Love, A" (Schroeder, Wyche), 128–29
Billington, Michael, 102–3
Billy Elliot (John, Hall), 62–63
Bizet, Georges, 52, 210–11
Blackboard Jungle, The (1955 film), 128–29
Black Crook, The (Baker, Barras), 143–44
blackface, 19–20, 115–16
Black Rider, The (Waits, Wilson, Burroughs), 120–21, 130–31, 141–50, 146*f*, 151, 152–53, 154
   "Briar and the Rose, The ," 147
   "But He's Not Wilhelm," 147–48
   "Chase the Clouds Away," 147–48
   "Crossroads," 146–47
   "Gospel Train," 146–47
   "I'll Shoot the Moon," 147
   "In the Morning," 147–48
   worldwide productions and success, 148–49
Blue Man Productions, 21–22
blues, 7–8, 20–21, 43, 68, 142, 146–47
Bock, Jerry, 193, See also *Anatevka*; *Fiddler on the Roof*; *Fiedler auf dem Dach, Der*
Boltanski, Luc, 29
Bombay Dreams (Rahman, Black), 68
Borchert, Thomas, 77–78
Boublil, Alain, 6–7
"Boy like That, A"/ "I Have a Love" (*West Side Story*), 211
Brachtel, Beni, 191
Brantley, Ben, 19–20, 24, 27–28, 212
Brecht, Bertolt, 101–2, 107, 110, 126, 130–33, 143–44, 158, 164, 179, 197, 223. See also *Aufstieg und Fall der Stadt Mahagonny*; *Baal*; *Dreigroschenoper, Die*; Eisler, Hanns; *Good Person of Szechuan, The*; *Happy End*; *Jasager, Der*; *Mother Courage*
Breger, Udo, 144–45
Breglio, John F., 18–19, 20–21, 55–56
Breth, Andrea, 204–5
"Briar and the Rose, The" (*The Black Rider*), 147
Briegleb, Till, 232–33
Brigadoon (Loewe, Lerner), 177
"Bring Him Home" (*Les Misérables*), 78–79
British Forces Broadcasting Services (BFBS), 128–29
Broadway Across America (production company), 19–20
Broadway League, 16–17
Broadway-style musical, definition, 3, 5–16, 31–32
Brouwers, Fred, 77
Brown, Timothy Scott, 129–30
Brug, Manuel, 189–90
Bruns, Klaus, 218
BTS (K-pop boy group), 46
Büchner, Georg, 107
Burgtheater (Vienna), 180–81, 182*f*, 184–85, 184*f*
Bürk, Barbara, 151–52
Burke, Kenneth, 10–12
Burkhard, Paul, 112–13, 167, 169–70
   schwarze Hecht, Der, 157–58, 180
Burroughs, William S., 141–42, 144–45, 147
Burston, Jonathan, 26–27, 78–79
"But He's Not Wilhelm" (*The Black Rider*), 147–48

Cabaret (Kander, Ebb), 52, 57, 119–20, 145
Caesar, Irving, 13
Cage aux Folles, La (Herman, Fierstein), 119–20, 243–44
   "Best of Times, The," 243–44
   "Look over There," 243–44
   "Song in the Sand," 243–44
Cage, John, 153, 172, 178
Caird, John, 217–18
Callas, Maria, 94–95, 230

cancel culture, 191
Candide (Bernstein, etc.), 189, 215–22
   "Auto-da-fé," 219–20
   German-language premiere (Vienna 1976), 216–17
   "Glitter and Be Gay," 218
   "King's Barcarolle," 221–22
   Kosky production (Komische Oper 2018), 189, 215, 217–22, 219*f*
   "Make Our Garden Grow," 216–17, 221–22
   Martin (character), 220–21
   "Nothing More than This," 221
   Royal National Theatre version (1989), 217
   Scottish Opera version (1988), 217, 221
Candide (Voltaire novella), 215–17
"Cannon Song" (*Die Dreigroschenoper*), 230
capitalism, 42–43, 45, 49, 89, 91, 122–25, 130–31, 133, 134–35, 185–86, 225, 229
   critique in East German musicals, 121–27
   critique in *Linie 1*, 135–36
Carletti, Alessandro, 218
Carlson, Marvin, 143
Carmen (Bizet), 52, 210–11
Carousel (Rodgers, Hammerstein), 21–22, 169
Castor et Pollux (Rameau), 189–90
   Kosky production (Komische Oper 2011), 189–90
Castorf, Frank, 133, 154–56, 158, 235–36
   Ring des Nibelungen, Der, production (Bayreuth 2013), 235–36
Cats (Lloyd Webber, Eliot), 6–7, 12–13, 52, 109–10, 144–45, 188
   Hamburg production, 149
   Korean premiere (1994), 52
   Vienna premiere (1983), 120–21
Cavalli, Francesco, 220
Cha Ji-yeon, 101–2
Chakrabarty, Dipesh, 38–39
Chang, Sarah, 77
changga (Western-style songs), 38–39
changgeuk (Korean opera), 39, 41–42, 49–50, 80–81, 102–3, 241–42

changjak (homegrown Korean musicals), 38, 44–45, 57–58, 71–72
Chaplin, Charlie, 158–59, 185, 195
Charell, Erik, 12–13, 167
"Chase the Clouds Away" (*The Black Rider*), 147–48
Chatterton, Thomas, 94–95
Chekhov, Anton, 39–40
Chess (Ulvaeus, Rice), 62–63
Chiapello, Eve, 29
Chicago (Kander, Ebb), 57–58
Chicago Tribune, 24
Childs, Lucinda, 143–44
Chinese Opera. See *jingju*
Cho Kwang-hwa, 95
Cho, Francisca, 92–93
Choe Sang-Hun, 19–20
Choi Yu-jun, 38–39, 48, 70, 71–72, 79–80, 100–1, 102–3
Chopin, Fryderyk, 89
Chorus Line, A (Hamlisch, Kleban), 5
Chun Doo-hwan, 44–45
Chung, Myung-whun, 77
Chung, Sung Hwa, 61–62, 78–79
Chungmu Art Hall (Seoul), 75
Churchill, Frank, 174
Claessens, Benny, 204–5, 234*f*, 236, 238–39
Clark, Victoria, 77–78
Clarke, Kevin, 236, 243–44
classism, 121
Clayton, Allan, 219*f*
"Climb Ev'ry Mountain" (*The Sound of Music*), 59–60
Cobain, Kurt, 84
Cockettes, the, 202, 203*f*
codification, 29
Cohen, Greg, 147
Cold War, x, 4–5, 32, 37–38, 50–51, 52, 88, 107, 114–16, 117, 125–27, 129–30, 193–94, 222
Cole, Nat King, 42–43
Collins, Phil, 27–28
colonialism, 37, 38–39, 40, 41–43, 48, 50–51, 81, 82, 92–93, 94, 216
Comedian Harmonists, 165–67
commedia dell'arte, 186
"Commitment" (Adorno), 179

Contemporary Gugak Orchestra, 79–80
Conti, Bill, 22–23
"Cool" (West Side Story), 209–10
Copland, Aaron, 126, 210–11
Cornish, Matt, 143, 156
Coughlin, Bruce, 217
Covid, 140, 229
Craymer, Judy, 57
Creedence Clearwater Revival, 96–97
Crossroads (1986 Hill film), 146–47
"Crossroads" (Johnson), 146–47
"Crossroads" (*The Black Rider*), 146–47
CUNY Graduate Center, ix
curtain call, 186–87

Dada, 158–59, 164–65
Dance of the Vampires (Steinman, Ives), 17–18.See also *Fearless Vampire Killers, The*; *Tanz der Vampire*
Davids, Matthias, 223, 225–28
    Lady in the Dark production (Staatsoper Hannover 2011), 226
    Lady in the Dark production (Wiener Volksoper 2021), 223, 225–28
Days, The (그날들) (Kim, Jang), 80–89, 96
    "Becoming Dust," 85–86
    "Flowers," 85–86
    "Letter That Did Not Get Sent, A," 87
    plot and structure, 84–85
    "Though I Loved You," 87–88
"Dear Officer Krupke" (*West Side Story*), ix–x
Debussy, Claude, 210–11
Degenhardt, Franz Josef, 130–31
De Quincey, Thomas, 141–42, 146–47
der die mann (Fritsch), 159–60
De Schutter, Marjan, 234f, 237
Deseure, Karel, 235–36
deterritorialization of musical, 16–18, 30–31
Deutsche Bank, 225
Deutscher Bühnenverein, 108–10
"Deutschland: Ein Wintermärchen" (Heine), 232–33
Dialectic of Enlightenment (Adorno, Horkheimer), 185
Didwiszus, Rufus, 195
Dietrich, Marlene, 175–77

Die Welt. See *Welt, Die*
Dippel, Roland, 122–24, 128
Disney (The Walt Disney Company), 26, 27–28, 30–31
Disney Theatricals, xii–xiii, 17, 21–22, 25–28, 29, 33
Disney, Walt, 30–31, 174, 226–27
Disney+ channel, 15–16
Divine, 31–32
Doctor Zhivago (Simon, Weller), 55–56
Dolginoff, Stephen, 55
Doll's House, A (Ibsen), 154–56
    Fritsch production (Oberhausen 2010), 154–56, 160
Dompke, Christoph, 201–2
Don Giovanni (Mozart, da Ponte), 217–18
    Kosky production (Wiener Staatsoper 2021), 217–18
Dongmulwon (folk-rock band), 83–84
Dongyang Gozupa, 79–80
Donizetti, Gaetano, 100–1
Donovan, Ryan, 243
Dostal, Nico, 188–89
Douwes, Pia, 77–78
Drake, Alfred, 78–79
Dreamgirls (Krieger, Eyen, Bennett), ix, 18–19
    Apollo Theater version of Seoul production, 18–21
    Black musical, as, 19–20
    deracialization in Seoul production, 19–21
    film version (2006), 18–19
    Seoul production (2009), ix, 18–21, 55–56
Dreigroschenoper, Die (Weill, Brecht), xii, 29–30, 109–10, 134–35, 170, 223–25, 228–31
    "Cannon Song," 230
    Kosky production (Berliner Ensemble 2021), 190–91, 223, 228–31
Dürrenmatt, Friedrich, 159
Dylan, Bob, 83–84, 85–87, 130–31

Ebb, Fred, 145, 147. See also *Cabaret*; *Chicago*
Eckert, Franz, 38–39
Edinburgh Festival, 165–67

Ed Sullivan Show, 43
Eggert, Moritz, 111–12
"Einheitsfrontlied" (Eisler, Brecht), 132–33
Einzige und sein Eigentum, Der (Hartmann, PC Nackt), 151–52
Eisler, Hanns, 130–33
Elektra (Strauss), 180–81
elitism, 24–25, 230, 238
Empire State Building, 31
E-Musik (serious music), 111–13
  U-Musik (entertainment music), distinction between, 111–13, 190–91, 201–2
Endgame (Beckett), 183–85, 217–18
Engel, Erich, 228–29
Engel, Lehman, 10
Engels, Friedrich, 151–52
Ensemble Sinawi, 79–80
"Er ist's" (Wolf), 177
"Erstes Liebeslied eines Mädchens" (Wolf), 175–77, 176f
Escher, M.C., 88
"Es wird mir heiß und kalt" (*Der schwarze Hecht*), 170–71
Euripides, 49–50
Everett, William A., 243
Evita (Lloyd Webber, Rice), 52, 62–63
"Eye of the Tiger" (Survivor), 22–23

fan culture, 23, 26–28, 30–31, 46, 48–49, 51, 53f, 76, 83, 84–85, 86–87, 128–29, 242–43
Fancy Free (Bernstein, Robbins), 126
fascism, 22–23, 32, 134–35, 229, 233–34, 236, 238
"Fatal Marksman, The" (De Quincey), 141–42
Faust (Gounod), 52
Fearless Vampire Killers, The (1967 Polanski film), 17–18
Fela! (Kuti, Jones), 68
Felsenstein, Johannes, 194–95
Felsenstein, Walter, 188, 192, 193–96
  Fiedler auf dem Dach, Der production (Komische Oper 1971), 193–95
Feuerwerk (1954 film), 167
Feuerwerk, Das (Burkhard), 112–13

Feydeau, Georges, 156
Fiddler on the Roof (Bock, Harnick), 5, 52, 119–20, 194–95, 207–9
Fiedler auf dem Dach, Der (Bock, Harnick, trans. J. Felsenstein), 193–96, See also *Anatevka*; *Fiddler on the Roof*
  Jewish identity, representation of, 194–95
Finding Mr. Destiny (2006 Jang musical), 83
Finian's Rainbow (Lane, Harburg), 177
Fisher, Eddie, 167
Flack, Roberta, 177
Flaherty, Stephen, 21–22
Fledermaus, Die (Strauss), 13–15
Floh de Cologne (Krautrock group), 131–32
"Flowers" (*The Days*), 85–86
Fluxus, 158–59, 164–65
folk-rock, 43, 83–84, 85–86, 133–34
Follies (Sondheim, Goldman), 85, 201–2
4.48 Psychosis (Kane), 151–52
  Rasche-van Wersch production (Berlin 2020), 151–52
Frankenstein (1931 Whale film), 74–75
Frankenstein (Lee, Wang), 72, 73f, 76, 79, 80–81, 85–86
  "Wounded," 74–75
Frankenstein (Shelley), 72–74, 141–42
Frankfurter Allgemeine, 173–74, 222
Frau, die weiss, was sie will!, Eine (Straus), 188–89
"Freischütz, Der" (Apel, Laun), 141–42, 144–45
Freischütz, Der (Weber), 141–42, 143–44
  Fritsch production (Zurich 2016), 154
Freud, Sigmund, 95–96, 169–70, 225–26
Friedrichstadtpalast (Berlin), 202–3, 222
Fritsch, Herbert, x–xi, 151–87, 234–35
  Amphitryon production (Berlin, Schaubühne 2019), 151–52, 160
  Beaver Coat, The, production (Schwerin 2010), 154–56, 157–58
  biography, 158
  der die mann (Volksbühne 2015), 159–60
  Doll's House, A, production (Oberhausen 2010), 154–56, 160

Freischütz, Der, production (Zurich 2016), 154
Jagdgesellschaft, Die, production (Frankfurt 2022), 160
King Arthur production (Zurich 2016), 154, 163–64
Murmel Murmel (Volksbühne 2012), 159, 161, 164–67, 166*f*
"Nonsense in Residence" (Kopatchinskaja multimedia event 2022), 178
Pfusch (Volksbühne 2016), 157–58, 161
Physicists, The, production (Zurich 2013), 159
(s)panische Fliege, Die, production (Volksbühne 2011), 154–56, 155*f*, 164–65
schwarze Hecht, Der, production (Zurich 2014), 157–58, 167–72, 168*f*, 180
Trilogie der Sommerfrische production (Munich 2014), 163
Valentin (with Wertmüller) (Hamburg 2017), 164–65
Wer hat Angst vor Hugo Wolf? (Zurich 2016), 157–58, 162*f*, 172–77, 176*f*
Zelt (with Jakisic) (Burgtheater 2019), 157–58, 161, 180–87, 182*f*, 184*f*
Frühlingsstürme (Weinberger), 188–89
Fun Home (Tesori, Kron), 204–5
Funny Girl (Styne, Merrill), 23

"Gangnam Style" (Psy), 48, 71–72
Garfunkel, Art, 85–86
Garland, Judy, 94–95
GEMA (German copyright collective), 111–12
Genatt, Simone, 56–57
Geomungo Factory, 79–80
German Composers' Union, 111–12
German Copyright Administration Act, 111–12
German Economic Miracle (*Wirtschaftswunder*), 128, 133–34
German Expressionism, 144–45
Germany, 107–244
    arts, state subsidization of, xii, 24–25, 32, 107–13, 116–17, 119–20, 121, 142–43, 149–50, 151, 163–64, 188, 189–90, 191, 193–95, 199–200, 201–2, 204–5, 222, 226
    distinction and codification between E-Musik (serious music) and U-Musik (entertainment music), 111–13, 190–91, 201–2
    history, 107–9
    musicals, history of, 114–21
    prejudice against musicals, xi–xii, 24–26, 77–78, 111–13, 115–16, 189–90, 191–93, 194–95, 222
    US culture, importing of, x, 114–20, 128–30
Germany, East (German Democratic Republic) (GDR), 107–8
    musicals, history of, 114–15, 121–28
Germany, West (Federal Republic of Germany) (FRG), 107–8
    musicals, history of, 114–21
Gershwin, George, 52, 126–27, 186. See also *Porgy and Bess*; *Rhapsody in Blue*
Gershwin, Ira, 10–11, 52, 186. See also *Lady in the Dark*; *Porgy and Bess*
"Gesang Weylas" (Wolf), 174–75, 177
Gewandhaus Orchestra (Leipzig), 193–94
Giebel, Julia, 208*f*, 211–12
Gilbert, Robert, 117, 167
    My Fair Lady, German-language version, 117–18
Girl from the North Country (Dylan musical), 86–87
Glass, Philip, 143–44
Glinka, Mikhail, 210–11
"Glitter and Be Gay" (*Candide*), 218
globalization, 49, 52
Gobé, Mark, 29
Goethe, Johann Wolfgang von, 114–15, 172–73
Golbeck, Carsten, 140
Goldoni, Carlo, 156, 163
"Gonna Fly Now" (Conti), 22–23
Good Person of Szechuan, The (Brecht), 101–2
Gordy, Berry, 46–47
gospel music, 7–8, 20–21, 31–32
"Gospel Train" (*The Black Rider*), 146–47

Go Trabi Go (Walenciak, Golbeck), 140
Gounod, Charles, 52
Grand Macabre, Le (Ligeti), 200–1
    Kosky production (Komische Oper 2003), 200–1
Grande, Ariana, 112
Grant, Mark, 28
Grateful Dead, 132–33
"Greensleeves" (traditional), 98–99
Grey, Joel, 145
Grimm, Jakob and Wilhelm, 133–34, 226–27
    "Snow White," 226–27
GRIPS Theater, 53–54, 134–36. See also *Linie 1*
    Left History, A (*Eine linke Geschichte*), 134–35
Grosch, Nils, 115–16
Großes Schauspielhaus (Berlin), 12–13
gugak (traditional Korean music), 38–39, 41, 44–45, 47–48, 70–72, 79–80
Gundlach, Daniel, 241, 243–44
Günther, Ingo, 151–52, 160–61, 165
Guthrie, Woody, 130–31
Guys and Dolls (Loesser), 52, 53–54
Gypsy (Styne, Sondheim), 9, 67–68
    "Rose's Turn," 9

Hair (Rado, Ragni, MacDermot), 5, 15–16, 62–63, 112, 119–20, 121, 128, 137–38
Hairspray (Shaiman, Wittman), 31–33, 57
    German-language premiere (St. Gallen 2008), 32
    Staatstheater Braunschweig production (2017), 31–32
    "You Can't Stop the Beat," 31–32, 33
Hairspray (Waters film), 31–32
Haley, Bill, 128–29
hallyu (Korean Wave), 38, 45–52, 65, 66–67, 71–72, 81–82, 89–90
    elitist cultural aspirations, 49–50
    origins, 45–46, 89–90
Hamilton (Miranda), 5, 15–16
    Hamburg production (2022), 15–16
Hamlet (Shakespeare), 119
Hammerstein, Oscar II, 59–60, 62–64. See also *Carousel*; *King and I, The*; *Oklahoma!*; *Show Boat*; *Sound of Music, The*; *South Pacific*

han (sadness, melancholy), 70–71, 72–75, 80–83, 84–86, 87–88, 89–91, 93–94, 97–99, 100, 102–3
Han A-reum, 61–62
Han Dong-jun, 87
Hanswurst, 164
Happy Days (Beckett), 183–84
Happy End (Weill, Brecht, Hauptmann), 224, 230–31
    Sommer production (Renaissance Theater 2022), 223, 224–25
Harkness, Nicholas, 93–94
Harnick, Sheldon, 193. See also *Anatevka*; *Fiddler on the Roof*; *Fiedler auf dem Dach, Der*
Hart, Lorenz, 143–44, 169
Hart, Moss, 10–11, 226
Hartmann, Sebastian, 151–52
    Einzige und sein Eigentum, Der, production (with PC Nackt, Berlin 2022), 151–52
Hass-Triptychon—Wege aus der Krise (Berg, Brachtel), 191
    Mondtag production (Gorki Theater 2019), 191
Hauptmann, Elisabeth, 224
Hauptmann, Gerhart, 154–56
    Beaver Coat, The, 154–56
Healy, Patrick, 16–17, 51, 76
Heine, Heinrich, 232–33
Heiße Ecke—Das St. Pauli Musical (Lingnau, Wohlgemuth), 140
"Hellhound on My Trail" (Johnson), 146–47
Hellman, Lillian, 215–17
Hello, Dolly! (Herman), 119–20, 125
    Korean tour (1965), 52
Helmi, Bettina, 181–82
Hemingway, Ernest, 144–45
Herbert, Victor, 12–13
Herman, Jerry. See also *Cage aux Folles, La*; *Hello, Dolly!*
Hero: The Musical (영웅) (Oh, Han), 58–59, 61–67, 71–72, 78–79, 81–82, 83, 85–86
    Japanese occupation, depiction of, 64–66
    "My Beloved Son, Thomas," 63–64
    transnational musical style in, 62–66

INDEX 295

Herrera, Brian, 206–7, 211
Herr Fressack und die Bremer Stadtmusikanten (Hoffmanns Comic Teater; Ton Steine Scherben), 133–34
Heymann, Birger, 29–30, 134–35
Heyward, DuBose, 52
Hill, Walter, 146–47
Hinterm Horizont (Lindenberg jukebox musical), 21–22
Hinton, Stephen, 224, 225, 229, 233
hip-hop, 7–8, 15–16, 67, 84
Hirschfeld, Magnus, 203–4
Hitler, Adolf, 232–33
Hochzeitstag, Der (AKA *Soul Mate*) (Lim), 49–50
   Oper Frankfurt production (2006), 49–50
Hoffmanns Comic Teater, 131–33. See also Krautrock; Reiser, Rio; Ton Steine Scherben
   Herr Fressack und die Bremer Stadtmusikanten, 133–34
Hof-Theater (Bad Freienwalde), 243–44
Holden, Stephen, 144–45
Holiday, Billie, 94–95
Hollaender, Friedrich, 197–99
Hollywood, 6, 12, 15–16, 25–26, 48, 55, 114–15, 144–45, 185, 212
Holm, Celeste, 115–16
Holy Roman Empire of the German Nation, 107
homophobia, 238
homosexuality, 175–77, 199–205, 227–28, 241
   Kosky, Barrie, reflected in work of, 199–205
   Olim and Severin in *Der Silbersee* as gay couple, 236–39
Hong Hae-ran, 77
Hong, Euny, 50–51
Hong, Hei-Kyung, 77
Hopp, Max, 195, 198f, 199
Horkheimer, Max, 185
Horwitz, Dominique, 145, 146f
"House of the Rising Sun, The" (traditional), 98–99
Howard, Keith, 41–42, 45
Hubrich, Susanne, 226

Hughes, Erika, 135–36
hung (joy), 81–82
Hwang, David Henry, 27–28
Hwang, Sumi, 77
"Hymn of Death" (사의찬미) (Yun Simdeok song), 40, 41, 94

"I'll Shoot the Moon" (*The Black Rider*), 147
Ibsen, Henrik, 154–56
"Ich hab in Penna" (Wolf), 175
Ich war noch niemals in New York (Jürgens jukebox musical), 21–22
Im Kwontaek, 80–81, 89–90. See also *Seopyeonje* (1993 film)
Importance of Being Earnest, The (Wilde), 122–25
Im weissen Rößl (Benatzky, Charell), 12–16, 191. See also *White Horse Inn*
   Weise production (Düsseldorf 2013), 191
   worldwide productions and success, 12–13
In Frisco ist der Teufel los (Masanetz, Schneidereit), 121–24, 125–28
   Xonga Miller (character), 125–27
"In the Morning" (*The Black Rider*), 147–48
Indecent (Vogel), 204–5
Intangible Cultural Heritage of Humanity, 39, 41–42, 91, 102–3
"It's a Small World" (Sherman, Sherman), 30–31, 32–33
Ito Hirobumi, 61–62, 63–64, 66
Ivanovici, Iosif, 40

Jackson, Shirley, 229
Jagdgesellschaft, Die (Bernhard), 160
   Fritsch production (Frankfurt 2022), 160
Jakisic, Matthias, 180–81
Jambinai, 79–80
James, Brian d'Arcy, 77–78
James, David E., 97
Jang, Yu-jeong, 83
Jansen, Wolfgang, 115–16, 117–18, 207–9
Jantschitsch, Eva, 191

Japan, x, 37, 38–39, 40–41, 42–43, 45–46, 55–56, 71–72, 78–79. *See also* kabuki
  Korea, occupation of, 37, 38–39, 40, 55, 57, 82, 92–93, 94. See also *Hero: The Musical*; *Last Empress, The*
Jasager, Der (Weill, Brecht), 110
jazz, 6–8, 12–13, 40–41, 68, 79–80, 95, 113, 114, 147–48, 164, 165–67
Jefferson Airplane, 132–33
Jekyll & Hyde (Wildhorn, Bricusse), 55–56
Jelly's Last Jam (Morton, Wolfe), 102–3
Jensen, Simon, 166f
Jeon Hye-rin, 94
Jesus Christ Superstar (Lloyd Webber, Rice), 55–56, 62–63, 120–21
  Seoul premiere (1980), 52
Jewish identity, 82, 117–18, 178, 188–89, 194–95
  Fiedler auf dem Dach, Der (Felsenstein production), as presented in, 194–95
  Kosky, Barrie, in work of, 195–99, 231–32
Ji Chang-wook, 83, 88
jingju (Peking Opera), 9–10, 39, 160, 236–37
Jo, Sumi, 77
John, Elton, 172, 174–75
Johnson, Robert, 146–47
  "Crossroads," 146–47
  "Hellhound on My Trail," 146–47
  "Me and the Devil Blues," 146–47
Jones, Chris, 24
Joplin, Janis, 94–95
Jordan, Julia, 55
Juchem, Elmar, 116
jukebox musicals, 5–6, 21–22, 67, 68, 80–81, 83, 86–87, 133, 151–52, 157–58, 163, 172–77
Jung, Carl, 169–70
Jürgens, Udo, 21–22

kabuki, 9–10, 39–40, 141, 148–49
Kafka, Franz, 179–80, 229
Kaiser, Georg, 232–33, 234, 238–39
Kálmán, Emmerich, 12–13
Kander, John, 145, 147. See also *Cabaret*; *Chicago*
Kane, Sarah, 151–52

Karl, Andy, 24
Katz, Elihu, 27
Katz, Micky, 197–99
Kavoori, Anandam, 48–49
Kay, Hershy, 217–18
Keaton, Buster, 180
Keine Macht für Niemand (Ton Steine Scherben), 132–33
Kermit the Frog, 200–1
Kern, Jerome, 12. See also *Show Boat*
Kerst, Andreas, 111–12
Kessel, Corinne, 144
Killick, Andrew, 39–40, 92, 97
Kim, Hee Gab, 59–60
Kim, Hee-sun, 46–47
Kim, Jason, 67
Kim, Joseph, 46
Kim, Kyung Hyun, 20–21, 37–38, 48, 62–63, 68
Kim, Patti, 43
Kim, Sandra So Hee Chi, 82
Kim, Youna, 47–49, 81–82
"Kim Kwang Seok" (Die Orsons song), 84
Kim Kwang-seok, 80–81, 83–84, 85–88, 94
Kim Min-gi, 53–54, 139–40, See also *Subway Line 1*
  "Morning Dew," 53–54
Kim Sisters (Korean girl group), 43
Kim Sook, 59
Kim U-jin, 40, 94
Kim Young-sam, 45
King and I, The (Rodgers, Hammerstein), 61–62
King Arthur (Purcell), 154, 163–64
  Fritsch production (Zurich 2016), 154, 163–64
King Lear (Shakespeare), 231–32
King, Carole, 177
"King's Barcarolle" (*Candide*), 221–22
Kinky Boots (Lauper, Fierstein), 55–56, 62–63
Kiss Me, Kate (Porter), ix, 5, 109–10
  Frankfurt production (1955), 116–17
  Kosky production (Komische Oper 2008), ix, 189, 190–91, 199–203, 203f, 205, 207
  standard repertoire in Germany, as, 116–17, 119–20

Wiener Volksoper production (1956), 225–26
Klabunde, Lisa, 136*f*
Klemperer, Otto, 190
klezmer, 147
Klitschko (2011 documentary), 23–24
Klitschko, Vitali and Wladimir, 23–24
Klotz, Volker, 112–13
Knapp, Raymond, 8, 207–10, 217
Koch, Wolfram, 155*f*, 158–59, 163–64
Koegler, Horst, 125
Kollege Klatt—Rock Story (Lokomotive Kreuzberg), 131–32
Komische Oper, ix, 188–203, 196*f*, 198*f*, 203*f*, 208*f*, 219*f*, 223, 228–29
　Felsenstein, Walter at, 193–95
　Kosky, Barrie, at, 188–93, 196*f*, 198*f*, 203*f*, 208*f*, 219*f*
　Selam Opera! initiative, 214–15
Kopatchinskaja, Patricia, 178
Korea. *See also* Korea, North; Korea, South
　Japan, occupation by, 37, 38–39, 40, 55, 82, 92–93, 94. *See also Hero: The Musical*; *Last Empress, The*
Korea National Opera, 49–50
Korea, North, 37, 43–44, 54–55
Korea, South, 37–103, 115–16
　arts, state subsidization of, 49, 52, 75
　electricity, introduction of, 40
　gugak (traditional music), 38–39, 41, 44–45, 47–48, 70–72, 79–80
　jazz, influx and influence of, 40–41
　Ministry of Foreign Affairs and Trade, 49
　musicals in, 37–38
　natural imagery, artistic use of, 43–44
　trot (popular song form), 41
　United States in, 37–38
　US culture, importing of, x, 38–45
　US-style musicals, history of, 51–54, 55–57
　Western classical music, influence of, 40–41, 43, 44–45
　Western music, performers of, 77–79
　Westernization, 38–45
Korea Times, 41–42
Korean Consulate General, 59
Korean Cultural Service, 59
Korean Enlightenment, 41–42
Korean Jazz Band, 40–41
Korean Musical Awards, 88, 91
Korean War, 37–39, 52, 64, 90–91, 97
Korean Wave. *See hallyu*
Koreanness, 41–43, 46–51, 66–68, 79–83, 89–90, 94. *See also gugak*; *han*; K-pop
Kosky, Barrie, ix, 111–12, 188–222, 223, 226, 228–33
　Anatevka production (Komische Oper 2017), 189, 190–91, 193–99
　Aufstieg und Fall der Stadt Mahagonny production (Komische Oper 2021), 190–91, 196*f*, 197, 198*f*, 223, 228–29, 231–32
　Ball im Savoy production (Komische Oper 2013), 188–89
　Barrie Kosky's All-Singing, All-Dancing Yiddish Revue (Komische Oper 2022), 197–99
　Beckett-Schoenberg triple bill (Komische Oper 2020), 217–18
　Candide production (Komische Oper 2018), 189, 215, 217–22, 219*f*
　Castor et Pollux production (Komische Oper 2011), 189–90
　Don Giovanni production (Wiener Staatsoper 2021), 217–18
　Dreigroschenoper, Die, production (Berliner Ensemble 2021), 190–91, 223, 228–31
　Frau, die weiss, was sie will!, Eine, production (Komische Oper 2015), 188–89
　Frühlingsstürme production (Komische Oper 2020), 188–89
　Grand Macabre, Le, production (Komische Oper 2003), 200–1
　homosexuality in work of, 199–205
　Jewish identity in work of, 188–89, 195–99, 231–32
　Kiss Me, Kate production (Komische Oper 2008), 189, 190–91, 199–203, 203*f*, 205, 207
　Komische Oper, at, 188–93, 196*f*, 198*f*, 203*f*, 208*f*, 219*f*

Kosky, Barrie (*cont.*)
   Moses und Aron production (Komische Oper 2015), 197, 231–32
   operetta, on, 190
   Perlen der Cleopatra, Die, production (Komische Oper 2016), 188–89
   schöne Helena, Die, production (Komische Oper 2014), 202–3, 205
   West Side Story production (with Pichler, Komische Oper 2013), 189, 190–91, 206–9, 208*f*, 211–15, 226, 228–29
Kotschenreuther, Hellmut, 117, 135–36, 137–38, 139–40
K-pop, 38, 41–42, 44–48, 49–50, 51–52, 62–63, 66–67, 71–72, 76, 81–82, 83, 95, 102–3
KPOP (Park, Kim), 66–68, 76
   "This Is My Korea," 67
Krafft-Ebing, Richard von, 203–4
Kraftwerk, 130–31
Kramer, Lawrence, 172–73
Krautrock, 128–34, 135–36. See also Amon Düül; Floh de Cologne; Kraftwerk; Lokomotive Kreuzberg; Tangerine Dream; Ton Steine Scherben
   Agitrock, as branch of, 130–31
Kröger, Uwe, 77–78
Kudlich, Hans, 226
Kugelmann, Cilly, 197
Kurt, Stefan, 145
Kushner, Tony, ix
Kwon, Seung-Ho, 46

La Cage aux Folles. See *Cage aux Folles, La*
Laages, Michael, 182–83
Lacan, Jacques, 226–27
Lady in the Dark (Weill, I. Gershwin, Hart), 10–12, 13–15, 222–24, 225–29
   Charley Johnson (character), 227–28
   Davids production (Hannover 2011), 226
   Davids production (Wiener Volksoper 2021), 223, 225–28
   Dream sequences, 169, 226–27
   Liza Elliott (character), 10–12, 223–24, 225–28
   "My Ship," 11–12, 223–24, 227–28
   "Princess of Pure Delight, The," 226–27
   "Saga of Jenny, The," 10–12
Lalo, Édouard, 210–11
Landestheater Linz, 226
Langhoff, Shermin, 213–14
Las Vegas, 43, 174–75
Last Empress, The (명성황후) (Kim, Yang, Yi), 17–18, 58–64, 65, 71–72, 83, 87, 102–3
   Japanese occupation, depiction of, 65–66
   "Rise, People of Chosun," 59–60, 65–66
Laun, Friedrich, 141–42
Laurel and Hardy, 158–59, 180
Laurents, Arthur, 206–7, 211
Lawrence, Gertrude, 10–11
Layne, Priscilla, 126–27
Le Pen, Marine, 22–23
Lee Ja-ram, 100*f*, 101–2
Lee Kee-woong, 42–43
Lee, Hyunjung, 31, 58–59
Lee, Yusun, 139–40
Left History, A (*Eine linke Geschichte*) (GRIPS Theater), 134–35
Lehár, Franz, 12–13
Lehmann, Hans-Thies, 112
leitmotifs, 91, 158, 209–10
   Seopyeonje musical, use in, 91, 97–99
Lenau, Nikolaus, 172–73
Lenin, Vladimir, 195
Leninism, 129–30
Lerner, Alan Jay, 117. See also *Brigadoon*; *Love Life*; *My Fair Lady*
"Letter That Did Not Get Sent" (*The Days*), 87
Lewis, Jerry, 158–59
"Lexicon Rhetoricae" (Burke), 10–11
Lie, John, 41, 45–46, 47–48
Lie, Tom Erik, 220
Liebes, Tamar, 27
Liedermacher (German protest singer-songwriters), 130–31, 136–37. See also Biermann, Wolf; Degenhardt, Franz Josef
Ligeti, György, 178, 200–1
"Light of Songs, The" (Yi short story), 90–91
Lim Jun-hee, 49–50, 79–80

Lincoln Center, 58–59
Lindenberg, Udo, 21–22
Lingnau, Martin, 140
Linie 1 (Ludwig, No Ticket, Heymann), xii, 29–30, 53–54, 120–21, 128, 130–31, 134–41, 136*f.* See also *Subway Line 1*
  "Berlin Song," 136–37
  Korean adaptation as *Subway Line 1* (Kim), xii, 53–54, 139–40
  "Mut zum Träumen," 139
  political content, 135–37
  Seoul production, 29–30
  song forms in, 137–39
  "Waiting," 137–39
  "Wilmersdorf Widows," 137
  worldwide productions and success, 29–30, 134–35
Lion King, The (Disney film), 30–31
Lion King, The (John, Rice), xii, 3, 5, 6–7, 16, 25–26, 27, 188
  Chinese cultural elements in Shanghai premiere, 26
  Chinese premiere, 26
  Hamlet, as variation of, 112
Lion, Margo, 175–77
"Literature Sausage" (Roth), 164–65
Lloyd Webber, Andrew, 6–7, 120–21, 144–45
Loewe, Frederick, 177. See also *Brigadoon*; *My Fair Lady*
Lohengrin (Wagner), 147–48
Lokomotive Kreuzberg (Krautrock group), 131–32
  Kollege Klatt—Rock Story, 131–32
Longbottom, Robert, 18–19
"Look over There" (*La Cage aux Folles*), 243–44
Lorde, Audre, 238
Loreau, Thierry, 77
Loriot, 158–59
"Lottery, The" (Jackson), 229
Love Life (Weill, Lerner), 222–23, 225–26
Lucia di Lammermoor (Donizetti), 100–1
Ludwig, Volker, 29–30, 134–35
Luft, Friedrich, 114–15, 116–17
Luker, Rebecca, 77–78
Lulu (Berg), 205
Lund, Peter, 140

LuPone, Patti, 77–78

Macbeth (Verdi), 59–60
MacBride Report, 25–26
MacDonald, Laura, 26–28, 243
"Macht kaputt, was euch kaputt macht" (Ton Steine Scherben), 132–33
Maciel, Ronni, 151–52
Mackintosh, Cameron, 17, 21–22, 25–26
mad scene, 100–1, 146–47
Mahler, Gustav, 172–73
"Make Our Garden Grow" (*Candide*), 216–17, 221–22
Making of a Musical, The (Engel), 10
Mamma Mia! (ABBA, Johnson), 53–54, 163, 186
Man of La Mancha (Leigh, Darion), 57–58, 119–20
Manzel, Dagmar, 199
Maoism, 129–30
Marthaler, Christoph, 152–53, 162–63
Martin Guerre (Schönberg, Boublil), 62–63
Martin, Mary, 52
Marx Brothers, 158–59, 165–67, 185
Marx, Karl, 151–52
Marxism, 44–45, 129–32, 133–34
Masanetz, Guido, 121–22, 125–28
  In Frisco ist der Teufel los, 125–28
  Wer braucht Geld?, 125–26
Massary, Fritzi, 197–99
Matusitz, Jonathan, 24–25
Mauceri, John, 215–16, 217
Maxim Gorki Theater, 191, 213–14
Mayerhofer, Alfred, 202
McCarthyism, 216
McClary, Susan, 162–63
McDonald, Audra, 77–78
McDonaldization of Society, The (Ritzer), 26–27
McMillin, Scott, 8, 10–11
McMusical, 28
McTheatre, 26–29
"Me and the Devil Blues" (Johnson), 146–47
Meehan, Thomas, 21–22
megamusicals, 5–7, 62–63
Mehr-BB Entertainment, 109–10

Mehrling, Katharine, 77–78
Meinardus, Ronald, 50–51
Mein Freund Bunbury (Natschinski, Degenhardt), 121–25, 123f
  Importance of Being Earnest, The, based on, 122–25
  My Fair Lady, as model for, 125
  West German telecast (1970), 124–25
melodrama, 9–10, 39–40, 92, 97, 112–13, 141–42, 154–56, 234
Merchant of Venice, The (Shakespeare), 242–43
Merkel, Angela, 211–12
Merman, Ethel, 77–78
#MeToo, 191, 227–28
Metropol-Theater (Berlin), 114, 117–18, 125–26, 128, 197–99
Meyer, Carsten, 163, 172, 174–75, 177
Michelangelo Buonarotti, 175
Midsummer Night's Dream, A (Shakespeare), 170–71
Migenes, Julia, 207–9
Miller, Arthur, 115–16
Miller, D.A., 100–1
Ministry of Foreign Affairs and Trade (South Korea), 49
Minjung movement, 44–45
minyo (folk songs), 41–42
Miracle on the Han River, 43–44
Misérables, Les (Schönberg, Boublil), 6–7, 52, 53f, 57–58, 62–63, 72
  "Bring Him Home," 78–79
  Korean revival (2013), 78–79
misogyny, 91, 101–2. *See also* artist, myth of suffering; *Seopyeonje*
Miss Piggy, 200–1
Miss Saigon (Schönberg, Boublil), 62–63
Miss Sara Sampson (Lessing), 158
Mitchell, Brian Stokes, 77–79
Mitchell, Joni, 85–86
Mock-O'Hara, Johannes, 23
Molière, 151–52, 156, 160
  Amphitryon, 160
Momix, 165–67
Mondtag, Ersan, 191, 204–5, 223–24, 232–39
  Baal production (Berliner Ensemble 2019), 191
  Hass-Triptychon production (Gorki Theater 2019), 191
  Silbersee, Der, production (Opera Ballet Vlaanderen 2021), 191, 223–24, 232–39, 234f
Monroe, Marilyn, 42–43
Monteverdi, Claudio, 220
Monty Python, 158–59
Mörike, Eduard, 174–75. *See also Wer hat Angst vor Hugo Wolf?*; Wolf, Hugo
"Morning Dew" (Kim), 53–54
Morrison, Matthew, 77–78
Moses und Aron (Schoenberg), 197, 231–32
  Kosky production (Komische Oper 2015), 197, 231–32
Mother Courage (Brecht), 101–2, 195–96
Motown, 20–21, 43, 46–47
Mozart, Wolfgang Amadeus, 231
muette de Portici, La (Auber), 236–37
Müller, Ida, 235–36
Müller, Ulrich, 142–43
Mumbly Cartoon Show, The, 164–65
Muppet Show, The, 200–1
Murder Ballad (Jordan, Nash), 55
Murmel Murmel (Fritsch, Volksbühne 2012), 159, 161, 164–67, 166f
Music Man, The (Willson), 102–3, 207–9
Mutual Defense Treaty (US and South Korea), 37–38
"Mut zum Träumen" (*Linie 1*), 139
"My Beloved Son, Thomas" (*Hero: The Musical*), 63–64
My Fair Lady (Loewe, Lerner), 122–24, 128, 135–36
  class conflict in, 119
  German-language version, 117–20
  German premiere (1961), 117
  history in Germany, 117–20
  Mein Freund Bunbury, modeled after, 125
"My Ship" (*Lady in the Dark*), 11–12, 223–24, 227–28
Mystère musical coréen, Le (2012 documentary), 77

Na Hye-seok, 94
Na Hyo-shin, 79–80

Nash, Juliana, 55
National Changgeuk Company, 49–50
National Gugak Center (Seoul), 79–80
Natschinski, Gerd, 121–26
   Mein Freund Bunbury, 121–25, 123f
Nazism, 12–13, 107–8, 114–16, 128–30, 135–36, 137, 139–40, 178, 199
Nenning, Günther, 192–93
Nestroy, Johann, 164
Neuköllner Oper (Berlin), 140
Newman, Barnett, 173–74
New York State Theater, 58–59
New York Times, 16, 18–20, 21, 24, 27–28, 37–38, 51, 55–56, 57–58, 76, 79, 188, 189–90, 193–94
New York World's Fair (1964), 30–31
Nichols, Robert, 39–40
Nielsen, Ken, ix
No, No, Nanette (Youmans, Caesar, Harbach), 114–15
Noland, Kenneth, 163, 165–67
"Nonsense in Residence" (Kopatchinskaja-Fritsch multimedia event), 178
Norman, Jessye, 143–44
North Korea. *See* Korea, North
No Ticket (band), 134–35
Not I (Beckett), 217–18
"Notes on 'Camp'" (Sontag), 201–2
"Nothing More than This" (*Candide*), 221
"Nur die Nacht" (*Aufstieg und Fall der Stadt Mahagonny*), 231–32

OD Musical Company (Korean production company), 18–19, 21, 24, 55–56
Oedipus the King (Sophocles), 95–96, 231–32
Offenbach, Jacques, 117, 205
   schöne Helena, Die (*La belle Hélène*), 202–3
O'Hara, Kelli, 77–78
Oh Jeong-hyuk, 83
Oh Sang-joon, 61–62
Oh, Youjeong, 45–46
Oklahoma! (Rodgers, Hammerstein), 5, 115–16, 122–24, 169, 177
   East German premiere (1978), 116
   State Department-sponsored Germany tour, 115–16

West German premiere (Theater des Westens 1978), 116
"Ol' Man River" (*Show Boat*), 126–27
"O mein Papa" ("Oh! My Papa") (*Das Feuerwerk*), 167, 170
O'Neill, Eugene, 15–16
On the Town (Bernstein, Comden, Green), 126
One Touch of Venus (Weill, Nash), 110
Ong Keng Sen, 49–50
opera, xii–xiii, 5–7, 8–10, 12–13, 15–16, 38, 49–50, 52, 59–60, 62–63, 72–74, 77–78, 81–82, 100–1, 102–3, 107, 108–10, 113, 116–18, 126–27, 141–44, 148–50, 151, 153, 154, 156, 160, 163–64, 169–70, 178, 188, 189–90, 191, 192, 193–95, 197, 200–2, 203–5, 207–10, 211, 214–17, 222, 223–24, 225–26, 228–29, 230–31, 232–33, 234–36, 237
Oper am Gänsemarkt (Hamburg), 107
Opera Ballet Vlaanderen, 191, 223, 234f, 238
Opéra Comique, 188
Oper Frankfurt, 49–50
   Hochzeitstag, Der (AKA *Soul Mate*), production (2006), 49–50
operetta, xii–xiii, 5–7, 9–10, 12–16, 107–9, 110, 111, 112–13, 114–18, 119, 120–24, 125–27, 134–35, 137–38, 142, 147–48, 149–50, 151, 153, 162–63, 164, 167, 170, 172–73, 178, 188–93, 197–202, 203–4, 205, 207–10, 216–18, 222, 223–24, 225–26, 228–29, 230, 232–33
   Kosky, Barrie on, 190
Operettenhaus (Hamburg), 21–22
Opernwelt, 189–90
Orbán, Viktor, 22–23
Orpheus, 94–95
Orsons, Die (German hip-hop band), 84
Ostermeier, Thomas, 157
Othello (Shakespeare), 242–43

pacifism, 129–30
Palmer, Lilli, 167
pansori (traditional Korean theatrical genre), 39, 47–48, 49–50, 80–82, 89–91, 92–94, 95–96, 97, 100–3, 241–42

Paoli, Gino, 163
Park Chung-hee, 41–42, 43–45
Park Jiha, 79–80
Park, Dong Woo, 83
Park, Helen, 67
Pasolini, Pier Paolo, 236
Paulsen, Harald, 230
PC Nackt (né Patrick Christensen), 151–52
   Einzige und sein Eigentum, Der, production (with Hartmann, Berlin 2022), 151–52
Peace in Asia, 66
Pearl Sisters (Korean girl group), 43
Peking Opera. See *jingju*
pentatonicism, 38–39, 41, 59–60, 63–64, 66, 79–80, 95
Perlen der Cleopatra, Die (Straus), 188–89
Perón, Eva, 59–60
Petrie-Martell, H.W., 231
Peymann, Claus, 157–58
Pfusch (Fritsch), 157–58, 161
Phantom (Yeston), 72
Phantom of the Opera, The (Lloyd Webber, Hart), 3, 5, 6–7, 9, 12–13, 16, 144–45
   Korean productions, 72
Physicists, The (Dürrenmatt), 159
   Fritsch production (Zurich 2013), 159
Piaf, Edith, 94–95
Pichler, Otto, 189, 202, 205, 218
Pierre et Gilles, 236
Pierrot Lunaire (Schoenberg), 217–18
Pilobolus, 165–67
Pink Floyd, 132–33
Platt, Len, 12–13
Playbill, 67
Poiger, Uta, 114–15
Polanski, Roman, 17–18
pop opera, 142
Porgy and Bess (G. Gershwin, I. Gershwin, Heyward), 115–16
   Korean premiere (1962), 52
   State Department-sponsored European tour, 115–16
   Zurich production (1945), 115–16
Porter, Cole, ix, 186, 199–200, 202. See also *Kiss Me, Kate*
postmigrant theatre, 206, 213–15

Prado, Pérez, 210
Presley, Elvis, 128–29, 172, 174–75, 197–99
   "Big Hunk o' Love, A" (Schroeder, Wyche), 128–29
Preuß, Hans, 115–16
Price, Leontyne, 115–16
Prince, Harold, 215–16
"Princess of Pure Delight" (*Lady in the Dark*), 226–27
"Proud Mary" (Fogerty), 96–97
Psy (K-pop star), 48
psychedelic rock, 43, 132–33
Psychology and Religion (Jung), 169–70
Pulitzer Prize, 215–16

Queen Elisabeth Music Competition, 77

Rabenalt, Arthur Maria, 119
racism, 31–32, 48, 121, 203–4, 206–10, 211, 214–15, 238
ragtime, 6–8
Ragtime (Flaherty, Ahrens, McNally), 59–60
Rameau, Jean-Philippe, 189–90
Rasche, Ulrich, 151–52
   4.48 Psychosis production (with van Wersch, Berlin 2020), 151–52
Rau, Milo, 157
Raupach, Matthias S., 243–44
Ravel, Maurice, 210–11
Really Useful Group, 21–22
Rebellato, Dan, 26–27
Rebstock, Matthias, 153
Reckwitz, Andreas, 40
Regietheater, 142–43
Reiber, Bastian, 158–59
Reich, Steve, 161
Reinhardt, Max, 192, 232–33
Reiser, Rio (né Ralph Möbius), 131–32. See also *Herr Fressack und die Bremer Stadtmusikanten*; Hoffmanns Comic Teater; Krautrock; Ton Steine Scherben
   coming out, 133
   Rio Reiser—Mein Name ist Mensch (jukebox musical), 133
Renaissance Theater (Berlin), 223, 225

Rent (Larson), 62–63
Rhapsody in Blue (Gershwin), 190–91
Rheingold, Das (Wagner), 171–72
Richard Rodgers Theatre, 27–28
Richter, Falk, 204–5
Richter, Gerhard, 163, 195
Rimini Protokoll, 157
Rimsky-Korsakov, Nikolai, 210–11
Ring des Nibelungen, Der (Wagner), 171–72
 Castorf production (Bayreuth 2013), 235–36
Ringst, Rebecca, 218, 229–30
Rio Reiser—Mein Name ist Mensch (jukebox musical), 133
Risch, Mandy, 111–12
Rise and Fall of the City of Mahagonny, The (Weill, Brecht). See Aufstieg und Fall der Stadt Mahagonny
"Rise, People of Chosun" (The Last Empress), 59–60, 65–66
Rita und Paul (Ton Steine Scherben), 132–33
Ritzer, George, 26–27
Road Runner (Warner Brothers cartoon character), 185–86
Robb, David, 130–31, 132–33
Robbins, Jerome, 194–95, 207, 209–10
Robeson, Paul, 126–27
Rockaby (Beckett), 217–18
rock 'n' roll, 7–8, 15–16, 22–23, 29–30, 31–32, 43, 44–45, 46–47, 68, 79–80, 85–86, 91, 95, 99, 111, 114–15, 128–30, 134–36, 151, 175
"Rock around the Clock" (Haley), 128–29
Rock in Deutschland (reference book), 131–32
rock musicals, xii, 4–6, 62–63, 77–78, 86–87, 119–21, 128, 137–38, 143–44, 191
rock operas, 121–22, 131–32
rock song structures, 62–64, 137–38
Rocky (1976 Stallone film), 21–22
 "Gonna Fly Now" (Conti), 22–23
Rocky Horror Picture Show, The (1975 film), 119–20
Rocky Horror Show, The (O'Brien), 119–20
Rocky III (1982 film), 22–23
 "Eye of the Tiger" (Survivor), 22–23

Rocky: Das Musical (Flaherty, Ahrens, Meehan) (original German production), 17–18, 21–24, 31
 Apollo Creed (character), 31
 Hamburg setting, 23
Rocky the Musical (Flaherty, Ahrens, Meehan) (Broadway production), 17–19, 23–24, 55–56
Rodgers and Hammerstein musicals, lack of popularity in Germany, 115–17
Rodgers and Hammerstein Organization, 116
Rodgers, Richard, 59–60, 62–64, 143–44, 169. See also Carousel; Hart, Lorenz; King and I, The; Oklahoma!; Sound of Music, The; South Pacific
Roesner, David, 148–49, 151–53
Rois, Sophie, 155f
Rolling Stones, 128–30, 132–33
Rom, Friedrich, 180–81
Romberg, Sigmund, 12–13
Romeo and Juliet (Shakespeare), 132–33
Ronell, Ann, 174
Ronen, Yael, 191
 Slippery Slope: Almost a Musical (Gorki Theater 2021), 191
Roos, Hanne, 234f
"Rose's Turn" (Gypsy), 9
Rosenfeld, Ruth, 163–64, 168f, 170, 172, 173–74, 175–77, 176f
Rosenkavalier, Der (Strauss), 207–9
Roth, Dieter, 164–67
 "Literature Sausage," 164–65
 Murmel Murmel, 164–67, 166f
 "Steeple Cheese (A Race)," 164–65
Rothe, Hans, 232–33
Routledge Companion to Musical Theatre, The (MacDonald, Donovan, Everett, eds.), 243
RuPaul's Drag Race, 205

(s)panische Fliege, Die (Arnold, Bach)
 Fritsch production (Volksbühne 2011), 154–56, 155f, 164–65
sächzgischt Giburtstag, De (Sautter), 167
Sacre du printemps, Le (Stravinsky), 161
"Saga of Jenny, The" (Lady in the Dark), 10–12

Salvation Army, 122–24, 224, 225
Sams, Eric, 172
Sartre, Jean-Paul, 179
"Satisfaction" (Jagger, Richards), 128–29
Sautter, Emil, 167, 169–70
SB Circle, 79–80
Schauspiel Düsseldorf, 191
Schauspielhaus Zürich, 162*f*, 168*f*, 176*f*
Scheidleder, Hermann, 181–82
Schenker, Hans, 155*f*
Schiffer, Marcellus, 175–77
Schiller, Friedrich, 107, 108–9
Schlager, 125, 152–53, 164
Schneider, Romy, 167
Schoenberg, Arnold, 142–43, 153, 197, 217–18, 231–32
Schönberg, Claude-Michel, 6–7
schöne Helena, Die (Offenbach)
 Kosky production (Komische Oper 2014), 202–3, 205
Schuler, Carol, 158–59, 175–77, 176*f*
Schütte, Uwe, 128–30
schwarze Hecht, Der (Burkhard)
 "Es wird mir heiß und kalt," 170–71
 Fritsch production (Zurich 2014), 157–58, 167–72, 168*f*, 180
 plot, 167–69
Schwitters, Kurt, 178
Seeger, Pete, 130–31
segyehwa (South Korean capitalist globalization), 49
Selam Opera! (Komische Oper initiative), 214–15
Sellers, Peter, 158–59
Seopyeonje (1993 Im film), 80–81, 90–92, 95–96, 101–3
"Seopyeonje" (Yi short story), 90–91
Seopyeonje (서편제) (musical) (Yun, Cho), 80–83, 85, 89–103, 100*f*, 241–42
 leitmotifs, use of, 97–99
 Simcheong (*pansori* narrative), staging of, 90–91, 92–93, 97, 99–101, 241–42
sexism, 121, 225–26, 238
Sgt. Pepper's Lonely Hearts Club Band (Beatles album), 132–33
Shaiman, Marc, 31–32
Shakespeare, William, 156, 199–200, 232–33, 242–43

shamanism, 39, 59–60, 63–64, 81–83, 85, 92–93, 95–96, 97, 99
Shanghai Disneyland, 26
Sharifi, Azadeh, 213–14
Shaw, George Bernard, 39–40
Shelley, Mary, 72
Sherman, Robert B. and Richard M., 30–31
Shin, Chun-soo, 18–21, 24, 55–56
Shin, Dohyun (Gracia), 40, 57–58
Shin, Hyunjoon, 46–47
shinpa (Western realism), 39–40
shinpaguk (melodrama), 39–40
Show Boat (Kern, Hammerstein), 5, 9, 12, 57
 "Ol' Man River," 126–27
Shuffle Along (Blake, Sissle), 62–63
Siedhoff, Thomas, 115–16
Sienknecht, Clemens, 151–52
Silbersee, Der (Weill, Kaiser), 110, 191
 "Ballad of Caesar's Death, The," 237
 Leipzig premiere (1933), 232–33, 238
 Mondtag production (Opera Ballet Vlaanderen 2021), 191, 223–24, 232–39, 234*f*
 Olim and Severin (characters), 233–34, 236–39
Simcheong (*pansori* narrative), 90–91, 92–93, 97, 99–101, 241–42
 Seopyeonje (musical) (Yun, Cho), use in, 90–91, 92–93, 97, 99–101, 241–42
Simon, Paul, 85–86
Sin Chae-hyo, 92
Slippery Slope: Almost a Musical (Ronen), 191
Smeets, Roger, 203*f*
Snow White and the Seven Dwarfs (1937 Disney film), 226–27
"Snow White" (Brothers Grimm), 226–27
"Solidaritätslied" (Eisler, Brecht), 131–32
Solomon, Alisa, 139
Sommer, Sebastian, 223, 224–25
 Happy End production (Renaissance Theater 2022), 223, 224–25
Son, Chang-Hee, 70–71
Sondheim, Stephen, ix–x, 22–23, 85, 136–37, 190–91, 201–2, 217. See also *Assassins*; *Candide*; *Follies*; *Gypsy*; *Sweeney Todd*; *West Side Story*

song categories, 10
song forms, 10–12, 227–28
   Linie 1, in, 137–39
"Song in the Sand" (*La Cage aux Folles*), 243–44
Song Yooguen, 100*f*
Sontag, Susan, 201–2
Sophocles, 95–96
Sorrows of Young Werther, The (Goethe), 94–95
Soul Mate (AKA *Der Hochzeitstag*) (Lim), 49–50
soul music, 7–8, 19–21, 22–23, 31–32
Sound of Music, The (Rodgers, Hammerstein), 52, 102–3, 116
   Korean premiere (1992), 52–53
South Korea, *See* Korea, South
South Korean Ministry of Culture and Tourism, 59
South Pacific (Rodgers, Hammerstein), 57, 61–62
Soziale Marktwirtschaft, 17–18
Spiegel, Der, 112, 144–45, 149
Spielberg, Steven, 206–7, 211–12
Spoliansky, Mischa, 114, 175–77, 188–89, 191
   Alles Schwindel, 191
Staatskapelle Dresden, 193–94
Staatsoper Hannover, 226
Staatsoperette Dresden, 190–91, 205
Stage Entertainment, 17–18, 21–24, 25–26, 27–28, 29, 109. See also *Hamilton*; *Hinterm Horizont*; *Ich war noch niemals in New York*; *Rocky: Das Musical*; *Rocky the Musical*; *Tarzan*; *Wunder von Bern, Das*
Stallone, Sylvester, 21–22, 23–24
Star Wars, 236
Starlight Express (Lloyd Webber, Stilgoe), 149
   Bochum production, 149
State Department (US), 115–16
States, Bert, 218
Statue of Liberty, 30–32
Steckel, Jette, 204–5
"Steeple Cheese (A Race)" (Roth), 164–65
Stella Entertainment, 21
Stern (magazine), 23

Sternfeld, Jessica, 27–28, 62–63, 121
Stirner, Max, 151–52
Stöck, Katrin, 121–22
Stolz, Robert, 164
Stonewall, 201–2
Straus, Oscar, 188–89, 205
Strauss II, Johann, 7
Strauss, Richard, 172–73, 180–81
Street Scene (Weill, Hughes), 110, 222–23
Strindberg, August, 39–40
Stringer, Julian, 102
Subway Line 1 (Kim) (Korean adaptation of *Linie 1*), 53–54, 139–40
Süddeutsche Zeitung, 203–4
Suh Nam-dong, 81
Summer, Donna, 177
surrealism, 158–59
Survivor (rock band), 22–23
Sweeney Todd (Sondheim, Wheeler), 75
Swoboda, Andreas Renee, 243–44
Symphonic Fantasia Korea (Ahn), 40–41

Tagesspiegel, 189–90, 202–3
Tageszeitung, Die, 147–48
Taming of the Shrew, The (Shakespeare), 199–200
Tangerine Dream, 130–31
Tanz der Vampire (Steinman, Kunze), 18. See also *Dance of the Vampires*; *Fearless Vampire Killers, The*
tap dance, 6–7
Tarzan (Collins, Hwang), 27–28
   Stage Entertainment production (Hamburg 2008), 27–28
Tati, Jacques, 158–59
Tauber, Richard, 197–99
Taylor, Millie, 8, 9
Tchaikovsky, Pyotr Il'yich, 89
Tempest, The (Shakespeare), 242–43
Tewinkel, Christiane, 222
Thalia Theater (Hamburg), 24–25, 120–21, 141, 146*f*, 147–49
Theater am Schiffbauerdamm (Berlin), 223, 228–29
Theater an der Wien, 120–21
Theater des Westens (Berlin), 116, 117, 125

Theater Neue Flora (Hamburg), 27–28
Third Generation (1980s Korean artistic movement), 44–45
"This Is My Korea" (*KPOP*), 67
"Though I Loved You" (*The Days*), 87–88
Three Little Pigs, The (1933 Disney cartoon), 174
Threepenny Opera, The (Weill, Brecht). See *Dreigroschenoper, Die*
Thrill Me (Dolginoff), 55, 57–58
TikTok, 231
Timbers, Alex, 21–22
Tin Pan Alley, 6–7, 121, 142
Titania-Palast (Berlin), 115–16
Tolstoy, Leo, 39–40
Ton Steine Scherben (Krautrock group), 131–34. *See also* Hoffmanns Comic Teater; Krautrock; Reiser, Rio
  Herr Fressack und die Bremer Stadtmusikanten, 133–34
  Keine Macht für Niemand, 132–33
  "Macht kaputt, was euch kaputt macht," 132–33
Tony Award, 55–56, 199–200, 207–9
Traviata, La (Verdi), 52
Trial, The (Kafka), 229
Trilogie der Sommerfrische (*The Holiday Trilogy*) (Goldoni)
  Fritsch production (Munich 2014), 163
Trojan Women, The (Euripides), 49–50
  Ong production (National Changgeuk Company 2016), 49–50
trot (Korean popular song form), 41
Trump, Donald, 22–23, 32
Tudor, Daniel, 70–71, 81–83
Turandot (Puccini), 236–37
"Twist and Shout" (Medley, Berns), 175

U-Musik (entertainment music), 111–13
  E-Musik (serious music), distinction between, 111–13, 190–91, 201–2
Uncle Sam, 31
UNESCO, 25–26, 41–42, 91, 102–3
UNICEF, 30–31
Urban, Erich, 6
USO (United Service Organizations), x
Uyghur Muslims, 236–37

Valentin (Fritsch, Wertmüller), 164–65, 167
Valentin, Karl, 153, 158–59, 164–65
van Gogh, Vincent, 94–95
van Tongeren, Wietske, 77–78
van Wersch, Nico, 151–52
  4.48 Psychosis production (with Rasche, Berlin 2020), 151–52
Variety, 19–20, 59–60
vaudeville, 6–7, 113, 141–42, 144–45, 147, 199, 200–1, 217–18
Verdi, Giuseppe, 52, 64
Vereinigte Bühnen Wien, 17–18, 21–22, 29, 55, 62–63, 109–10
Verfremdungseffekt, 164, 224
"Vergine degli angeli, La" (*La forza del destino*), 64
Viebrock, Anna, 152–53
Vienna Actionists, 158–59, 164–65
Vienna Waits Productions, 18–19
Vietnam War, 112, 134–35
Vinge, Vegard, 235–36
Vinuesa, Roman, 170
virtuosity, 78–79, 100–1, 144–45, 151–52, 158–59, 165–67, 170, 183–84
vocal styles, 77–79
Volksbühne (Berlin), 133, 154–58, 155f, 164–65, 166f, 178
Vollmer, Joan, 144–45
Voltaire, 215–17, 221

Wagner, Richard, xii–xiii, 78–79, 97–98, 108–9, 113, 147–48, 153, 231
Waiting for Godot (Beckett), 180, 217–18
"Waiting" (*Linie 1*), 137–39
Waits, Tom, 141–42, 146–49
Waldbühne (Berlin), 128–29
Walenciak, Dominik, 140
Wallace, Lew, 72
Walter, Bruno, 190
Warfield, William, 115–16
Warmbrunn, Harald, 155f
Waters, John, 31–32, 236
"Waves of the Danube" (Ivanovici), 40
Weber, Carl Maria von, 141–42
Webern, Anton, 209–10
Wehlisch, Kathrin, 230

Weill, Kurt, 10–11, 12–13, 110, 126–27, 130–31, 147, 190–91, 197, 222–23. See also *Aufstieg und Fall der Stadt Mahagonny*; Brecht, Bertolt; *Dreigroschenoper, Der*; *Happy End*; *Jasager, Der*; Kaiser, George; *Lady in the Dark*; *Love Life*; *One Touch of Venus*; *Silbersee, Der*; *Street Scene*
Weimar Republic, 107–8, 114, 164
Weinberger, Jaromir, 188–89
Weise, Christian, 191, 204–5
  Alles Schwindel production (Gorki Theater 2017), 191
  Im weissen Rößl production (Düsseldorf 2013), 191
Welker, Sebastian, 32
Wellershoff, Marianne, 112, 116
Wells, Elizabeth A., 210
Wells, John, 217
Welt, Die, 189–90, 205
"Wenn die beste Freundin" (Spoliansky, Schiffer), 175–77
Wer braucht Geld? (Masanetz), 125–26
Wer hat Angst vor Hugo Wolf? (Fritsch, Zurich 2016), 157–58, 162f, 172–77, 176f
Wer spielte was? (Deutsche Bühnenverein), 110
Wertmüller, Michael, 164
West Side Story (Bernstein, Sondheim, Laurents, Robbins), ix–x, 5, 23, 62–63, 188, 206–15
  "America," 211
  "Boy like That, A"/ "I Have a Love," 211
  "Cool," 209–10
  critical reception, historical, 207–9
  "Dear Officer Krupke," ix–x
  German touring production (1961), 207–9
  Kosky-Pichler production (Komische Oper 2013), 189, 190–91, 206–10, 208f, 211–15, 226, 228–29
  Laurents revival (Broadway 2009), 206–7
  Spielberg film (2021), 206–7, 209, 212–13
  standard repertoire in Germany, as, 119–20
  van Hove revival (Broadway 2020), 206–7, 209, 212
  Wiener Volksoper production (1968), 207–9
  Wise film (1961), 207–9
Whale, James, 74–75
Wheeler, Hugh, 215–16
White Horse Inn (Benatzky, Charell, Caesar), 12–16, 14f, See also *Im weissen Rößl*
"Who's Afraid of Red, Yellow and Blue" (Newman paintings), 173–74
"Who's Afraid of the Big, Bad Wolf?" (Ronell, Churchill), 174
Who's Afraid of Virginia Woolf? (Albee), 173–74, 200–1
"Why Don't We Do It in the Road?" (Beatles), 158
Wicked (Schwartz), 53–54
Wiener Blut (Strauss), 7
Wiener Staatsoper, 207–9, 225–26
Wiener Volksoper, 190–91, 205, 225–26
  Kiss Me, Kate production (1956), 225–26
  Lady in the Dark production (2021), 225–28
  West Side Story production (1968), 207–9
Wiens, Wolfgang, 144–45
Wilbur, Richard, 215–16
Wild, Hubert, 163–64, 168f, 170, 180–81
Wilde, Oscar, 124
Wildhorn, Frank, 55
Wilk, Richard, 3–4
Williams, John, 62–63
Williams, Tennessee, 115–16
"Wilmersdorf Widows" (*Linie 1*), 137
Wilson, Robert, 141–42, 143–45, 148–49, 153, 154, 204–5, 228–29
Winter Garden Theatre, 23–24
Winter Sonata (Korean television series), 45–46, 81–82
Wittman, Scott, 31–32
Wohlgemuth, Heiko, 140
Wolf, Hugo, 172–77. See also Mörike, Eduard; *Wer hat Angst vor Hugo Wolf?*
  "Alles endet, was entstehet," 175
  "Er ist's," 177

Wolf, Hugo (*cont.*)
   "Erstes Liebeslied eines Mädchens,"
     175–77, 176*f*
   "Gesang Weylas," 174–75, 177
   "Ich hab in Penna," 175
Wolf, Stacy, 101–2
Wollman, Elizabeth, 62–63, 121
Woo-Cumings, Meredith, 54–55
World Bank, 17–18
World Trade Organization, 17–18, 45
World War I, 6, 12, 13–16, 107–8, 203–4
World War II, xi–xii, 4–5, 37, 107–8, 112–13, 114–15, 158–59, 178, 217–18, 222–23
"Wounded" (*Frankenstein*), 74–75
Wu, Yilun (Della), 243
Wunder von Bern, Das (2003 film), 21–22, 112
Wunder von Bern, Das (musical) (Lingnau, Ramond), 21–22

xenophobia, 24–25, 238
Xi Jinping, 236–37

Yang, In Ja, 59–60

yangak (modernized Western music), 41, 70, 71
Yegrin Akdan (Korean musical production company), 52
Yeston, Maury, 72
Yi Chung-jin, 89–91
Yi Sang, 94
Yi, Mun Yol, 59–60
"You Can't Stop the Beat" (*Hairspray*), 31–32, 33
"You'll Never Walk Alone" (*Carousel*), 64
Youens, Susan, 172–73
YouTube, 45–46, 48, 51, 71–72, 76, 241–42
Yuh, Ji Hyon (Kayla), ix, 19–20, 52, 242
Yun Il-sang, 95
Yun Sim-deok, 40–41, 94
Yun, Ho Jin, 3, 38, 58–59, 60–61, 62–63, 66

Zappa, Frank, 172
Zaufke, Thomas, 140
Zelt (Fritsch, Jakisic), 157–58, 161, 180–87, 182*f*, 184*f*
   curtain call, 186–87
Zimmer, Hans, 62–63
Zwach, Sabrina, 171–72